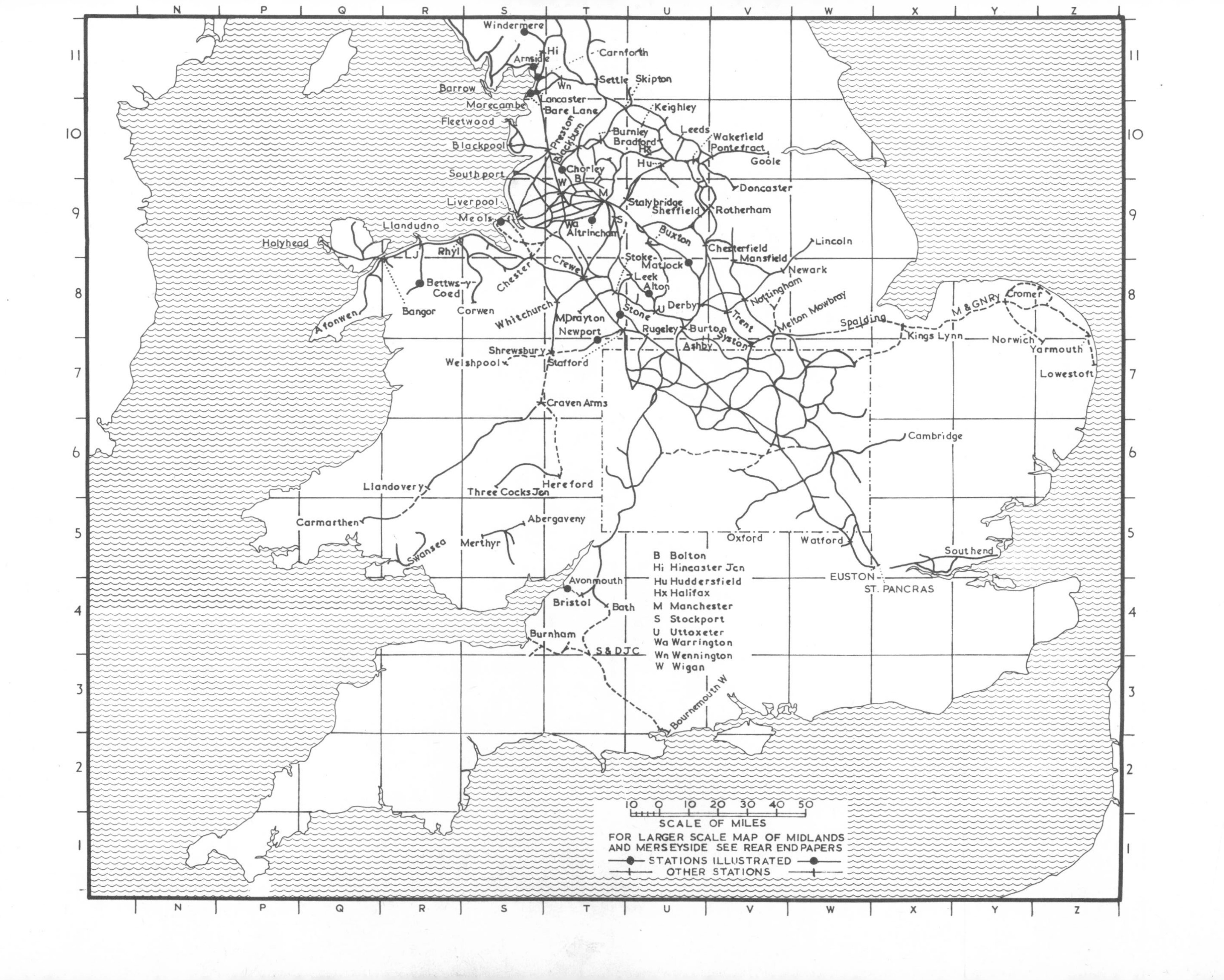

Windermere
Hi
Arnside
Carnforth
Barrow
Wn
Settle
Skipton
Morecambe
Lancaster
Bare Lane
Keighley
Fleetwood
Preston
Blackburn
Burnley
Bradford
Hx
Leeds
Wakefield
Pontefract
Goole
Blackpool
Hu
Southport
Chorley
W
B
M
Doncaster
Liverpool
Meols
Stalybridge
Sheffield
Rotherham
Wa
Altrincham
S
Llandudno
Holyhead
Buxton
Chesterfield
Mansfield
Lincoln
LJ
Rhyl
Stoke
Matlock
Newark
Crewe
Chester
Leek
Alton
Bettws-y-Coed
Nottingham
Melton Mowbray
M & GNRy
Cromer
Corwen
Bangor
Derby
U
Afonwen
Whitchurch
M Drayton
Stone
Trent
Spalding
Newport
Rugeley
Burton
Syston
Kings Lynn
Norwich
Yarmouth
Ashby
Shrewsbury
Welshpool
Stafford
Lowestoft
Craven Arms
Cambridge
Llandovery
Three Cocks Jcn
Hereford
Carmarthen
Abergaveny
Swansea
Merthyr
Oxford
Watford
Southend
Avonmouth
EUSTON
ST. PANCRAS
Bristol
Bath
Burnham
S&DJC
Bournemouth W
B Bolton
Hi Hincaster Jcn
Hu Huddersfield
Hx Halifax
M Manchester
S Stockport
U Uttoxeter
Wa Warrington
Wn Wennington
W Wigan
10 0 10 20 30 40 50
SCALE OF MILES
FOR LARGER SCALE MAP OF MIDLANDS
AND MERSEYSIDE SEE REAR END PAPERS
STATIONS ILLUSTRATED
OTHER STATIONS
N P Q R S T U V W X Y Z
1 2 3 4 5 6 7 8 9 10 11

C000300519

An Historical Survey of Selected

LMS STATIONS

Layouts and Illustrations

Volume I

by

Dr. R. Preston Hendry MRCS LRCP BA (Cantab)

&

R. Powell Hendry LLB FCA

Oxford Publishing Co.

ISBN 086093 168 4

Typeset by Aquarius Typsetting Services, Wheatley

Printed by S & S Press Ltd., Abingdon, Oxfordshire

Published by:
Oxford Publishing Company,
Link House,
West Street,
Poole, Dorset.

Portrait of a city terminal. The radiating pattern of roof girders, glazed and unglazed areas, rolling stock, track, platforms and even paving slabs makes an arresting composition in this portrayal of Liverpool Exchange station in 1977. The numerous trains and generous station facilities make a marked contrast with the peace and quiet of Marton station illustrated opposite, yet both were on the same system, the London, Midland & Scottish Railway, and these two scenes capture the diversity of that far-flung empire. Both exercised a fascination upon those interested in the railway station, and it is a sad thought that despite their very different nature, they have shared a common fate, closure.

Portrait of a country station. The location is Marton station on the Rugby—Leamington branch of the former LNWR, and the date is June 1959, but this peaceful railway scene recalls a bygone era when the branch line and the country station were a way of life. The view is taken looking towards Rugby from the Up platform, and although typical of so much, it is also unusual, for this platform which starts at ground level in the distance, is supported on piles above an embankment from where the illustration is taken. A few yards behind the camera, it extends high over a nearby main road on a bridge. As was so often the case, even the most minor station could offer the unusual.

▼

Contents

Preface

In a single volume, one can but scratch the surface of a subject as vast and as complicated as LMS stations. The London, Midland & Scottish Railway was, by a considerable margin, the largest of the grouped companies, and in this volume alone, the stations range in geographical spread from the Bristol Channel to the northern fastnesses of Sutherland. Even to seek to cover every aspect of the stations chosen would be impossible within acceptable bounds, and further selection is inevitable. Each of the 80 passenger stations and 2 associated junctions, making 82 locations in all, are covered by one or more illustrations, historical and operational details, and plans. In some cases, the scale plans and signalling plans are concurrent or similar, although perhaps separated by decades, showing the strength of tradition on the railways. Others, of the 60 plus signal box layouts, show dramatic differences to the accompanying scale plans, permitting one to study the changing face of Britain's railways.

Stations have been selected, varying from the tiny, such as Padbury or Binton to the large, including Coventry, Carnforth, and Liverpool (Exchange). In date, stations stretch from the dawn of the railway age to the 1930s, and a historical perspective is given in each case. In view of the sheer size and spread of the LMSR, it would not be possible for the authors to have specialised in the history of the entire LMSR *and* its constituents. We have, therefore, had recourse to the standard works on the constituent companies for basic details, augmented by historical data gleaned from contemporary sources wherever appropriate, as for example in the case of the Morecambe-Bare Lane or Rugby-Market Harborough line doublings. In the individual case histories, we have consulted a wide range of material, including the former Board of Trade inspecting officers' reports, signalling alteration drawings, rating plans, sectional appendices, public and working timetables and signal box diagrams. Station facility details are listed for each station covered, and these give a useful guide to the sort of traffic handled.

Without the historical backdrop, it is difficult to fully comprehend stations such as Wansford, Byfield, Morcott or Lea Hall, each of which represents a clear phase in station development. That having been said, equal or greater importance is attached to the workings of the station. As with the railway locomotive, the station existed for a *purpose*, and without considering that purpose no study would be complete. It would be pleasant to give full passenger and freight service details, but once again, one must be selective, and the yardstick adopted is the stopping passenger services. Although no definite rules can be laid down, these give a rough measure of the station's significance as a traffic centre. In the majority of cases, we have avoided reference to previously reprinted historical timetables etc., so that readers desiring more information can augment the details given by reference to reprints in their own possession.

Train service data has been augmented or occasionally supplanted by other items of interest. The signalling installations at certain locations such as Erdington, Liverpool (Exchange) or Tamworth are given prominence in view of their interest or significance.

Acknowledgements

As with any historical work, acknowledgements are due to many individuals, not least the countless railway officials, from regional Public Relations Officers and Engineers of the LMR and Scottish Regions, through district officers, to Area Managers, station masters, station staff and signalmen etc. In many cases it is not possible to provide names, and in other cases the passage of the years has witnessed retirements or transfers to other posts. To all of the railwaymen, whose co-operation was whole-heartedly given, we would record our thanks.

Outside the railway services, we are indebted to various fellow enthusiasts including Messrs. M. Christensen, R. D. Foster, D. Collins, K. A. Miller and the directors of Oxford Publishing Co. The OPC/BR Joint Venture facilities have provided much useful information and in some cases the possibility of checking or amplifying information already in the authors' possession.

Our sincere thanks also go to Mrs. Elaine Hendry for her patience in putting up with a husband and son whose joint idea of a family day out was to descend upon railway stations near or far. Few people can have a more expert or first-hand knowledge of that neglected subject, the railway station car park, for whilst some visits could be made by train, many had to be by car owing to the infrequency of many rural services.

Bibliography and Further Sources of Information

Brief mention of some sources of reference has already been made in the preface. The first and most generally available reference work, for the majority of readers, will be the various standard or localised histories of the pre-group companies. The LMS constituents are reasonably, but not fully, covered in this respect, there being a number of notable gaps. Original and more detailed research is possible through records held in official hands, including the Public Record Office, County Archives and local libraries or museums. Many local libraries have local newspaper files, and these are a useful, if time consuming, research tool, especially for the years prior to 1860, when any railway 'event' tended to be treated as important news. Parliamentary acts, copies of which are to be found in a few libraries, are another useful source of data. Enthusiasts require the *Private* and *Local* rather than the Public and General Acts, as railway legislation was private as opposed to state business.

Official railway information in the form of public and working timetables, sectional and general appendices, engineers' plans and signal plans are further important sources of detail, as are the various reprints of historical material which appear from time to time.

Finally, the model and prototype press produce a vast amount of information over and above that listed, and periodicals, and the various specialist societies, whose officers are listed therein, are another useful source of information. The authors have not yet encountered a society solely devoted to the study of, say, *goods yard cranes* but most other aspects of railway activity are covered by specialist groups, and many of the larger companies by Company societies. These bodies frequently publish their own historical bulletins and have invaluable archives.

Notes to the Layout Diagrams

1. The scale drawings are the 'A' plans. In a number of cases, two scale plans are provided.
2. The signalling diagrams are the 'B' plans, and are *not* to scale. Their prime function, as with an actual signal box diagram, is to display the signalling details, and proportion and scale are sometimes incompatible with clarity.
3. Other supporting drawings, maps etc., are sometimes provided.
4. The scale of the 'A' plans is indicated, as is the date or approximate period of the plan where definitely known.
5. The 'B' plan dates relate to the official diagrams from which they originate, or to a known time at which the layout was shown. Signalling and pointwork for certain disconnected, disused or lifted lines is sometimes shown, the relevant work being indicated.
6. In using the 'A' scale plans, it is important to remember that a small scale drawing cannot be relied upon to give measurements to the nearest few inches. Even original 30 or 40 foot plans are not *that* reliable, and were not intended to be used for such purposes. One experienced 19th century railway engineer observed that the *only* reliable scale plan was an unmounted rolled drawing on paper. Folding, repeated use, or damping and mounting on linen (as was frequently done for strength), was detrimental to accuracy, and to this list, we must add storage for 100 years or more. *Overall, the plans give a satisfactory and reliable impression of the station, but they were never intended to give exact sizes of items such as water columns or gates, to take an extreme example.*
7. The 'B' signalling plans have, for the most part, been prepared from original material, and verified back to the same. Such diagrams are thought to be correct, although it is amusing to record that a few signal box diagram inaccuracies came to light during the preparation of the book. One MR diagram, hanging in the authors' darkroom, shows a crossover in such a manner that, no matter how the points were set, a train would have to run through one set of blades. Readers are referred to Stamford and Liverpool Exchange for similar discrepancies.
8. Both minor and major changes in signalling at stations have occurred, without layouts having necessarily been altered. Signals have been renewed, sometimes in a different location and to a different configuration, and transfer of ground signals from one side of the line to the other is not uncommon. It is thus possible that the signalling shown may differ from information in other sources. This does not mean that either source is wrong – it may simply be the result of changes.
9. Certain signalling details should be mentioned, as being liable to trip the unwary. Ground signals are sometimes shown on SB diagrams as *discs*, other times as *miniature arms*. These indications have been followed in the 'B' plans (in the absence of clear evidence to the contrary), although it should be understood that they are frequently symbolic, rather than exact representations of the type of signal in situ. Thus official records may err.
   Wherever possible, spares and spaces have been distinguished, and when both terms appear, are as given. Sometimes, however, official diagrams group spares and spaces under the overall heading of spare.
   The selection of the term *signal box* or *ground frame* is usually straightforward, but in few cases the choice is not so simple, and we have adopted the view that if it looks and behaves like a signal box that it is shown as such. The subject is open to argument, and like the classic question of how to define the front and rear of a steam locomotive, is deceptively simple. Peculiarities such as the 'Fairlie' locomotive can play havoc with nice logical definitions, and provide a locomotive with a front at each end and a rear in the middle! Signal boxes and ground frames are a similar case.

Introductory Review

In the last years of steam, the phrase pre-group achieved an almost magical significance. To see and to photograph a locomotive dating from those halcyon days was an especial thrill to enthusiasts, who might travel hundreds of miles for just such a chance. There is still one sphere in which the influence of the past lingers on, and this is the railway station. Many lines have been torn up and stations obliterated, and wayside stations on other routes have gone, or been modernised, but throughout the country, the work of the civil engineers of the past lives on. Their contribution to the railway scene was immense, and in studying it, one becomes ever more conscious of railway history.

In locomotive design, it is possible to point to great strides forward such as the multi-tubular boiler or superheating. In station design, the picture is rather different. There is a gradual evolution from the early layouts to those which would commend themselves to a modern railwayman. It is a case of survival of the fittest, with the best features multiplying and the worst dying out. Station development is also a history of incredible reconstruction. Locomotive engineers were talented at rebuilding and modernising locomotives, but no CME ever took a 'Bury' 0-4-0 as the basis of a 'Deltic'. In their own way, the railway civil engineers did just that, taking the stations of the 1830s, 40s and 50s and gradually transforming them in to the layouts of recent times. Sometimes old stations were swept away in massive rebuilding projects, especially on main lines where quadrupling was carried out. In other cases, circumstances precluded a thorough rebuild, and one could look deep into the past. In examining LMS stations, it is useful to begin with a short review of the trends which have influenced station design over the past 150 years, and by which all of the stations in this book have, in some way, been influenced. Although few stations show traces of every factor, most show evidence of some, and their study, in the light of the wider considerations, can be rewarding.

The first fifty years, from 1825 to 1875, were devoted to the creation of the basic network, and to learning how to operate the most complex organisations of their day. Locomotives and rolling stock were small and trains short; stations were, as a result, extremely cramped by modern standards, and platforms were low or even non-existent. Buildings were small and often at ground level. The marshalling of trains was often carried out by use of wagon or carriage turntables. Signalling and block telegraph only developed to an appreciable extent towards the end of the period, and operating methods were hazardous. Wagons were frequently transferred from sidings on one side of a double track main line to those on the opposite side by means of two wagon turntables and a short length of inter-connecting track passing through the running lines by means of square crossings. Until the advent of reliable signalling, block telegraph and adequate brakes, such shunting moves must have been hazardous in the extreme!

By 1875, the pioneering days were over, and the main network, with a few notable exceptions, was complete. Henceforth the emphasis was to be on filling in the gaps with branch lines, and upon bigger and better stations, to cope with the steady increase in traffic, and the larger and heavier rolling stock. Large stretches of single line were doubled, and quadrupling gathered momentum, especially after 1880. Facilities, which in the 1850s had been the last word in comfort and convenience, were regarded as abominable, (one station was actually so described!), and at big stations where congestion was too severe – or public resentment too fierce – wholesale reconstruction took place. Elsewhere the tempo was slower, but even on minor branch lines, platforms (or a portion of them) were raised to the more modern heights and facilities updated.

By the start of this period, the early days of glorious, if misplaced, optimism were on the wane. Railway management had a grasp of the realities of the situation, one of which was that country branch stations were not, and were never likely to become, financial goldmines. The ornamentation which was characteristic of early stations, great and small, was increasingly confined to the great, and even there, the practical rather than the picturesque took a firm hold.

On the LNWR, this change was particularly apparent, perhaps as a result of the economical and astute chairmanship of Sir Richard Moon. The exuberance which had led to stations such as Wansford or Fenny Stratford was gone, and a more economical style was in evidence, and stations of this period, such as Padbury, provided what was necessary without superfluous flourishes. This trend towards simplicity continued, and Morcott is typical not just of LNWR practice, but of the many wayside stations opened by the railway companies from the 1890s.

Apart from the suppression of ornament, the new thinking was evident in the reduced scale of accommodation provided. In the early days it was unthinkable for a passenger travelling first class to have to share a waiting room with persons travelling third class, and separate accommodation was a necessity. Gradually attitudes changed, and communal facilities were provided. In this century the trend has continued, with separate accommodation being phased out.

Changes in layout design which had commenced prior to 1875 intensified. Coaching stock increased in size, and the short turntables which had sufficed in the 1850s fell out of use for marshalling stock in passenger stations, although they remained popular in goods yards for much longer. Block telegraph and interlocking made great progress, and the provision of wagon turntables and square crossings through running lines went out of favour, and station remodellings of the 1880s and 1890s frequently included the removal of such connections. (At Brandon & Wolston on the London & Birmingham main line, it was not until 1903, however, that the Civil Engineer dealt with the square crossings!)

The concentration of signal and point levers into signal boxes, and the emergence of block telegraph working, contributed materially to safety, but brought a number of constraints to layout design, not the least of which were the Board of Trade regulations governing the distance at which points could be worked from a box. To comply with these rules, railway engineers developed basic design patterns for layouts, which although capable of infinite detail variation, can be recognised time and again.

At wayside stations on double track lines, the typical layout was a pair of platforms with a yard at one end, which was reached off trailing connections. The signal box was either at the yard end of the platforms, or if the goods accommodation was very long, part way down the yard. Any connections at the opposite end of the station were kept to a minimum, and were often worked by ground frame released from the cabin.

On single lines, the format differed. At passing places, the cabin was usually on a central or nearly central site, with the yard coming off as a trailing connection at one end. As the loop points could not be placed at more than the regulation distance, this central site enabled the maximum length of loop to be worked in. On a few lines, this was not enough. Usually this was where special conditions prevailed. On the Highland Railway, the traffic only warranted a single track in most places, but long trains had to be operated from time to time, and as these were too long to pass at a one-box layout, it was necessary to provide two boxes, one at each end. Invariably one box controlled the yard connections as well as the crossing points at its respective end, and was much the larger of the two. This arrangement was adopted in the old days when wages were not a major source of concern, but has proved to be a considerable headache in recent times. The appearance of motor worked points enabled many second boxes to be abolished, and closures have thinned the ranks of the survivors.

The wider use made of goods running loops as opposed to trailing refuge sidings in the latter part of the period, greatly facilitated operation, although refuge sidings continued to be laid in, even on new lines, up to the turn of the century. In the early days, when railway working was largely a matter of trial and error, unlocked facing points had constituted a serious risk, and railwaymen's memories, coupled with the hostility of the Board of Trade to facing connections, gave the refuge siding an unnecessarily long life. Gradually the convenience of goods loops won converts and new connections were laid in. As the points were invariably beyond the range of existing boxes, the end result was a considerable increase in the number of signal cabins, until power operation became possible.

A trend which is frequently forgotten was the increasing separation of the railway from the public. In the early days road and footpath level crossings — even on busy lines — were readily accepted. By the 1870s, Parliament was less enthusiastic about level crossings, and bridges were demanded in new schemes, where level crossings would have sufficed twenty years earlier. The public, after the initial doubts about the 'railway age', welcomed any new line with open arms; then the reaction set it. Rates and fares were excessive, carriages and services were inadequate, but perhaps the most popular target of all was the level crossing in busy towns. The gentry and the commoner might frequent separate waiting rooms, but all were united in their detestation of level crossings. The Midland Railway endured a vitriolic correspondence over their level crossing at Melton Mowbray, the President of the Board of Trade was grilled in Parliament about the level crossing at Altrincham on the Manchester, South Junction & Altrincham Railway, and the Warwickshire County Council took the LNWR to court over a crossing at Atherstone, to give but three examples!

The third phase of railway station history, from 1923 to the present day, started with the grouping. Both nationally, and on the newly formed London, Midland & Scottish Railway, it was a trying time. The dislocations of World War I, and the boom, recession and grouping had no sooner occurred than there was the threat of road competition, the General Strike and then the depression. For each of the 'Big Four', money was tight, and what little there was had to be spent on the replacement of locomotives and carriages worn out with war traffic, and on the permanent way. Stations were well down the list, and as the nineteenth century engineers had tended to build 'for ever', the companies took advantage of this to concentrate on the spheres in which expenditure was vital. As traffic no longer rose almost annually, there was little need to enlarge facilities, other than where new housing estates created an entirely new market. One such development was at Lea Hall, on the outskirts of Birmingham. An entirely new station was constructed. It was a complete break with traditional design, and heralded the modern notion of functionalism — it was, in other words, hideous.

Superficially, the most obvious effects of the new phase were the attempts to graft an LMS image on to existing stations. LNWR signal boxes lost their lettering mounted on the front, in favour of a Midland type end nameboard. LMS style station nameboards appeared at many stations as did tubular post signals. The changes were little more than window dressing, for with traffic no longer increasing, and with buildings adequate for decades to come, there was no call for large scale expenditure. The LMS station scene was in essence the LNWR, Midland, Furness, Highland etc., scene with a fresh coat of paint and some different initials. Unlike the GWR, who 'Great Westernised' everything in their sway, be it locomotive or station, the LMS had no outstanding station trademarks to proclaim its ownership with the clarity of fittings such as signals, signal boxes, footbridges, awnings, seats etc. on the GWR. On the LMS, such additions as there were tended to blend into the background.

With the reduced level of new work, station design trends up to 1948 are less clear-cut. Where new stations appeared or old stations were rebuilt, (e.g. Lea Hall or Meols), current architectural thinking, with reinforced concrete and steel window frames, predominated. Overdue improvements were made elsewhere, with better lighting and sanitary facilities in demand. A few lightly-used stations were simplified or even closed, but it was not until the BR era that wholesale closure was to begin. One major development, affecting operation rather than station layouts, was the appearance of colour light signalling. Mostly, this was confined to distants on fast main lines, but by the late 1930s, several stations had received MAS or Multiple Aspect Signalling. Other changes included the abolition of some block posts without siding connections, and their replacement by Intermediate block signals controlled by an adjacent signal box. Some, including Erdington and Tamworth, are described.

BR at first followed the LMS pattern. There was a new symbol to become accustomed to on stations and paperwork. It was a sausage of the appropriate regional colour. Eventually the sausage fell out of favour and was supplanted by the current double arrow logo. There were a few closures in the early 1950s, but it was not until the Beeching era that station casualties began to mount at an alarming rate. Vast stretches of secondary line were ripped up, and on the main lines, wayside stations fell victim to retrenchment. Of the survivors, many were altered out of all recognition, with goods yards torn up, signal boxes demolished and platforms swept bare, or left with a 'bus shelter' type of structure. For the station enthusiast it was a sad time. Happily, even after all these years of Beeching, rationalisation and basic railway, there is still much to see and to photograph.

One important influence upon station design which has been touched upon above, but not properly explored, was the Board of Trade. The names of the inspecting officers of the Board, Col. F. H. Rich, Major Marindin, Col. H. A. Yorke etc., are remembered today chiefly on account of the Board of Trade accident reports, and perhaps for their inspections of new lines, but it is seldom recalled that almost any alteration to passenger facilities or running lines, no matter how trivial, was subject to Board of Trade inspection and approval. The files of the Board provide an absorbing insight into the complex relationship between the railways and the Board of Trade, and make one wonder how so few inspecting officers were able to discharge such an immense workload, for their inspections were no mere formality. Time and time again, an inspecting officer records that lever 'X' should be locked against lever 'Y', or that a lamp post should be moved to improve sighting of a certain signal.

At times the requirements were almost pedantic, and must have infuriated railway officers, but on the whole, the inspecting officers exercised a very beneficial rule over the railways of Britain. Perhaps their greatest achievement was to set a standard below which none might fall, and which over the years was gradually raised. Runaway catch points, station nameboards, adequate passenger facilities, high platforms, clocks visible to the passengers, correct interlocking, staff working on single lines; all were Board of Trade requirements. Railway engineers were at times irritated with the requirements, but accepted the verdict. The inspecting officers were not, of course, all-powerful, and as well as the requirements which they could insist upon, there were many matters in which agreement, rather than coercion, was called for. Often they were successful, sometimes the companies rebelled. When Col. Yorke inspected the Seaton Junction station of the LNWR prior to the opening of the Uppingham branch, he suggested that better waiting facilities be provided on the down platform. Given the limited passenger potential at the station, Euston did not see the advantage of providing additional accommodation, and commented, 'My directors believe the existing accommodation fulfils all the requirements of the traffic conducted at that station at the present time, and they are not, therefore, at the moment prepared to entertain the proposal to increase it.' Col. Yorke commented, 'I do not see that anything more can be done. The responsibility must rest with the Company.'

'Elementary my dear Watson' Sherlock Holmes would have enjoyed a field day at Kettering station had he spared the time from crime fighting, to investigate railway stations, for in this view is all the evidence that the maestro would have needed to deduce much about the station's past. As the sleuth said, 'the little things are infinitely the most important' and they are there in profusion. So my dear reader, it is up to you; the answers Holmes would have perceived appear in due course as in the best detective story, but the clues await your evaluation.

It is our hope that this book will not be seen as a mere catalogue of facts and figures, interesting though these may be. Our ambition is to record something of the diversity of LMS stations, in terms of size, traffic, origins and area. We have covered the two dominant constituents, the LNWR and Midland, in considerable depth, as together they contributed the greater share of facilities to the LMS, and it was their influence which tended to dominate LMS thinking after the grouping.

If we were to attempt to cover every other constituent or absorbed line, we would do no more than scratch the surface, without giving any very clear idea of a particular company. Accordingly, we have selected certain other lines, and explored them to a degree which would only be possible after several volumes if a slavish sense of proportion were to be adopted. As one of the most influential of the intermediate companies, the Lancashire & Yorkshire Railway has received extended coverage, and we have described the busy LYR line between Liverpool and Southport. Amongst the smaller systems, the Highland and Stratford-upon-Avon & Midland Junction receive pride of place, both being relatively neglected in the past. Mention is also given to the Furness, CKPR and 'Knotty' as well.

One objective to which we have attached great importance is the recording of comprehensive signalling data. The wholesale slaughter of branch lines since the 1950s, coupled with the relentless spread of power box working, has made enormous inroads into mechanical signalling of railways, and much information has been destroyed or is scattered in private collections.

One group of readers to whom we hope this book will be of interest is railway modellers. Layout design, whether in prototype or model form is a complex business. When building a locomotive, the modeller usually has comprehensive data plus a keen sense of proportion. With a model layout, a sense of proportion is difficult to achieve — our prototype viewpoint is the worm's eye view, our model viewpoint, a bird's eye view, and the authors are certain that this dissimilarity in perspectives contributes greatly to the difficulty in producing a good layout. Many model layouts would not commend themselves to a practical railwayman, although it is only fair to add that the same applied to many genuine stations, and a useful exercise with layouts, model or real, is to run through the moves which are likely, to see just how easy or difficult they are! Several stations have been included with the individual modeller, or club, in mind. Some of the Highland stations would provide an unusual subject, whilst stations such as Brinklow or Flitwick would make impressive exhibition layouts, in the smaller scales. For a really ambitious club project, Liverpool Exchange would offer a real challenge, and with trains constantly arriving and departing would hold the spectator's interest. When it has been done well, the modelling of a terminal (or a large through station such as Coventry) has resulted in some truly memorable layouts. In the case of these larger stations we have provided comprehensive signalling details, partly because such information deserves to be put on record, and partly because the convenient signalling of a really large station with full mechanical equipment is a highly skilled, but dying, art.

Features of Signal Box Diagrams

The signal diagram below, is intended to depict a wide range of typical signalling features to be found at a passenger station of modest size in manual signalling days. A steep gradient and level crossing have been included, as these allow for further 'demonstration' features. The Up line signalling (against the gradient) is kept to a minimum, whilst the Down line is more comprehensively signalled, with no fewer than five stop signals as opposed to two in the other direction. Ordinarily, there would be a rough balance in both directions, but the need for braking distances or other factors could lead to such a result. The positioning of the distant signals is also dependent upon line speed, sighting and gradients, and is less on a rising grade than on a falling grade. A level crossing is added at the right-hand side of the diagram, both to show a typical crossing cabin, and to illustrate the slotting of signals, where boxes were relatively close. In the Up direction, the limited number of signals at the station, and reduced braking distances obviate the need for such measures. In the Down direction two typical slots are shown. As signal 28 is well under half a mile in advance of the level crossing, it would not be possible to put the station distant the Down side of the gates; therefore it must be placed on the same post as the home signal for the crossing box (the crossing box signals being shown in outline only). This signal is 'slotted' by level crossing box signal No. 3 (L3) by means of multiple counter weights, so that 29 will only clear when station box No. 29 is pulled and the crossing home, L3, is pulled. This is to avoid the confusing indication, which might otherwise arise of L3 at danger and 29 at clear. Although the crossing signalman does effectively share control of 29 with his neighbour, it is not technically his signal. As distant 29, even though it is located on the crossing home post L3, is only 790 yards from signal 28 on a falling grade, it is essential that there should be an outer distant, and this signal, No. 30, is combined with the crossing distant, L4. For No. 30 to clear, both boxes have to be able to pull the appropriate levers, so this signal is not only worked by both boxes, but 'belongs' to both. It is sometimes said that a distant indicates the position of the next 'home' signal. This is incorrect. A distant signal indicates that all the relevant running signals at a particular box are 'off', i.e. 1 is 'led' by 2 and 3; 29 is led by 28, 27, 26, 25 and 24. An outer distant is led by an inner distant (30 by 29). Where an Intermediate Block signal is installed, this has its own 'distant' (see 23 and R23). A distant is thus independent of an 'IB'. In certain cases, e.g. junctions or single lines where special caution is required, distants may be fixed (e.g. Kenilworth Junction or Keswick).

In the demonstration layout, slotting is confined to distant signals, but where two or more boxes work one station, usually a large and complicated one, stop signals can also be slotted, so that two boxes share control over one signal. For examples, see Coventry and Liverpool Exchange. A triple slot, by three boxes, appears under Chorley.

The numbering of the levers in the layout follows standard practice, with Up and Down signals grouped at opposite ends of the frames and other signals grouped by the relevant cross overs, e.g. 7, 8 and 9. Where facing point locks are required, these adjoin the point lever. Early signalling layouts sometimes grouped all Up running signals and then all Up shunt signals, followed by points, FPLs etc. and then Down shunt and Down running signals, to give a red, black, red frame pattern. As points were widely separated from their appropriate signals it had little to commend it. The layout is partially track circuited on the Down line. IB signals were always track circuited, whilst home or starting signals remote from the box tended to be so treated before other sections easily seen by the signalman. The fireman's plunger and D sign on signal 28 was an alternative and cheaper method of advising the signalman of the presence of a train. In the absence of either system, the fireman was required to go to the box to remind the signalman of his train, so that it would not be overlooked and another train accepted. Comprehensive track circuit layouts to modern standards are seen at Fenny Compton and Carnforth. The exact opposite, working a busy station with hardly any modern aids, is illustrated at Coventry. Other signalling details are noted in the drawing itself, e.g. ground frame release, yellow shunt signals, co-acting arms etc.

Further details of track circuit indications, different arrangements of slips etc. are given in the signalling notes. As certain of the signalling plans show arrangements which have been out of fashion for many years, some mention is made of these, including the placing of running signals for different routes vertically on the same post, instead of on a bracket signal as latterly. Locating Up and Down signals on the same post was also more common in the old days than in recent times, whilst a number of pre-group railways used ringed arms for slow lines, and added S to shunt signals etc.

Plan devised to show many typical features, nomenclature, numbering, slotting, co-acting arms, I.B.s, etc.

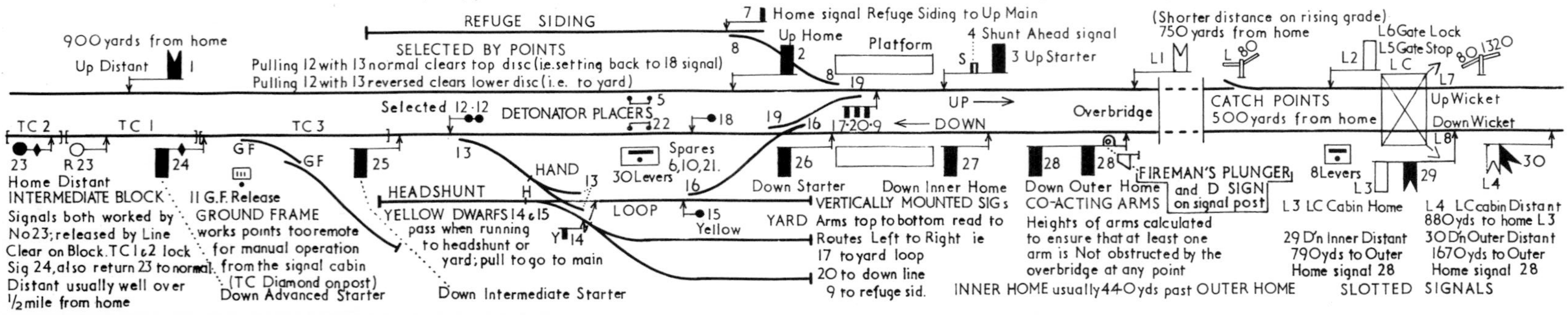

List of Stations and Facilities

Page	Station	Map Ref.	Facilities	Crane *Tons Cwt*	Notes
10	Adderley Park	D6	G P	—	
12	Ainsdale	A5	G P	—	LYR
	Ainsdale	A5	P	—	(LNWR)
14	Alcester	D4	G P F L H C	1 0	MR & (GWR)
15	Alton	U8	G P L H	8 0	
17	Altrincham	T9	G P F L H C	5 0	MSJ&AR
		—	P	—	(CLC)
18	Arnside	S11	G P F L H C	3 0	
20	Atherstone	E7	G P F L H C	5 0	
22	Avonmouth Dock	T4	P	—	
23	Banbury (Merton Street)	G3	G P F L H C	5 0	
26	Bare Lane	S11	G P	—	
27	Berkswell	E6	G P	—	
28	Bettws-y-Coed	R8	G P F L H C	4 0	
29	Binton	D4	G P F L H C	2 0	
30	Birdingbury	F5	G P L H C	—	
31	Birkdale	A5	G P	5 0	LYR
			P	—	(LNWR)
32	Birkenhead North	A1	G P L	—	WR
			G L	—	Birkenhead Jct.
34	Boat Of Garten	R18	G P F L H C	1 10	HR
			G P F L H C	1 10	GNSR
36	Bonar Bridge	Q20	G P F L H C	2 0	
37	Brandon & Wolston	F6	G P F L H C	3 0	
38	Brinklow	G6	G P F L H C	—	
40	Brora	R20	G P F L H C	3 0	
42	Buckingham	H3	G P F L H C	5 0	
44	Byfield	G4	G P L H	—	
46	Canley Halt	E6	P	—	
48	Carnforth (passenger)	S11	P H C	—	LNWR, FR, Midland
	Carnforth (goods)		G F L	10 0	LNWR, FR
52	Chester Road	D7	G P	—	
54	Chorley LYR Station	T10	G P F L H C	10 0	LYR
	Chorley LYR Station		P H C	—	(LNWR)
	Chorley LNW goods		G F L	5 0	LNWR
56	Coundon Road	F6	G P	—	LNWR
			G	—	(Midland)
58	Coventry LNW Station	F6	G P F L H C	25 0	LNWR
	Coventry LNW Station		P	—	(Midland)
	Coventry MR goods		G F L	5 0	Midland
62	Dingwall	Q19	G P F L H C	4 0	
65	Dunrobin	R20	P F H C	—	Private station
66	Erdington	D7	G P L	5 0	
68	Ettington	E4	G P F L H C	—	
70	Fearn	R19	G P F L H C	1 0	
71	Fenny Compton SMJ	F4	G P L H	—	
74	Fenny Stratford	K3	G P L H	3 0	
76	Flitwick	L3	G P	1 5	
78	Four Oaks	D7	G P F L H C	—	
80	Gravelly Hill	D7	P	—	
82	Hall Road	A3	P	—	LYR (& LNWR)

Page	Station	Map Ref.	Facilities	Crane *Tons Cwt*	Notes
84	Hampton- in- Arden	E6	G P F L H C	5 0	
86	Harlington	L2	G P F L H C	1 10	
88	Hillside	A5	P	—	
89	Invergordon Station	Q19	G P F L H C	1 0	
	Harbour Branch		G	—	
90	Kenilworth	E5	G P F L H C	5 0	
92	Kenilworth Junction	E5		—	
93	Keswick	S12	G P F L H C	4 0	CKPR, LNWR, NER
95	Kettering	K6	G P F L H C	10 0	
98	Ketton	K8	G P F L H C	10 0	Midland
			P	—	(LNWR)
100	Kineton	F4	G P F L H C	2 0	
102	Lairg	Q20	G P F L H C	1 0	
103	Lea Hall	D6	P H C	—	
104	Leamington Spa Avenue	F5	G P F L H C	—	Crane at Milverton
107	Lentran	Q19	G P F L H C	—	
108	Lichfield City	D8	G P F L H C	10 0	
110	Liverpool Exchange	A1/S9	P H C	—	LYR
			P H C	—	(Midland)
116	Luffenham	K8	G P F L H C	1 10	Midland
			G P F L H C	—	(LNWR)
118	Market Harborough	J7	G P F L H C	5 0	MR
			G P F L H C	5 0	LNWR
			G	—	(GNR in LNW station)
122	Marston Green	E6	G P L H	—	
124	Marton	F6	G P F L H C	—	
127	Marton Junction	F6		—	
128	Matlock	U8	G P F L H C	15 0	
130	Meols	S9	P	—	
132	Milverton	F5	G P F L H C	7 0	
134	Morcott	K8	G P F L H C	—	
136	Narborough	G7	G P F L H C	1 10	LNWR
			G F L	1 10	MR
138	Newport	T7	G P F L H C	5 0	
141	Padbury	H2	G P L H	—	
142	Stamford	L8	G P F L H C	10 0	MR & (LNWR)
144	Stone	T8	G P F L H C	8 0	
146	Sutton Coldfield	D7	G P F L H C	5 0	
148	Sutton Park	D7	G P F L H C	1 10	
149	Tamworth High Level	E8	G P F L H C	5 0	MR Station
149	Tamworth Low Level	E8	G P F L H C	10 0	LNWR Station
152	Theddingworth	H6	G P F L H C	—	
154	Verney Junction	J2	G P	—	LNWR & Met/GC Jt.
156	Wansford	L7	G P F L H C	1 15	LNWR
			P H C	—	GNR
158	Welford & Kilworth	H6	G P F L H C	1 5	
160	Wellingborough	K5	G P F L H C	5 0	
163	Windermere	S11	G P F L H C	5 0	
166	Woburn Sands	K3	G P F L H C	5 0	
168	Wylde Green	D7	P	—	

Note: *Station facilities given as in 1912/20 except for LMS-opened stations such as Lea Hall*
Where companies exercising running powers enjoyed partial facilities, or separate goods depots etc. these are indicated, running power companies being shown in brackets.

G – Goods
P – Passenger & Parcels
F – Furniture vans etc.
L – Live Stock
H – Horse Boxes
C – Carriages by Passenger Train

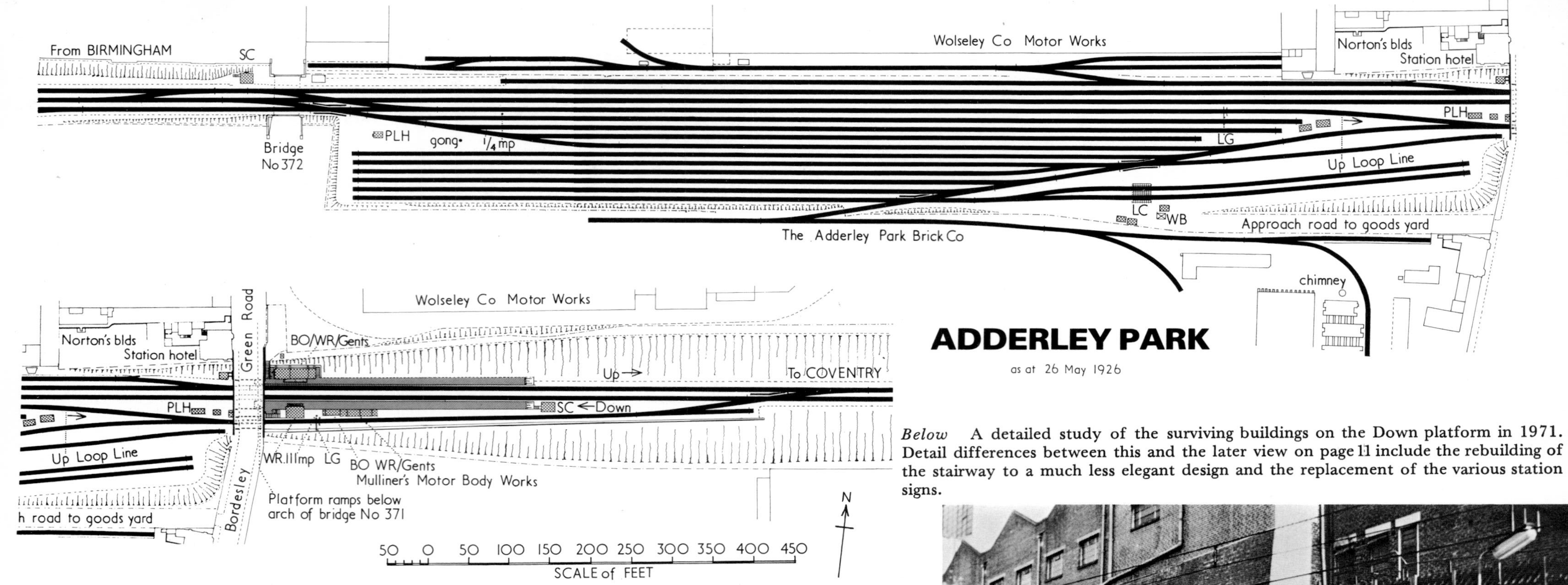

Below A detailed study of the surviving buildings on the Down platform in 1971. Detail differences between this and the later view on page 11 include the rebuilding of the stairway to a much less elegant design and the replacement of the various station signs.

ADDERLEY PARK *(Map Ref. D6)*

Adderley Park is the last station before New Street on the London & Birmingham main line, and is also the south-east outpost of the complex network of multiple lines and junctions which comprise the two mile approach into New Street. It is not an original L&B station, dating instead from 1st August 1860. At this time, Birmingham was expanding rapidly, and the new station was intended to serve mixed industrial and housing developments. The passenger platforms were sited to the east of Bordesley Green Road, which was carried over the line by an overbridge. Access to the platforms is via steps from the roadway, and a booking office was provided on each platform.

Goods traffic was first handled in 1877, and the yard, marshalling sidings and carriage sidings are to the west of the roadbridge on the south side of the line. Access to the yard is off the Up goods loop, which runs from Grand Junction (where the MR/LNWR routes into New Street converge) to Adderley Park. As well as the marshalling sidings (246 wagons) and coal yard (60 wagons), there were a number of private sidings. The Garrison Farm Brickworks (later Midland Brickworks), and Adderley Park Brickworks were reached off the Up loop, but the most interesting sidings came off the Up main itself. These served Brown Marshalls' Britannia Railway Carriage Works, one of the leading carriage and wagon manufacturers in Britain. Later the site passed to Wolseley Motors and then to Austin.

In 1895, nine Down and twelve Up trains called at Adderley Park. By 1944 there were fourteen trains each way, and today, it is a stopping place on the Euston–Birmingham local service.

The station cabin was closed on 4th June 1966, during the commissioning of New Street Power Box. A second small cabin, No. 2, existed on the Up side at the western end of the yard, but this had vanished by 1929. The Up loop was eventually converted into an Up and Down through siding, a facing lead being laid in to the Down main.

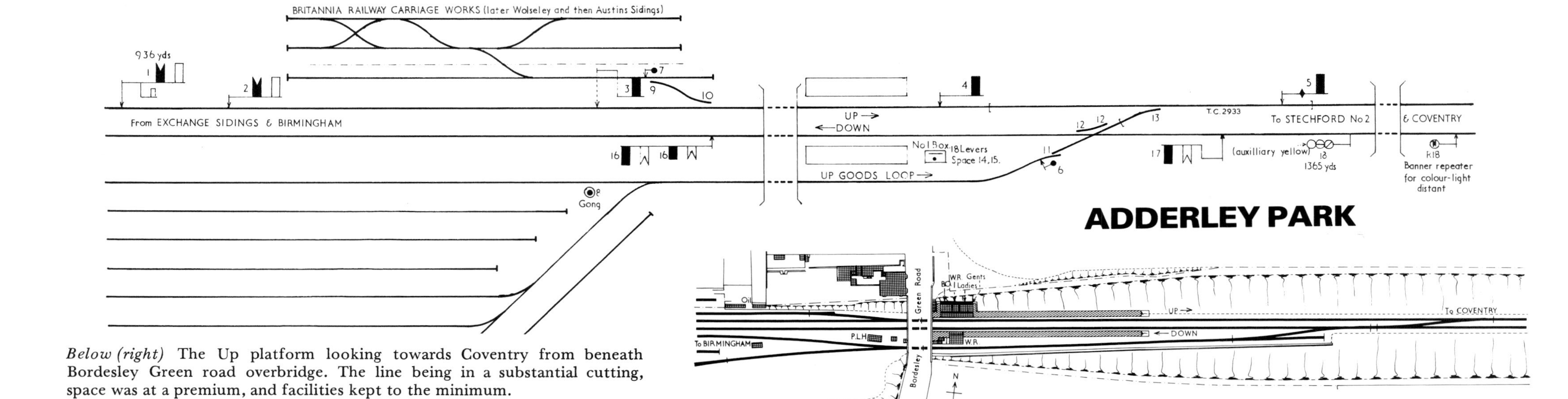

Above Adderley Park as modified by BR with the conversion of the former Up loop into an Up and Down road, a change made possible by the modern preference for single leads and facing points rather than slips. It will be noted that the signal box has fallen victim to New Street Power Box.

Below (right) The Up platform looking towards Coventry from beneath Bordesley Green road overbridge. The line being in a substantial cutting, space was at a premium, and facilities kept to the minimum.

Below The Down platform looking towards Coventry in 1977. Space was even more restricted on this side, and instead of a fairly gentle sloping approach from the road, a narrow timber staircase which reversed direction at the mid-point was necessary. The buildings were even smaller, and the retaining wall in the background became necessary when the Up goods loop was added, making it an expensive piece of track.

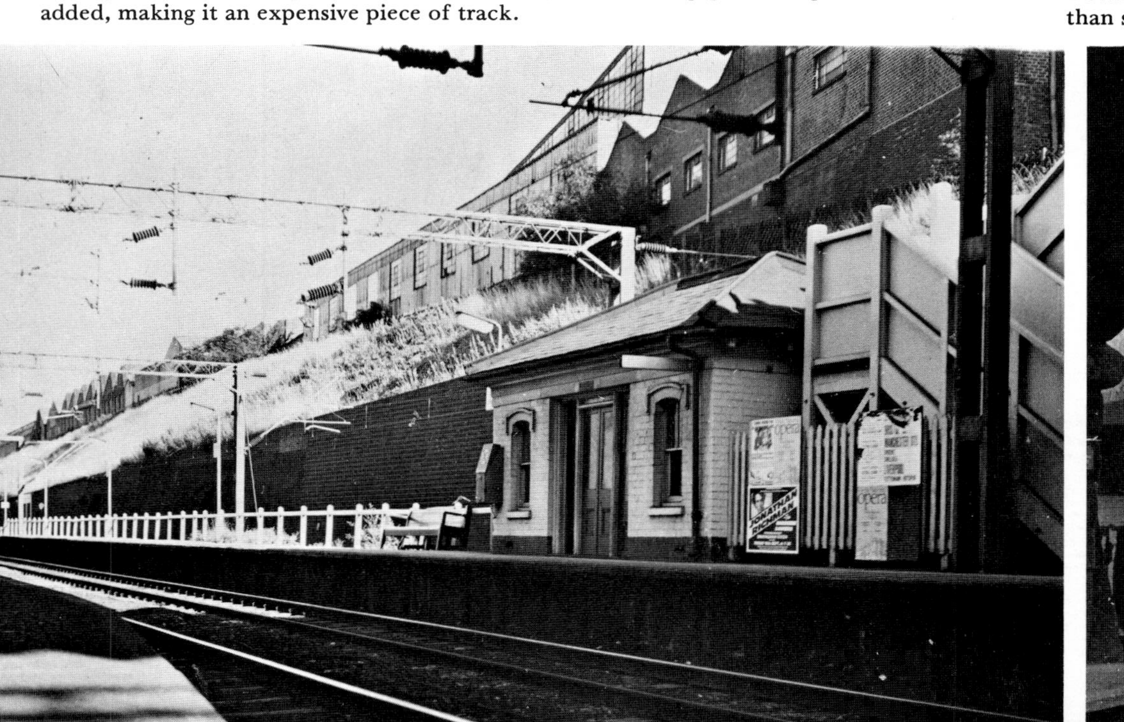

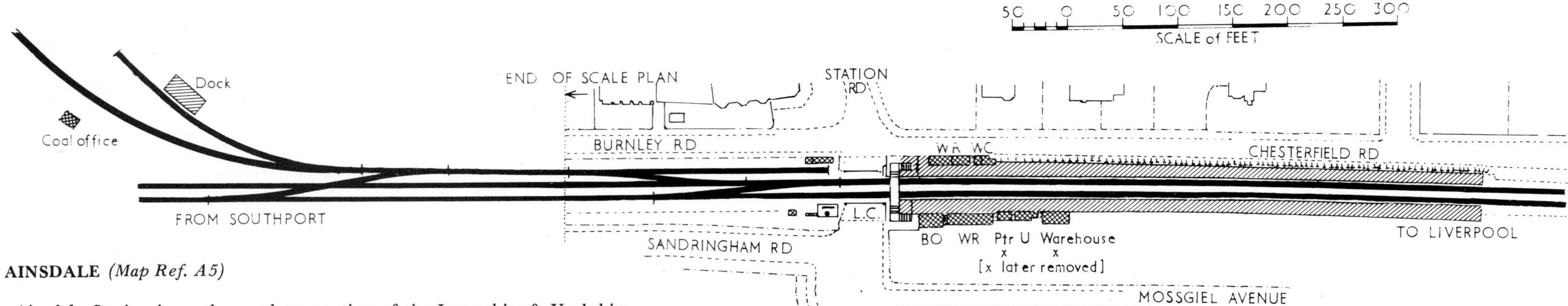

AINSDALE

AINSDALE *(Map Ref. A5)*

Ainsdale Station is on the northern portion of the Lancashire & Yorkshire Railway Liverpool–Southport line. The Liverpool, Crosby & Southport Railway was authorised in July 1847, and the section from Waterloo to the outskirts of Southport opened to public traffic on 24th July 1848. The line was initially single, but was doubled by September 1852. Ainsdale was one of the original stations.

As Southport developed as a holiday resort and high class residential centre, and the bare fields around Seaforth, Waterloo and Crosby gave way to neat housing development, traffic built up rapidly. The Liverpool approaches were quadrupled, but even so the position soon became critical again. Short workings from Liverpool to Crosby ran every quarter of an hour and to Southport every half hour. The goods traffic to and from the docks, plus the Manchester and Ormskirk services, meant that some drastic solution was essential if the appproaches to Liverpool Exchange were not to become unworkable. Additional running lines in an already highly built up area were one expensive solution. Electrification was the other possibility and on 22nd October 1902, orders were given to electrify. The first test trains ran on 29th December 1903; partial electric services commenced on 22nd March 1904, and full working on 13th May. In steam days, the express services on the 18½ mile route took 25 minutes and local services 55 minutes. The express schedule remained at 25 minutes, but the enormous acceleration of the electric stock enabled the local time to be cut to 37 minutes, despite there being thirteen intermediate stops. A 14% increase in traffic took place in the first year, and the new service provided a boost to residential growth north of Crosby. The area around Ainsdale Station with its post-1900s architecture is convincing proof of the success of the scheme.

The spectacular 25 and 37 minute schedules were subsequently eased to around 35 and 45 minutes respectively, the expresses, by the 1920s, calling at more stations than in pre-war days. When the LMS replaced the original L&Y stock during World War II, these schedules were maintained, although war conditions led to the suspension of the fast services. The 1944 timetable gave stations such as Ainsdale seventy trains each way, with 7 minute headways during the rush hour and 20 minutes out of peak.

A small goods yard, closed on 28th November 1966, existed at the north side of the station level crossing. This could only handle general goods, particularly domestic coal, and not livestock, horse boxes or furniture vans. A private siding, 53 chains in length, ran from the yard to a corn mill on the Liverpool Road. Work began on this line in 1851, although Parliamentary approval was not actually obtained until 1853!

Ainsdale level crossing and signal box looking towards Southport in April 1977. Although the yard has been lifted, the point blades are still in situ.

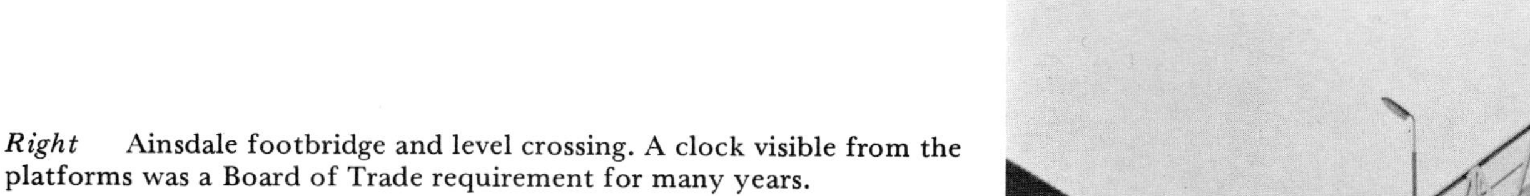

Right Ainsdale footbridge and level crossing. A clock visible from the platforms was a Board of Trade requirement for many years.

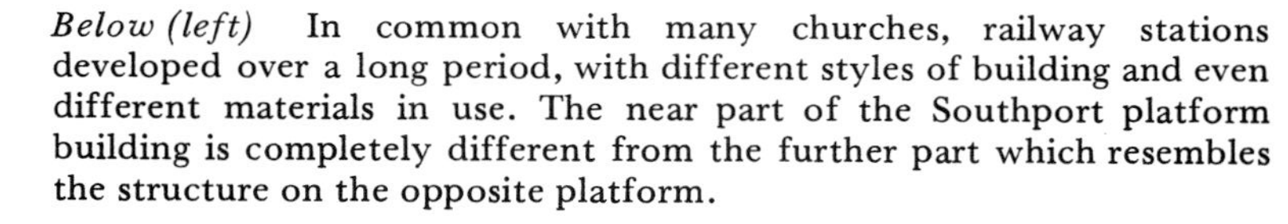

Below (left) In common with many churches, railway stations developed over a long period, with different styles of building and even different materials in use. The near part of the Southport platform building is completely different from the further part which resembles the structure on the opposite platform.

Below (right) A further study of Ainsdale reinforces the message, the Up and Down gents being of brick, in stark contrast to the main buildings. Even the lamp standards differ, that on the left being an ornate metal standard, whilst reinforced concrete appears opposite.

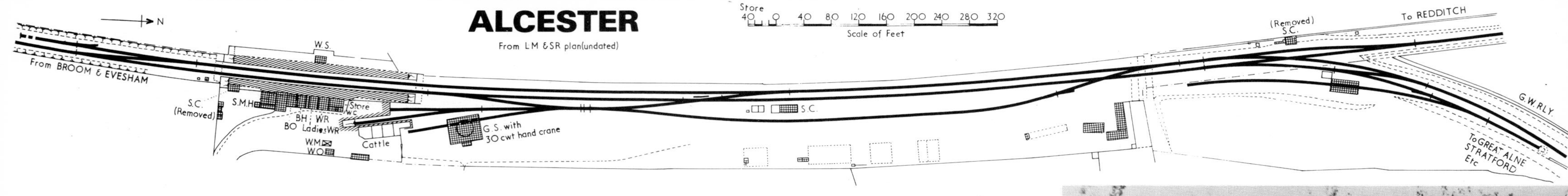

ALCESTER *(Map Ref. D4)*

The Barnt Green and Ashchurch branch of the Midland Railway was built piecemeal, and although it provided an apparent relief route to the Lickey incline on the MR Birmingham–Gloucester main line, its single track and speed restrictions, as severe as 15 mph in places, reduced its significance to branch line status. The line was built in three sections, the final portion, from Evesham to Redditch via Alcester, being authorised as the Evesham & Redditch Railway in 1863. The Evesham–Alcester section was opened in June 1866, and the line extended north to meet the Redditch branch in 1868. These companies were in the Midland orbit, and the E&R taken over in 1882. In the meantime, the GW inspired Alcester Railway had been busy, opening its short branch from Bearley Junction to Alcester in September 1876, the AR being formally vested in the GWR two years later. As a junction station, Alcester thus received Midland trains on the long Barnt Green–Ashchurch route, and GW workings from Bearley, a small locomotive shed being located almost opposite the junction signal box at Alcester for the branch engine. The GW branch was closed from 1917 to 1923 as a war-time economy measure. Services were again suspended on 25th September 1939 and the branch finally closed in 1951. Trains on the Midland route continued until 1st October 1962, freight workings lingering until 6th July 1964.

In October 1905, the Midland provided seven passenger trains in each direction, whilst the GWR offered five workings to and from Bearley. Under LMS auspices the station and junction signal boxes were replaced by a central cabin in the yard, working under single line token arrangements to Broom Junction and Studley. By 1944, the GW service had ceased and the LMS service had dropped to five through trains, and an early morning working from Redditch to Alcester and back north through to Birmingham.

Alcester — vignette of a country station, with floral display.

The station and yard looking towards Redditch; a freight train shunts in the yard, the engine being to the right of the LMS-built signal box.

Facilities on the northbound platform were simple but attractive.

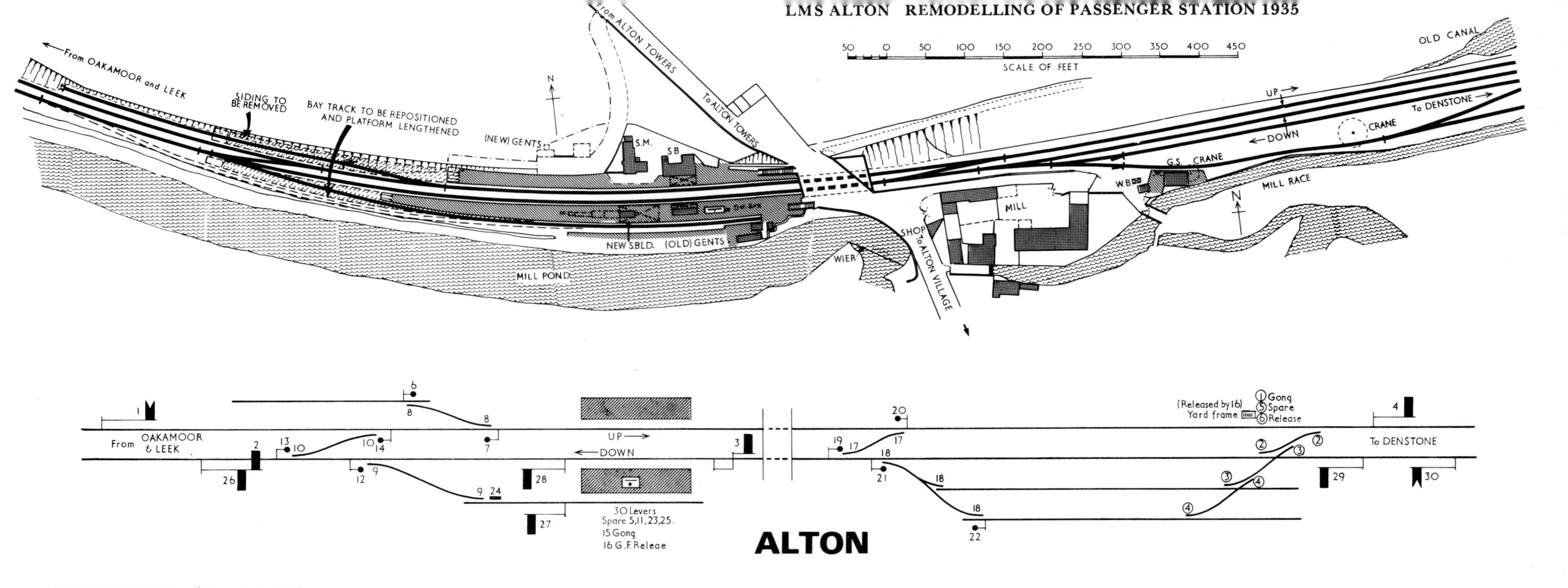

ALTON TOWERS *(Map Ref. U8)*

The Churnet Valley Railway was one of several routes authorised in June 1846, and which laid down the framework of the North Staffordshire Railway. The line ran from North Rode, near Macclesfield, through Leek and Alton to Uttoxeter, and opened on 13th July 1849. It became renowned for its attractive scenery and its equally charming stations, Alton frequently being attributed to the noted Victorian architect, A. W. Pugin. As Pugin had been involved in the design of nearby Alton Towers, seat of the Earl of Shrewsbury, this would have been appropriate, but the story has never been wholly satisfactorily explained.

The station was situated on a curve, and this, together with the rising ground to the north and mill pond to the south, necessitated a long narrow layout, but set off the remarkable buildings to perfection. Because of the Mill Race and canal, access to the goods yard was awkward, but the combination of mill ponds, mill, railway and a rising backdrop would make the station ideal for a model, especially as it is on such a convenient curve!

In NSR days the traditional service was four workings each way on weekdays, with a Sunday service geared to holiday needs. By 1944 there were six trains each way over the Oakamoor–Uttoxeter portion of the Churnet Valley line, with two trains on Sundays (as day tripper traffic was being discouraged).

The scale plan shows enlargements proposed by the LMSR, and emerged from the architectural assistant's office in 1935. The station then lacked an adequate road approach, the platforms were only about 500 feet long, and half of that was less than standard height, whilst the Down platform boasted five earth closets – hardly the thing for a tourist station! The rebuilding sought to eliminate all these defects. Whilst repairs were charged to revenue, improvements constituted a continuing drain on capital, and in the late thirties the LMS estimated that sundry station improvements throughout the system would swallow over half a million pounds within a relatively short period.

Alton was renamed Alton Towers in 1954. In 1960, the northern section of the line from Leeds to North Rode was closed, and the southern section, on which Alton Towers was located, followed suit on 4th January 1965. The track was subsequently lifted, but happily Pugin's glorious station was not demolished.

Overleaf
Alton Towers looking towards Uttoxeter in the late 1950s. The pantiled roof of the station buildings and the old oil lamp are captured in reflection as well as in life. Alton is customarily attributed to Pugin, one of the great Gothic revivalists of the early Victorian era, but the station is Florentine rather than Gothic in concept, although rock faced stone replaced the more customary stucco. As Pugin worked with Sir Charles Barry on the Houses of Parliament, and as Trentham Station is customarily attributed to Barry, it is possible that Alton may be a strange mixture of the two, an odd result of two men of differing tastes affecting each other's creation. The nearer building in the illustration, with tower and balcony, is the station master's house, the station building being further down the platform, graced by a canopy. The road bridge carries the road from Alton Towers to Alton village over the line.

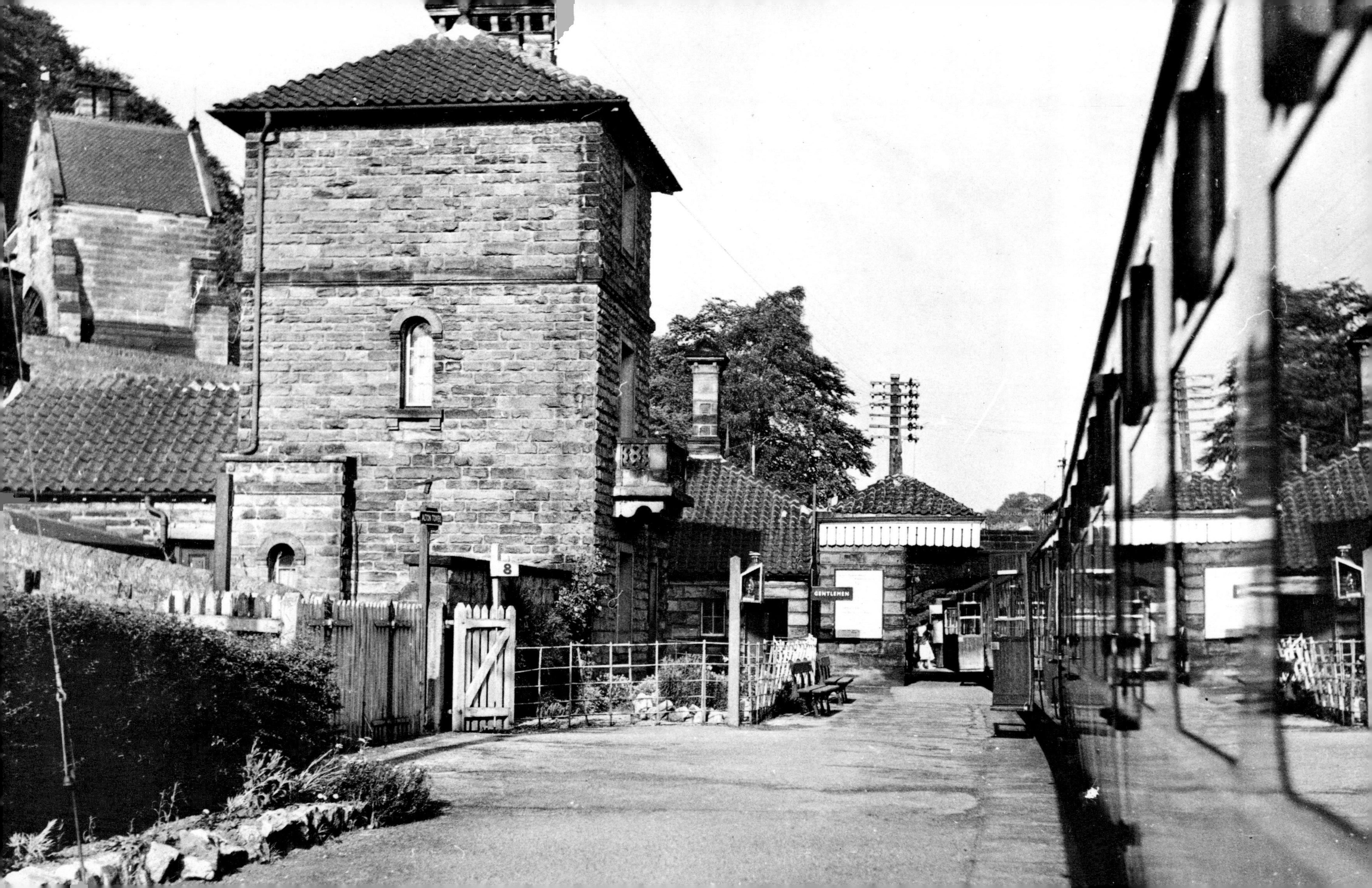
8
GENTLEMEN

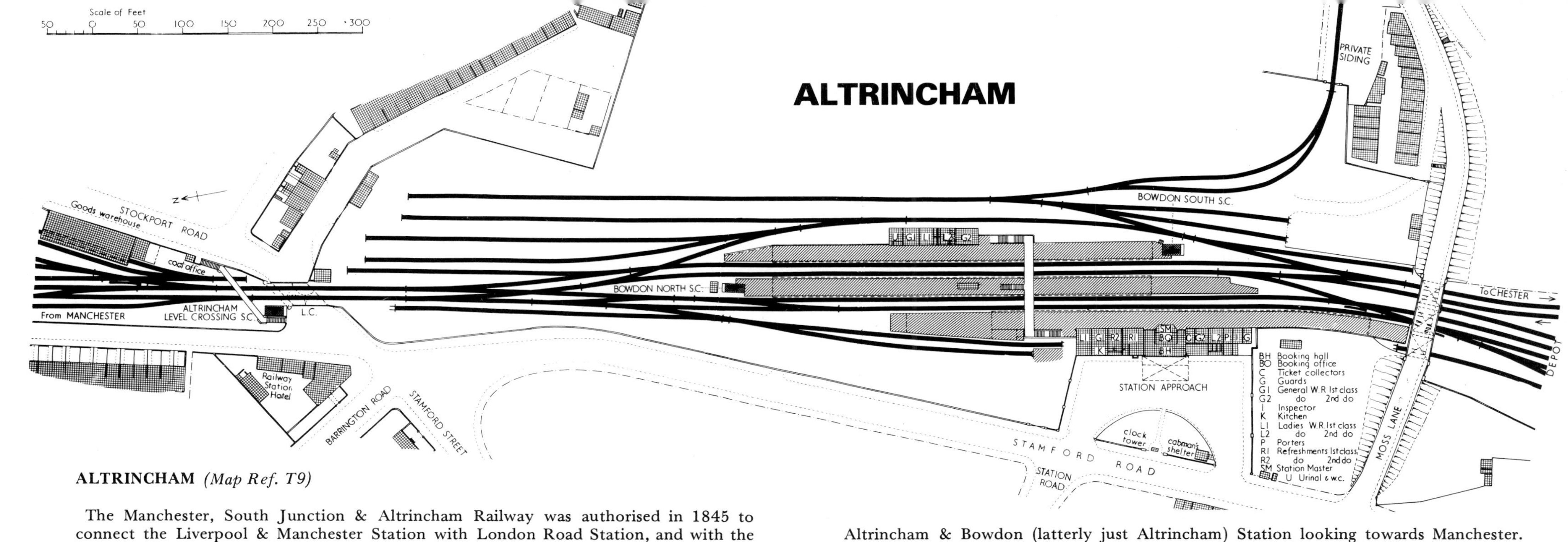

ALTRINCHAM *(Map Ref. T9)*

The Manchester, South Junction & Altrincham Railway was authorised in 1845 to connect the Liverpool & Manchester Station with London Road Station, and with the small town of Altrincham. In 1845-46 the various mergers forming the LNWR and the MS&LR took place, the MSJ&AR becoming a subsidiary of these two. The section from Oxford Road Station to Altrincham was opened on 20th July 1849. In the 1850s, the MS&L was seeking pastures new, and backed the Cheshire Midland Railway which was to carry the line on from Altrincham to Northwich, with extensions out to Chester in view. The Altrincham–Knutsford portion of the CMR was opened on 12th May 1862, the extension diverging from the MSJ&AR between Bowdon and Altrincham Stations. In 1863, the Cheshire Midland passed to the Cheshire Lines Committee, upon which the MS&LR, GNR and Midland were ultimately to have equal shares. The CLC route reached Chester in 1874, by which time Altrincham had become a fashionable suburb of Manchester.

On 3rd April 1881 the old Bowdon and Altrincham Stations were closed, and a new station, Altrincham & Bowdon, opened in between. Two platforms were provided for the CLC trains and two for the MSJ&AR workings, the station being worked from a level crossing box and two station cabins. The crossing was a constant cause of complaint, and even led to a question in Parliament. The MSJ&AR did prepare plans for a road flyover diverting Stamford Road and losing the sidings at the north end of the station, but the work was never carried out. A private tramway from the station to Altrincham Gas Works was authorised in 1893 and opened within two years. This ran along Moss Lane, and was worked by horse, sentinel lorry, steam and diesel locomotives before its closure in 1958. In May 1931, the MSJ&AR was electrified on the 1,500 volt DC overhead system, the original electric stock remaining in use until 1971 when the line was re-electrified on the more modern 25kV AC system. By the late 1930s, there were over one hundred trains each way on the MSJ&AR and about fifteen to twenty over the CLC. Both passenger services survive.

Altrincham & Bowdon (latterly just Altrincham) Station looking towards Manchester. The lines in the foreground served the MSJ&AR car shed, which was the original Altrincham Station. The lines on the right are the CLC tracks to Chester.

ARNSIDE

c.19 Apr 1956

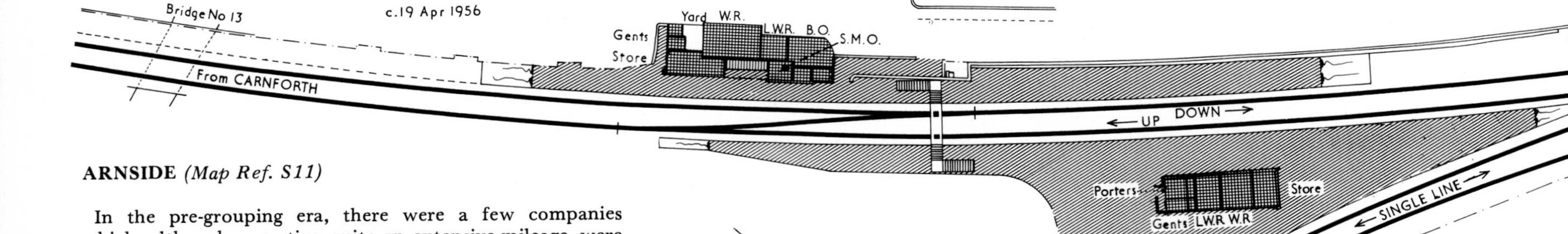

ARNSIDE *(Map Ref. S11)*

In the pre-grouping era, there were a few companies which, although operating quite an extensive mileage, were still very local in *their* direction and management. The Furness Railway was one such concern. Its main line ran from Carnforth to Barrow and Whitehaven, and was built up piecemeal over a number of years.

The section from Ulverston to Carnforth, where it joined the LNWR, was built by the Ulverston & Lancaster Railway (incorporated 24th July 1851), and opened to goods on 10th August 1857, and to passengers on 16th August. The route adopted necessitated the crossing of the Leven and Kent estuaries, and the line was correspondingly costly to construct.

Arnside (pop. 1,154) lies on the east bank of the Kent estuary, and was in Westmorland on the narrow neck of land which gives that county access to the sea. The station is in a picturesque location beside the water. Its significance increased considerably after 26th June 1876, when the line to Hincaster Junction came into use. Both connections from the FR to the LNWR West Coast Route thus converged on Arnside.

The Furness, well aware of the needs and attributes of its territory, described Arnside thus in its guides. 'This is Arnside, a winsome little town with many natural advantages, not the least amongst these being reckoned its position on a lovely bay and beneath the shoulder of the wooded hill called Arnside Knott'.

In 1905, seven main line services in each direction called at the station, together with five workings over the Hincaster branch. In later years the services improved. In 1927 there were six branch trains, mostly running between Kendal and Grange, but some starting further afield. On the main line the service varied, there being eighteen northbound trains, a number of which were short workings only as far as the next station, Grange.

Even in 1938, there were still six trains over the branch. However, changed conditions resulted in the Hincaster passenger service being suspended on 4th May 1942, with the route officially closing on 1st March 1953. Carnforth line services continue to call at Arnside. Freight services to Sandside, on the branch, ran until 1968, private siding traffic lingering even longer.

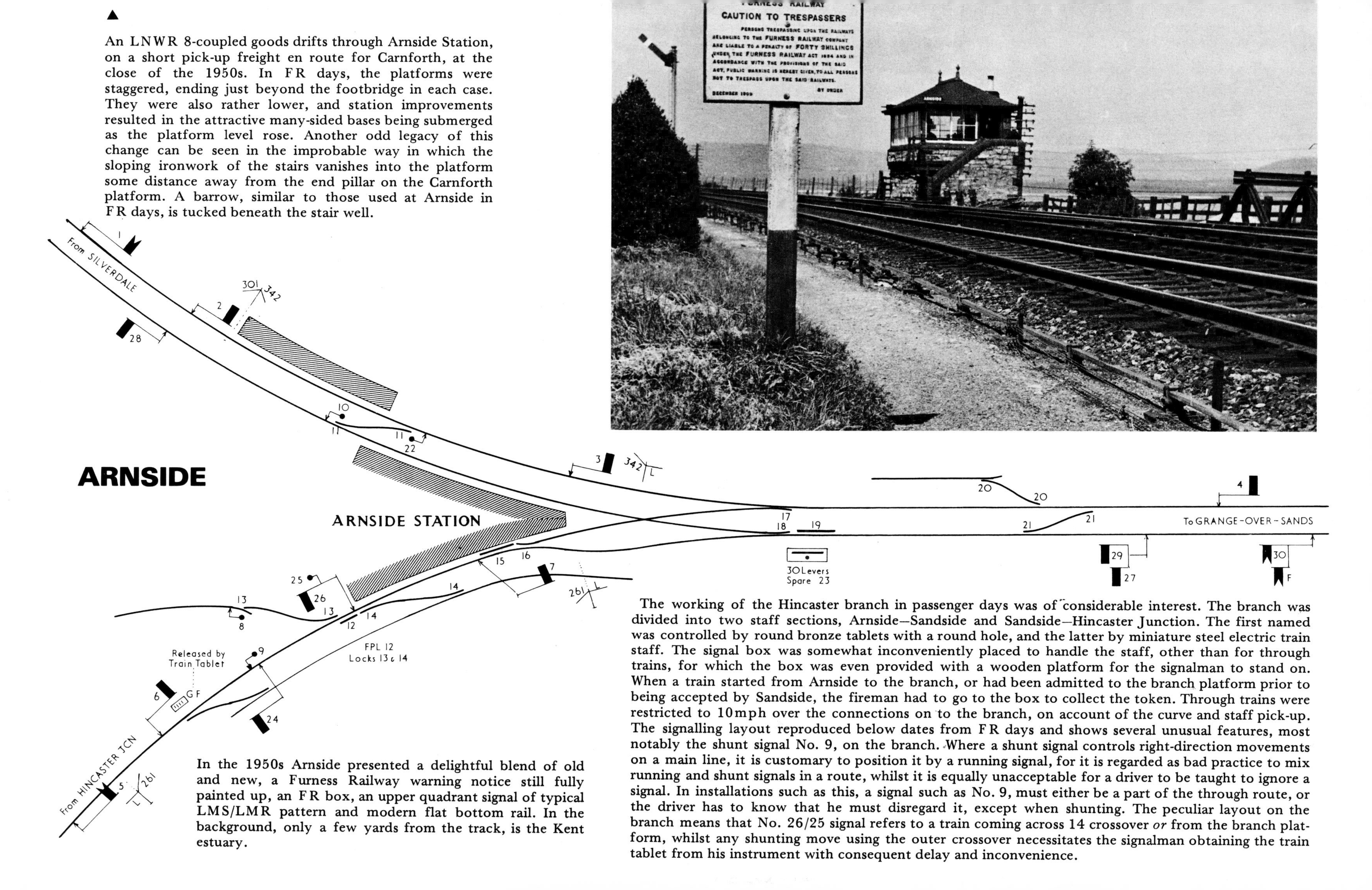

▲ An LNWR 8-coupled goods drifts through Arnside Station, on a short pick-up freight en route for Carnforth, at the close of the 1950s. In FR days, the platforms were staggered, ending just beyond the footbridge in each case. They were also rather lower, and station improvements resulted in the attractive many-sided bases being submerged as the platform level rose. Another odd legacy of this change can be seen in the improbable way in which the sloping ironwork of the stairs vanishes into the platform some distance away from the end pillar on the Carnforth platform. A barrow, similar to those used at Arnside in FR days, is tucked beneath the stair well.

ARNSIDE

In the 1950s Arnside presented a delightful blend of old and new, a Furness Railway warning notice still fully painted up, an FR box, an upper quadrant signal of typical LMS/LMR pattern and modern flat bottom rail. In the background, only a few yards from the track, is the Kent estuary.

The working of the Hincaster branch in passenger days was of considerable interest. The branch was divided into two staff sections, Arnside—Sandside and Sandside—Hincaster Junction. The first named was controlled by round bronze tablets with a round hole, and the latter by miniature steel electric train staff. The signal box was somewhat inconveniently placed to handle the staff, other than for through trains, for which the box was even provided with a wooden platform for the signalman to stand on. When a train started from Arnside to the branch, or had been admitted to the branch platform prior to being accepted by Sandside, the fireman had to go to the box to collect the token. Through trains were restricted to 10mph over the connections on to the branch, on account of the curve and staff pick-up. The signalling layout reproduced below dates from FR days and shows several unusual features, most notably the shunt signal No. 9, on the branch. Where a shunt signal controls right-direction movements on a main line, it is customary to position it by a running signal, for it is regarded as bad practice to mix running and shunt signals in a route, whilst it is equally unacceptable for a driver to be taught to ignore a signal. In installations such as this, a signal such as No. 9, must either be a part of the through route, or the driver has to know that he must disregard it, except when shunting. The peculiar layout on the branch means that No. 26/25 signal refers to a train coming across 14 crossover *or* from the branch platform, whilst any shunting move using the outer crossover necessitates the signalman obtaining the train tablet from his instrument with consequent delay and inconvenience.

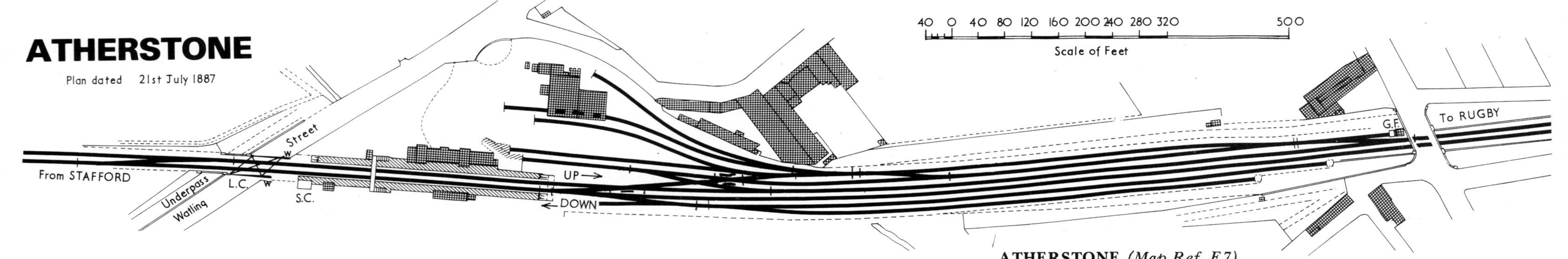

Atherstone Station looking towards Stafford from the Up platform in the 1950s, with the Holyhead road overbridge visible in the distance. The Up and Down awnings are quite dissimilar, revealing the station's piecemeal ancestry, and whilst the supports for the Down canopy are quite normal, the forest of supports on the Up side shows clearly.

ATHERSTONE *(Map Ref. E7)*

Atherstone was one of the original Trent Valley Railway stations of 1847. The TVR was authorised in 1845, brought into limited use on 15th September 1847, and into full use on 1st December that year. At that time, the line was double track, and remained thus for many years. Periodic additions were made to the layout during the nineteenth century, most notably in 1887 when the Up platform was extended and the Up yard enlarged.

In the LNWR (Additional Powers) Act 1892, permission was obtained to quadruple 7 miles 4 furlongs between Tamworth and just north of Atherstone level crossing. This level crossing, over the A5 Holyhead road, had, for many years, been a bone of contention between the local authorities and the LNWR. Finally in 1898-99, the Warwickshire County Council took the LNWR to court, and obtained an injunction prohibiting them from running trains across the road at more than 4mph!

The Tamworth–Atherstone quadrupling came into use on 1st July 1901, and powers for the Atherstone–Nuneaton section were obtained in the LNWR Act of 1902. The Act also authorised the company to divert and carry Watling Street over the railway and the Coventry canal, by means of a bridge, and to close up the old level crossing. This latter task was completed in September 1903.

The old signal box at the north end of the station, together with the Down platform, was swept away during the quadrupling, and a new timber building and signal box erected. A 1909 stage work sketch for the quadrupling is reproduced.

The new cabin was centrally situated, and was carried on girders, one set of supports being on the Down platform, the others in a slightly enlarged 'six foot' between the fast lines. Access to the box was via a catwalk from the Down side. Any girder box was of interest, but what made the Atherstone example even more remarkable, was the superstructure, which possessed the extended roof and barge boards of post-1904 LNWR boxes, but the shallower windows reminiscent of earlier designs.

Another unusual aspect of the station was the short awning on the Up side. The supports for this were placed very close together (inconveniently so), and were considerably less than the regulation six feet from the platform edge.

The goods yard was closed in May 1964, although the passenger station remained in use. Since 2nd October 1972, it has been unstaffed.

In the stage work plan reproduced below, it is possible to see how the old Down platform, evident in the 1887 scale plan, was replaced by a new platform two tracks away, and a new signal box erected on its site. Although authorised in 1902, the Nuneaton–Atherstone quadrupling was still under way in 1909, being opened sectionally.

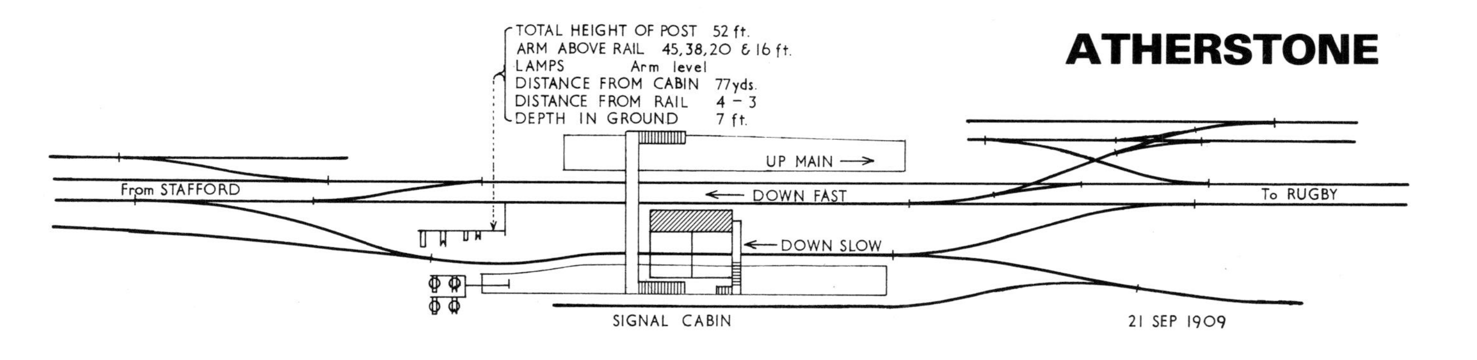

The original Trent Valley stations were the work of J. W. Livock, an excellent but somewhat neglected architect, and were Elizabethan or Jacobean in style. Atherstone followed the Elizabethan manorial style with steeply pitched roofs, tall patterned chimneys and alternate bands of patterned slates.

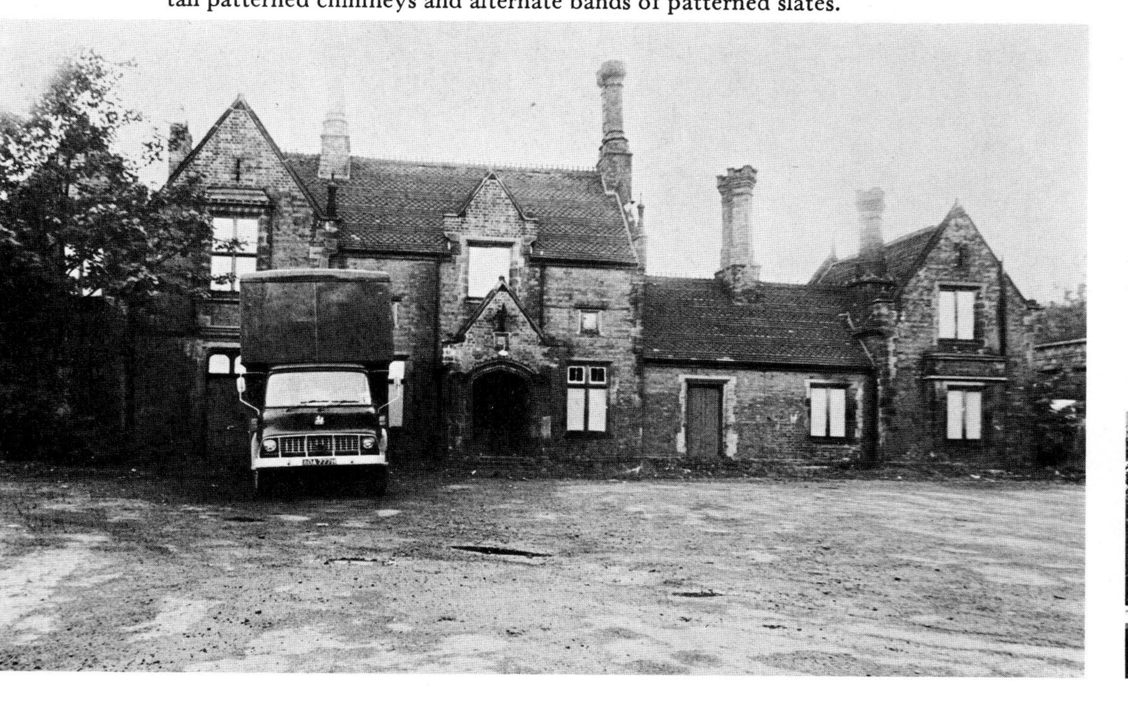

Although vandalism, neglect and disuse, after Atherstone was made an unstaffed halt, had taken their toll by the late 1970s, the removal of the awning on the Up platform enables one to appreciate Livock's design once again, in this evening study looking towards Rugby. A 'bus shelter' edifice beyond the building is all that the present day passenger can expect.

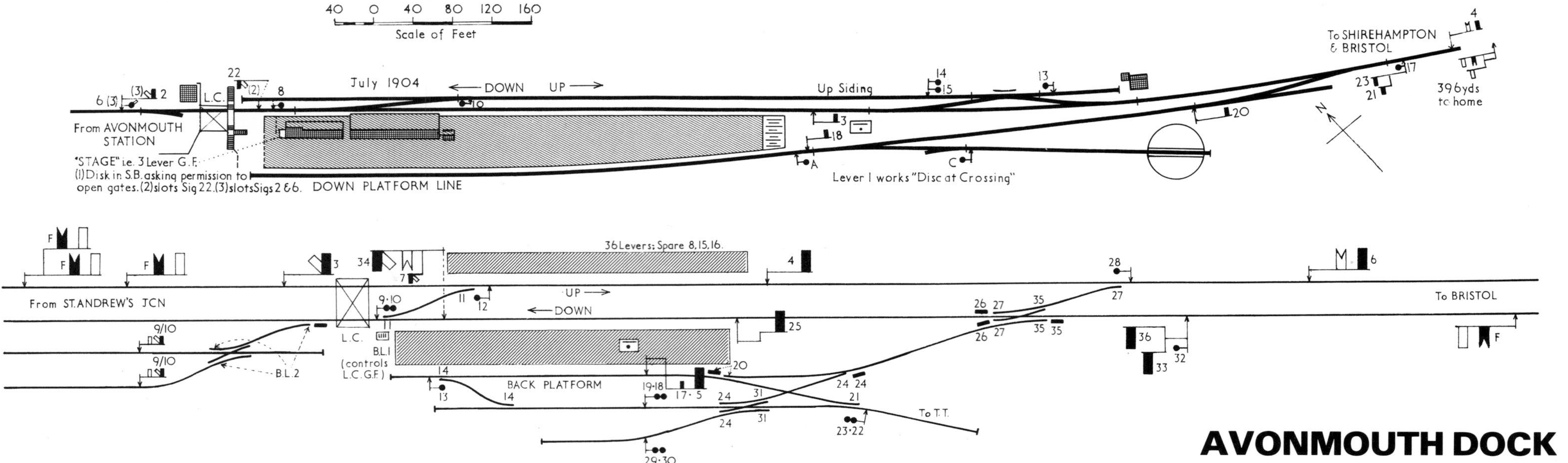

AVONMOUTH DOCK

AVONMOUTH DOCK *(Map Ref. T4)*

Of all the stations owned or part owned by the LMSR, Avonmouth Dock was one of the strangest. It lies on the Clifton Extension Railway on the outskirts of Bristol, the first portion of which opened on 6th March 1865 as the Bristol Port Railway & Pier Co. The BPR&P was isolated from the rest of the railway network, and soon fell on hard times. Plans to extend to a junction with the MR and GWR were taken over by those companies and a joint line opened on to the BPR&P in 1877. Owing to the deplorable condition of the lesser company's track, it was not feasible to inaugurate through passenger services. Finally, the MR obtained powers to rebuild the line, and through workings commenced on 1st September 1885. A new Avonmouth Dock Joint Station was opened to the east of the old BPR&P edifice (which, however, remained in use until 1903). The GWR provided a service from Temple Meads, and the Midland from St. Philip's, but the latter was withdrawn after only thirteen months on 1st October 1886. Henceforth, Avonmouth Dock was a joint station *not* served by Midland trains (other than for excursions).

Despite this reverse, the MR retained a keen interest in the station, and the MR (Additional Powers) Act of 1890 authorised the MR and GWR to purchase the BPR&P. In 1903-04, major improvements were effected. The line from Shirehampton to near Avonmouth Dock was doubled in May 1903, and an additional bay platform added at the Dock Joint Station the following year. Despite the lack of Midland involvement with the passenger service, the plans for the rebuild emanated from Derby, and it was the MR general manager's office who notified the Board of Trade when the work was ready for inspection.

During the 1914-18 war, the area assumed great military importance, and the existing platform was extended in December 1917, and a third (Up) platform added on 15th July 1918. The shelter on this platform was utilitarian and did not add to the overall appearance of the station.

In the early days the through services between Avonmouth and Bristol were relatively few in number. In 1887, shortly after the MR workings ceased, the GWR provided six trains into the Joint Station, and even in 1905 there were no more than eleven trains from Temple Meads. Although a GWR service, the line was shown in Bradshaw as *Great Western and Midland*, and details of the GWR services still graced the LMS public and working timetables in the 1940s! By 1944, there were some thirty trains a day from Temple Meads to Avonmouth Dock.

The original BPR&P service from Avonmouth to Clifton (situated almost directly beneath the suspension bridge), survived the introduction of through trains and the GW-MR take-over. The traditional service was about nine or ten trains a day, but this came to an end in the 1920s when the Clifton terminus was closed.

Avonmouth Dock Station from the 1918 platform, looking towards St. Andrew's Junction and Avonmouth Station. All three platform faces are exceptionally wide, the canopies on the Down platform and bay being to an unusual design with two quite different sections. The level crossing ground frame hut — a mini signal box in fact — can just be made out at the left hand end of the footbridge which overshadowed it. The differing constructional style of the Down platform is noteworthy, and the abrupt change in materials reflect the piecemeal extensions effected to the station.

BANBURY (Merton Street) *(Map Ref. G3)*

Right The driver of No. 80040 holds his billy of tea as he chats to his fireman on the platform shortly prior to departure for Bletchley, in this evocative 1953 scene. A member of the station staff sees that all is well at the far end of the platform. The cladding to the station roof had only just been removed at the date of the photograph, and the supports had not yet been repainted. A fresh coat of paint lightened and brightened up the station greatly. The three types of construction utilised for the platform are apparent; transverse planking for the original section within the train shed, Staffordshire blue paving bricks for the first extension and longitudinal timbering for the final additions. Although the locomotive and stock are more modern, the scene would not have surprised a regular traveller of the 1850s, although he might have looked askance at the train shed robbed of its covering. Although less than a third of that period has elapsed since the view was taken, it is an altogether different age. Such was the permanence, and then the sudden impermanence of the railway scene.

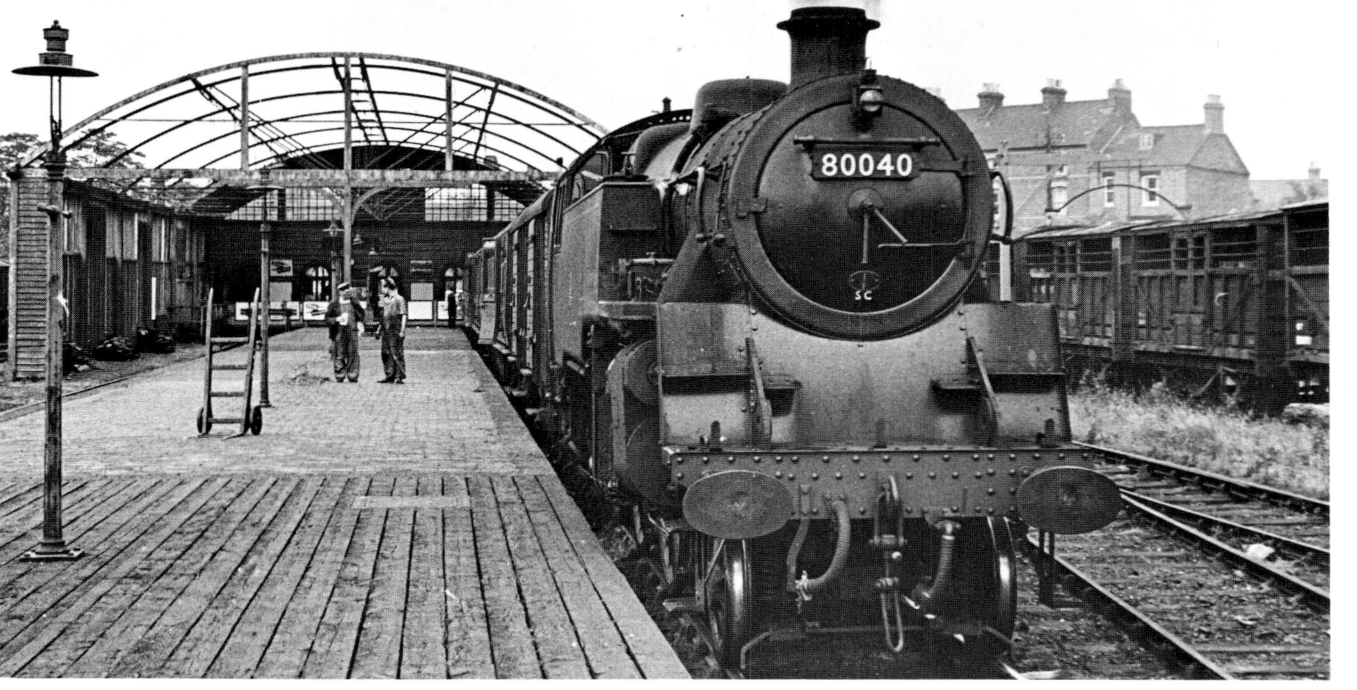

Below The LMS image; experiments to create a recognisable LMS station nameboard got under way in 1934, but it was not until 1938 that the Hawkseye sign went into mass production. In the decade which remained to the company, it became widespread. Originally the lettering was black, the ground being coated in a myriad of tiny yellow glass spheres to improve night visibility. Normal signs were 4 feet long, but **BANBURY (MERTON ST)** was too long, necessitating a longer sign, seen here after BR had chipped the beads off to impose London Midland Region maroon paint.

Below right The exterior of Merton Street Station in 1953. The LONDON MIDLAND & SCOTTISH RAILWAY lettering on the roof board (which had replaced an LNWR title), had not been altered by BR, nor had the poster boards been altered. The pedimented ends to the station offices are unusual in a timber building, but echo the adjoining GWR station which was built in 1850 with an overall roof in the form of a portico, with prominent pediments. Perhaps Merton Street got its pediments and train shed in retaliation!

BANBURY LNWR

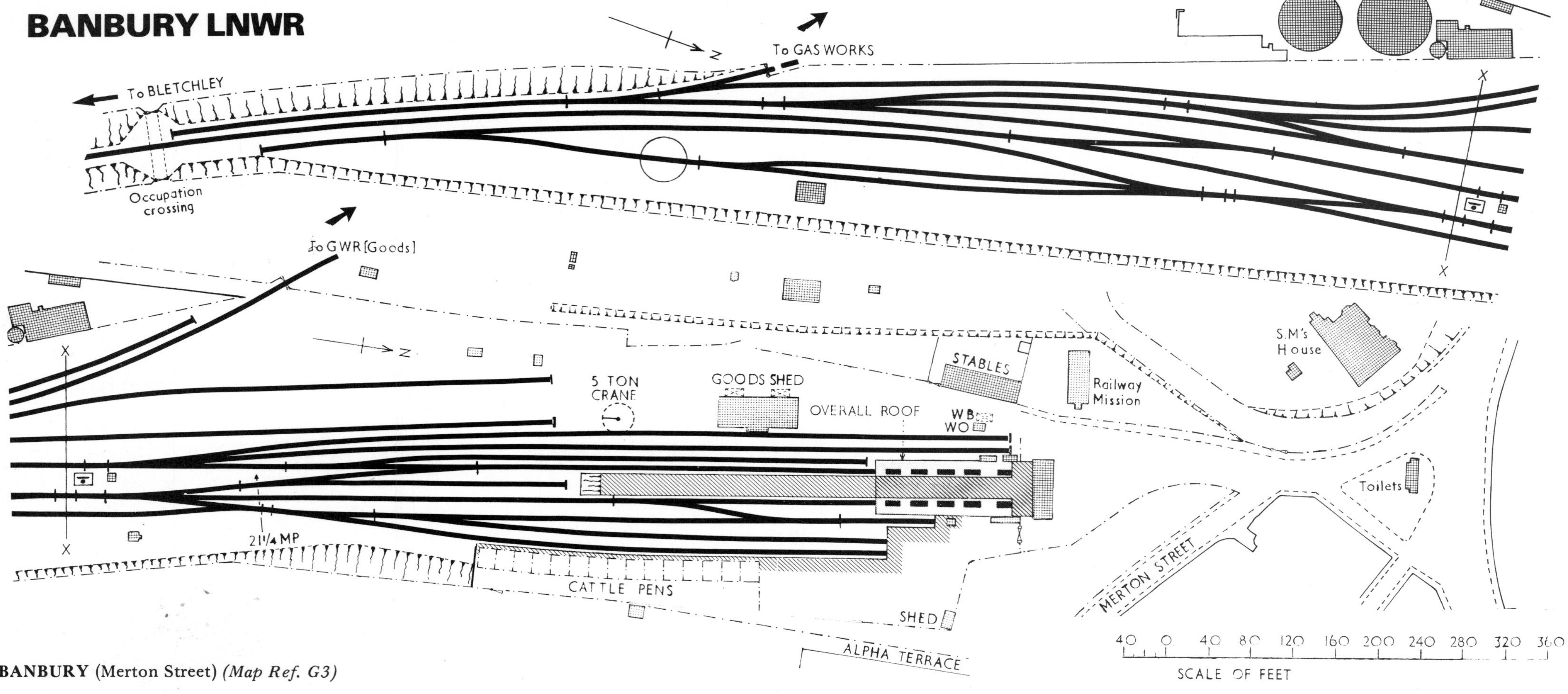

BANBURY (Merton Street) *(Map Ref. G3)*

The location of Merton Street Station, tucked away behind its GWR rival in Banbury reflected its secluded and peaceful atmosphere. Merton Street was at the end of a 21¼ mile single track branch from Verney Junction, and because of its sparse service, most folk travelling to or from Banbury patronised the GWR.

Banbury was a market town with a population of some 20,000, historically best known for its medieval cross, and popularly for its cakes! The North Western station was one of the two termini of the Buckinghamshire Railway, and opened on 1st May 1850. The main buildings were of timber construction with a short timber, steel and corrugated iron train shed. There was a single island platform, a goods yard, exchange sidings and a small motive power depot.

The train shed was the most interesting feature of the station. It was in the form of a shallow arch, the curved members being supported by the framework for the side walls, and by tie rods radiating out from a longitudinal tie rod and transverse tie rods above the platform. The upper section of the town end was partially glazed, but the country end was not, illumination from below the roof level being judged sufficient. The curved roof was clad in corrugated galvanised sheeting, the whole design reflecting economy and the early view that train sheds did not need much glazing. Had the station been built a few years later, a steel framed, glazed structure would have been the order, had Banbury been judged worthy of a train shed at all, as for minor stations they fell out of favour quite early.

Train services from Merton Street ran over the Bucks line to Verney Junction and Bletchley, and via Cockley Brake on to the Stratford-upon-Avon & Midland Junction Railway to Towcester. Although a byway, Merton Street acquired a joint atmosphere due to these foreign workings, and the SMJ locomotives were almost as common a sight in Banbury as LNWR stock.

In 1895, there were five passenger departures daily to Bletchley and three to Towcester. The same basic pattern prevailed in 1909, but with the added refinement of a through coach between Banbury and Euston. This left Merton Street on the 9.40 am, arriving in London at 12 noon. The return working left Euston at 4.05 pm, was slipped at Bletchley, and arrived back in Banbury at 6.32 pm.

The LMS maintained the five-train service on the Verney line, but traffic fell away on the SMJ section, and by 1938 there were but two trips a day. The Towcester service ceased on 2nd July 1951, and that to Buckingham on 2nd January 1961.

The station remained in existence for many years after closure, gradually becoming more and more overgrown, with its platform projecting out like a forgotten pier into a sea of weeds.

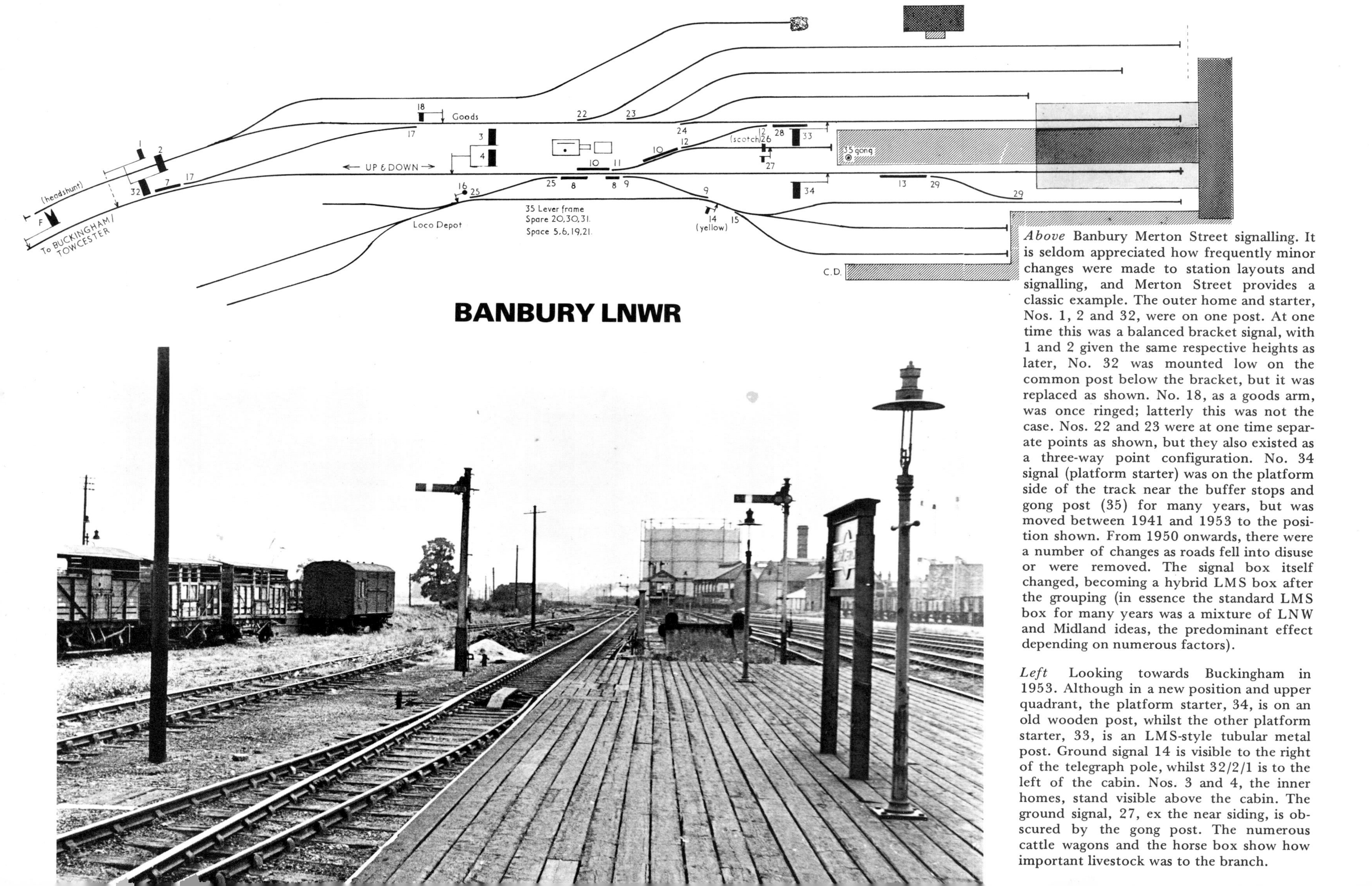

Above Banbury Merton Street signalling. It is seldom appreciated how frequently minor changes were made to station layouts and signalling, and Merton Street provides a classic example. The outer home and starter, Nos. 1, 2 and 32, were on one post. At one time this was a balanced bracket signal, with 1 and 2 given the same respective heights as later, No. 32 was mounted low on the common post below the bracket, but it was replaced as shown. No. 18, as a goods arm, was once ringed; latterly this was not the case. Nos. 22 and 23 were at one time separate points as shown, but they also existed as a three-way point configuration. No. 34 signal (platform starter) was on the platform side of the track near the buffer stops and gong post (35) for many years, but was moved between 1941 and 1953 to the position shown. From 1950 onwards, there were a number of changes as roads fell into disuse or were removed. The signal box itself changed, becoming a hybrid LMS box after the grouping (in essence the standard LMS box for many years was a mixture of LNW and Midland ideas, the predominant effect depending on numerous factors).

Left Looking towards Buckingham in 1953. Although in a new position and upper quadrant, the platform starter, 34, is on an old wooden post, whilst the other platform starter, 33, is an LMS-style tubular metal post. Ground signal 14 is visible to the right of the telegraph pole, whilst 32/2/1 is to the left of the cabin. Nos. 3 and 4, the inner homes, stand visible above the cabin. The ground signal, 27, ex the near siding, is obscured by the gong post. The numerous cattle wagons and the horse box show how important livestock was to the branch.

BARE LANE

10 April 1900

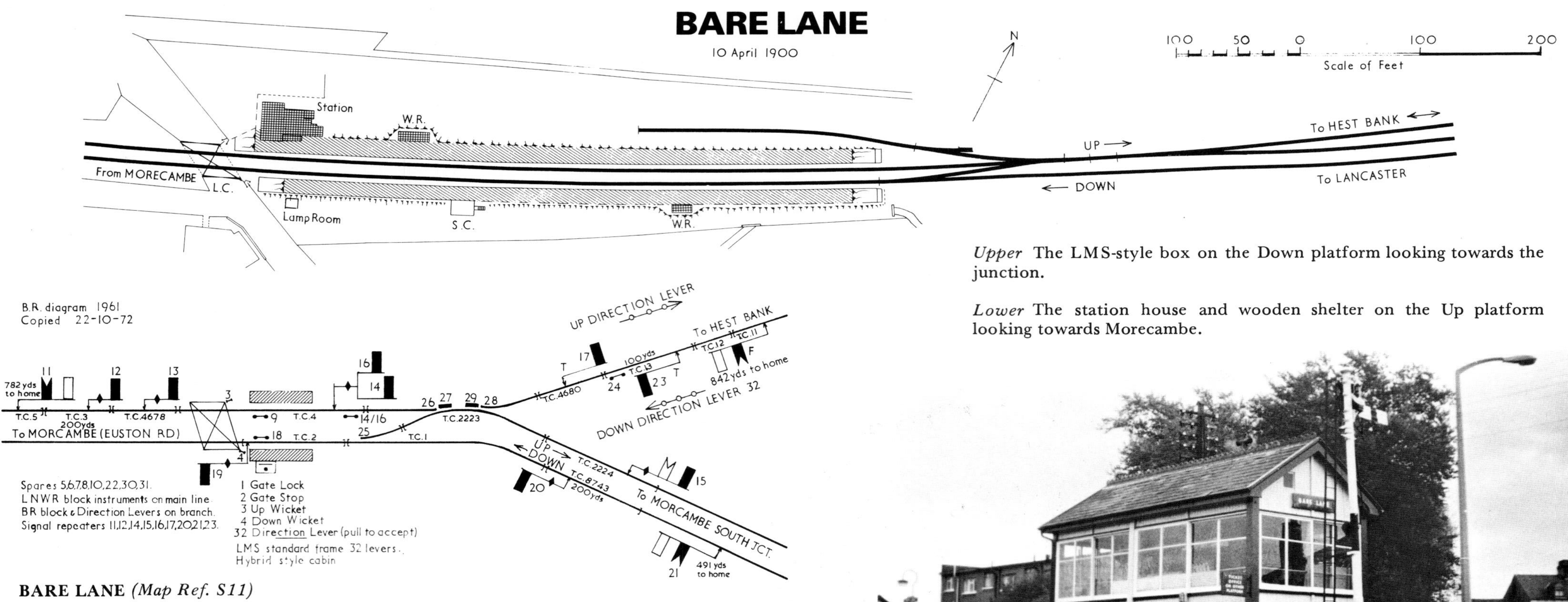

Upper The LMS-style box on the Down platform looking towards the junction.

Lower The station house and wooden shelter on the Up platform looking towards Morecambe.

BARE LANE *(Map Ref. S11)*

The short single track branch which diverges from the West Coast main line at Hest Bank, just north of Lancaster, dates back to the days of the Lancaster & Carlisle Railway. It was authorised in 1859, although not opened until 8th August 1864. It was expected that an export traffic in coke and other minerals from the north-east would develop at Morecambe, and the line was built as double track, but was later singled. In 1887, the LNWR obtained powers to build a double track curve from the south on to the branch. This was 55 chains in length and left the main line at Morecambe South Junction, running to the only intermediate station on the line at Bare Lane. Here it joined the still single line into the LNWR station at Morecambe (Euston Road). The absurdity of a double and a single track leading on to a single track section was remedied in 1891 when the 1 mile 16 chains into Morecambe were re-doubled. The portion from Bare Lane to Hest Bank remained single.

A short siding was laid in off the Up line in 1900, so providing freight facilities. The North Western cabin situated part way down the platform was replaced, in LMS days, by a hybrid box adjacent to the level crossing gates. When the single track line was not in use, this cabin could be switched out as a block post. A miniature electric train staff controlled movements over the branch, the staff being round and steel-coloured. This method of working survived the replacement of Hest Bank box in the 1950s by a new structure, 165 yards further north, but was superseded some years later by 'direction lever' working. A direction lever was provided at each cabin, which, when pulled, locked its counterpart in the other box, and, at the same time, freed the appropriate signals on the single line section.

In the 1890s, sixteen or seventeen trains called at Bare Lane in each direction. The majority of these used the South curve into Lancaster, but three or four traversed the single track section to Hest Bank and Carnforth. The service was subject to considerable seasonal variation, and excursion workings were common. Despite the existence of the competitive Midland Railway electrified route from Lancaster (Castle) and Green Ayre, the line continued to carry a good service in LMS days, and has in fact outlived its Midland rival.

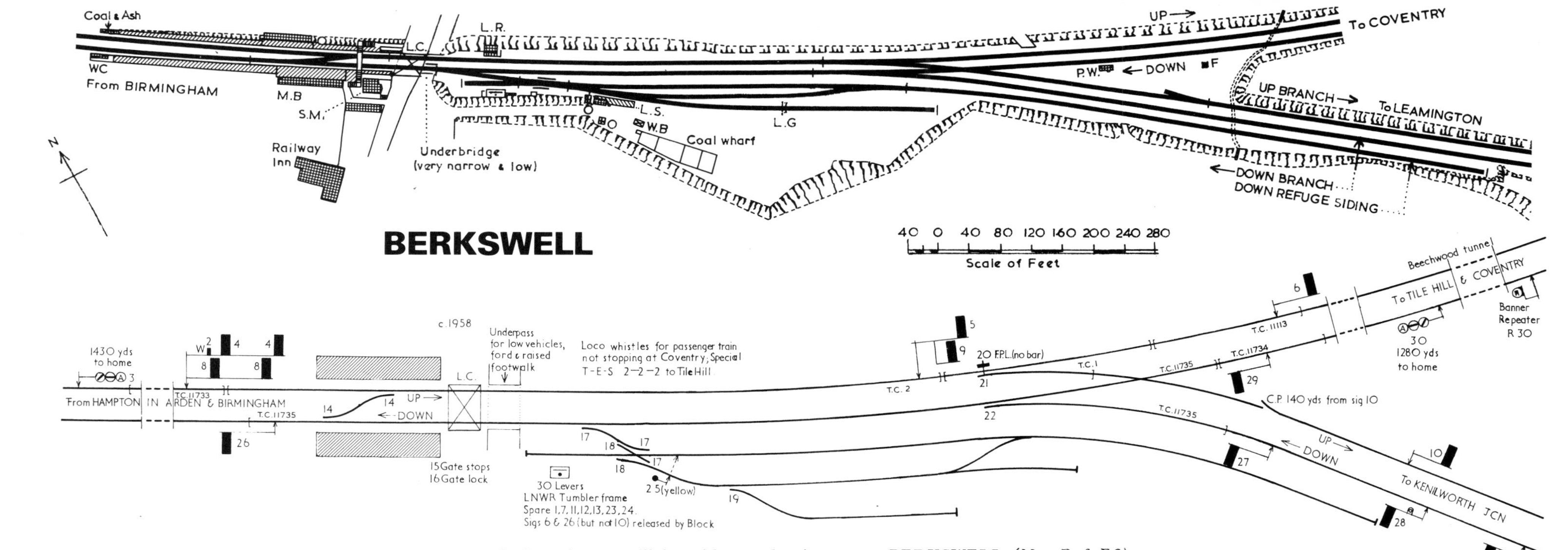

Berkswell Station looking towards Coventry, with L&NWR platform lamps still in evidence, despite electrification. The left-hand, or Up, platform dates from shortly before World War I, and the buildings, although of customary North Western pattern, display many differences from their counterparts on the Down side, which are to a much earlier pattern.

BERKSWELL *(Map Ref. E6)*

When the London & Birmingham main line opened between Birmingham and Rugby in 1838, wayside stations were few in number, and it was not until October 1844 that the decision was taken to open a halt at Docker's Lane. Platforms and a booking hut appeared a short while later. In 1847, the LNWR obtained powers to build a line from Kenilworth to Docker's Lane, but this scheme was subsequently abandoned.

The next event of any significance was the renaming of the station as Berkswell on 1st January 1853. Goods traffic was first handled in 1865, and in 1881, powers were once again obtained for a Kenilworth–Berkswell branch, which opened to goods on 2nd March 1884, and to passengers on 2nd June.

Early photographs show the platforms to have been staggered, with the Up platform being on the south side of the level crossing opposite the signal box. In 1911 plans were prepared to improve the station, and the Up platform was transferred to the north side of the crossing, and an overbridge added. Commodious buildings were erected on the new platform, and these included a separate booking office (not used as such latterly).

Under the LMSR, the station became Berkswell & Balsall Common, but has now reverted to Berkswell.

With the implementation of the Coventry power box scheme, Berkswell signal box became a crossing frame controlling the level crossing and connections on to the Kenilworth branch, which was subsequently closed and has now been lifted.

In 1895 there were eight Down and eleven Up trains. By 1944, the growth in commuter traffic in the Birmingham and Coventry area had resulted in the service being increased to fifteen workings each way. A number of trains diverged at Berkswell on to the Kenilworth–Leamington line, so providing a service from Birmingham that was competitive with the GWR.

BETTWS-Y-COED

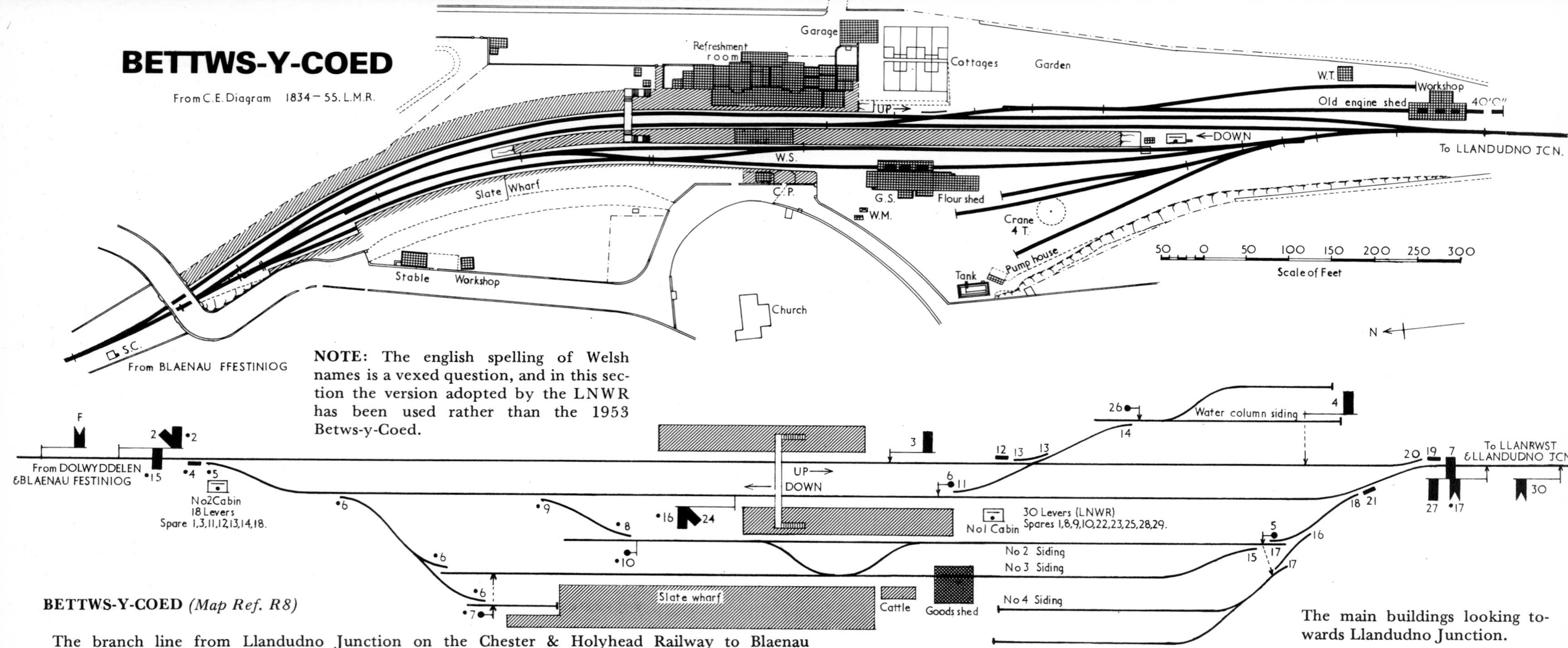

NOTE: The english spelling of Welsh names is a vexed question, and in this section the version adopted by the LNWR has been used rather than the 1953 Betws-y-Coed.

The main buildings looking towards Llandudno Junction.

BETTWS-Y-COED *(Map Ref. R8)*

The branch line from Llandudno Junction on the Chester & Holyhead Railway to Blaenau Ffestiniog was constructed in three stages. The first, the Conway & Llanrwst Railway, was incorporated in 1860, and opened the 11¼ miles to Llanwrst in June 1863. In 1867, the C&LR was taken over by the LNWR, and the line completed to Bettws-y-Coed, a further 3¾ miles, on 6th April 1868. On 22nd July 1879, the line was pushed through Blaenau Ffestiniog despite the severe engineering works involved, including the 3,726 yard Ffestiniog tunnel. The magnitude of these works made it appear likely that the extension would be constructed as a narrow gauge line, in which case it would have tied up with the Ffestiniog Railway from Portmadoc. This was not to be however, and after some distress at the high cost, the LNWR completed it as a normal branch and Bettws, instead of becoming a transhipment point, became an ordinary wayside station, with one platform.

A second platform was added in 1898, but as this was on the far side of the line from the village, and access to it necessitated passengers using a footbridge, the LNWR retained dual direction signalling through the main platform. This, despite its obvious convenience and the increased safety, as passengers did not have to climb the stairs unless trains were crossing, was an anathema to the Board of Trade, and the company were ordered to remove the wrong direction signalling forthwith. In many cases the Board of Trade requirements were beneficial. Here, they were entirely ludicrous, and merely served to inconvenience the public and add – marginally – to the risk of using the station. In 1895, the LNWR provided seven trains between Llandudno Junction and Blaenau Ffestiniog with an extra short-working from the junction to Bettws. By the summer of 1927, there were eleven trains to Blaenau and a dozen to the junction. Most had a four or five minute wait at Bettws, but a couple hung around for fourteen minutes.

BINTON

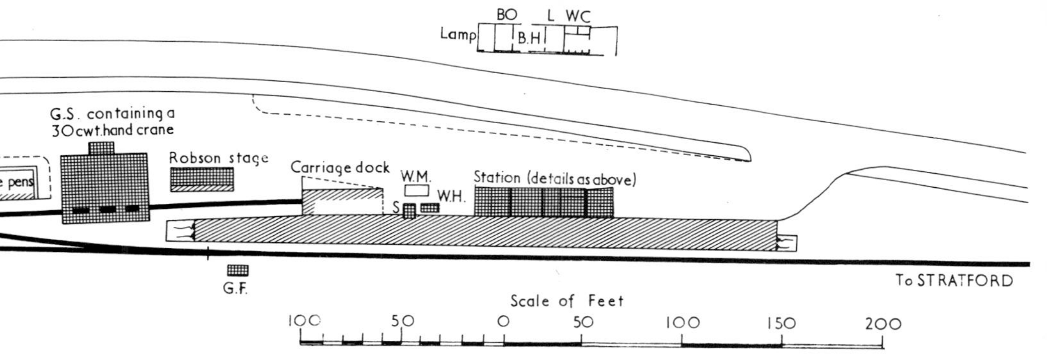

BINTON *(Map Ref. D4)*

On old railway maps an obscure line meanders across country from Broom Junction, near Evesham, to Ravenstone Wood Junction near Northampton. It serves no major town en route, and is variously lettered the East & West Junction Railway or the Stratford-upon-Avon & Midland Junction Railway.

The first section of the E&WJ opened in 1871, and by 1873 the line from Stratford in the west to Towcester in the east had been completed. Alas, receipts were depressing, and the E&WJ optimistically promoted an extension from Stratford to Broom, on the Midland Railway. The new company formed to build the line, the Evesham, Redditch & Stratford-upon-Avon Junction Railway was incorporated in 1873, and the line opened in 1879. By this time the E&WJ had got into such difficulties that it had withdrawn its own passenger services, and these did not recommence until 1885. In the meantime, the E&WJ had been working the ER&SJ, but not actually paying that company any traffic receipts, so that *they* in turn went into receivership in 1886! The companies staggered on from year to year, a re-organisation in 1908-10 helping somewhat.

Traffic over the Broom line, both local and through, was light, and the sections east and west of Stratford were treated as separate entities. In 1905 four trains ran over the ER&SJ in each direction – a typical service. The LMS made efforts to retain the branch, running four trains as late as 1938, by which time motor competition had made considerable inroads. The difficulties created by war conditions resulted in the service being curtailed to one train in each direction, and even this meagre service ended on 16th June 1947, and Bidford and Binton, the two intermediate stations, were temporarily closed. The closure was made permanent on 23rd May 1949. Freight traffic ceased in March 1960, and the line was subsequently lifted. The buildings remain in good condition and were (1979) in use as contractors' premises.

Binton Station looking towards Stratford circa 1951. The E&WJ did not have the money to go in for lavish layouts or architectural grandeur, and Binton typifies the plain but adequate country stations which came into fashion from the 1860s onwards.

The platform and goods shed looking towards Broom and Bidford. Brick edging to the platform, with a gravel surface, was an economical way of finishing a station, and was used by many companies for their wayside stations.

BIRDINGBURY

c. 1894

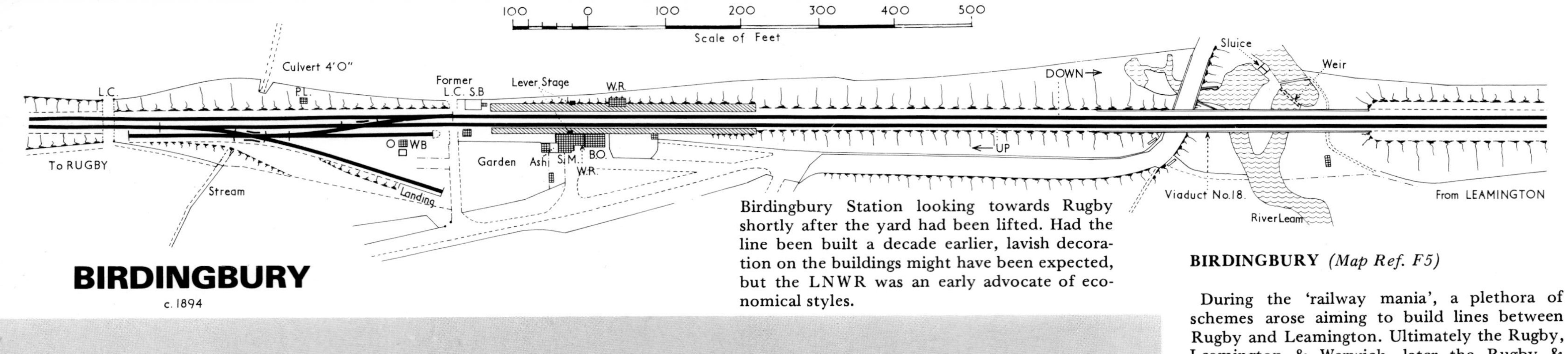

Birdingbury Station looking towards Rugby shortly after the yard had been lifted. Had the line been built a decade earlier, lavish decoration on the buildings might have been expected, but the LNWR was an early advocate of economical styles.

BIRDINGBURY *(Map Ref. F5)*

During the 'railway mania', a plethora of schemes arose aiming to build lines between Rugby and Leamington. Ultimately the Rugby, Leamington & Warwick, later the Rugby & Leamington Railway emerged triumphant. The R&L obtained its Act on 13th August 1846, but within weeks the shareholders met to discuss the sale of the line 'on such terms and conditions as may be determined', to the LNWR. The sale took place on 17th November 1846. The North Western began work, but there were frequent delays, which caused much local resentment, and it was not until 1st March 1851 that the line was opened. Birdingbury and Marton were the only intermediate station, until Dunchurch was opened to passengers in 1871.

Originally the R&L was single, but doubling was carried out in the 1880s. Until 1893 a private level crossing existed at the Rugby end of Birdingbury Station. The driveway leading to this crossing, although private property, was used by the LNWR under agreement as an access to the goods yard. The agreement granted a right of way to all vehicles 'except those propelled by steam'. The goods yard closed in August 1953 and was lifted shortly thereafter.

Birdingbury closed to passengers on 15th June 1959, when the Rugby & Leamington local service was discontinued. The line from Rugby to Southam via Marton Junction remains open for cement works traffic.

The scale plan, prepared in the 1880s and updated to the 1950s (!), shows two small lever stages, one on each platform. These slotted the running signals, and allowed station staff to work the running signals even when the box was closed. When the signal box was open, they were left pulled.

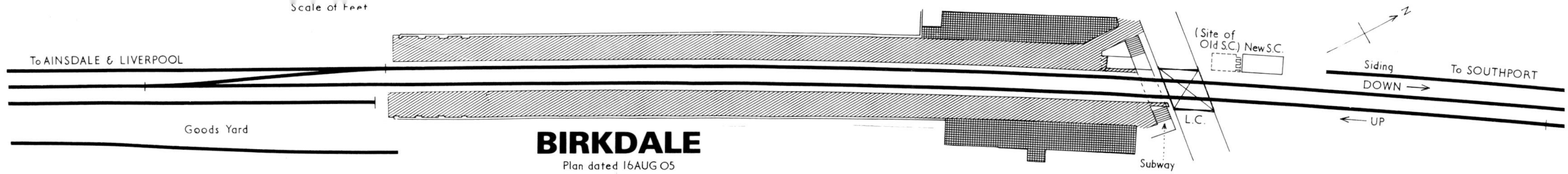
Scale of Feet
To AINSDALE & LIVERPOOL
Goods Yard
(Site of Old S.C.) New S.C.
Siding
To SOUTHPORT
DOWN
UP
L.C.
Subway
N

BIRKDALE
Plan dated 16AUG05

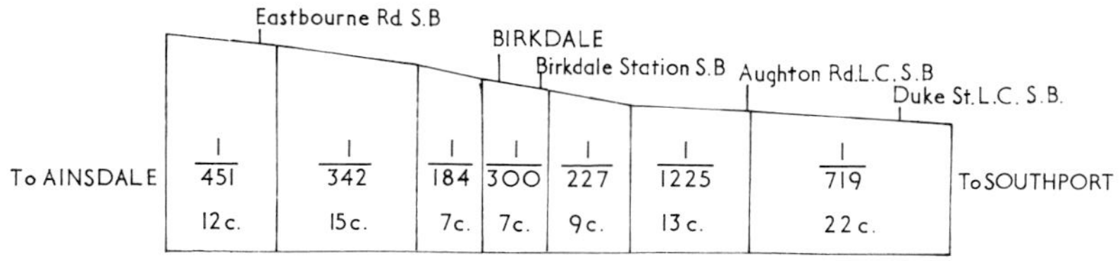
Eastbourne Rd. S.B
BIRKDALE
Birkdale Station S.B
Aughton Rd.L.C.S.B
Duke St.L.C.S.B.
To AINSDALE
To SOUTHPORT
1/451 12c.
1/342 15c.
1/184 7c.
1/300 7c.
1/227 9c.
1/1225 13c.
1/719 22c.

BIRKDALE *(Map Ref. A5)*

When the Liverpool, Crosby & Southport Railway opened out of Southport in 1848, Birkdale was not of sufficient importance to warrant a station, and it was not until 1851 that facilities were provided. Today, Birkdale is a fashionable suburb of Southport and Liverpool, and boasts an internationally famous golf course.

The station with its trim canopies, subway for pedestrians, and ornamental flower tubs, is well kept, and in harmony with Birkdale itself. As the entrance to the subway obstructs the signalman's view to the south, the box is partially overhung, i.e. the working floor overhangs the front wall of the locking room. The station was known as Birkdale Park from 1854 until 1865.

The LYR provided passenger and freight services. The LNWR possessed running powers from Bootle to Southport, and were entitled to use the passenger, but not the freight facilities at intermediate stations. A private siding, Lloyds siding, existed near to the station.

◀ *Upper* The platforms and level crossing at Birkdale, looking almost due north towards Southport. Unusually for a station with a level crossing, Birkdale is provided not with a footbridge but a subway. This served the needs of pedestrians and of passengers, and the platform entrances, with their iron gates, are visible to the left and right of the crossing gates. Minimum clearance was left for the platform ramps which were connected by a narrow timber crossing to save staff having to use the subway.

◀ *Lower* The signalman is prompt in closing the gates as an ex-LMS electric set accelerates out of Birkdale towards Southport. The deplorable condition of the road surface, which has crumbled away from the rails in many places and is patched, is the result of excavations for utility services, and is noteworthy; it would make a superb feature for a model railway, whilst the need to provide a conduit for signal wires and point rodding should not be overlooked. At Birkdale this is covered by timber shuttering running across the road in line with the boardwalk to the box.

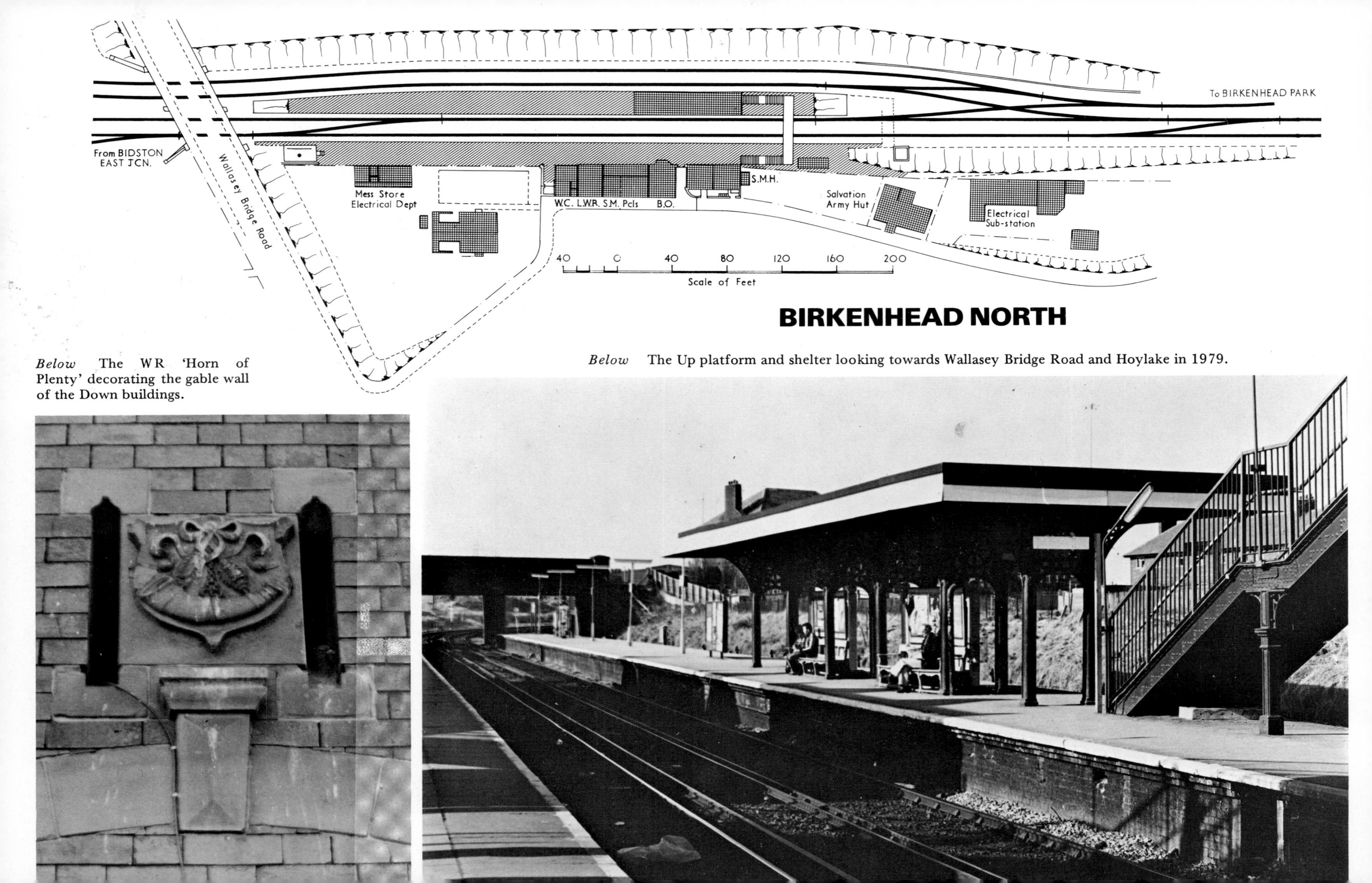

BIRKENHEAD NORTH

Below The WR 'Horn of Plenty' decorating the gable wall of the Down buildings.

Below The Up platform and shelter looking towards Wallasey Bridge Road and Hoylake in 1979.

BIRKENHEAD NORTH

No. 1 S.C.

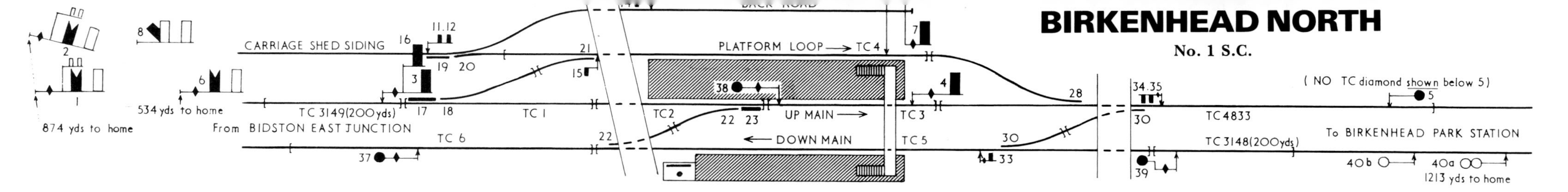

BIRKENHEAD NORTH *(Map Ref. A1)*

The development of suburban railways from Liverpool under the Mersey to Birkenhead, and into the Wirral peninsula, is a complex story, the many threads of which were not finally united until 1948. The development of what is now an integral route fell in three phases, the first being the authorisation of the Hoylake Railway, which was to run from Hoylake on the north west coast of the peninsula, to twin termini on the north and south sides of Birkenhead Docks, the northernmost line extending almost to the banks of the Mersey at Seacombe, whilst the southern limb was to terminate inland at Bridge Road in Birkenhead. The Birkenhead Dock–Hoylake section was opened on 2nd July 1866. The construction of a line under the Mersey to connect Liverpool with the residential districts of Birkenhead was much desired, and an independent company, the Mersey Railway, began work in 1872 on a line from Liverpool James Street to Hamilton Square, Birkenhead. This left the Mersey and the Wirral lines separated, and a link was agreed, the Mersey line extending on to Birkenhead Park, whilst yet another concern, one of three to bear the Wirral title (!), providing the Birkenhead Park–Birkenhead Docks section. Both parts of the connecting link were opened on 2nd January 1888, the old Hoylake Railway passenger station becoming a part of Birkenhead North locomotive shed. In 1891 the Hoylake Railway (by then renamed the Seacombe, Hoylake and Deeside) and the short Wirral railway (which contributed the Docks–Birkenhead Park section) were merged into a new Wirral Railway Co. In 1903, the Mersey Railway electrified its whole route, clean and comfortable stock replacing the grimy steam trains. The Wirral sought powers to follow suit but did not have the cash, and passengers had to change trains at Birkenhead Park until 1938, when the LMS electrified the Wirral section, and joint LMS-Mersey Railway working was instituted into Liverpool. The Mersey Railway, which was outside the grouping, came into the fold with nationalisation in 1948.

Birkenhead Docks has been known by many titles, Bridge Road in the early days, and Birkenhead North latterly. The old passenger station lay to the north of the present station, and was incorporated into the locomotive depot for many years. It was to the west of Bridge Road and was separated from Birkenhead Dock goods by the connection on to the Mersey Docks railways.

Below The Up and Down platforms and footbridge looking towards Birkenhead Park. The footbridge, which is less than the regulation six feet from the edge of the platform loop is the same one as in the illustration on the opposite page, but is seen prior to the removal of the covering over the stairs and walkway. The pre-cast concrete lamp in the foreground is of the type introduced by the LMS in 1938, whilst the Wirral 'horns' can be seen in the gable ends of the main buildings on the Down platform.

BOAT OF GARTEN

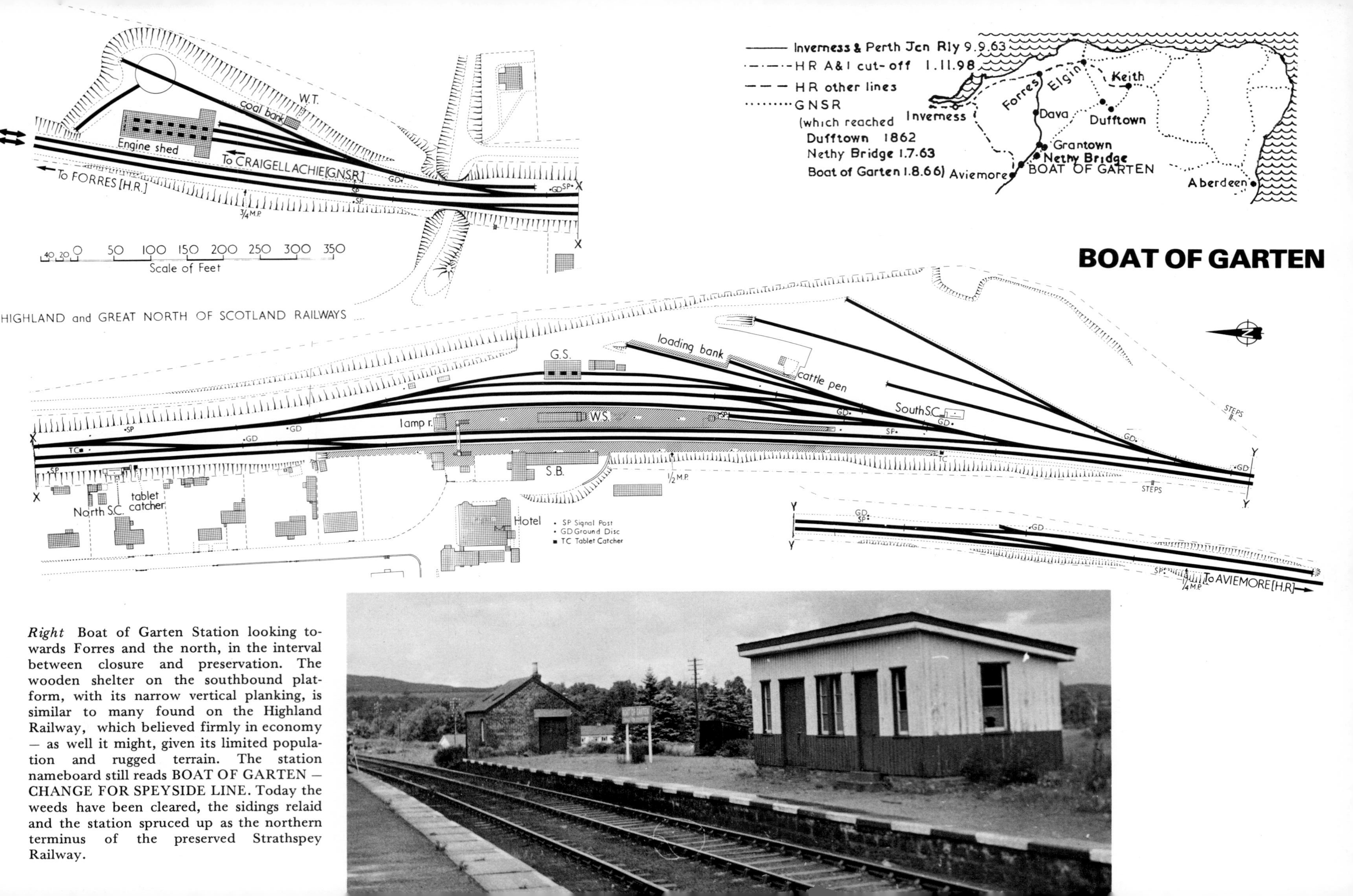

Right Boat of Garten Station looking towards Forres and the north, in the interval between closure and preservation. The wooden shelter on the southbound platform, with its narrow vertical planking, is similar to many found on the Highland Railway, which believed firmly in economy — as well it might, given its limited population and rugged terrain. The station nameboard still reads BOAT OF GARTEN — CHANGE FOR SPEYSIDE LINE. Today the weeds have been cleared, the sidings relaid and the station spruced up as the northern terminus of the preserved Strathspey Railway.

BOAT OF GARTEN *(Map Ref. R18)*

Between Perth and Inverness, the forbidding mass of the Grampians rises up, a daunting challenge to road or railway engineers. It is no wonder that the building of a line across such terrain was eschewed for many years, but in 1860 the Inverness & Perth Junction Railway was formed to construct a route from Forres on the Inverness—Aberdeen line to Dunkeld, a short distance north of Perth. The I&PJR opened on 9th September 1863. The new line climbed through the pass of Killiecrankie, then via Dalwhinnie and Kingussie to Aviemore and along the valley of the Spey before the final ascent to Dava summit and so to Forres. The first station north of Aviemore was Boat of Garten, a village of some 400 souls.

In the 1880s dissatisfaction with the roundabout route to Inverness crystallised into proposals for a rival line, and reluctantly, the Highland Railway (into which the I&PJ had been merged) obtained powers for a direct Aviemore—Inverness cut-off. This opened on 1st November 1898, leaving the Aviemore—Forres section a backwater.

In the 1860s, the Great North of Scotland Railway, the near neighbour and hereditary enemy of the Highland had been extending its influence from the east. In 1862, the GNSR reached Dufftown, then on to Nethy Bridge, and finally on 1st August 1866 into the HR station at Boat of Garten.

There were three platforms and a short bay at the south end of the station. GNSR trains used the back face of the Up platform upon which there was a modest timber shelter. The yard was quite extensive and included standage roads and a run round for the GNSR, as well as public sidings. A two road locomotive shed with a turntable and the usual facilities was reached off the GNSR line at the north end of the station.

In December 1905, the GNSR provided three trains a day and the Highland five northbound and six southbound. By the late 1930s there were four workings on the HR and three over the GNSR Speyside branch. The branch goods service comprised two class D freights in each direction. The most famous freight workings from Boat of Garten were, however, to the south. They were the 'Boat' goods, made up of whisky traffic from the distilleries along both the Highland and Speyside lines.

The old main line closed to passengers on 18th October 1965; passenger services over the GNSR ceased at the same time, and this might well have been the end of the story. However, Scottish enthusiasts, mindful of the success of preservation schemes south of the border, formed the Strathspey Railway Co. to reopen the section from Aviemore to Boat of Garten, and given the popularity of Aviemore as a holiday centre, the line should have an assured future.

Above The commodious South signal box which controlled the yard connections.

Below The timber North box looking towards Forres.

The northbound platform and main buildings looking towards Forres, with the southbound shelter visible on the extreme right. The North signal box is visible in the distance just beyond the shelter. The black and white edging to the platforms is an effective and neat feature.

BONAR BRIDGE

LMS SCOTTISH DIVISION
HIGHLAND DISTRICT

From Tain
From INVERNESS
BOT office
BOT store
loading bank
ash pit
G.S.
South SC.
W.T.
high water mark
Post office
Balnagown Arms hotel
Agents house
G.S.
B.O.
Refresh'ts
W.R.
G. St.W.R.
To Bonar Bridge
North S.C.
To Culrain
To WICK
Bonar Bridge

50 0 50 100 150 200 250 300 350
Scale of Feet

The main buildings and Agent's house at Bonar Bridge Station looking north, together with two splendid platform barrows.

BONAR BRIDGE *(Map Ref. Q20)*

To the north of Inverness lies the desolate terrain of the northern Highlands of Ross, Cromarty, Sutherland and Caithness, counties which were tragically affected by the clearances which followed the rebellion of 1745. To build railways into such poor country required great courage, but construction of the Farther North main line began in the 1860s. Dingwall was reached in 1862, Invergordon in 1863, and in the same year the Ross-shire Extension Act was passed. The first section of this line opened to Meikle Ferry in June 1864, and trains steamed into Bonar Bridge Station (actually sited in Ardgay village) on 1st October 1864. After a delay of four years, the Sutherland Railway took the line on to Golspie, but Bonar Bridge remained something of a frontier post with its commodious refreshment rooms and other facilities. These included a goods shed and generous loading bank accommodation. The station was worked from two signal cabins, a north and south box, as was normal Highland policy. Curiously, the northbound platform was only two thirds of the length of the southbound platform.

In October 1905 three trains called at Bonar Bridge in each direction daily. They all stopped for between seven and ten minutes; no doubt it was a welcome opportunity for passengers to stretch their legs on the long journey between Inverness and Wick. By 1938 the halt had been cut to no more than four minutes, and as well as the three long-distance trains there was a terminating train from Inverness in the afternoon. The return working appears to have started at Tain, 14 miles to the south.

The station was renamed Ardgay, after the village in which it is actually located, in the

BRANDON

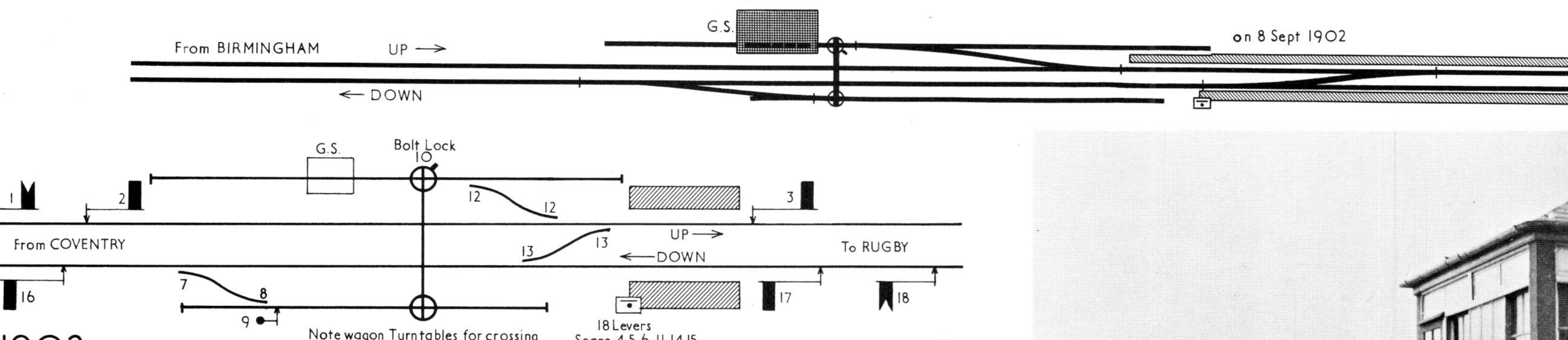

BRANDON

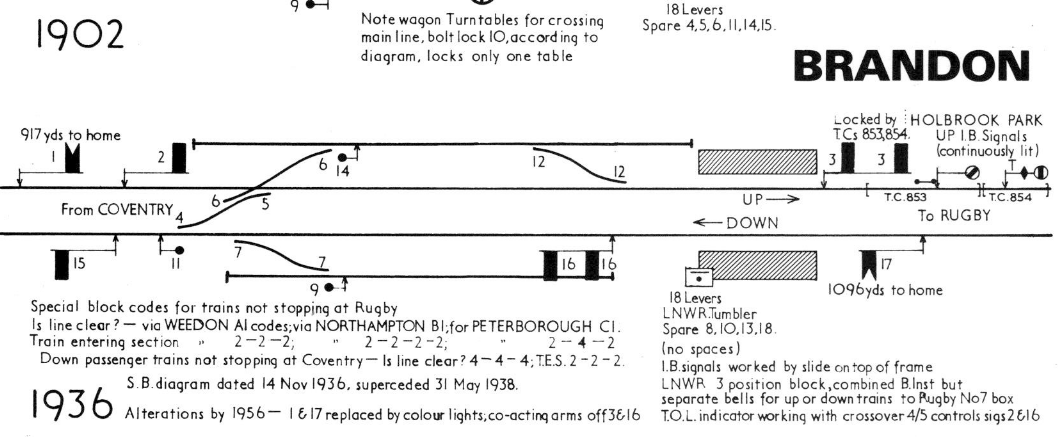

917yds to home
From COVENTRY
UP →
← DOWN
To RUGBY
Locked by T.Cs 853,854.
HOLBROOK PARK
UP I.B. Signals
(continuously lit)
T.C.853
T.C.854
1096yds to home
Special block codes for trains not stopping at Rugby
Is line clear? — via WEEDON A1 codes; via NORTHAMPTON B1; for PETERBOROUGH C1.
Train entering section " 2-2-2; " 2-2-2-2; " 2-4-2
Down passenger trains not stopping at Coventry — Is line clear? 4-4-4; T.E.S. 2-2-2.
S.B. diagram dated 14 Nov 1936, superceded 31 May 1938.
1936
Alterations by 1956 — 1 & 17 replaced by colour lights; co-acting arms off 3 & 16
18 Levers
LNWR Tumbler
Spare 8, 10, 13, 18.
(no spaces)
I.B. signals worked by slide on top of frame
LNWR 3 position block, combined B.Inst but separate bells for up or down trains to Rugby No7 box
T.O.L. indicator working with crossover 4/5 controls sigs 2 & 16

Below A southbound express roars through Brandon.

Above Brandon & Wolston box in 1964.

BRANDON & WOLSTON *(Map Ref. F6)*

Brandon was on the L&B Birmingham—Rugby section, which opened to passenger traffic on 9th April 1838, and was the only station in the 11½ miles separating Coventry and Rugby. It was replaced, on 29th October 1879, by a new station, Brandon & Wolston, on an adjacent site.

Unlike the minor stations west of Coventry, Brandon never developed any significant suburban traffic, and was closed to passengers on 12th September 1960.

A small goods yard was provided on the Up, and a single siding on the Down side. Until 1903 these were joined by a pair of wagon turntables and a short section of inter-connecting track passing through both running lines by means of square crossings. The survival of such an archaic arrangement on the main line at so late a date is remarkable, especially as the LNWR had been suppressing such connections on country branches in the 1880s!

The signal cabin was another early relic, possibly from the 1879 rebuilding. It survived the modernisation of 1903, and the next sixty years as well, and its final demise was as a result of the Rugby power box scheme. Brandon & Wolston box was closed during the implementation of stage 1 of the power box commissioning on 12th-14th September 1964. Until the Up siding was finally taken out, the box was replaced by a ground frame adjacent to the siding.

Although the through service carried over the L&B line was immense, Brandon merited little more than branch line status as far as stopping trains were concerned. In 1895 there were five trains each way daily, less than one third of the services enjoyed by stations west of Coventry. Even at the close of the Edwardian era, there were no more than eight or nine trains. In LMS days the picture improved, and by 1938 there were about a dozen stopping trains in each direction.

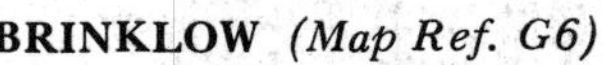

BRINKLOW

In contrast to the larger stations on the Trent Valley line, Brinklow possessed a modest and severely plain station building, the road frontage of which is illustrated below. The front and side walls (and chimneys) were of brick, and the building straddled the running lines. The title BRINKLOW STATION was carved into panels above the windows flanking the central entrance, and the station (still supporting LMS timetable boards) is seen shortly after nationalisation.

BRINKLOW *(Map Ref. G6)*

Brinklow, or Stretton as it was named until 1870, was the first station north of Rugby on the Trent Valley line. The TVR was authorised in 1845, and a limited service commenced in September 1847, but it was not until 1st December that full services started and Stretton station opened.

The enormous increase in traffic over the Trent Valley resulted in the Up third line being added between Bulkington and Rugby on 14th August 1871. At first this was purely a goods line, but it was upgraded as a slow line in June 1876. For twenty years the treble track (plus the Birmingham route) was adequate, but it was a growing struggle, and in the LNWR (Additional Powers) Act of 1899, authority was given to widen 13m 4f 2c 50 1 of the Trent Valley line between Rugby and Nuneaton. Other than for the sections between Rugby and Brinklow and Attleborough Sidings and Nuneaton, this work was never carried out, the quadruplings elsewhere and the newer and more powerful engines introduced from the turn of the century, reducing the need for continuous quadruple track.

The station buildings at Brinklow were perched on the roadbridge, and steps led down to the platforms, the facilities thereon being of the simplest kind. The yard was on the Up side, and could accommodate 38 wagons, whilst a further 25 could be stabled in the dead-end off the Down slow.

In 1895 six Down and five Up trains called at Brinklow. By 1946 there were four Down and three Up workings, with a ten hour gap in the middle of the day between two of the Up services. Not surprisingly, the station closed to passengers on 16th September 1957 and to goods on 20th February 1961. The signal box was closed during stage 1 of the Rugby power box commissioning on 12-14th September 1964.

Right An unrebuilt 'Royal Scot' brings a moment of life to an otherwise tranquil scene at Brinklow in the thirties. The layout on the left-hand of this illustration, looking towards Rugby, is little altered from the 1880s, other than for a cross over from the Up third line to the Up main. The track on the right, passing out of sight behind the hedge, is the end of the Down slow line which terminated just short of the signal box. For the detail lover, the wheelbarrow on the right hand side of the barrow crossing is lettered LMS.

Below Brinklow Station looking south with late afternoon shadows creeping across almost to the third line. Except for a few lamps, seats and the small hut on the Down platform, passenger facilities were confined to the main buildings. Had the LNWR wished to extend the quadruple track northwards through the station, the bank on the right hand side of the line would have been excavated.

Below right Looking towards Stafford. The booking clerk has the station window open on a warm 1930s summer day, but as is apparent from the blackening of the paintwork, it was not the best way to admit clean air! Even a southbound train, such as the special in this scene, headed by an unrebuilt 'Royal Scot', No. 6144 *Honourable Artillery Company*, added its quota of grime. Although the front of the station building was brick, the rear wall was timber, whilst the steps to the platform were roofed in curved corrugated iron, an uninspiring combination. The timber stage visible on the extreme right is beyond the third line, and is a milk dock. It was connected to the road by a sloping path.

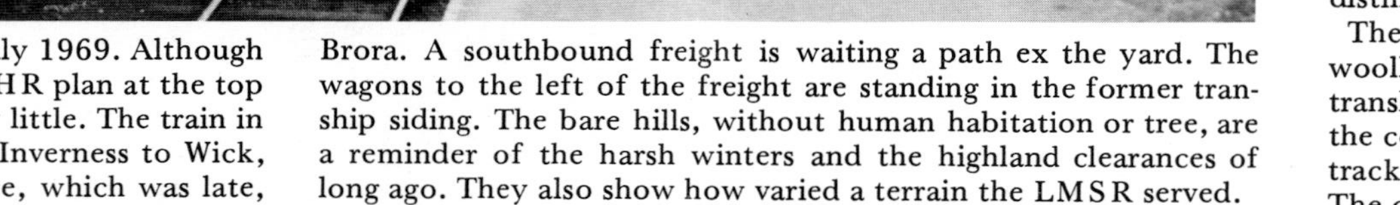

The scale plan, from a 1913 HR survey, emphasises the great length of the more important stations on the Inverness–Wick line. In common with many Highland stations, tow rope shunting was authorised, and HR men were adept at moving up to *sixteen* wagons at a time in this manner. Wire ropes were sometimes used, but the older men preferred the natural ropes, for whilst they did not have the same breaking strain, they would give warning that they were about to break, in contrast to the wire ropes which went without any warning signs. To avoid confusion between staff sections, the North line was divided into alternate Key Token and Electric Tablet sections, the Helmsdale–Brora section being key token, and the southern section, to Golspie, being worked on round tablets.

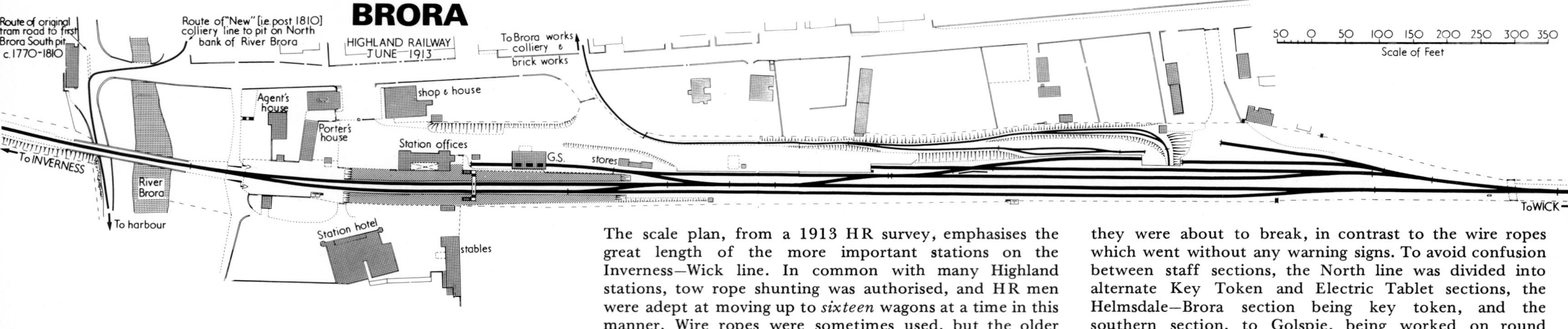

Brora Station looking towards Wick on 9th July 1969. Although more than half a century has elapsed since the HR plan at the top of the page, the layout has changed remarkably little. The train in the foreground is the morning working from Inverness to Wick, awaiting the corresponding southbound service, which was late, to the considerable annoyance of the crew who switched over at Brora. A southbound freight is waiting a path ex the yard. The wagons to the left of the freight are standing in the former tranship siding. The bare hills, without human habitation or tree, are a reminder of the harsh winters and the highland clearances of long ago. They also show how varied a terrain the LMSR served.

BRORA *(Map Ref. R20)*

Although the farther north main line of the Highland Railway did not reach Brora until 1st November 1870, a railway, or rather an industrial tramroad, had existed in the village for about a century, making Brora one of the first places in the highlands to be rail served. The tramroad ran from the first Brora colliery on the south bank of the river down to the harbour. This colliery was closed in 1810, and was replaced by a new pit on the north bank. The western portion of the tramway was relaid to this working.

In 1870, the Duke of Sutherland obtained powers to construct a standard gauge line from Golspie to Helmsdale, and Brora opened later that same year. The Duke took over the colliery, a brickworks and the tramway, and constructed a branch from the station yard, past an engineering works which he set up, to a junction with the earlier line. The works later became a wool mill, and coal passed from the colliery to the harbour, mill or station exchange sidings. The harbour branch fell out of use in 1914, as a result of the war, and was removed in 1920. George Seaton, a former Highland man, recalls that 'a branch line broke off about 300 yards from the pit and ran alongside the coalpit road to the road bridge over the Brora river, thence to Brora Harbour where the trolley loads were transferred to small cargo boats for shipment'. He adds, 'the colliery was Brora's lifeline, and also provided cheap fuel for the local distillery'.

The deathblow to the system came in 1947, when the woollen mill switched to electric power, for by this time tranship traffic at the station was negligible. All except the colliery lines were closed and later lifted, although some track remained in situ in the station yard for many years. The colliery closed only recently.

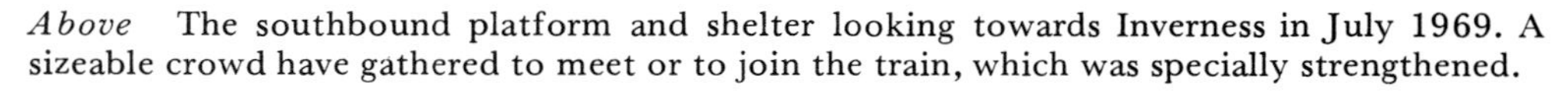

Above The southbound platform and shelter looking towards Inverness in July 1969. A sizeable crowd have gathered to meet or to join the train, which was specially strengthened.

Right The South signal box at Brora looking towards Inverness. As standard HR practice was to install staff instruments in the station office, the cabins did not act as block posts. The station master was responsible for handling the train staffs and Manson's exchange apparatus (for tablets or key tokens) was installed at many stations, the 'snatchers' at Brora being at the south end of the loop, near the platform ramp for both lines.

Below Brora goods shed, typical of many such structures on the Highland section.

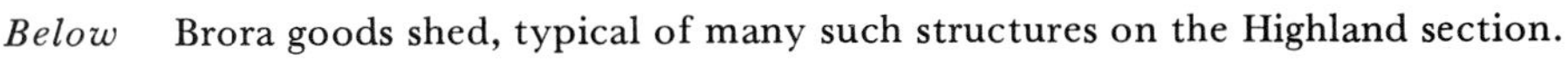

BUCKINGHAM

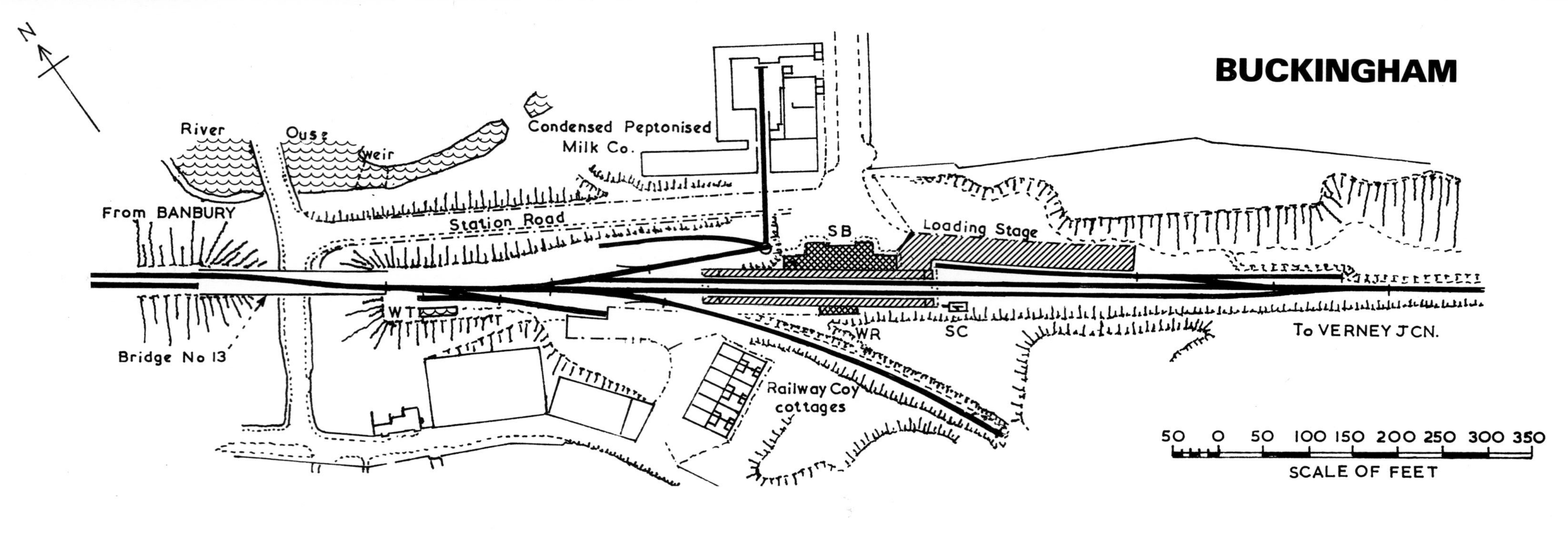

BUCKINGHAM *(Map Ref. H3)*

Buckingham is a picturesque county town with a population of 4,200 located in delightful countryside. It boasts many fine buildings, including a handsome gaol (not used as such for many years). The station was on the LNWR (originally the Buckinghamshire Railway) branch from Verney Junction to Banbury, and opened to passengers on 1st May 1850. The station buildings were in a pleasant cream stone. Goods facilities at the passenger station were very limited, as a separate goods yard existed a short distance to the north, on a site originally used by the contractors as a depot during the construction of the line. The yard was controlled from two ground frames, released by the train staff.

The passenger station was worked from a cabin at the south end. The original LNWR box was burnt down on 25th August 1931, and replaced by an LMS hybrid type. A private siding led from the station across Station Road into Messrs. Thew Hooker & Gilbey Ltd., Condensed Peptonised Milk factory. This siding was reached off a wagon turntable which also gave rise to another CPM siding on station premises. The latter was paved in old sleepers.

In 1895, there were five trains each way. By 1909 a number of additional short workings to and from the south existed. This pattern endured into LMS days, but by the early 'fifties there were but three or four trains a day north of Buckingham, and it looked as if the end was in sight. BR, in an unusually determined mood, drafted two single unit railcars onto the branch in 1956, and passenger figures quadrupled! By 1959, there were no fewer than *seven* return workings a day between Buckingham and Banbury, but rising costs eventually caught up with this brave experiment, and on 2nd January 1961 the northern section closed, to be followed on 7th September 1964 by the Verney—Buckingham portion.

Left Looking towards Banbury from the dock siding; note the head of the rails curved up at the buffer stops, and the low platforms.

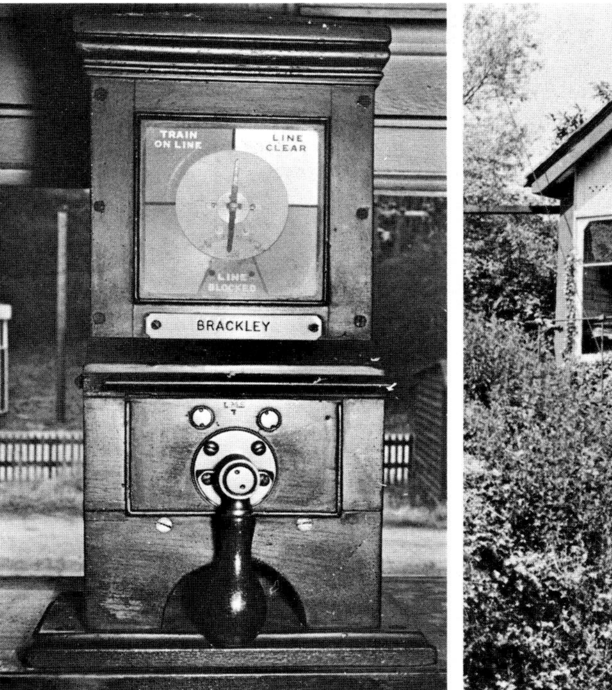
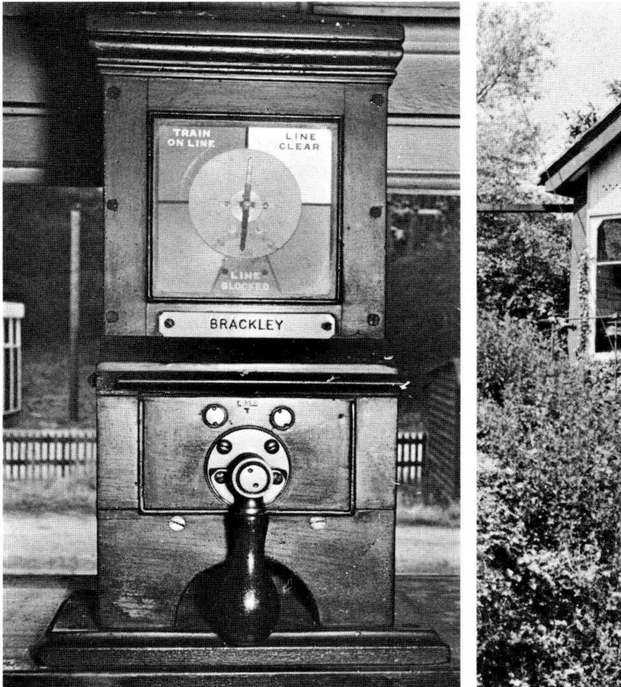

Above left Signalling equipment at Buckingham, included this lovingly maintained single needle block telegraph instrument.

Above The LMS hybrid box which replaced the LNW box after the 1931 fire.

Above right Right up to closure, the Buckingham–Verney Junction section retained miniature Webb-Thompson electric train staff equipment with red painted staffs.

Left The original timber buildings were replaced, in 1861, by mildly Italianate buildings by J. W. Livock, a pale creamy brick predominating. Note the classical pediments.

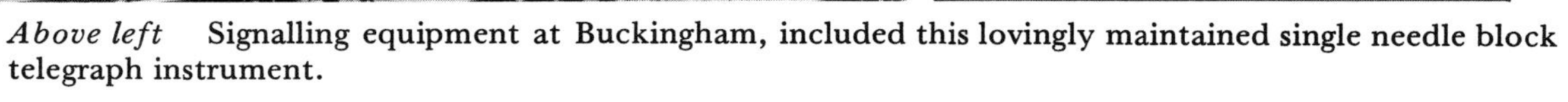

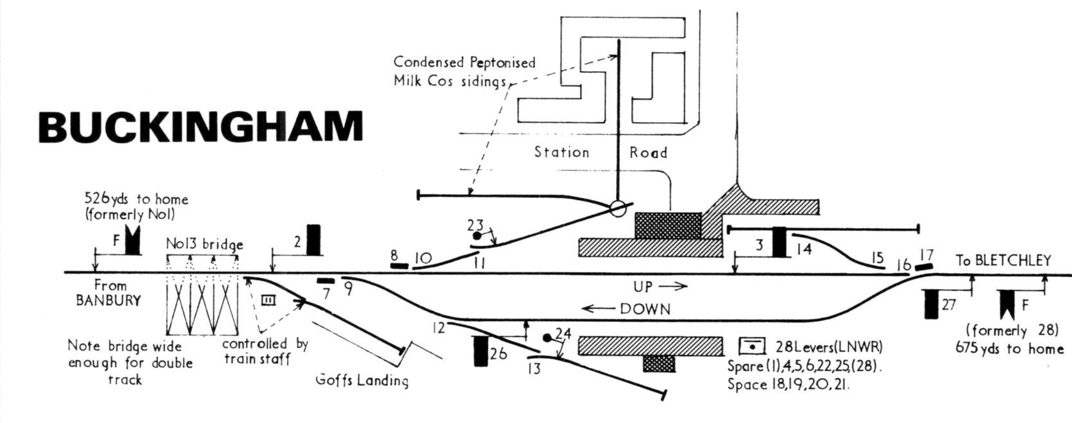

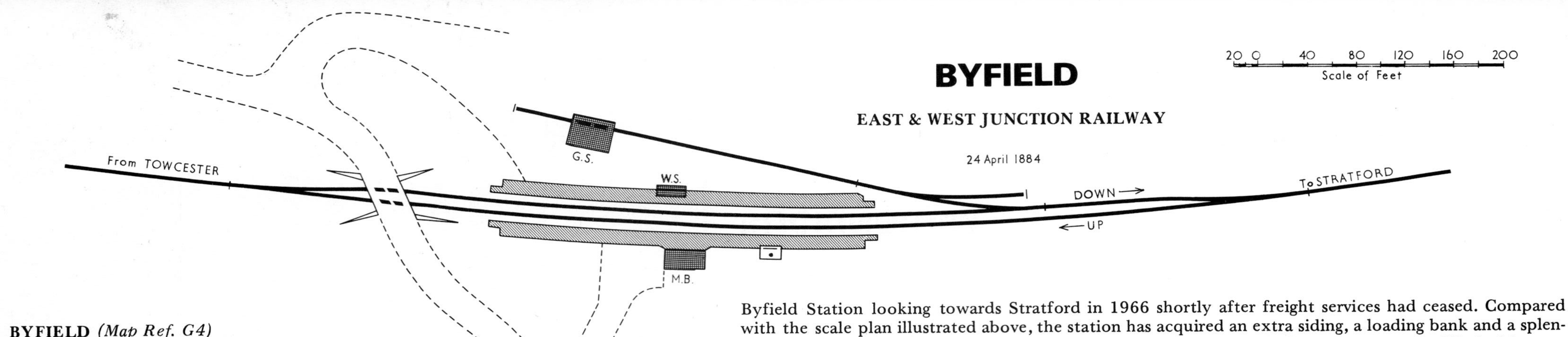

Byfield Station looking towards Stratford in 1966 shortly after freight services had ceased. Compared with the scale plan illustrated above, the station has acquired an extra siding, a loading bank and a splendidly period 30 cwt hand crane with rolling counterbalance box. The latter were usually filled with scrap iron, and the crane is similar to those used on early 4-wheel mobile rail cranes.

BYFIELD *(Map Ref. G4)*

The East & West Junction Railway (later the Stratford-upon-Avon & Midland Junction Railway) was opened in sections between 1871 and 1873, from Stratford to Towcester. Byfield lies on the section between Fenny Compton and Towcester, and was opened on 1st July 1873.

Unlike many companies, the E&WJR was highly standardised in its station design, and of the eight stations on its original 33¼ mile line, no fewer than five were carbon copies of one another. Byfield was to the classic pattern, with a small brick station building, a passing loop, single siding and goods shed. Another unifying feature was that most stations, including Byfield, were located by an over-bridge, for level crossings were less acceptable in the 1870s than had formerly been the case. A second siding was eventually added in the yard, as were a lay-by and shunting neck to the loop. A 1½ ton crane was another late addition (see photograph).

In 1876, two trains called in each direction, but in 1877 passenger services were suspended and the line became more and more woe-begone. Services recommenced after eight years, and the opening of the GCR London Extension brought additional traffic in the form of connecting services to and from Woodford GC. Some of these ran through to Stratford, others terminated at Byfield. In 1905 there were four main line trains and two Woodford–Stratford services, plus the shuttle.

In 1946 there was a through train each way in the morning, and a short working, from Towcester to Byfield and back, in the afternoon. In the evening convenient connections were made from Stratford and from Towcester to Woodford, but passengers from Towcester for the Stratford line had 1¼ hours in which to explore the village before the Woodford–Stratford train appeared!

It was, perhaps, hardly surprising that the line closed to passengers on 5th April 1952. Through freight services ended on 1st March 1965. Little remains today of what was a very pretty station with a complicated, albeit infrequent, train service.

BYFIELD

From Railway Signal Co. diagram

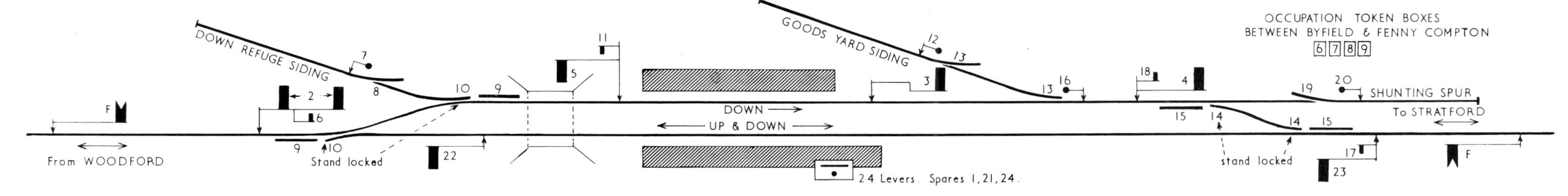

The station buildings at Byfield looking towards Towcester, the coach body being a late addition, a second body being added by the goods shed. As with Binton on the Stratford–Broom extension, money was in short supply and the buildings at Byfield, Ettington, Fenny Compton and Moreton Pinkney were to a standard but unpretentious design. The nearest block with three windows is the station office, access being via a door on the side wall beneath the awning. A long wooden counter divided the office into a section for traders and for the station agent. A second door off the covered area led into the general waiting room where passengers booked their tickets. Although a diminutive building, this was a cut above Buckingham, where passengers had to queue in the roofed but otherwise unprotected circulating area. A diminutive Ladies' room, or more properly a kind of porch, provided access to the ladies' toilet, the window to which was the right-hand window beneath the sloping roof in the view on the previous page. A small unroofed urinal and an enclosed gents' toilet completed the facilities.

The signal box was an equally delightful structure, built of timber with superb extensions at each end, seemingly to house the electric train staff instruments. The Fenny Compton–Byfield section was worked with blue ETS and the Byfield–Woodford West Junction with red ETS. Under the LMS, long-section working was provided with miniature ETS equipment, so that Byfield box could be switched out. As a cross-country route, the SMJ made connection with the GWR at Stratford and Fenny Compton, with the GC near Byfield, with the LNWR at Cockley Brake (on the Verney Junction–Banbury branch) and at Roade and Blisworth, and with the Midland at Broom and Ravenstone Wood. At the grouping it passed to the Midland division of the LMS, providing a useful if circuitous LMS freight route between London and Bristol/South Wales. As a preserved line it would have been ideal.

CANLEY *(Map Ref. E6)*

Canley Halt, on the western outskirts of Coventry on the London & Birmingham main line, is a genuine LMS station, having been opened to passengers on 30th September 1940, primarily to serve the nearby Standard Motors Co. and other important factories which were of great strategic importance during World War II. As a war-time measure, economy in labour and materials was vital and the station has retained its 'austerity' appearance. Although officially named Canley Halt, the prior existence of Canley Gates signal box led to confusion even in the official mind, with some LMS and BR sources referring to Canley Gates (Halt). Canley has also been the subject of numerous proposals over the years, many unfulfilled, for improvements such as footbridges, road bridges etc. to try to reduce congestion over what was a busy road crossing even thirty years ago. The station has never handled general goods, as Coventry Station, with its extensive freight facilities, was little more than a mile away. The existence of several factories, primarily associated with the motor industry, led to numerous proposals for private sidings, and one of the most interesting plans of the LMS period is depicted. This pre-dated the establishment of the passenger station, and whilst the latter is not covered, a footbridge is postulated. The rush of pedestrians at works closing times used to be vast, and the folly displayed by many in crossing the lines without looking, or in front of a train, was a constant source of complaint by railwaymen, whilst the crossing gates also suffered from damage from motor vehicles. When Coventry power box was commissioned in the early sixties, Canley Gates became a fringe box, the signal box layout showing it thus. On 2nd-4th July 1966, the Coventry PSB area was extended to meet up with the phase 3 commissioning of New Street PSB, and Canley, Tile Hill and Berkswell were added to Coventry panel.

The booking office and level crossing looking towards Coventry.

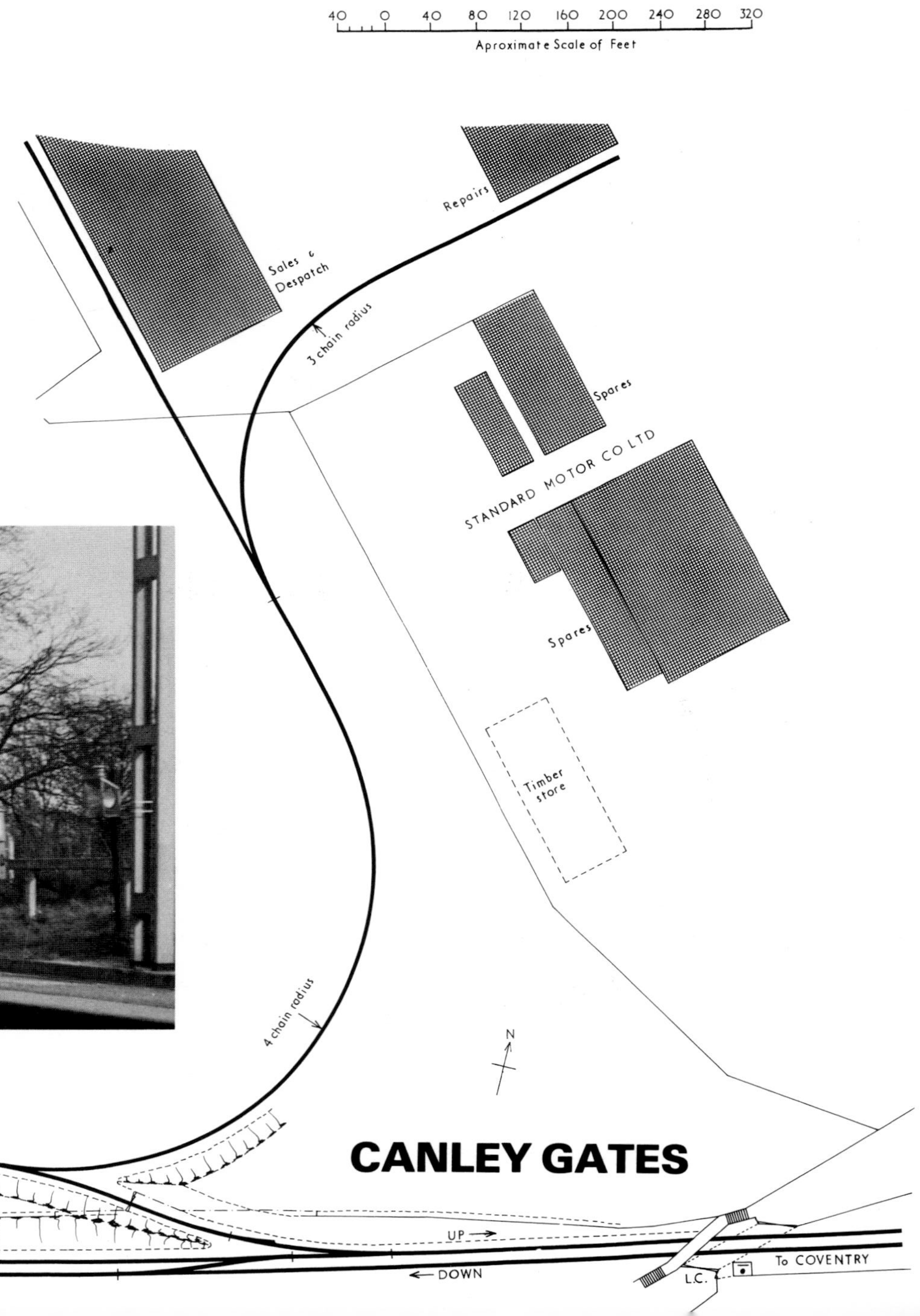

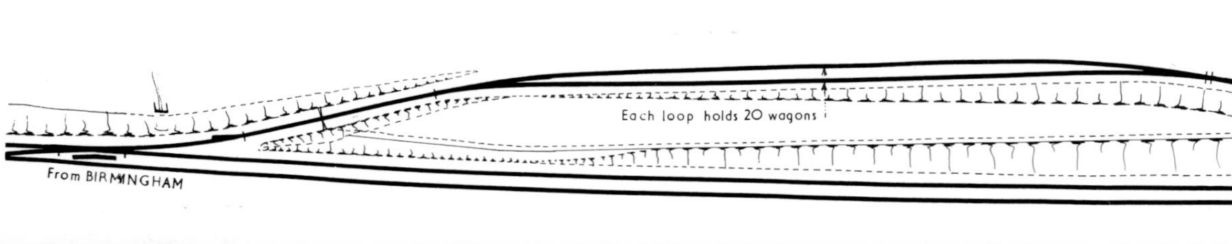

CANLEY GATES

40 0 40 80 120 160 200 240 280 320
Aproximate Scale of Feet

Repairs
Sales & Despatch
3 chain radius
Spares
STANDARD MOTOR CO LTD
Spares
Timber store
4 chain radius
N
Each loop holds 20 wagons
From BIRMINGHAM
UP
DOWN
L.C.
To COVENTRY

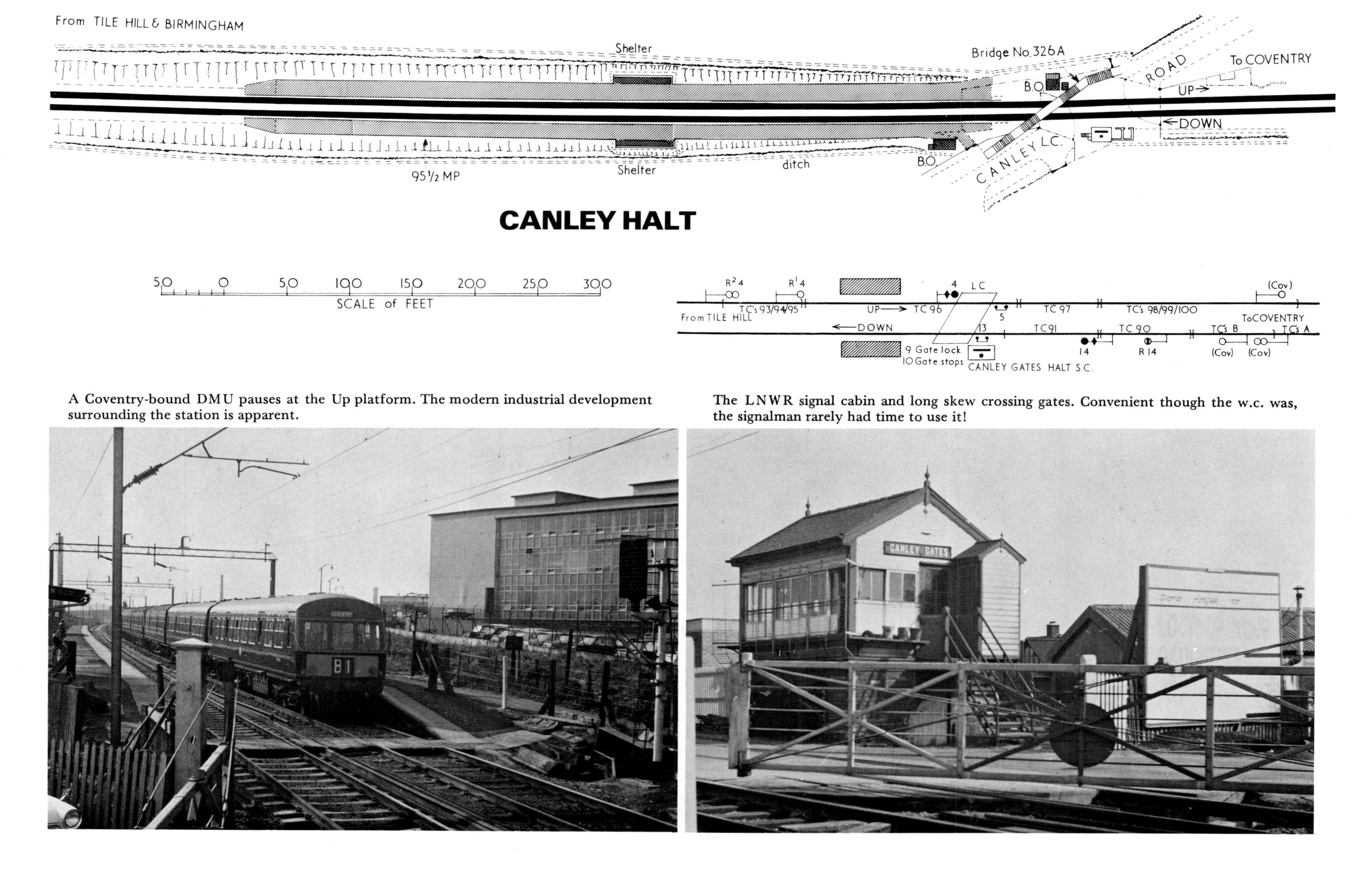

A Coventry-bound DMU pauses at the Up platform. The modern industrial development surrounding the station is apparent.

The LNWR signal cabin and long skew crossing gates. Convenient though the w.c. was, the signalman rarely had time to use it!

Looking from the 1938 LMS platform at the divergence of the Barrow line *(left)* and the F&M joint line to Wennington *(right)*. The footbridge, not indicated on the original survey, gives access to *Steamtown*.

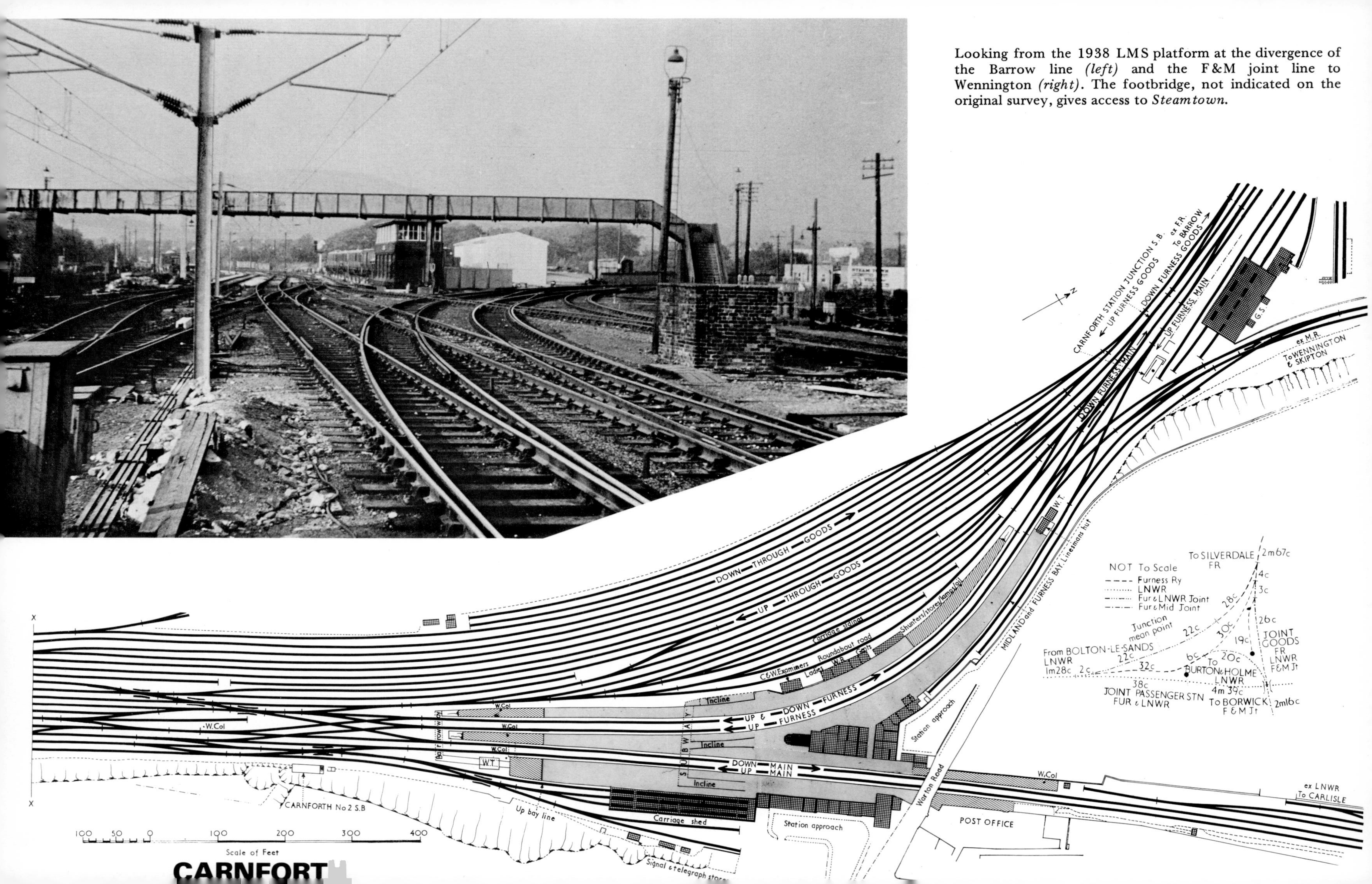

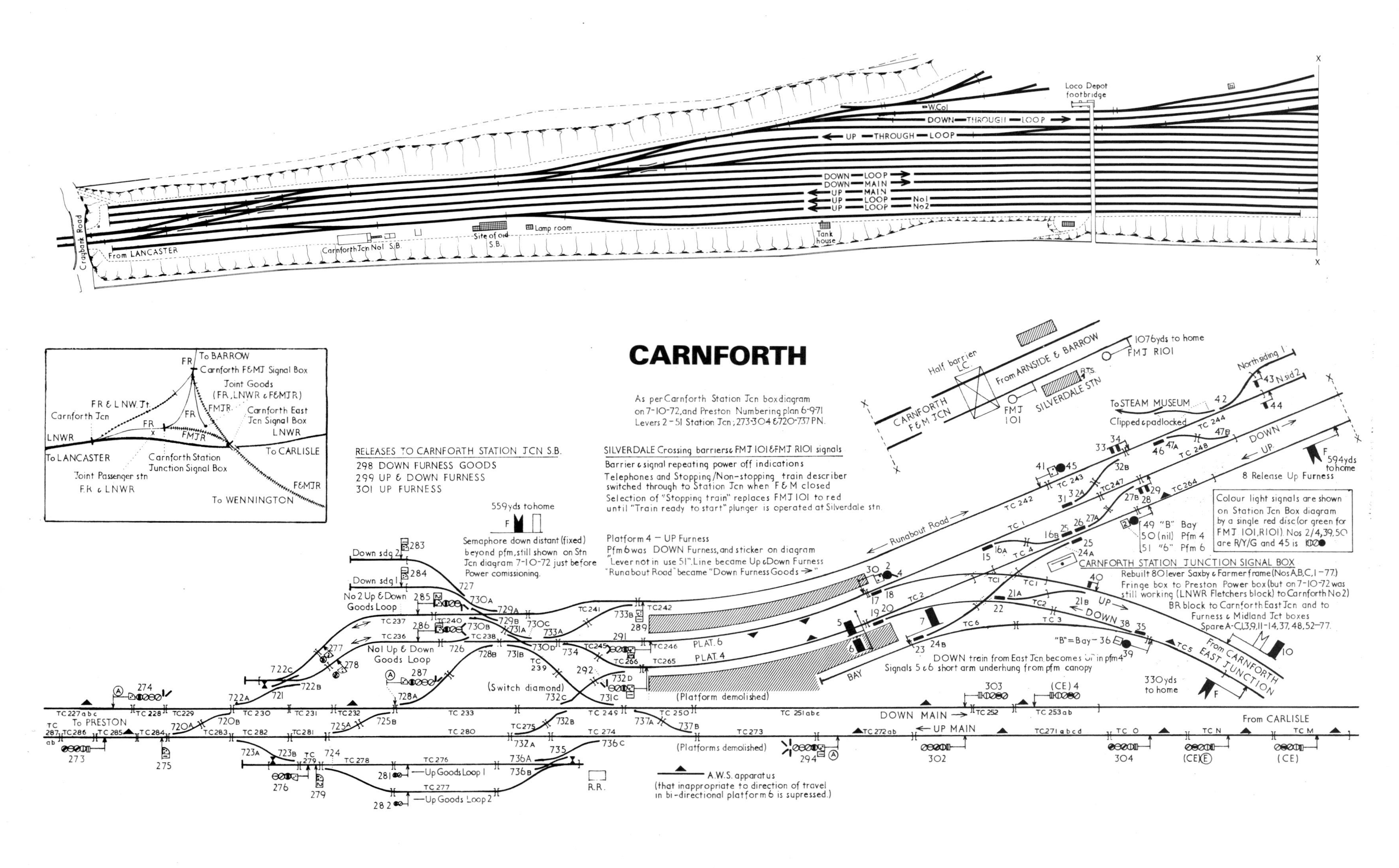

CARNFORTH
As per Carnforth Station Jcn box diagram on 7-10-72, and Preston Numbering plan 6-9-71
Levers 2 - 51 Station Jcn; 273-304 & 720-737 PN.
RELEASES TO CARNFORTH STATION JCN S.B.
298 DOWN FURNESS GOODS
299 UP & DOWN FURNESS
301 UP FURNESS
SILVERDALE Crossing barriers & FMJ 101 & FMJ R101 signals
Barrier & signal repeating power off indications
Telephones and Stopping/Non-stopping train describer switched through to Station Jcn when F & M closed
Selection of "Stopping train" replaces FMJ 101 to red until "Train ready to start" plunger is operated at Silverdale stn
559yds to home
Semaphore down distant (fixed) beyond pfm, still shown on Stn Jcn diagram 7-10-72 just before Power comissioning.
Platform 4 – UP Furness
Pfm 6 was DOWN Furness, and sticker on diagram "Lever not in use 51". Line became Up & Down Furness
"Runabout Road" became "Down Furness Goods"
CARNFORTH STATION JUNCTION SIGNAL BOX
Rebuilt 80 lever Saxby & Farmer frame (Nos A,B,C,1-77.)
Fringe box to Preston Power box (but on 7-10-72 was still working (LNWR Fletchers block) to Carnforth No 2)
BR block to Carnforth East Jcn and to Furness & Midland Jct boxes
Spare A-C,1,3,9,11-14,37,48,52-77.
Colour light signals are shown on Station Jcn Box diagram by a single red disc (or green for FMJ 101, R101). Nos 2/4,39,50 are R/Y/G and 45 is
8 Release Up Furness
594yds to home
330yds to home
49 "B" Bay
50 (nil) Pfm 4
51 "6" Pfm 6
"B" = Bay – 36
DOWN train from East Jcn becomes UP in pfm 4
Signals 5 & 6 short arm underhung from pfm canopy
A.W.S. apparatus
(that inappropriate to direction of travel in bi-directional platform 6 is supressed.)
From LANCASTER
Craglank Road
Carnforth Jcn No1 S.B.
Site of old S.B.
Lamp room
Tank house
Loco Depot footbridge
W.Col
DOWN THROUGH LOOP
UP THROUGH LOOP
DOWN LOOP
DOWN MAIN
UP MAIN
UP LOOP No1
UP LOOP No2
To BARROW
Carnforth F&MJ Signal Box
Joint Goods (FR, LNWR & F&MJR)
Carnforth East Jcn Signal Box
FR & LNW Jt
Carnforth Jcn
LNWR
To LANCASTER
Carnforth Station Junction Signal Box
Joint Passenger stn F.R. & LNWR
To CARLISLE
F&MJR
To WENNINGTON
Half barrier L.C.
CARNFORTH F&M JCN
From ARNSIDE & BARROW
SILVERDALE STN
FMJ 101
FMJ R101
1076yds to home
To STEAM MUSEUM
Clipped & padlocked
North siding 1
N sid 2
Runabout Road
PLAT. 6
PLAT. 4
BAY
From CARNFORTH EAST JUNCTION
Down sdg 2
Down sdg 1
No 2 Up & Down Goods Loop
No1 Up & Down Goods Loop
(Switch diamond)
(Platform demolished)
(Platforms demolished)
To PRESTON
DOWN MAIN
UP MAIN
From CARLISLE
Up Goods Loop 1
Up Goods Loop 2
R.R.

CARNFORTH

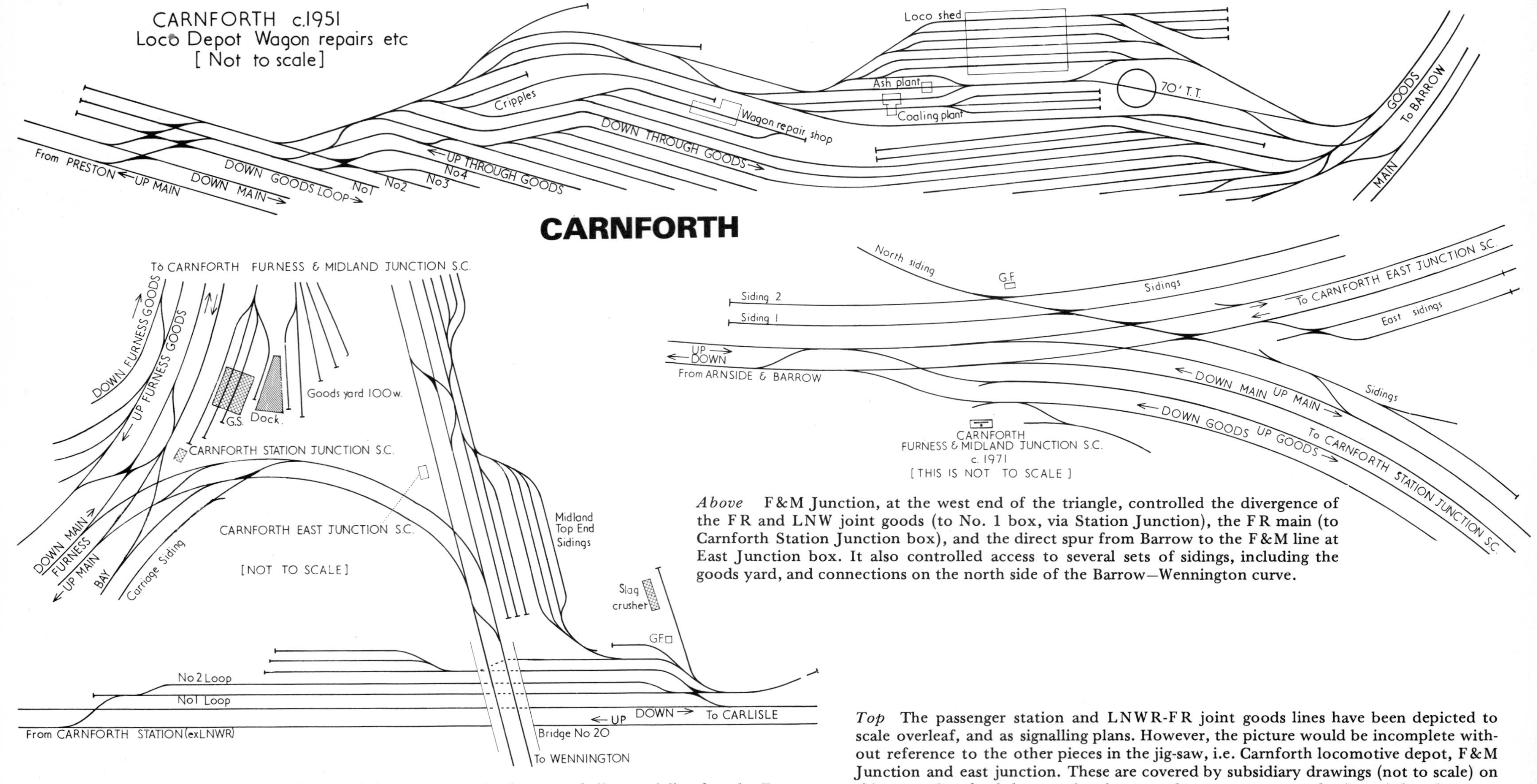

Above F&M Junction, at the west end of the triangle, controlled the divergence of the FR and LNW joint goods (to No. 1 box, via Station Junction), the FR main (to Carnforth Station Junction box), and the direct spur from Barrow to the F&M line at East Junction box. It also controlled access to several sets of sidings, including the goods yard, and connections on the north side of the Barrow—Wennington curve.

Above Carnforth East Junction is one of the most complex layouts of all, especially after the Furness to the North connections were laid in, during the war. These were later demoted from through lines to sidings, but the facilities to the north of the passenger station remained extensive. Carnforth East Junction box was located in the 'V' of the junction between the curve into Carnforth Station (working to Station Junction) and the direct line to Barrow (working to F&M Junction). A group of exchange sidings came off the Barrow line just opposite the box. Although through running had ceased by the date of the plan above, it was still possible to exchange traffic with the West Coast main line via the Top end sidings and the LNW No. 1 and 2 loops. The goods yard sidings in the middle of the triangle, and also a slag crusher, added still further complications.

Top The passenger station and LNWR-FR joint goods lines have been depicted to scale overleaf, and as signalling plans. However, the picture would be incomplete without reference to the other pieces in the jig-saw, i.e. Carnforth locomotive depot, F&M Junction and east junction. These are covered by subsidiary drawings (not to scale) on this page. Carnforth locomotive depot, as known to most enthusiasts, is largely a product of the LMS, replacing separate sheds owned by each constituent. The LNWR and FR sheds were to the south and to the west of the replacement LMS shed, whilst the Midland depot was located on the Wennington line. The upper layout plan commences by the LNWR No. 1 box, which controlled the divergence of the LNWR main lines and the joint LNW and FR goods. (The passenger junction was worked from No. 2 box). Wagon repair facilities existed at the south end, and access to the shed could either be via the connections by No. 1 box, or — at the north — between Carnforth Station Junction and F&M Junction.

CARNFORTH *(Map Ref. S11)*

Carnforth is perhaps best known to enthusiasts for *Steamtown*, but it has been an important junction for almost the whole of its history. The first line through Carnforth was the Lancaster & Carlisle Railway, which opened on 22nd September 1846. The L&CR was leased, and later absorbed into the LNWR. In 1851, the Ulverston & Lancaster Railway was authorised to construct a line from Ulverston to a junction with the L&CR. This line, later absorbed into the Furness Railway, opened to passengers on 16th August 1859. In the early days, Haematite iron ore passed south off the FR to the Black Country and coke northwards to the furnaces around Barrow.

The third line into Carnforth was the Midland & Furness Joint Railway from Wennington (on the MR). This gave the Furness a route to the south independent of the LNWR, but, far more important, it gave the Midland direct access to Barrow and the Barrow Steam Navigation services to Ireland and the Isle of Man. The Wennington line opened on 6th June 1867 and, until the opening by the MR of Heysham harbour in 1904, carried heavy boat traffic. Although a joint line, train services were provided by the Midland. Carnforth Station was enlarged when the F&M line opened, and was thereafter owned jointly by the Furness and North Western companies, all, that is, except for the Up West Coast platform, which remained LNWR property. The FR line diverged from the main line at the south end, and ran through the station on a sharp curve, the Furness through platform being beneath an elegant overall roof (removed by the LMS). Beyond the platform, one route led west to Barrow and the other east to Wennington. A bay platform led into the Wennington line, and an avoiding line for the Midland Barrow services completed the triangle north of the station. The locomotive depot was not depicted on the original station plan.

The LMS, in 1938, added a second through Furness line platform with a hideous concrete shelter. Prior to this, all Up and Down through trains had to use one platform face. Two years later, a chord was laid in from the Barrow line to the L&C in a north facing direction.

Passenger services still operate over all three routes, although local services calling at Carnforth are now confined to the ex Furness side of the station, the West Coast platforms having been closed and partially demolished. In pre-group days, between ten and fifteen trains called at Carnforth in each direction from each line. This included a number of express or semi-fast services on the main line. Collectively, the trains on the three routes, together with the goods and light engine movements, made Carnforth a difficult station to work, and there were, in all, six signal boxes. Three were on the LNWR side, and the other three on the FR and FR/MR section. The latter were located at each of the angles of the triangular junction. The main line boxes were eventually replaced by Preston power box.

Above The station approach in the angle of the LNW and Furness lines.

Below left Carnforth Station Junction signal box looking towards the F&MJ line.

Below right The LMS platform *(left)* and the FR platform and Wennington bay *(right)* looking north.

CHESTER ROAD *(Map Ref. D7)*

Chester Road Station is situated on the Aston–Sutton Coldfield branch of the LNWR, immediately adjacent to a girder bridge carrying the line over the nearby main road from which it takes its name. It was opened to passengers on 1st December 1863, eighteen months after the other stations on the branch. Due to the steady outward spread of the Birmingham conurbation, it developed as a useful suburban station, even though less than a mile separates it from Erdington to the south and Wylde Green to the north. The station is on a curve, and is subject to a 50mph speed restriction, one of several on the route. Wooden LNWR buildings with separate booking facilities were provided for each platform. The Up platform is hemmed in by a minor road parallel to the track, and access is via a flight of steps, but there is adequate space on the Down side for a gently inclined approach.

After the Sutton branch was extended to Lichfield City in 1884, services fell into an established pattern. There were two main types of train; through workings which ran semi-fast from Birmingham to Sutton, and then all stations to Lichfield, and short workings calling at all stations and terminating at Sutton or the next station to the north, Four Oaks. In 1895, Chester Road handled seventeen stopping trains in each direction. By 1927, there were some twenty eight workings each way. Following a brief period of declining importance, the line is now seen as an important part of the Birmingham suburban network, train services being provided by BR on behalf of the West Midlands Passenger Transport Executive, which in common with the PTEs in other Metropolitan counties is responsible for establishing a co-ordinated road and rail passenger transport network.

For many years, the southern section of the Sutton branch has been controlled from Erdington signal box by means of strategically located IB, or Intermediate Block signals, a full account of which appears under Erdington. Goods facilities at Chester Road survived until 1958, the yard being on the Up side, controlled by Annett's key from a ground frame on the Up platform.

Chester Road Station looking due south on a peaceful summer afternoon in 1977, the high rise blocks of the modern Birmingham skyline in stark contrast to the enduring timber architecture of the LNWR. It is a sobering thought that buildings such as these have been a feature of the scene from the days of the Ramsbottom DX goods, down to the diesel multiple unit era!

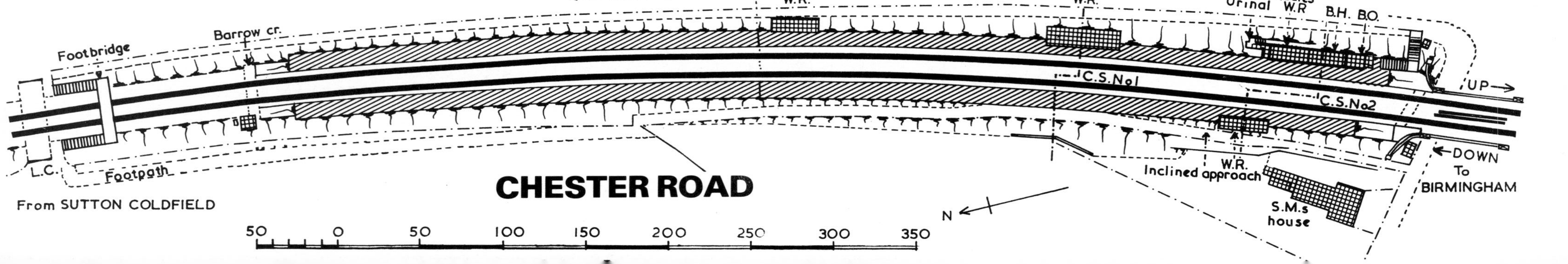

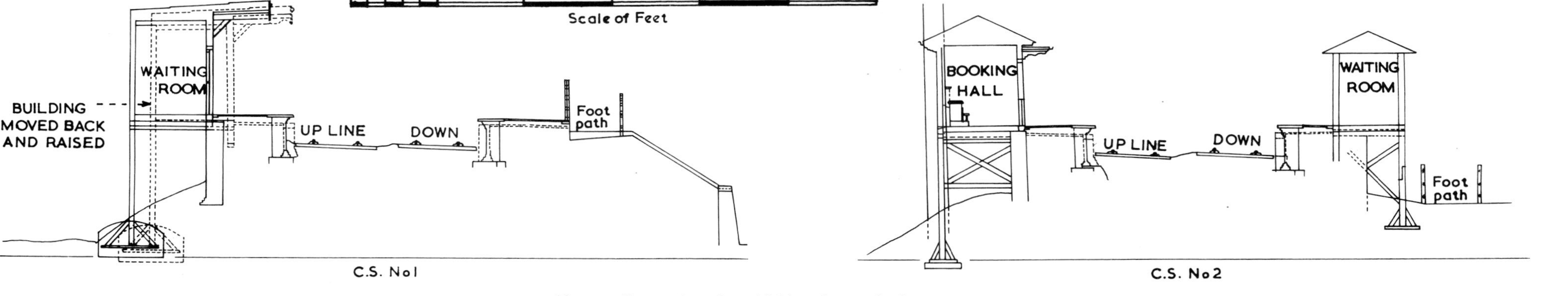

Above Even in the 1860s, low platforms were still common, and whilst these survived into recent times in many places, the LNWR and LMS spent a good deal of money on improving stations over the years. Sometimes a complete rebuild was necessary, but on occasion old structures could be reused, and the cross-sections above show how such a project could be tackled. In cross-section No. 1, the building is physically moved backwards and raised, whilst the platform is also rebuilt. At cross-section No. 2, the alterations are less drastic, the platform being raised a little, and the excessive slope towards the line removed.

Below The booking hall and waiting room on the Up platform looking towards Sutton. From a study of cross-section No. 2 *(above right)* it will be seen that the building is supported on massive timbers bedded into the embankment, and Chester Road is a useful station at which to study this mode of construction. A brick building would be extremely costly to build in such circumstances. For a model railway, an embankment station, especially if the structural timber work was visible from the rear, would make a fine subject.

Below The Down and Up platforms looking from the Chester Road bridge. The Erdington Up distant signal is visible just beyond the far end of the Up platform. In this view it is possible to see the platform surfaces sloping *away* from the line. The slope is necessary to throw off rainwater, and in early days, platforms often sloped towards the track. By the 1890s, this was regarded as unsafe, and tragic proof to this view was afforded by the Wellingborough accident of 1898, when a mail barrow fell into the path of a train.

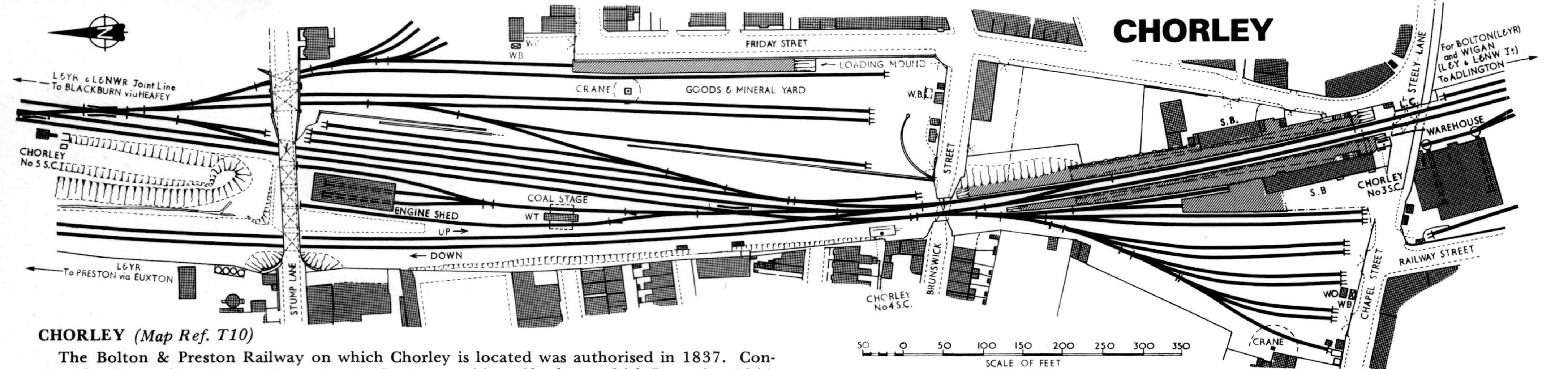

CHORLEY *(Map Ref. T10)*

The Bolton & Preston Railway on which Chorley is located was authorised in 1837. Construction began from the south, and trains first steamed into Chorley on 24th December 1841. North of the town, the awkward terrain held up work and it was not until 22nd June 1843 that the B&PR was opened through to a junction with the North Union Railway at Euxton, a few miles south of Preston. In 1844 the NUR and B&PR were amalgamated. Two years later the enlarged NUR was taken over by the LNWR/LYR, and the system operated jointly until the late 1880s when the West Coast main line south of Euxton Junction passed to the LNWR, the former B&PR to the LYR, and the portion from Euxton to Preston remained joint.

An additional route into Chorley came into being after much sparring between the LNWR and LYR. This was the Lancashire Union Railways which had originally been proposed as an LNWR backed route from Blackburn through Chorley to Wigan and St. Helens. The LYR opposed this with a Blackburn–Chorley line of their own, and in the end, Parliament authorised a joint LUR–LYR line from Cherry Tree Junction near Blackburn to Chorley and from Adlington (south of Chorley) to Boar's Head on the LNWR main line. Solely owned LUR lines ran on to the outskirts of St. Helens. The Blackburn line, which opened to goods in November and to passengers on 1st December 1869 joined the NUR just north of Chorley Station, and an LNWR goods depot, reached off the LUR, was established adjacent to the junction. In 1883, the LUR was vested in the LNWR, the effect being that joint LUR–LYR lines became LNWR–LYR.

The original Chorley Station was rebuilt in 1862. It was worked by a total of four signal boxes. Nos. 1 and 2 were to the south of the station and controlled goods connections; No. 3 worked the station level crossing and a gate from the platform on to the street by means of a 'gate control' lever. No. 4 box operated the junction with the LUR. Only 1,026 yards separated all four cabins!

As the B&P was the main LYR route from Manchester and East Lancashire to Blackpool, the Fylde Coast and Morecambe, there was an immense summer traffic as well as the usual services. During the summer of 1944 (when holiday travel was positively discouraged), the Manchester, Chorley, Preston & Blackpool services occupied no fewer than ten pages in the LMS public timetables, and on weekdays, let alone Saturdays, there were thirty main line departures from Chorley in the northbound direction. Thirteen trains left Chorley for Blackburn, some being through services, others originating at Chorley.

The Wigan–Chorley–Blackburn service ceased on 4th January 1960, and the stump of the LUR at Chorley provides access to sidings. Passenger services still operate over the B&P line. The station now comes under the control of Preston power box, only Chorley No. 3 surviving the advent of power working as a level crossing frame. Two new ground frames replaced Chorley's Nos. 1 and 4. These control access to the old Exchange sidings south of the station and the sidings reached off the LUR respectively.

Lower left Road repairs were not making access to the Down forecourt any easier!

Lower right Looking towards Preston. Chorley No. 4 box is on the left hand margin.

Above Looking towards Preston in 1981 from the foot of the Down platform. Compared with the early 1970s view on the previous page, Chorley No. 4 box has gone, the Up and Down cross over and yard connection (the old Blackburn branch) being worked by the 4-lever ground frame, with the signals controlled from Preston power signal box. The use of pre-group LNWR ground frames in modern signalling installations is one of the fascinating contrasts in the railway scene. The gas holder and chimneys testify to the industrial environment.

CHORLEY

Above Chorley No. 3 box survived as a crossing frame into the start of the eighties. The station was re-modelled in 1981 and the main buildings demolished.

Below Chorley No. 4 box from the divergence of the Preston and Blackburn lines.

COUNDON WHARF

This coal yard had a capacity for about 330 wagons in the clear in its 11 sidings.

The coal merchants offices are indicated, and the Ref. Nos. boundaries and areas (in sq. yds) of each plot of stacking ground are given. The areas varied from the modest 80 sq yd of Nos. 4 & 5 to the 800 of No. 14 (Co-op) & No. 10 (Brentnall & Cleland) and the 940 of No. 8 (Morton, this firm also rented plots 22, 23, 24 & 25).

Note plot 1 (600 sq yd) has been subdivided into No. 1 (190) No. 1A & 1B (each 100) and three unspecified remnants.

Access to the main line is controlled by a 2 lever ground frame with a gong.

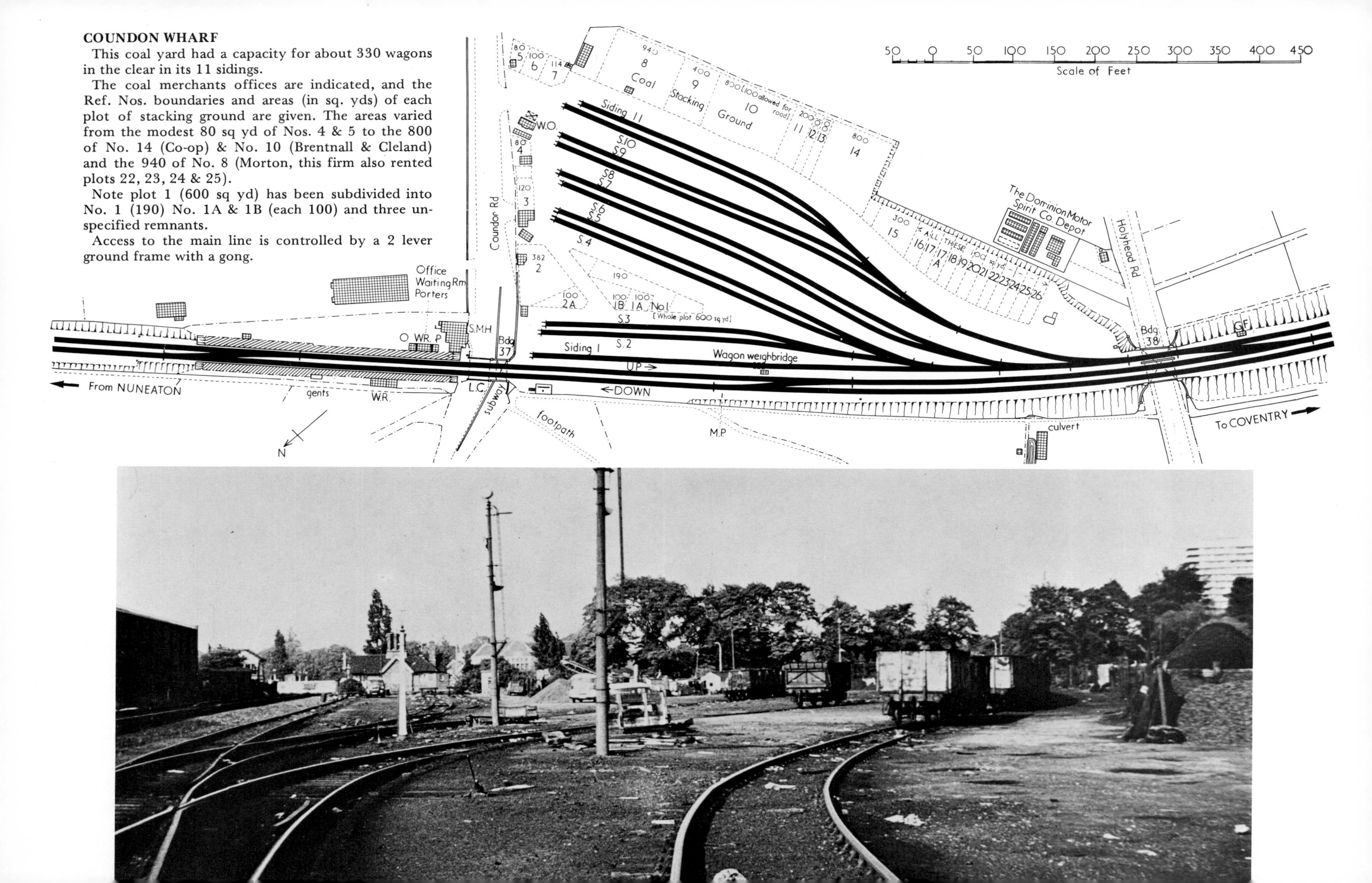

COUNDON ROAD *(Map Ref. F6)*

Coundon Road was the first station out of Coventry on the LNWR Coventry–Nuneaton branch. Parliamentary powers were obtained in 1846/47 and the line opened on 2nd September 1850. After the collapse of the Spon End Viaduct in January 1857, Counden Road (as the station was known until 1894) acted as terminus for the trains from Nuneaton. The line reopened as a through route in 1860.

The buildings were small and of archaic appearance, but the station, due to its location on the north side of Coventry within close walking distance of local industry, schools and the Coventry RFC ground, handled a useful volume of traffic until Coventry–Nuneaton local services were withdrawn on 18th January 1965. The line still carries freight traffic, and with the ever present problems of road congestion in the rush hours, proposals are heard from time to time that it should be reopened to passengers.

Coundon Road remains open for goods traffic, and the LNWR signal cabin acts as fringe box to Coventry. The yard connections are worked by a ground frame released from the box. The MR possessed goods running powers over the LNWR from Nuneaton.

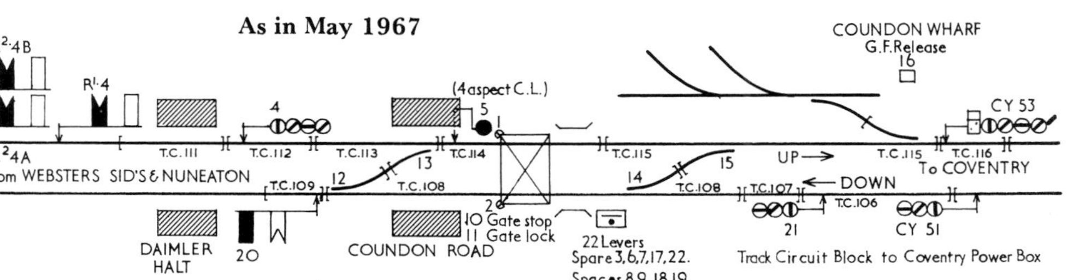

Above Coundon Road coal wharf looking towards Nuneaton. The signal box is visible, half in shadow to the left of the view adjoining the crossing gates. The track in the centre foreground leads to sidings 8–11. Illumination was provided to simplify shunting, especially during the long hours of darkness in mid-winter, when coal traffic was at its peak. The various *doglegs* on the yard tracks suggest that the rails have never been properly bent to the curves.

Right The station house looking west. Of stone construction with prominent quoins at the corners (the alternating large and small stones), this building reflected the age of the Coventry–Nuneaton line, for by the late 1850s ground level access would have been frowned upon. The building is not improved by the mixture of styles and alterations, with shallow arches above the windows, and non-matching brick chimneys.

COVENTRY

Above right Looking from the Up platform towards Coventry No. 1 box and Rugby, during reconstruction. The Down main line is closed and blocked by supports for the new footbridge. A new 4-doll gantry has been built on the platform to replace the LNW signals suspended from the Stoney Road overbridge (which was to be demolished). LNWR dwarf signals can be seen each side of the Up

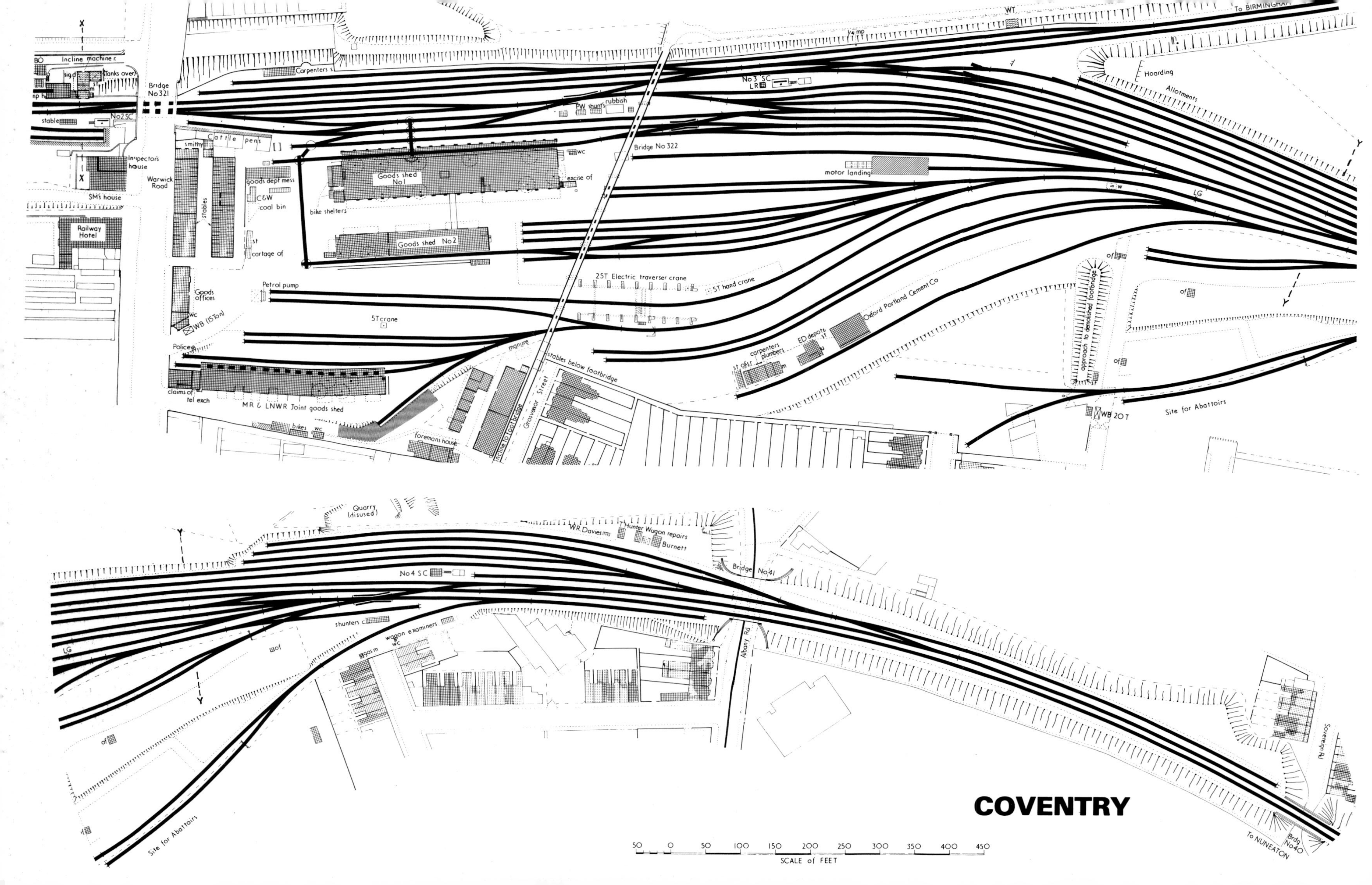

COVENTRY
To BIRMINGHAM
To NUNEATON
Bridge No 321
Bridge No 322
Bridge No 41
Brdg No 40
No 2 SC
No 3 SC
No 4 SC
Incline machine r.
Tanks over
Inspector's house
SM's house
Railway Hotel
Warwick Road
stable
smithy
Cattle pens
stables
goods dept mess
C&W
coal bin
cartage of
Goods shed No 1
Goods shed No 2
bike shelters
excise of
Carpenters s
PW shunts
rubbish
motor landing
Hoarding
Allotments
25T Electric traverser crane
5T hand crane
5T crane
Petrol pump
Goods offices
WB (15 Ton)
Police
claims of
tel exch
MR & LNWR Joint goods shed
bikes
foremans house
manure
stables below footbridge
Grosvenor Street
Incline to footbridge
carpenters
plumbers
ED depots
Oxford Portland Cement Co
approach to demolished footbridge
WB 20 T
Site for Abattoirs
Quarry (disused)
WR Davies
Hunter Wagon repairs
Burnett
shunters
wagon examiners
Albany Rd
Sovereign Rd
SCALE of FEET
50 0 50 100 150 200 250 300 350 400 450

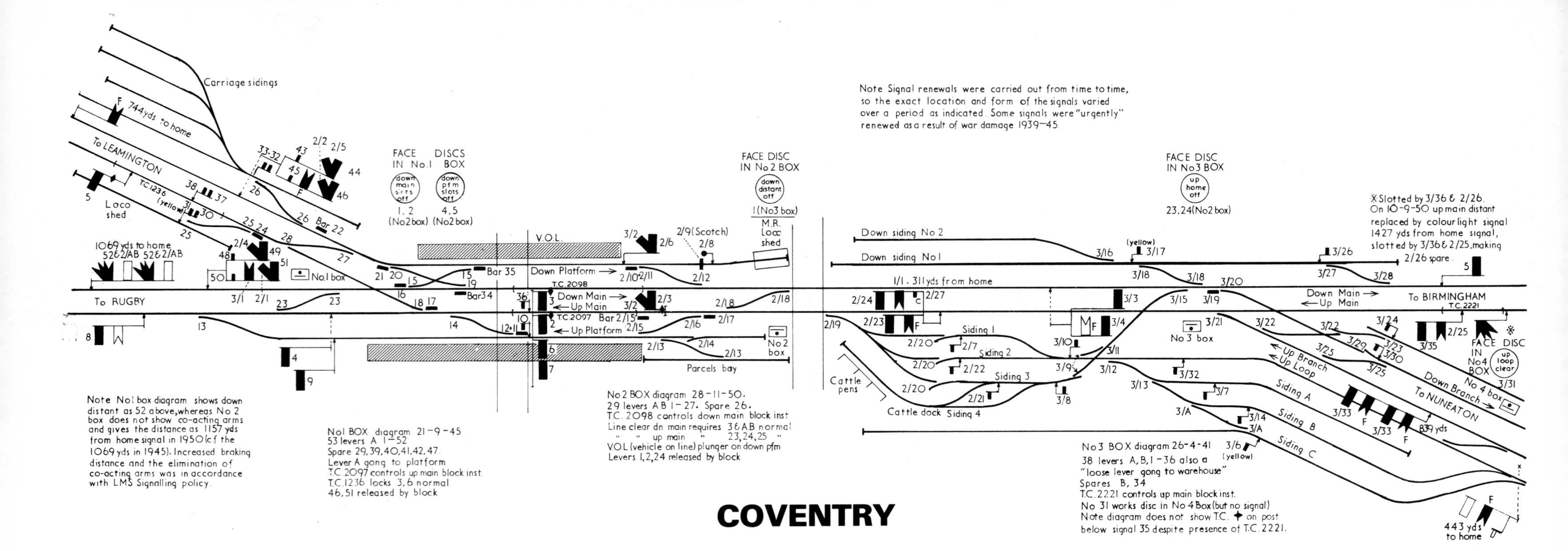

COVENTRY

COVENTRY *(Map Ref. F6)*

Coventry Station is on the London & Birmingham main line, 94 miles from Euston and some 18¾ miles from Birmingham. When the Birmingham—Rugby section of the L&B opened on 9th April 1838, the original Coventry Station was the Rugby side of the Warwick Road overbridge, but the facilities were so inadequate, that it was replaced in 1840 by a new station about 100 yards further east. There were four lines through the station, the centre lines being for through traffic, the outer ones were the platform roads. The buildings were long timber structures, 92 ft. 6 in. by 22 ft. 8 in. For a while these facilities sufficed, but the growth in main line traffic, together with the opening of the Warwick and Nuneaton branches put more pressure on the station. Extensive alterations were carried out in 1848-50 and again in the 1860s, 1880s, 1890s and 1901-04, but the basic plan remained the same. Under powers contained in the Railways (agreement) Act 1935, some improvements were effected on the Up side, but little was achieved on the Down side prior to 1939. It was thus not until the BR era, and the preparation for the 25 kV electrics that a brand new four platform station with MAS signalling came into being. Ironically this greatly enlarged station was still fairly new when the Nuneaton and Warwick lines lost their passenger services, so reducing train movements considerably!

The signalling of any large station is a complicated task, and the Coventry layout, as might be expected from its piecemeal origins, was by no means ideal. Coventry boxes, Nos. 1, 2 and 3 controlled the main line and station area (see signalling plan 'B'). No. 4 box was on the Nuneaton branch, and controlled various freight connections. Nearby boxes included Whitley Wharf and Humber Road Junction on the Rugby line and Gibbet Hill on the Leamington branch. Even in LMS days, there were no more than three track circuits in the station area, and reliance was placed upon the skill and vigilance of the signalmen. The station was thus both architecturally and operationally Victorian in the essentials up to its replacement. Communication between boxes was by means of block, telephone and face discs. The latter are indicated on the 'B' plan. The Up goods loop line from No. 4 to No. 2 boxes was controlled by telephone by the signalmen at Nos. 4, 3 and 2 boxes. In 1947, a signal department memo noted that, as through trains were not normally run over the loop, it should be renamed 'Up Through Siding', and that the indicator lettered 'UP LOOP CLEAR' in No. 4 box (controlled by lever 31 in No. 3 box) should be abolished. 'This indicator is never used, and is not necessary in view of special instructions to signalmen at boxes concerned'.

The parcels depot, opposite the MR locomotive depot, was on a very cramped site, and it was not uncommon for a bogie van to be located with one bogie each side of trap 14. It was safe, but hardly in accordance with the rules!

Prior to its demise, the old Coventry Station could have given points and a beating to any railway museum in the country. It possessed two engine sheds, one a normal LNWR depot, the other a one-horse effort reached by a facing lead off the Down platform. This had once been used by the Midland, who had running powers from Nuneaton. There were sundry bits of building dating back to the 1840s (or to Noah if one accepted local beliefs), and as a crowning glory, an Edward Bury fluted water column beside which a Midland 2F looked positively modern.

Above Looking towards Rugby, with 'Jubilee' No. 45647 *Sturdee* passing No. 1 box. The locomotive shed and Leamington line are to the right of the box.

Below Looking towards Rugby from the Up platform. The buffer stops protecting the supports for the new footbridge (in the four foot of the Down main) can be seen, as can the coach body which served as a temporary Down building during reconstruction. The engine, No. 40104, and parcels van were used to convey parcels and luggage between the Up and Down platforms whilst the usual luggage bridge (319A) was out of commission.

Above Temporary accommodation, during reconstruction, was provided in the large wooden chalet.

Below Looking past the former Midland engine shed *(left)* towards Warwick Road bridge (No. 321), Goods Shed No. 1 (visible through the arch), the venerable Coventry No. 2 signal box and the parcels depot. The box, which pre-dated the standard types which appeared in the 1870s, owed its survival to the cramped site and limited scope for layout extensions. Footbridge No. 322 is visible through the arch.

DINGWALL

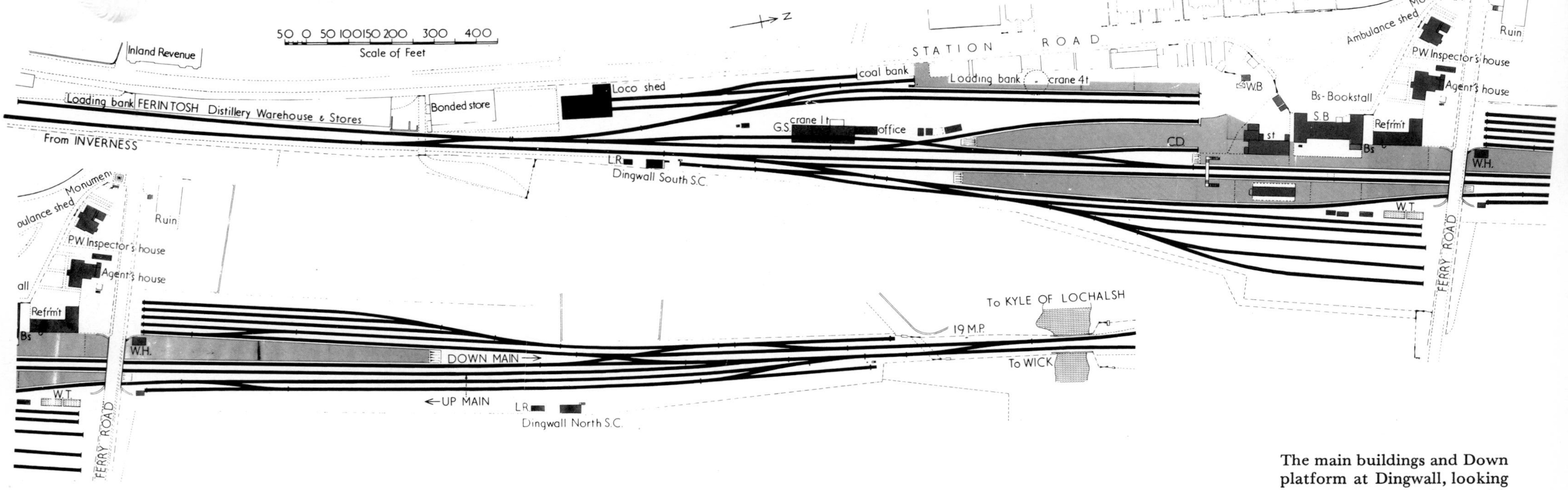

The main buildings and Down platform at Dingwall, looking towards the Kyle of Lochalsh and Wick, in 1969. A number of lorries and vans have drawn up on to the platform to await the arrival of the morning train to the Far North. The Ferry Road over-bridge, about which there was such controversy, can be seen to the right of the picture. The stepped gable wall on the near building was a feature as beloved to Scottish architects as the smokebox wingplates were to Scottish locomotive designers, whilst the glazed ridge and furrow awning was to be found in a few prestige locations. A similar, but even longer, awning was to be found at Strathpeffer as the branch served an affluent clientele. Both awnings were graced with radiating glazing bars on the gable ends.

◁ Looking south, towards Inverness, from the footbridge. The cattle dock and landing, although rather overgrown, were still in use. The diamond crossing of the goods shed line and back siding to the landing is visible just short of the timber built goods shed.

The Up platform and buildings looking from the footbridge towards Ferry Road. The bases of the water tanks at the Ferry Road end of the platform are visible to the left of the buildings.

DINGWALL *(Map Ref. Q19)*

South of the border, Dingwall (pop. 2,700) would not rate as a particularly important town, but in its context in the lightly populated highlands, it is a market town and administrative centre of note. Indeed its name, which is of Norse origin, refers to the meeting field and hill or thing-vollr. (Similar meeting hills were to be found at Tingwall in the Shetlands and Tynwald in the Isle of Man).

The Inverness & Ross-shire Railway was authorised in 1860, and opened as far as Dingwall on 11th June 1862. Owing to a dispute with a local landowner as to the manner of crossing Ferry Road, completion of the line to Invergordon was delayed until the 25th March 1863, and the company was forced to provide an overbridge (see scale plan). The first section of the Kyle of Lochalsh line opened in 1870, and the Strathpeffer branch, which diverged from the Kyle line just north of the town, in 1885.

The Strathpeffer trains ran into a bay platform at the north end of Dingwall Station. In 1905, there were six trains each way, in 1938, ten. By 1944 the service had become Saturdays only, and ceased altogether in 1946.

The Kyle line normally carried between two and four trains in each direction, whilst the Wick service was commonly composed of two or three through trains to Wick, and between one and four short-workings to Tain, Helmsdale, etc.

The main yard was on the Down side and included generous side loading and cattle facilities, for livestock traffic was formerly very heavy on market days. A private siding to the Ferintosh distillery and a two-road locomotive shed were reached off the Down yard. The facilities at the north end of the station included several storage roads, but these, in common with the loop into the second southbound platform, were lifted in later years, along with some of the Up sidings.

Dingwall goods yard and shed looking towards Wick. The track in the foreground is the shed head shunt and end loading track. The 4ton yard crane is visible part way along the long loading bank, whilst a second smaller crane was provided in the goods shed, which was of typical Highland design with vertical planking and capped joints. Dingwall is rather larger than the average HR shed with two sets of cart doors.

In a scene reminiscent of an earlier phase of railway operation, the locomotive of the 10.30 Inverness to Kyle of Lochalsh passenger train has left its train to pick up a parcels vehicle. It is seen backing on to the train from beneath the Ferry Road bridge, the small

Although the train service through Dingwall was infrequent, operation tended to be interesting due to the variety of movements and the close bunching of Wick, Kyle and Strathpeffer trains to provide good connections. All four routes radiating from the town were single track, the three main lines being worked by electric token equipment and the Strathpeffer branch by one engine in steam working with a staff key. North of the town, the Dingwall North—Achterneed and Dingwall North—Foulis sections were both controlled by key token equipment, whilst Dingwall South to Conon was operated with tablet equipment. In all cases the staff instruments were in the signal boxes, rather than in the station office as was the rule at minor stations. Normal station working was in force through the main platforms whilst the platform loop on the Up side was worked as a bi-directional road on single line block regulations, but without a staff.

As well as providing motive power for the Strathpeffer branch and sundry shunting duties, Dingwall shed also had to provide banking engines on the Kyle line out to Raven's Rock, west of Achterneed. The summit was located between Achterneed and Garve, and engines dropped off at Achterneed to return to Dingwall. As single line banking always presented problems, a description of the procedure when banking passenger trains is of interest. When leaving Dingwall, the bank engine was to be coupled to the train with the vacuum brake connected. At Achterneed station, the bank engine was uncoupled and the vacuum pipes disconnected, and when the train was ready to leave, the station master handed the Achterneed—Garve token to the train driver and a banking key to the driver of the banker. The latter could only be withdrawn from the instrument after a Garve token had been withdrawn, and once withdrawn, it protected the bank engine until it had returned to Achterneed, whereupon the token was replaced in the instrument, and the banker sent back under ordinary token working to Dingwall.

Another unusual operating feature concerned the cross over from the down main line to the cattle bank (see scale plan and illustration). These were not worked directly from Dingwall South box, but by a ball lever controlled by rod locking from the South box. The use of mechanical or electrical releases is not, of course, uncommon, but in such cases, the customary method is to work to a one or two lever ground frame. A few such installations existed on the HR, others being found at Blair Atholl and Elgin. As the yard was conveniently laid out, and engines about regularly, rope shunting was not permitted, in contrast to the smaller stations farther north.

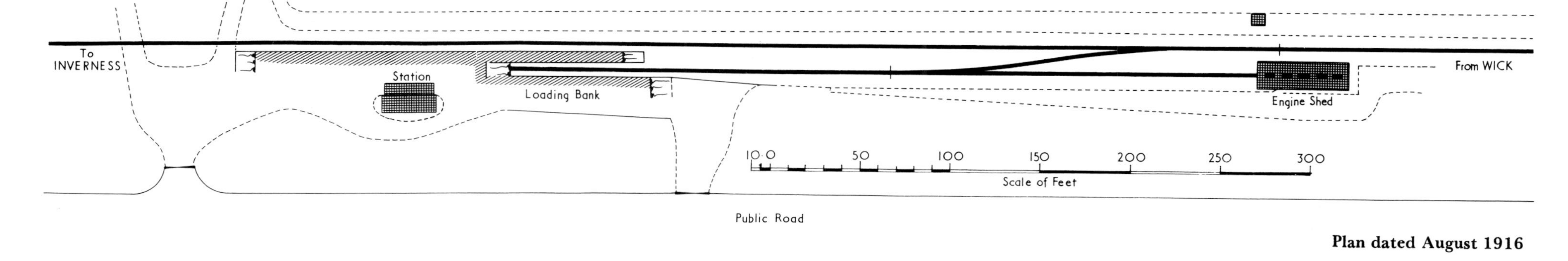

Plan dated August 1916

HIGHLAND RAILWAY
(PRIVATE STATION)

DUNROBIN

DUNROBIN *(Map Ref. R20)*

The third Duke of Sutherland was a staunch advocate of railway construction, and when it came to building railways into the barren highlands, his contribution, both in cash and in effort, was great. When the Sutherland Railway, which was empowered to build a line from Bonar Bridge to Brora, ran out of funds and stopped short at Golspie in 1868, the Duke stepped forward. In June 1870, he obtained powers to build a privately owned line from Golspie through Brora to Helmsdale. The Duke of Sutherland's Railway opened from Dunrobin, two miles north of Golspie, to the outskirts of Helmsdale on 1st November 1870, and, after the difficult approach into Golspie had been finished, was completed as a through route the following June. During this period, the line was worked by the Duke, but after the work had been completed, it was taken over by the Highland Railway.

This was not the end of the Sutherland involvement however, for until 1948, the Dukes retained the right to run their own rolling stock over the line and also to stop trains at Dunrobin, which, upon completion of the line into Golspie, became a private station serving Dunrobin Castle.

The original station building was constructed in log cabin style with projecting eaves. In 1902, this was replaced by the timber framed and gabled building illustrated. As well as the passenger facilities, the station possessed a short siding with a loading dock, and a small carriage shed, wherein the Duke kept his private saloons. Until 1902 there was also a signal cabin, but this was removed during the rebuilding, and the levers transferred to the station buildings for some years prior to their removal.

Public traffic was handled at Dunrobin in conjunction with the annual county crofters show in August, and, pre-war, as many as 1,500 passengers have used the station in a single day.

◁ The later buildings and loading bank at Dunrobin looking towards Inverness. It would be hard to fault this delightful chalet building in its picturesque setting. One could imagine the splendour as the ducal carriage arrived, the team groomed to perfection, and the special train awaiting to hurry south to Inverness or perhaps even further afield. Although official plans are usually to be relied upon, the 1916 HR survey, from which our scale plan is taken, makes a common but erroneous assertion — the shed at the Wick end of the station was not a locomotive shed, but a carriage shed for the ducal saloon, the locomotive being kept in a small shed at Helmsdale.

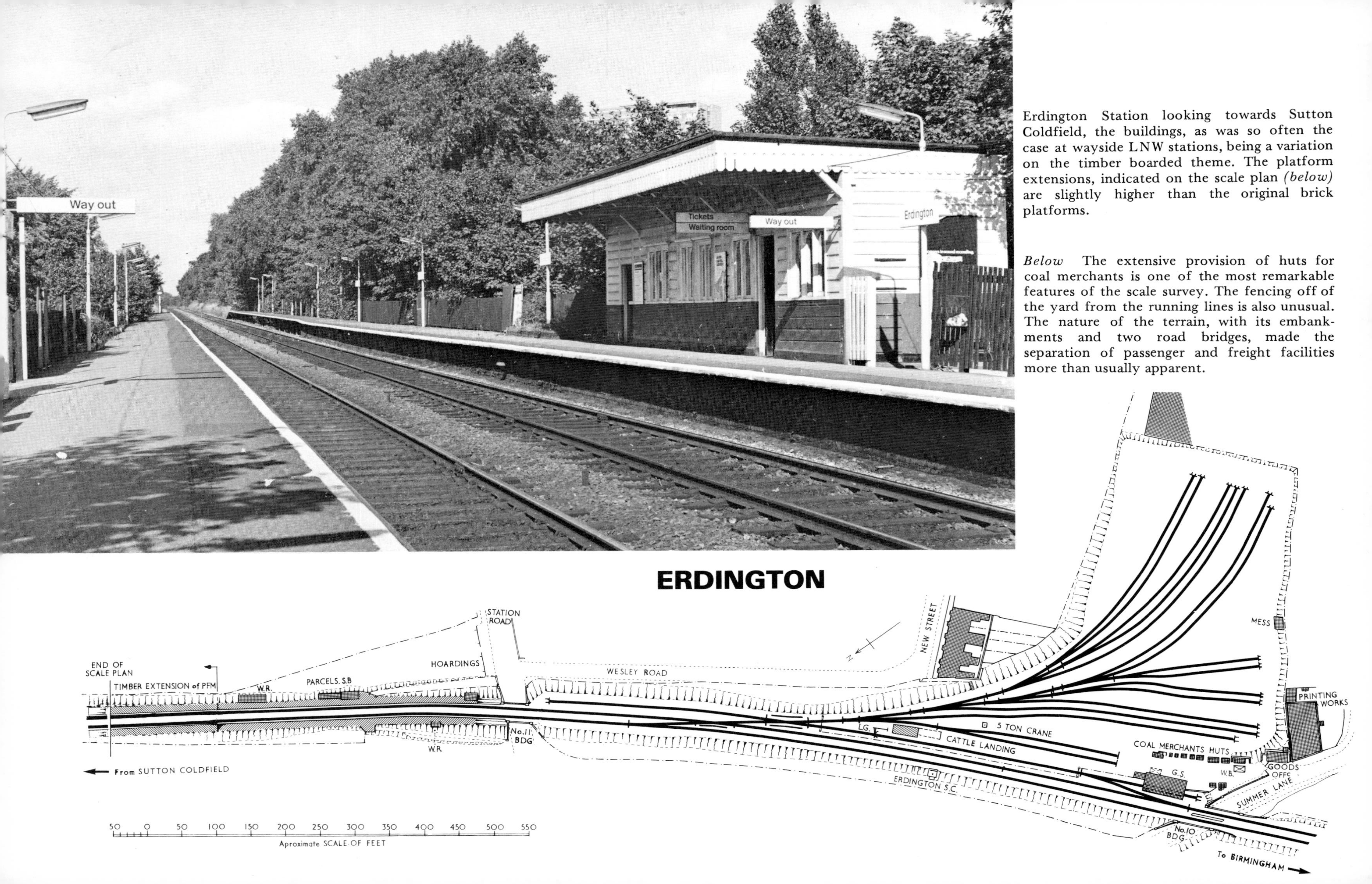

Erdington Station looking towards Sutton Coldfield, the buildings, as was so often the case at wayside LNW stations, being a variation on the timber boarded theme. The platform extensions, indicated on the scale plan *(below)* are slightly higher than the original brick platforms.

Below The extensive provision of huts for coal merchants is one of the most remarkable features of the scale survey. The fencing off of the yard from the running lines is also unusual. The nature of the terrain, with its embankments and two road bridges, made the separation of passenger and freight facilities more than usually apparent.

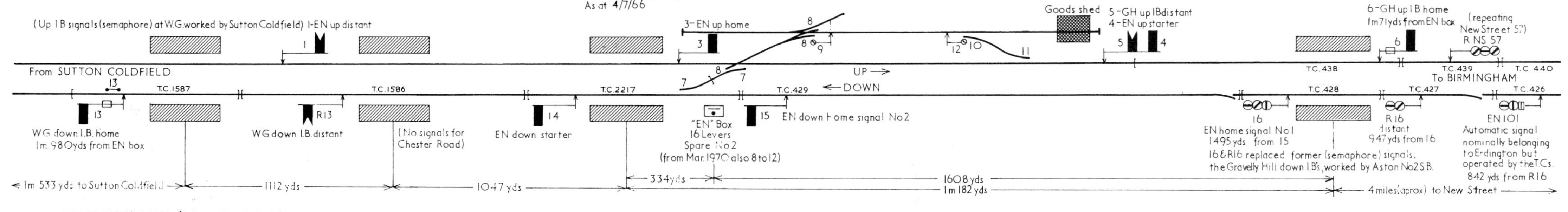

Above As Erdington box signals the Wylde Green—Gravelly Hill section, embracing four passenger stations, the signalling plan has been extended to cover these stations also. As with any such plan, signalling clarity, rather than scale, predominates, and the Up distant No. 1 was, in fact, quite close to Chester Road platform, whilst the box was approximately half way along the yard.

ERDINGTON *(Map Ref. D7)*

Erdington Station was one of the original stations on the Aston—Sutton Coldfield branch of the LNWR, and opened on 2nd June 1862. The passenger station is on Station Road, over which the line is carried by a single arch bridge, which as late as 1977, still carried traces of an 'L.M.S. ERDINGTON STATION' inscription. As at Chester Road, the line is on an embankment, and the timber buildings rest on massive wooden piles driven into the earth.

The signal box and goods yard are some distance to the south of the station. In order to handle the intensive commuter service on the Sutton branch in an economical manner, the block sections Aston No. 2—Erdington (2 miles 288 yards), and Erdington—Sutton (2 miles 1,266 yards), were split by Intermediate block signals at Gravelly Hill and Wylde Green respectively. These were semaphore signals controlled from the box in rear, Erdington being responsible for the Down Wylde Green and Up Gravelly Hill IBs. Sutton controlled the Up Wylde Green IB, and Aston No. 2, the Down Gravelly Hill IB.

During stage 3 of the commissioning of New Street power Box (for which Erdington is a fringe box) on 2nd-4th July 1966, the arrangements were modified. The Erdington Down distant was taken away, and a three aspect Down home EN 16 and distant REN 16 installed in lieu of the former Down Gravelly Hill IB. A two aspect fully automatic signal, EN 101 (EN indicating Erdington box area) was positioned 842 yards in rear of the new REN 16. RNS 57 is nothing to do with Erdington, being the distant for New Street PSB.

Right The main buildings looking towards Sutton Coldfield. In common with the timber buildings at Gravelly Hill, Chester Road and Wylde Green, they display several differences from the later more standardised LNWR structures. The corner posts are inconspicuous; the window frames are highly ornate (and quite unlike later frames) with twin or triple windows to a tall narrow design without horizontal division. The ornate tops to the windows do not feature in later buildings. Erdington is even more remarkable, for the roof is unlike its contemporaries (hipped roof); nor does it resemble the late 1870s design where the canopy and building flat roof both sloped to a central gutter in a mild 'V' form (see Theddingworth).

ETTINGTON

EAST & WEST JUNCTION RAILWAY

Ettington Station looking towards Towcester in the late 'twenties, a scene which vividly recaptures all the charm of rural lines in general and of the SMJ in particular. On a beautiful summer day, an LNWR 0-6-0 blows off in the Up platform waiting for a Down passenger train; a horsebox is lying in the yard, and the goods shed doors are open. In the distance can be seen the Down home signal, with its subsidiary arm added in 1911 for bi-directional working through the Up loop. Well tended flower beds and trim paintwork reflect the pride which Ettington staff still take in their station.

ETTINGTON *(Map Ref. E4)*

Ettington Station was on the Stratford–Kineton section of the East & West Junction Railway, and opened to traffic on 1st July 1873. Services were suspended between 1877 and 1885, and the station finally closed to passengers on 5th April 1952. Through freight services ceased on 1st March 1965, and the section between Stratford and Burton Dassett was subsequently lifted.

Ettington was to the standard E&WJ pattern with a passing loop and characteristic buildings. The goods shed is (1977) one of the few E&WJ structures to remain in good condition, the yard being used by timber merchants and agricultural dealers.

When the LMS came into being, the SMJ, as the E&WJ had by then become, was a natural addition to the Midland Division, as it provided a useful short-cut between the Bristol and St. Pancras routes, and was indeed used as such by the LMS in an attempt to win freight traffic from the GWR Bristol–London services! Despite its Midland Division ownership, the line became the haunt of L&Y and LNWR motive power as well as former MR engines, and our illustration shows a former LNWR goods at the far end of the loop.

As an economy measure, in 1911, long-section electric train staff equipment was installed between Stratford and Kineton, to allow Ettington box to be switched out. This was a very early example of such equipment. In 1937 the Stratford–Ettington (short-working) staff was round and painted red. The Ettington–Kineton staff was round and blue, and when Ettington box was closed, which at that time was between 9.30pm and 7.15am, a long-section token, coloured green, was used.

Signalling modifications in conjunction with the long-section working included making the Up loop bi-directional, and the provision of a switching-out lever. The method of working is explained in the notes to the 'B' signalling plan.

ETTINGTON

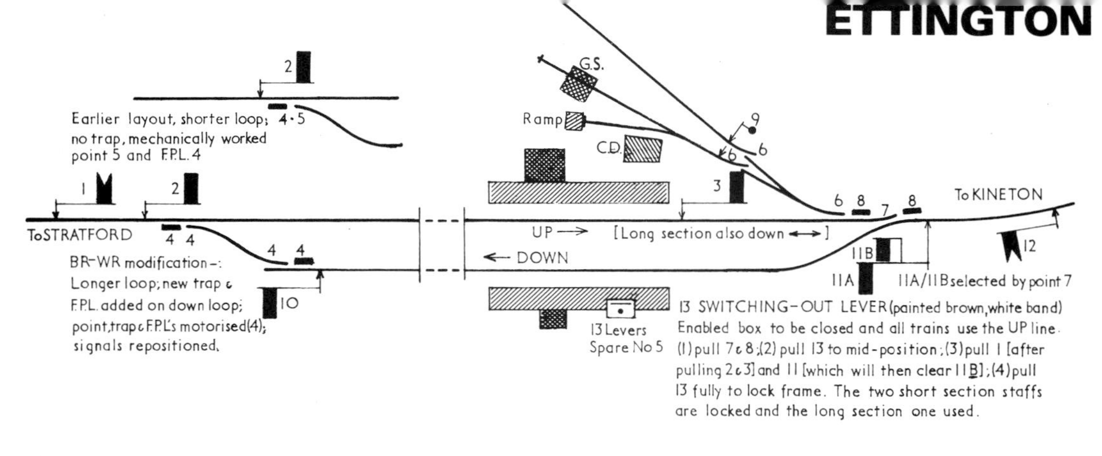

Earlier layout, shorter loop; no trap, mechanically worked point 5 and F.P.L. 4
4·5
ToSTRATFORD
BR-WR modification-: Longer loop; new trap & F.P.L. added on down loop; point, trap & F.P.L's motorised(4); signals repositioned.
10
G.S.
Ramp
C.D.
UP
DOWN
[Long section also down]
13 Levers
Spare No 5
To KINETON
11A/11B selected by point 7
13 SWITCHING-OUT LEVER (painted brown, white band)
Enabled box to be closed and all trains use the UP line. (1) pull 7 & 8; (2) pull 13 to mid-position; (3) pull 1 [after pulling 2 & 3] and 11 [which will then clear 11B]; (4) pull 13 fully to lock frame. The two short section staffs are locked and the long section one used.

Below When the newly formed SMJ board decided to order switching out equipment and long section staffs for Ettington in 1909, it was a bold step as the idea was still a novelty. The installation was inspected by the Board of Trade early in 1911 and by its latter years was regarded as positively archaic. Although the wooden case has been vandalised, enough remains of the equipment to gain an impression of its robust construction.

Below right The Railway Signal Co. frame at Ettington in February 1966. Although the line had been closed, and the box abandoned, the route is still set up correctly for the box when switched out, with Down signals 1, 2 and 3 off, point 7 pulled and locked by 8, the Down home 11 pulled (working the auxiliary arm) and the switching out lever 13. Spare 5 is also pulled.

Above Ettington signal box looking towards Towcester, in 1966. The staff exchange platform was added after the station was closed to passengers and the platform cut back.

FEARN

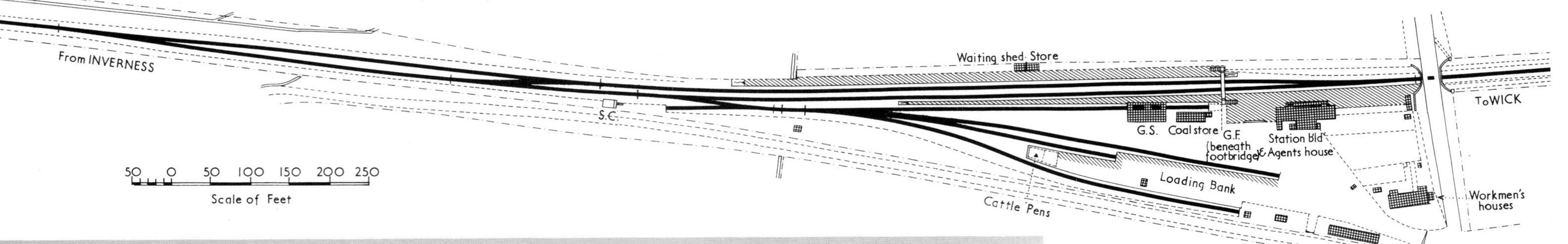

FEARN *(Map Ref. R19)*

Fearn is situated on the Highland Railway 'Farther north' line between Nigg and Tain, on what is only the second inland section after leaving Inverness. The line between Invergordon and Bonar Bridge was authorised in the Ross-shire Extension Act of 1863, and the southern portion, on which Fearn lies, opened on 1st June 1864.

It is a minor intermediate station typical of the smaller stations on this section. The station buildings and agent's house are of sturdy masonry construction, designed to stand the savage winter conditions encountered; they are provided with a small awning by the main entrance.

A common feature on this line is the way in which carts, lorries and even post office vans drive right on to the platform to meet the trains, as can be seen in the illustration.

One unusual aspect of the station layout is, that if a long southbound train is occupying the platform, it would block the departure of any northbound train. Normally at single line stations, the passing loop is made of sufficient length to ensure that a train in one platform does not foul one in the opposite direction. At Fearn, a road overbridge crosses the line just beyond the platform, and to extend the loop would have involved the rebuilding of this bridge.

Freight traffic handled by Fearn included farm produce, livestock and fish from the Tarbat peninsula. Heavy potato traffic — up to 40 wagons at a time — was handled in season.

◁ The main buildings at Fearn looking towards Inverness. The sidings, visible between the buildings and the footbridge, were on the Up side of the station facing towards Inverness, and to facilitate shunting by Down trains, a tow rope was kept at the signal box. Despite falling into disfavour, the method was quick and effective, and as one of the authors has proved, will even work well on a model railway. As with the prototype, a kinked rope is the quickest way to disaster, and one learns to care for the rope!

FENNY COMPTON

Plan 12 Dec 1884

From TOWCESTER
EAST & WEST JUNCTION RLY.
DOWN →
← UP
From OXFORD
GWR
S.B.
M.B.
W.S.
L.C.
L.C.
DOWN →
← UP
To STRATFORD E & WJ
GWR. To LEAMINGTON
20 0 100 200
Scale of Feet

Below Fenny Compton SMJ Station looking towards Stratford at the start of the 'fifties. On the extreme left is the opening underneath the platform for the point rodding and signal wires from the E&WJ signal box, as shown on the scale plan *(above)*. This was replaced, in 1931, by the LMS and GW joint box visible to the right of the level crossing. It was in turn replaced, in 1960, by a BR box. The building on the left is similar to others on the E&WJ, although these existed in left-hand and right-hand versions with other local differences and peculiarities. In 1873 when Colonel Yolland inspected the E&WJ, he complained that the Up (right-hand) platform was not the requisite 6ft. wide at one point. Had his ghost returned to the scene 80 years later, he would very probably have haunted the station in rage; it still wasn't 6ft. in the clear! The reason being that the GWR goods yard lay immediately beyond the fence.

FENNY COMPTON

Above The LMS/GWR joint box diagram in 1956. Comparison with the E&WJ layout of 1884 reveals several changes, mostly on the GWR, although the E&WJ yard has gained a siding, whilst a trap has been added on the Up loop. The Down GW platform has been moved to the Leamington side of the crossing to reduce congestion in the yard, and a second connection, from the yard to the GW Down main, has been laid in. A very short additional siding has been added, the Up and Down GW cross over moved out, and a refuge loop laid in on the Up side, opposite the new GW platform. The signalling plan on the following page shows the radical changes effected in 1960, when the Up SMJ platform was swept away and a third loop added, the old exchange sidings and GW yard replaced by a running junction, and the SMJ yard made accessible from the GW as well as from the SMJ. Most remarkable of all, the connection in to the SMJ yard, instead of trailing, had become a facing lead.

Above right Fenny Compton SMJ looking towards Byfield in 1951. From left to right; the GWR yard and cattle dock, the SMJ boundary fence (original by the look of it!), the exchange siding shunt signal and starter to Byfield, the *facing* points from the Up SMJ into the exchange sidings, the trailing connection off the Up SMJ to the yard, the Down loop and a smouldering embankment.

Right The LMS/GWR joint box and Up SMJ platform shelter, looking towards the GWR main line and Byfield. The signal box had two separate lever frames, one on each side of the box, both commencing with No. 1, the signal in the background being GWR frame No. 27. One wonders if the signalman drank GWR tea on the far side of the box, and LMS tea on the

FENNY COMPTON

28 February 1960

FENNY COMPTON *(Map Ref. F4)*

The East & West Junction Railway was for much of its life in a state of acute financial embarrassment, and with little money to spare, its relations with the inspecting officers of the Board of Trade were none too happy. It was a tradition which went back to the days prior to the line even being open! The first section of the E&WJ to be submitted for inspection was between Fenny Compton (on the GWR Birmingham main line) and Kineton. Colonel Hutchinson was deputed to inspect the line, and he baulked at deficient ballast, missing fish bolts, poor fencing, incomplete interlocking, inadequate station facilities and no station nameboards or clocks. On his second visit, he passed the line, subject to an undertaking from the company concerning Fenny Compton, where the E&WJ hoped to use GWR facilities until a joint station was built. The line opened on 1st June 1871.

Two years later, the E&WJ invited the Board of Trade to inspect the extensions from Kineton to Stratford, and from Fenny Compton to Towcester. On this occasion, Colonel Yolland descended upon the impecunious E&WJ. He soon noticed that the Up platform at Fenny Compton narrowed to no more than 2ft. 11in. at one place, instead of the requisite 6ft. This was because the GWR goods yard adjoined the platform, and the Colonel issued orders that, unless the GWR would agree to move their fence, the platform was to be shortened. As it was only 100 yards long in the first place, this was not very convenient, and as late as 1951, the platform was still less than the conventional width (see illustrations).

The E&WJ signal box was on the Up platform adjacent to the main buildings, but a joint LMS/GWR cabin was installed in 1931, which signalled both routes. This was in turn replaced by a BR (WR) box in March 1960. As passenger services over the SMJ ceased in 1952, the old Up platform was swept away, and a series of running connections laid in between the SMJ and WR lines. These were intended to facilitate through goods traffic, but a change of plans resulted in the line being closed as a through route in 1965. The only section which carries traffic today (1977) is from Fenny Compton to an army camp at Burton Dassett.

The Board of Trade's dislike of facing points is well known, and is illustrated by this comment from the inspecting officer's report: 'I have also recommended that the siding at Blakesley Station off the Down line should cross that line and join the Up instead of the Down line, and thus avoid an unnecessary pair of facing points'.

At Fenny Compton, this fetish was honoured in the case of the Down yard siding, which was laid in to the Up line, but the E&WJ/GWR exchange siding was reached off a facing connection at the end of the Up platform, instead of a trailing point off the Down line! This made nonsense of the whole exercise, but was passed without comment! (see scale plan 'A').

Looking towards Banbury and Towcester on 27th July 1964, after the dramatic 1960 reconstruction; locomotive No. 80072 has drawn into the Down and Up reception loop with an ore train. The illustration is taken from the Up SMJ crossing loop, and the Up GW platform is visible on the extreme left, whilst the disused Down SMJ platform is visible on the right. Signals prominent in this view comprise 56, 48 (off), 61 (ground disc), 33, 34/28/40/39. Also visible are Nos. 47, 55/6/12 and 10/8/13. The Great Westernising philosophy of the Western Region signal department will be noted! A few months after this impressive scene, the SMJ was closed as a through route, and the GWR passenger station lost its passenger service thereafter.

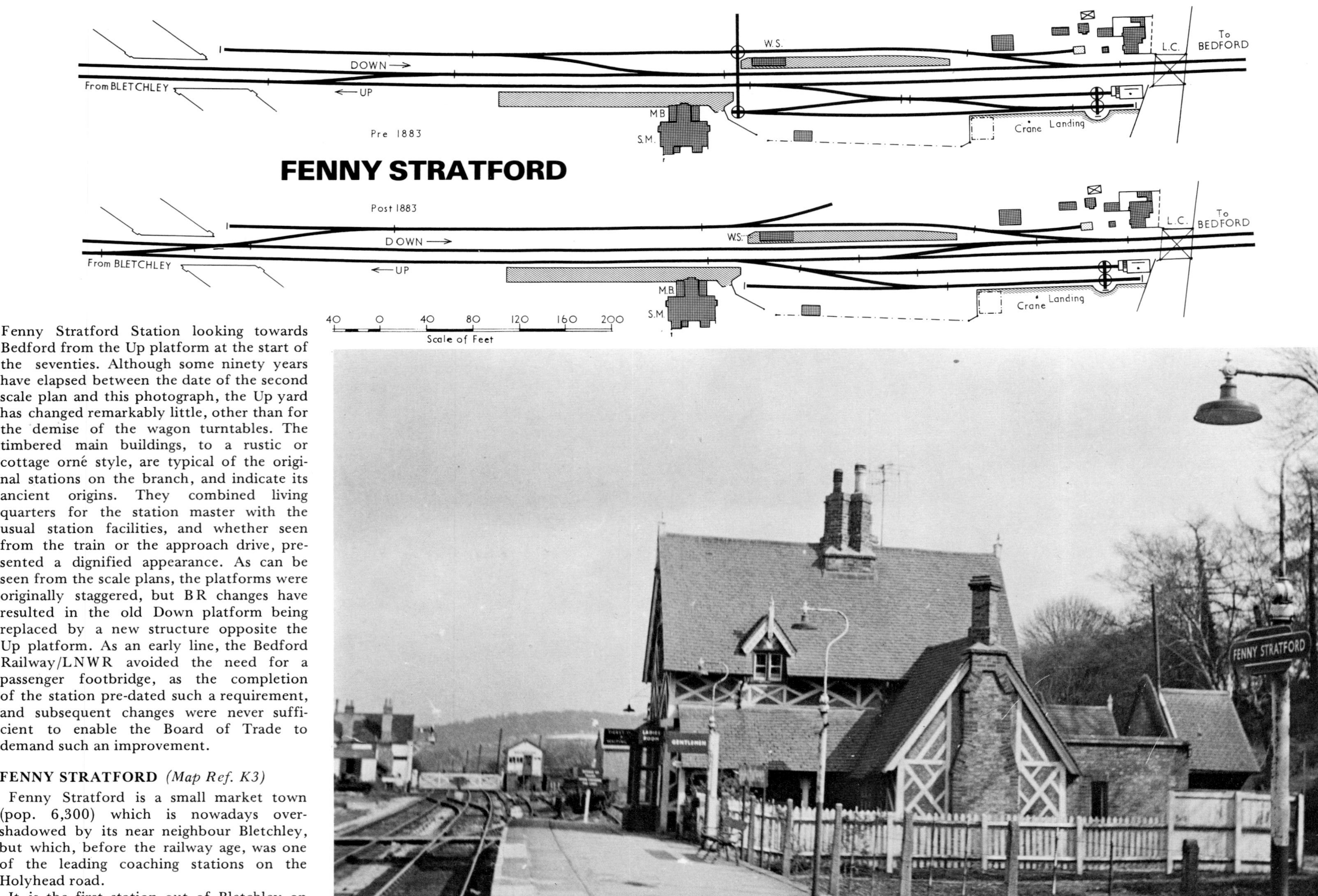

Fenny Stratford Station looking towards Bedford from the Up platform at the start of the seventies. Although some ninety years have elapsed between the date of the second scale plan and this photograph, the Up yard has changed remarkably little, other than for the demise of the wagon turntables. The timbered main buildings, to a rustic or cottage orné style, are typical of the original stations on the branch, and indicate its ancient origins. They combined living quarters for the station master with the usual station facilities, and whether seen from the train or the approach drive, presented a dignified appearance. As can be seen from the scale plans, the platforms were originally staggered, but BR changes have resulted in the old Down platform being replaced by a new structure opposite the Up platform. As an early line, the Bedford Railway/LNWR avoided the need for a passenger footbridge, as the completion of the station pre-dated such a requirement, and subsequent changes were never sufficient to enable the Board of Trade to demand such an improvement.

FENNY STRATFORD *(Map Ref. K3)*

Fenny Stratford is a small market town (pop. 6,300) which is nowadays overshadowed by its near neighbour Bletchley, but which, before the railway age, was one of the leading coaching stations on the Holyhead road.

It is the first station out of Bletchley on

the Bedford branch of the LNWR. The line was constructed by the Bedford Railway, the first sod being lifted in November 1845. The ceremonial opening was one year later, on 17th November 1846, and the line was worked from the outset by the LNWR.

The scale plans show the station prior to and after its 1883 rebuilding, during which the old square crossings through the running lines were removed. It is of interest to note that whilst this was carried out at Fenny Stratford as early as 1883, there were stations on the L&B main line where this was still to be done in 1900 (see Brandon & Wolston).

The picturesque timbered main buildings and agent's house are characteristic of the Bedford railway architecture, and are at ground or low level, with a ramp or steps leading up to the more modern high level platform.

A private siding formerly ran from opposite the station house, across the down yard to a wagon turntable near the roadway. A siding led off this turntable into Rowlands Bros. premises on the north side of the yard. Two narrow gauge industrial tracks led from the factory on to a loading bank on LNWR land.

The most significant change to the station layout since the 1880s has been the installation of the Bletchley flyover, to carry traffic from the Oxford line on to the Bedford branch, and so avoid a flat junction with the West Coast main line. This BR innovation has been of limited value because the Oxford and Bedford lines, which were intended to form a major east-west route, were downgraded to little more than local importance. The signalling 'B' plan shows the layout at Fenny Stratford upon the commissioning of Bletchley power box.

In the 1890s six stopping services called in each direction, the branch carrying some seven or eight trains at that time. By World War I, the local services had improved to about ten trains each way, some being LNWR steam railcars. This trend was resumed after the War, and by 1938 there were nineteen trains calling at Fenny Stratford, several of which were one-class motor workings.

FENNY STRATFORD

As in JUNE 1965

768yds to home BY 25
From BLETCHLEY
1892 yds to home BY 22
DOWN CAMBRIDGE FLYOVER →
← UP CAMBRIDGE FLYOVER
UP MAIN
DOWN MAIN
Cambridge Sidings Frame Release 7
112Oyds from signal ahead
To CAMBRIDGE
14 Gate Lock
15 Gate Stops
21,22 Wickets
22 Levers
Spare No16.
(NO ground signals)
73Oyds to home
1 Gong
Side loading dock

Note colour light signals shown as above on signal box diagram however
F.S. 17/18 is 4-aspect; R/Y being controlled by F.S; Y/YY/G by Bletchley.
BY 22&25 3-aspect; R/Y " " Bletchley; Y/G by F.S. No 4 or 2
F.S. 2 & 4 3-aspect; R/Y " " lever 2 or 4; the G clearing on pulling 3

A closer study of the level crossing, signal box and siding connections. Access into the Down sidings necessitated blocking the road crossing during shunting moves, a nationwide bone of contention between railway companies and road users, and whilst the Board of Trade could not demand that existing layouts should be altered, new connections of this sort were but rarely approved after the mid Victorian period. The layout as well as the buildings attested to the antiquity of the branch and the remarkably few changes over the decades.

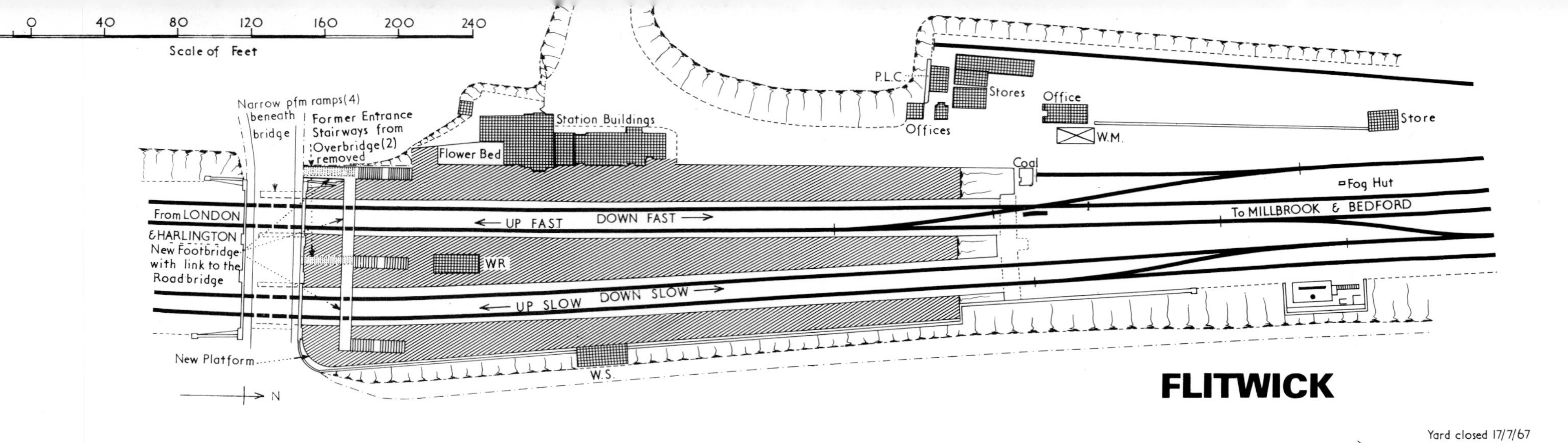

FLITWICK *(Map Ref. L3)*

Flitwick Station is 9½ miles south of Bedford on the MR Bedford–St. Pancras main line. Midland access to London was originally via the LNWR, but the MR Leicester–Bedford–Hitchin extension to the GNR opened in 1857. Congestion on the GNR south of Hitchin soon became so bad that in 1863, the Midland obtained powers for their own independent line into the metropolis. This new line was double track, and opened to goods on 8th September 1867, to local passengers on 13th July 1868 and to express services on 1st October. Traffic built up rapidly, and quadrupling started as early as 1875! Owing to the extensive engineering works required, the section from Bedford to Leagrave (on which Flitwick is located) was the last to be tackled south of Kettering.

The new goods lines were mostly laid in on the east side of the existing formation, but in certain locations, such as at Ampthill tunnel, the fast lines were transferred to a new alignment and the goods lines route through the old bores. In general, however, the older older engineering features are to be found on the westernmost or fast lines. Priority was given to the installation of the Up goods line to relieve the pressure on the Up main caused by slow heavy coal trains. Between Ampthill (to the north) and Flitwick, the Up goods came into use on 15th October 1893. It was extended to Harlington on 28th October 1894. The Down goods from Harlington to Elstow Junction (near Bedford) followed on 28th July 1895.

The new lines were intended for freight traffic, and in consequence no additional platforms were provided (other than in the south nearer London, and at certain major stations such as Kettering). With minor exceptions this remained the position until the implementation by BR on 11th January 1960, of a greatly augmented and accelerated diesel local service between St. Pancras and Bedford. The goods lines were upgraded to slow lines, and additional platforms added at Luton, Leagrave, Harlington and Flitwick.

One inconvenient result of the quadrupling in the 1890s was that the goods lines were to the east of the station, whilst the yard was on the west side. Operationally it would have been more satisfactory if the sidings had been transferred to the eastern side of the line, but road access etc. precluded this, and the inconvenience of having to shunt trains from the slow lines into the yard persisted until the station closed to goods in 1967. The movement of vehicles by tow rope was permitted to speed up the shunting of wagons detached off Up trains.

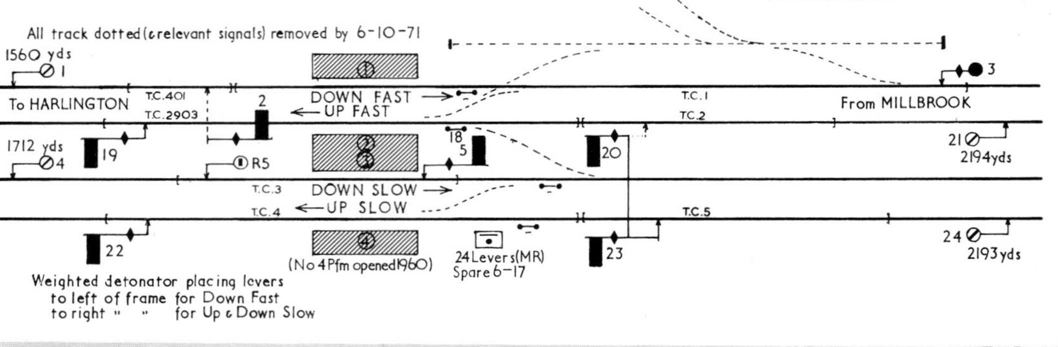

Above Flitwick Station from the Down fast platform in 1953. The station, which did not open until 1870, two years after the line was completed, was similar to its near neighbour Harlington, with an 'L' shaped building on the Down side, the twin storey Station Master's house forming the base of the 'L'. The ground was cut away and a retaining wall provided for the Up slow platform, many years before it was required.

Below Flitwick on 7th October 1971. The extra platform is in; there is a new footbridge and the lights have been replaced by concrete standards.

The goods yard and cabin at Flitwick looking north towards Bedford from the Up fast platform. At this time, the slow lines had not received platforms, and from the scale plan and illustrations it will be seen how very awkward shunting at Flitwick was. As with many places, the local pronunciation differed from the spelling, the 'W' being silent, to produce 'Flit-ick'. The signal box proclaims its Midland ancestry.

Below Flitwick looking north from the BR footbridge on 7th October 1971. Although the goods yard has gone, the platforms are still as well cared for as in the 'fifties, and the floral displays have been extended to the new No. 4 platform as well. The station is indeed a tribute to its staff.

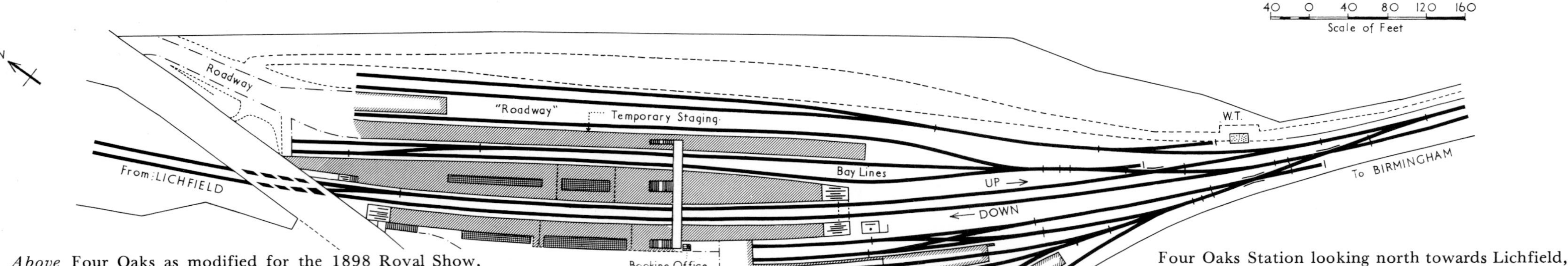

Above Four Oaks as modified for the 1898 Royal Show, long before that event called for a permanent site.

FOUR OAKS

Four Oaks Station looking north towards Lichfield, with a permanent way train headed by a Class 08 shunter on the north cross over. The station building is a development of the earlier rusticated boarding buildings found south of Sutton. The lean-to shelter over the ticket hatch provides a touch of individuality.

FOUR OAKS *(Map Ref. D7)*

This history of the southern portion of the Birmingham–Sutton Coldfield–Lichfield branch has already been detailed. In 1880, the LNWR obtained powers to extend the line from Sutton to Lichfield, and this section opened on 15th December 1884. The opening of the Sutton line in the 1860s had led to a rapid growth in population as the area developed as a suburb of Birmingham. This trend was repeated at Four Oaks, but further north, the area remained predominantly agricultural, and even today the service is much less frequent than in the south.

In June 1898 the station was specially enlarged in conjunction with traffic to and from the Royal Agricultural Show. A temporary wooden platform, served by two roads, was laid in on the east side of the line, together with several extra sidings. After the show, the excess passenger accommodation was removed, and the space used for sidings. The scale plan shows Four Oaks during the period that the show connections were in use. Such facilities would make an unusual addition to a model railway.

Some idea of the importance of Four Oaks as a terminating station under ordinary circumstances is given by the train services at different periods.

Southbound trains originating ex station named	*1909*	*1927*
Lichfield	10 (a)	14 (b)
Four Oaks	26	25
Sutton Coldfield	6	1

(a) Three of these trains terminated at Four Oaks.
(b) as above, certain Lichfield Motor trains ran only as far as Four Oaks.

The majority of the siding accommodation at Four Oaks was removed by BR, but with the intensification of the Birmingham services, some roads were restored in 1977 on the Up side of the station.

FOUR OAKS

As at 3 JULY 1976

716yds to home CP
240 6yds to home CP
1142 yds to home
From LICHFIELD CITY
T.C.3
440yds
T.C.2
23t
BLAKE STREET DOWN I.B. Sigs.
23a
BAY
UP MAIN →
← DOWN MAIN
CB
26 Levers. Spare 6,17 to 22.
T.C.1
To SUTTON COLDFIELD
C.P. 491 yds to home
902 yds to home

With the decline in local freight traffic and the rise of the DMU, Four Oaks lost its freight sidings on the Down side and the stabling roads on the Up side, but made a come-back in the late 'seventies as a result of the intensified suburban passenger services provided by BR at the behest of the West Midlands PTE. After a long period of decline, it was pleasant to see new track and new ballast going in. Amusingly, the sidings are in modern flat-bottom rail, whilst the main lines and bay platform are still chaired bullhead!

A delightful period piece visible in the previous view, and seen in close-up below. Curiosities such as this, on the Birmingham end of the Up platform, gave so many stations their charm and individuality, and it is good to see a few surviving into modern times.

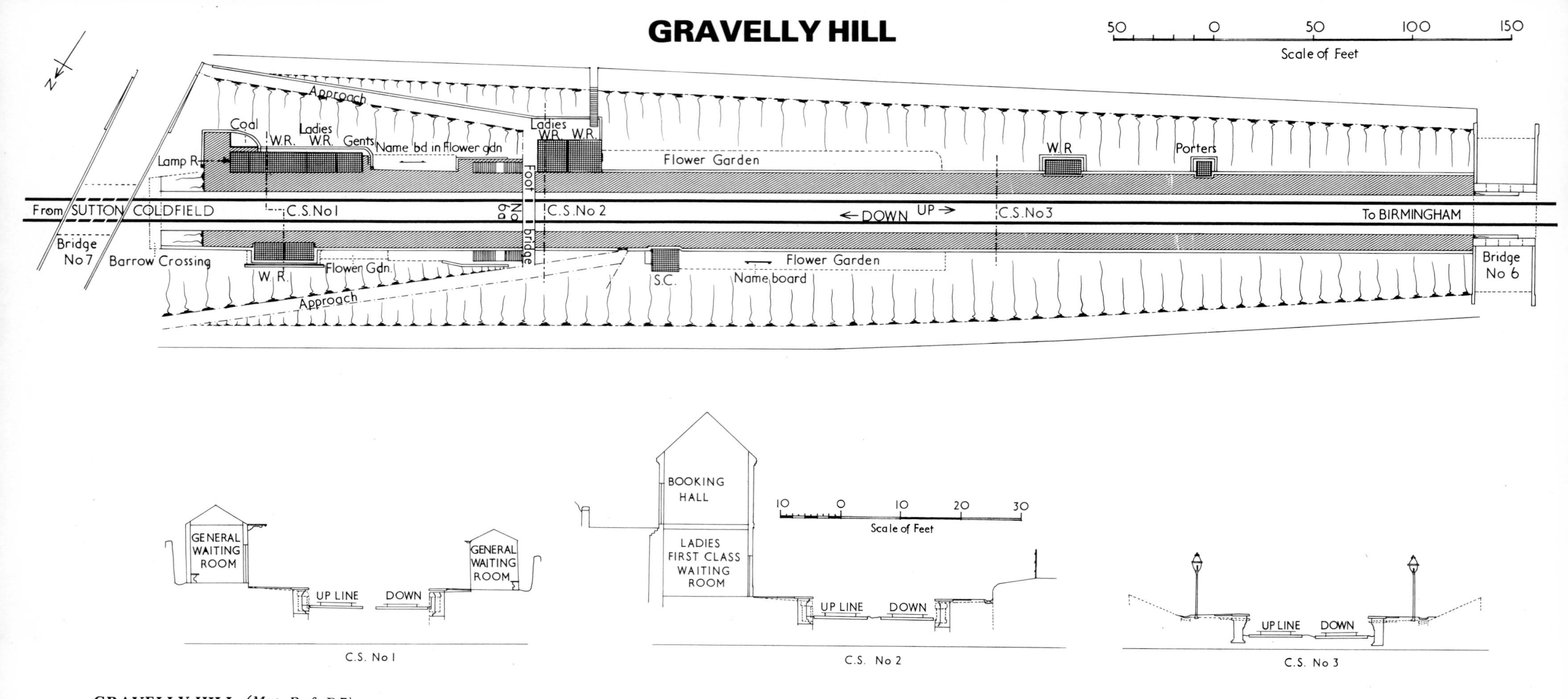

GRAVELLY HILL *(Map Ref. D7)*

The Gravelly Hill district of Birmingham is best known for its motorway intersection, the remarkable 'Spaghetti Junction', but it is also on the Birmingham–Sutton Coldfield branch of the LNWR, which in fact penetrates the northern extremity of the road complex. Gravelly Hill Station lies a short distance to the north of Spaghetti Junction, and is in a deep cutting. The two storey main buildings on the Up side are reached via Frederick Street, and the booking office is on the upper floor. A footbridge, adapted from the standard type of LNWR pedestrian overbridge, leads down to the two platforms. A second access path on the Down side leads to the footbridge and to the platform directly. Timber platform buildings, similar to those found at Chester Road and Erdington, were provided on both platforms, whilst the ground floor of the main building provided a 1st Class Ladies Waiting Room and an additional 1st Class General Waiting Room, giving Gravelly Hill the remarkable distinction of no fewer than five waiting rooms on the Up platform alone! Excessive though this may seem, many early stations were provided with separate 1st Class facilities, necessitating four waiting rooms at even a minor station.

The scale plan pre-dates the introduction of Intermediate Block signalling and shows a small signal cabin on the Down platform. With the overbridges at each end of the platforms, the signalmen must have enjoyed a remarkably poor view. Frustrating though the bridges must have been to the signalman, they do provide a natural scenic break for the modeller who has to work in a confined space, whilst the slope of the cutting on the Up side and the wooded nature of the area would facilitate a convincing model.

The three cross sections give a good idea of how compact the site is – a foot width would suffice in 'OO' gauge. The station opened on 2nd June 1862, train services being similar to other stations on the branch, such as Chester Road and Erdington. Signalling arrangements after the installation of IBs are commented upon under Erdington.

GRAVELLY HILL

Left The view from Bridge No. 7 looking towards Birmingham. Comparison of the 1970s study with the LNWR plan will reveal that the subsidiary timber buildings on the Up platform have fallen victim to rationalisation, the only apparent trace being the retaining wall on the left hand side of the picture. With the days long gone, when a small station could support a large staff, the well tended flower beds of North Western days are another memory. It is apparent, even from this elevated view close to the Down line, how restricted the signalman's view must have been.

Below The view from near the site of the signal box looking past the footbridge (No. 6A), road bridge No. 7 and on towards Sutton Coldfield. Two further overbridges can be seen in the distance, making this one of the few locations where it is possible to see five overbridges all within a short distance, four to the north, one to the south. The red brick main buildings on the Up side are neat but plain. The Down waiting room, of early LNWR rusticated boarding construction, is visible just short of the platform end.

HALL ROAD

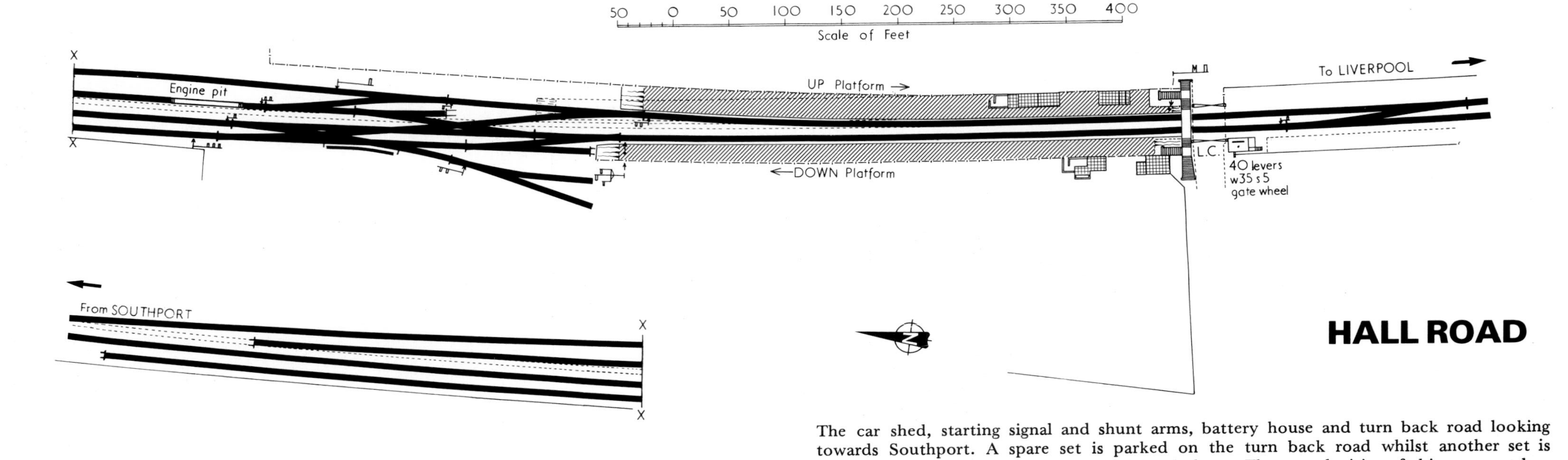

Hall Road Station looking towards Southport, 19th April 1977. The illustration provides a rare glimpse of the diagonal bars fitted for rigidity under the decking and stairs of the L&Y footbridges. It is also interesting to study the fixing of the lattice bars on the right hand staircase. In accordance with Board of Trade requirements, the nearer building on the Up (right-hand) platform boasts a clock. It also sports some rather ornate ridge tiles.

The car shed, starting signal and shunt arms, battery house and turn back road looking towards Southport. A spare set is parked on the turn back road whilst another set is stabled at the far end of the car shed head shunt. The complexities of this compact lay-out merit a prolonged study both of the plan and view. The facing lead from the Down main to the turn back road and the diamond crossing of the Down main and trailing lead from the car depot to the Up main almost coincide, making for a very complex piece of track.

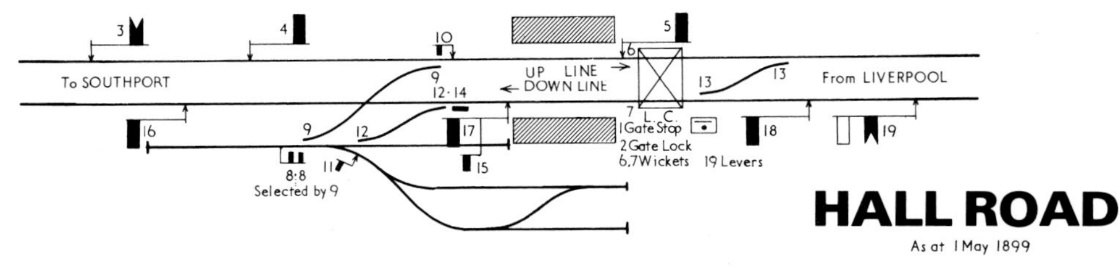

Above The short-lived 1899 re-signalling of Hall Road Station; within a short period the 19 lever box had been extended to accommodate a 40 lever frame, the scale plan on the previous page actually showing this extension.

Below left Hall Road looking towards Liverpool in April 1977. Either the commuters of Hall Road are exceptionally tidy or the station staff unusually conscientious, as there is not a piece of litter to be seen. The twin storey building on the right is a part of the offices and staff facilities of the electric depot. As remarked earlier, the footbridge is typical of L&Y design with lattice bars and overhead bracing. The latter extend to the bottom decking and are additionally strengthened by outriggers, some of which are curved, as in this case; others being more angular.

Below right Hall Road level crossing and signal box looking towards Liverpool Exchange. Research has failed to show if this is the pre-electrification box as enlarged, but the evidence is strongly supportive, both as to style, as it is in the Saxby & Farmer tradition, and because the method of supporting the opening for the point rodding and the brickwork show an abrupt change at the same point, approximately where the box would have needed to be extended to go from a 19 to a 40 lever frame.

HALL ROAD *(Map Ref. A3)*

Hall Road Station on the L&Y Liverpool–Southport line was a comparatively late-comer, not opening until 1874. It is 7¼ miles from Exchange Station, and was initially an ordinary wayside station with the usual trailing cross overs and siding. In May 1899, the L&Y advised the Board of Trade that the layout was being revised. The changes at this time included a facing connection from the Down line into a short neck, a trailing cross over on to the Up line, and an extra siding.

A more general reconstruction was carried out in 1903-04 in conjunction with electrification work. A new centre road was added for turn back trains at the north end of the station, and the electric running depot was established adjacent to the Down platform. Facing leads from the Down line led into the turn back road, the car depot head shunt, and connections from these lines ran in turn into the Up running line. The company applied for inspection of the new works on 14th March 1903, and they were passed by Colonel Druitt. He noted that the signal cabin had been extended and a new 40 lever locking frame installed. He concluded his report, 'I can recommend the Board of Trade to sanction the use of the new works in question'. Ironically, all the safety precautions were to prove in vain, as on 25th July 1905 a signalman's error was to result in one of the worst accidents in the history of the L&Y.

A local train arrived at Hall Road, unloaded, and then ran forward into the turn back road. A minute or so later the signalman accepted a Down express and found he could not clear his signals. He assumed that the points had not gone home and worked them again hoping to clear them, but in his haste inadvertently left them pulled. As the express approached, he flagged it past, rather than delay it whilst the route was examined. The driver on seeing the flag, accelerated rapidly and suddenly swung on to the siding and crashed into the empty stock. Twenty one lives were lost.

A battery sub-station was installed on the Down side north of the station in 1905. As well as smoothing out the power load peaks, the batteries were invaluable when a rotary sub-station was disabled, or when it was necessary to run special trains during the night shut down.

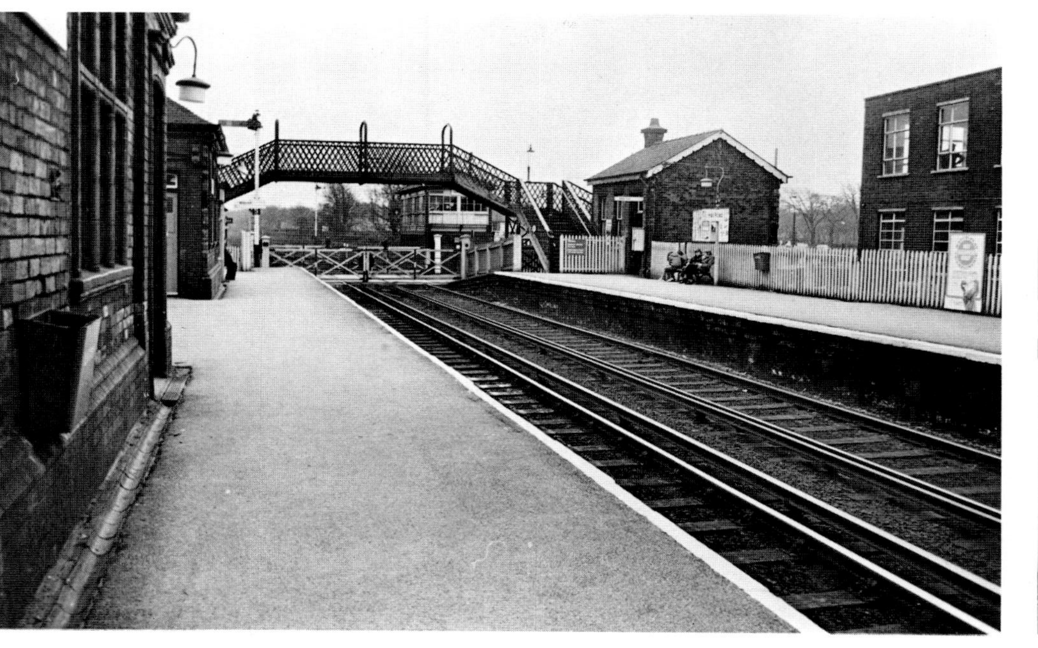

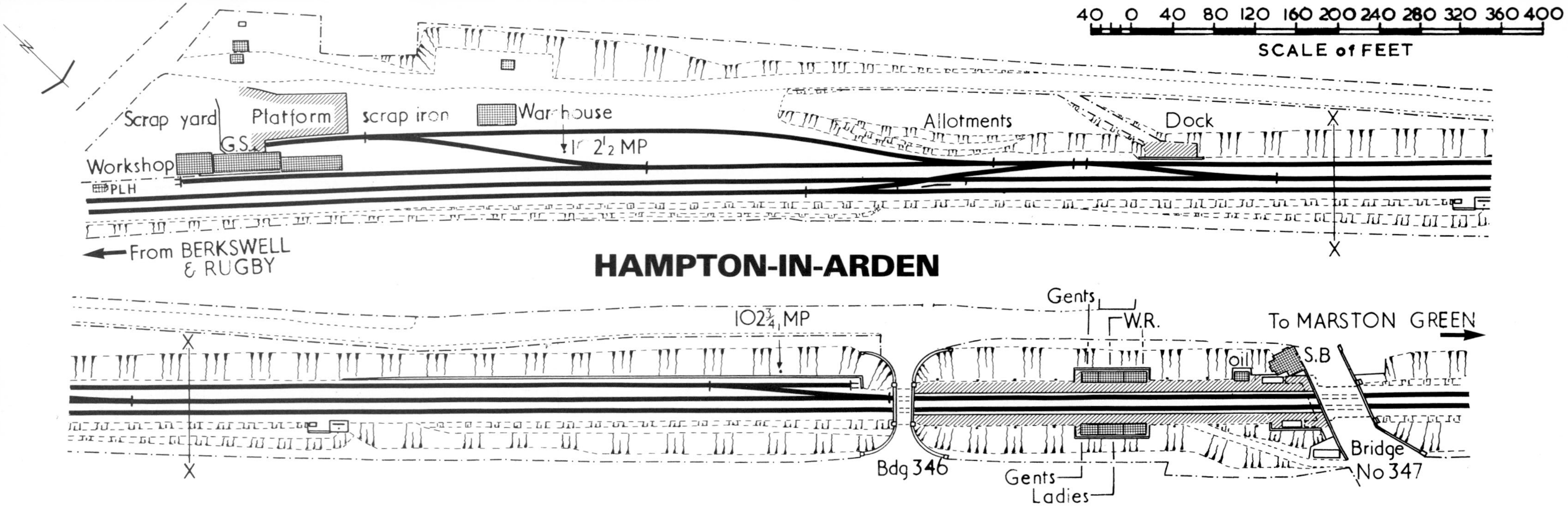

40 0 40 80 120 160 200 240 280 320 360 400
SCALE of FEET

Scrap yard
Platform
scrap iron
Warehouse
Allotments
Dock
G.S.
Workshop
PLH
1 in 2½ MP
← From BERKSWELL & RUGBY

HAMPTON-IN-ARDEN

102¾ MP
Gents
W.R.
To MARSTON GREEN →
Oil
S.B
Bridge No 347
Bdg 346
Gents
Ladies

HAMPTON-IN-ARDEN *(Map Ref. E6)*

The first station in the Hampton area opened in April 1838, when the London & Birmingham line to Rugby came into use. The following year, the Birmingham & Derby Junction Railway opened from Derby to Hampton, and established their own station alongside the L&B. The completion of competitive routes by Midland constituents soon robbed the Hampton line of its significance, and the Midland rapidly downgraded it to branch status. On 1st September 1884, the LNWR closed their original Hampton Station, replacing it by a new one, a quarter of a mile to the south east.

The new station was sited in a cutting between two road bridges. The station offices were built at road level to a mock medieval style with an ornate porch, the uppermost window of which was to the quatrefoil pattern. The platform accommodation conformed with the general style of LNWR timber buildings, but with the medieval theme superimposed once again, primarily in the case of details such as the window frames. The removal of the station awnings during electrification work, although disfiguring the buildings, enabled one to study these features much more clearly. These highly individual buildings were all swept away during the modernisation of the Birmingham line stations, to be replaced by functional but characterless modern counterparts.

The station serves a high class residential area, popular with both London and Birmingham business men, and even in North Western days, a number of semi-fast or express services called at Hampton-in-Arden. This tradition was maintained by BR until the opening of Birmingham International. As the station is in a deep cutting, with hardly a building in sight, this unexpected halt at what appeared to be a *very* minor country station came as a surprise to unsuspecting passengers, much to the amusement of regular travellers.

The Arden suffix, which historically is derived from the great forest of Arden which once covered much of Warwickshire, was adopted by the LNWR to avoid confusion between the LNWR and the Midland stations, the latter retaining its plain Hampton title. The LNWR passenger station cabin was named Hampton-in-Arden; a second cabin, Hampton, existed 815 yards to the west to control the connections on to the Midland branch.

HAMPTON-IN-ARDEN

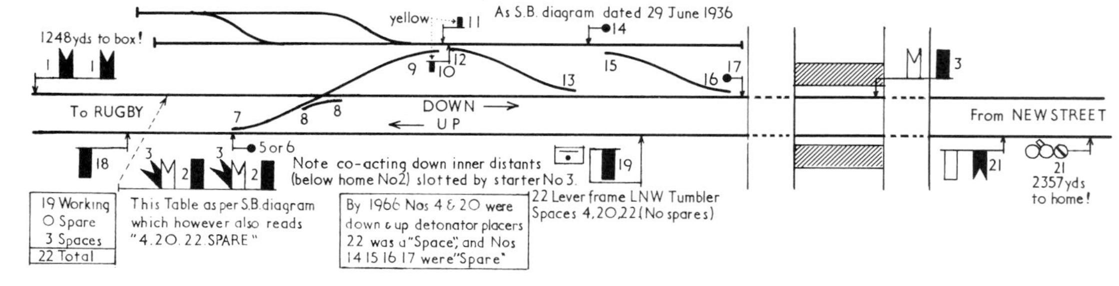

As S.B. diagram dated 29 June 1936
yellow
1248yds to box!
To RUGBY
DOWN
UP
From NEW STREET
5 or 6
Note co-acting down inner distants (below home No2) slotted by starter No 3.
2357yds to home!
19 Working
0 Spare
3 Spaces
22 Total
This Table as per S.B diagram which however also reads "4.20.22 SPARE"
By 1966 Nos 4 & 20 were down & up detonator placers 22 was a "Space", and Nos 14 15 16 17 were "Spare"
22 Lever frame LNW Tumbler Spaces 4,20,22 (No spares)

Previous page The road elevation of the mock medieval booking hall looking towards Rugby in 1966. The lancet windows above the doorway are grouped into a doublet, with the wall above the doublet being pierced with a neat quatrefoil window, the whole ensemble creating a plate tracery, also common in churches of the Early English Gothic period (1200-1300). A further link with this period is the steeply pitched roof. Even the barge boards and timbering reflect the ecclesiastical theme, the scissor beam construction on the end wall being occasionally found in early churches. The arched brace with horizontal collar beam at the apex of the arch is more common, but in this case it is surmounted by a vertical king-post and two sloping struts. The quadrant windows each side of the lancet windows have no normal counterpart in ecclesiastical design, and are necessary to widen the arch to allow for the side windows flanking the doors.

Above Hampton-in-Arden signal box looking towards Rugby in March 1966. From the scale plan it will be seen that the box occupied the classic position almost exactly mid-way between the Up and the Down connections. The only unusual feature was the provision of two trailing leads into the Down main. The yard itself was at the London end of all the connections, a good distance away from the station due to the lie of the land. When the station was rebuilt for Inter-city operation, the platforms required lengthening, and when it is realised that this study of the box is taken from the extended platform, it can be seen that the platform was more than doubled in length.

Left The platform buildings were a blend of standard LNWR design and special features to harmonise with the booking office on the road. Except for the brick base, which is atypical, the general design of this building on the Up platform, is normal. The window frames are unusually deep for their width, but these proportions, coupled with the decorative arches, repeat the lancet theme of the main building. This view, taken during the station rebuilding in March 1966, shows the canopy removed to provide adequate clearance for electrification. Although the stumps of the cast brackets look forlorn, the removal of the canopy permits a good view of the front elevation and of the roof construction.

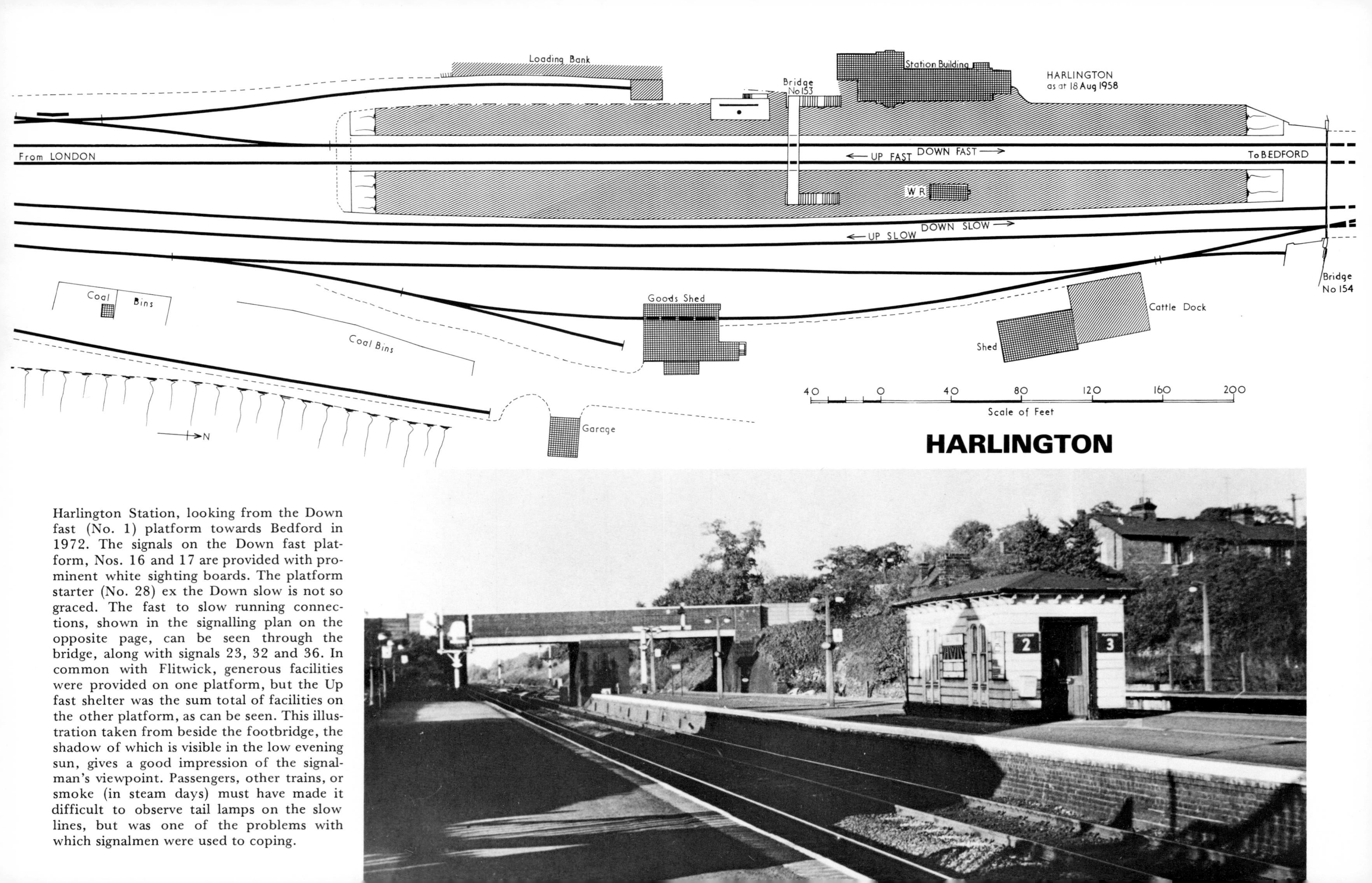

HARLINGTON

Harlington Station, looking from the Down fast (No. 1) platform towards Bedford in 1972. The signals on the Down fast platform, Nos. 16 and 17 are provided with prominent white sighting boards. The platform starter (No. 28) ex the Down slow is not so graced. The fast to slow running connections, shown in the signalling plan on the opposite page, can be seen through the bridge, along with signals 23, 32 and 36. In common with Flitwick, generous facilities were provided on one platform, but the Up fast shelter was the sum total of facilities on the other platform, as can be seen. This illustration taken from beside the footbridge, the shadow of which is visible in the low evening sun, gives a good impression of the signalman's viewpoint. Passengers, other trains, or smoke (in steam days) must have made it difficult to observe tail lamps on the slow lines, but was one of the problems with which signalmen were used to coping.

HARLINGTON *(Map Ref. L2)*

Harlington Station is situated on the MR St. Pancras main line between Bedford and Luton, and is three miles south of Flitwick (see page 76). Its history is similar to Flitwick, except that quadrupling was completed from Leagrave (to the south) some years before the Flitwick section. The Up and Down goods lines to Leagrave, where they joined existing quadruple track, came into use on 3rd August 1890. The Up goods from Flitwick was commissioned on 28th October 1894, and the Down goods on 28th July 1895. This marked the completion of a major multiple tracking exercise, and the Midland Railway Chief Engineer's report for 30th June 1895 reported proudly, (if a trifle prematurely), 'The widening between Bedford and London, including the tunnels at Elstree and Ampthill, is now completed, four parallel lines of way being thus opened for traffic between Glendon Junction and London, a distance of 75 miles'.

As with Flitwick, the goods lines were upgraded and an additional platform brought into use to accommodate the intensified local service inaugurated in 1960.

In LMS days, seven to nine trains called at Harlington in each direction.

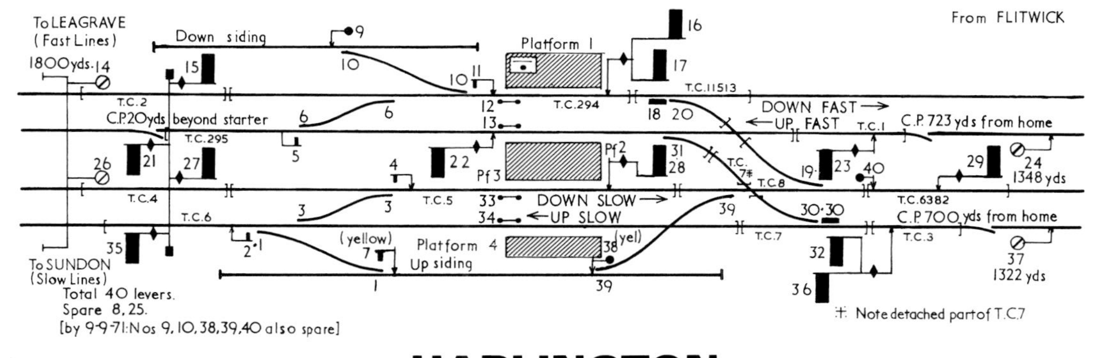

HARLINGTON

Right Harlington was one of the original stations on the MR London Extension Northern Contract, and although plain by Midland standards, was in a mellow red brick with segmented window arches with projecting keystones. In this view, taken from the station forecourt looking towards Bedford, the station offices are in view on the left, and the edge of the twin storey Station Master's house on the extreme right. The building was roughly in the shape of a reversed 'L', the projection of the station house into the forecourt forming the base of the letter. Numerous detail differences existed in the buildings, window arches varying from the rounded arches at the extreme left, through flattened arches in the foreground to flat topped windows in parts of the station house, a mixture of styles which was hardly necessary or elegant. The partially open window should be noted. It is not a feature which is often seen on model railway — perhaps there are no 'OO' fresh-air fiends!!

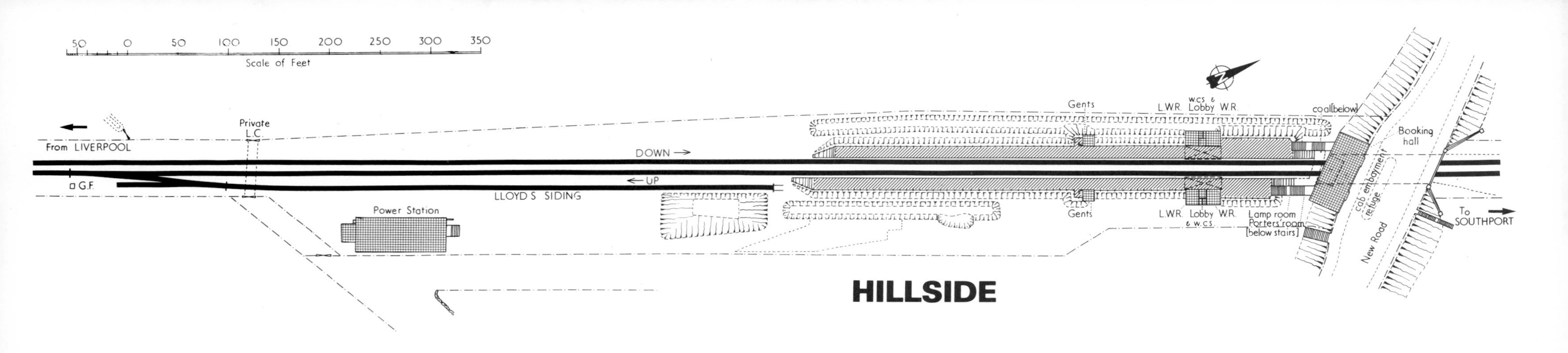

Looking from a Down ex-LMSR electric train towards Southport in April 1977, with the overbridge and main building in the distance, and the Up shelter in the foreground. The prominent ridge tiles were characteristic of LMS buildings of this period, as was the hipped roof. Within a few years, the concrete age had dawned (see Lea Hall and Meols) and LMS stations underwent a dramatic change in design.

HILLSIDE STATION *(Map Ref. A5)*

When the LMSR came into being in 1923, its first civil engineer was E. C. Trench, formerly of the LNWR. He held this position until 1927 when he retired. It was a period of consolidation, rather than of expansion or innovation, and the few stations to be opened or drastically rebuilt were built to proven styles with little ornament. In his final report, for 1926, Trench commenced on the completion of 'a new station at Hillside between Ainsdale and Birkdale'. The station was located by an overbridge over the former L&Y Liverpool–Southport line, and comprised a single storey brick booking office carried above the tracks and modest brick shelters on each platform. The main building had much in common with a partial rebuild of Acton Bridge Station the previous year, when a plain hipped roof brick building fronting onto a road overbridge had replaced a pre-group structure. The heavy cornice at the top of the chimneys was common to both stations and over emphasised the chimney stack.

The station is located on the south side of the main Liverpool–Southport road on the fringe of the built-up area, and within close proximity of three golf courses. It takes its name from the nearby Birkdale Hills, but as these are of the improved molehill variety, the name is somewhat misleading. However, as the surrounding countryside is mostly some 13-24ft. above sea level, they have some prominence.

A private siding, Lloyd's Siding, existed at the south end of the station on the Up side. The scale plan, which dates from the construction of the station shows this to be worked by a ground frame, but a temporary block post is recorded as existing here in 1937. Train service details are as recorded for other stations on the Liverpool–Southport section.

INVERGORDON

50 0 50 100 150 200 250 300
Scale of Feet

From INVERNESS
tank
SC
W.B.
Loco
G.S.
office
cattle pens
loading bank
3 ton crane
H.M. meat store
slaughter house
H.M. bonded store
saw mill yard
To HARBOUR
S.B.
Agent's house
Station approach
W.R.
SC
school

INVERGORDON *(Map Ref. Q19)*

Although Invergordon acted as temporary terminus of the Highland farther north line from 25th March 1863 until 1st June 1864, it is its subsequent history to which the greatest interest attaches.

Prior to 1914, Invergordon was a small village on the northern banks of Cromarty Firth. The firth was used by the Royal Navy to a limited extent, but it was with the establishment of Scapa Flow as the war base of the Grand Fleet, that Invergordon became of crucial importance. By the end of October 1914 the exertions of the naval harbour master had rendered the firth reasonably secure against submarine attack, and a large Admiralty floating dock was moved up from Portsmouth. So makeshift were the arrangements that dockyard workers were accommodated in a captured German merchantman! Railway traffic in conjunction with all this activity was immense and sustained, the pressure beginning with material trains in conjunction with anti-submarine defences. By 1916 much of Invergordon Station yard was in service use, and the pressure continued after the battle of Jutland with numerous refits to cope with. A second and later a third floating dock arrived, a new pier (with its own railway) was constructed, and a vast oil depot created. As well as a practice base, repair base and fuel store, Invergordon was used for leave purposes, with ships being sent down from Scapa Flow. The resultant leave specials added a further dimension to the chronic difficulties being experienced on the Highland in general, and at Invergordon in particular. A vast quantity of traffic was worked over the harbour branch which commenced in the goods yard. By 1916, military facilities in the yard included a bonded store, meat store and a proposed Admiralty salvage shed. A 40ft. engine shed was located adjacent to the goods shed, and this housed HR 2-4-0T No. 118 *Invergordon* during the war period.

Between August 1914 and August 1919 over 1,000 special trains were dealt with, and this included military as well as naval traffic, as large military camps were also established in the area. So vital was the area to the national defence that the whole of Scotland north of the Caledonian Canal was made a restricted area from 1916, and access forbidden without a permit.

The passenger station is situated on a curve, and although it no longer sees the vast crowds of seamen on their way to and from the vessels of the Grand Fleet, it retains its interest, partly on account of its unusual architecture. The Up shelter illustrated is quite unlike any of the other HR stations covered in this selection, and possesses some exceptionally fine spandrels supporting the canopy. Note also the black and white edging to the platform and the inevitable lorry drawn up awaiting traffic.

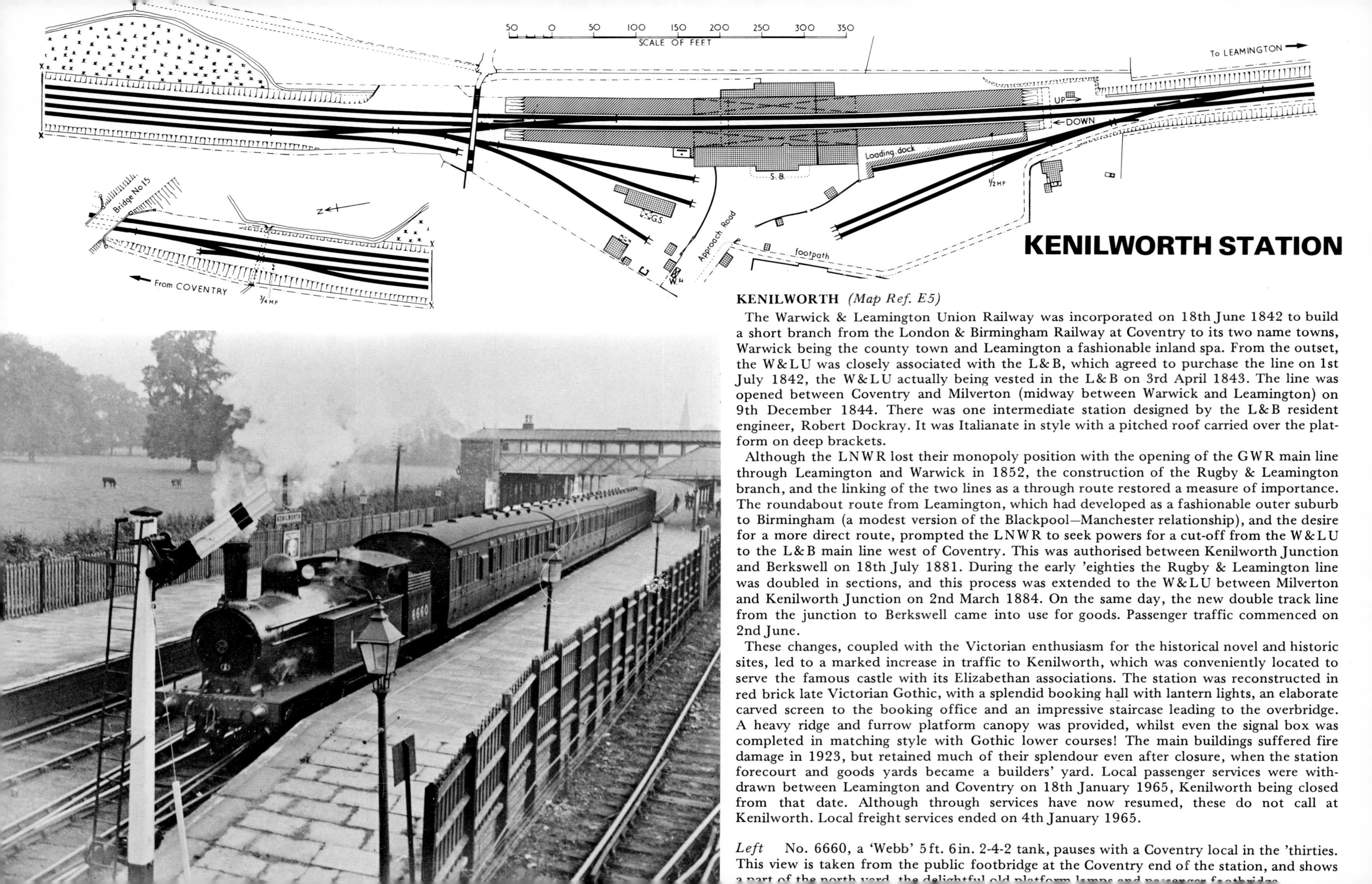

KENILWORTH STATION

KENILWORTH *(Map Ref. E5)*

The Warwick & Leamington Union Railway was incorporated on 18th June 1842 to build a short branch from the London & Birmingham Railway at Coventry to its two name towns, Warwick being the county town and Leamington a fashionable inland spa. From the outset, the W&LU was closely associated with the L&B, which agreed to purchase the line on 1st July 1842, the W&LU actually being vested in the L&B on 3rd April 1843. The line was opened between Coventry and Milverton (midway between Warwick and Leamington) on 9th December 1844. There was one intermediate station designed by the L&B resident engineer, Robert Dockray. It was Italianate in style with a pitched roof carried over the platform on deep brackets.

Although the LNWR lost their monopoly position with the opening of the GWR main line through Leamington and Warwick in 1852, the construction of the Rugby & Leamington branch, and the linking of the two lines as a through route restored a measure of importance. The roundabout route from Leamington, which had developed as a fashionable outer suburb to Birmingham (a modest version of the Blackpool–Manchester relationship), and the desire for a more direct route, prompted the LNWR to seek powers for a cut-off from the W&LU to the L&B main line west of Coventry. This was authorised between Kenilworth Junction and Berkswell on 18th July 1881. During the early 'eighties the Rugby & Leamington line was doubled in sections, and this process was extended to the W&LU between Milverton and Kenilworth Junction on 2nd March 1884. On the same day, the new double track line from the junction to Berkswell came into use for goods. Passenger traffic commenced on 2nd June.

These changes, coupled with the Victorian enthusiasm for the historical novel and historic sites, led to a marked increase in traffic to Kenilworth, which was conveniently located to serve the famous castle with its Elizabethan associations. The station was reconstructed in red brick late Victorian Gothic, with a splendid booking hall with lantern lights, an elaborate carved screen to the booking office and an impressive staircase leading to the overbridge. A heavy ridge and furrow platform canopy was provided, whilst even the signal box was completed in matching style with Gothic lower courses! The main buildings suffered fire damage in 1923, but retained much of their splendour even after closure, when the station forecourt and goods yards became a builders' yard. Local passenger services were withdrawn between Leamington and Coventry on 18th January 1965, Kenilworth being closed from that date. Although through services have now resumed, these do not call at Kenilworth. Local freight services ended on 4th January 1965.

Left No. 6660, a 'Webb' 5 ft. 6 in. 2-4-2 tank, pauses with a Coventry local in the 'thirties. This view is taken from the public footbridge at the Coventry end of the station, and shows a part of the north yard, the delightful old platform lamps and passenger footbridge.

Left A 'Johnson' goods, No. 3347, runs through Kenilworth on a pick-up goods in August 1936. In this view, looking from the Down platform towards Warwick, long shadows, from the low evening sun, pattern an otherwise bare platform.

Above Many Victorian architects were passionate admirers of Gothic design for churches. Here we see the Gothic ideal as applied to a signal box. Perhaps this is what a medieval LNWR might have looked like!

Left The main buildings looking from the approach road towards Leamington. The splendid lantern resulted in a light and pleasant interior to what would otherwise have been a gloomy building.

KENILWORTH JUNCTION *(Map Ref. E5)*

Kenilworth Junction was located 1,742 yards north of Kenilworth Station at the divergence of the 1844 W&LU route to Coventry and the 1884 cut-off line, which rejoined the L&B main line at Berkswell. Prior to the construction of the new line, the W&LU was single track, but during the building of the Berkswell curve, the W&LU was doubled from Warwick to the junction, the section north of Kenilworth Junction into Coventry remaining single. The double line was opened on 2nd March 1884, the same day as the Berkswell line opened to freight. Passenger services began via the new line on 2nd June 1884. Although the LNWR doubled the northern section of the W&LU from Coventry to a new signal box at Gibbet Hill in 1916, the intervening section, from Gibbet Hill to Kenilworth Junction remained single, largely, it is said, to provide an excuse to refuse the GWR access over LNWR metals into the city! Coventry passenger services ceased in 1965, and the Berkswell curve was closed altogether on 1st March 1969, and subsequently lifted. The Leamington–Coventry line is now worked as a single track branch, with an intermediate remotely controlled passing loop at Kenilworth Station, while Kenilworth Station, Kenilworth Junction and Gibbet Hill boxes have all gone. In former days, the Kenilworth Junction–Gibbet Hill section was controlled by full-sized Webb-Thompson electric train staff apparatus. The signal box diagram is prepared from the original signal box plan, retaining the proportions of the latter. In a number of cases, e.g. points 19, the proportions are rather misleading, whilst signal 16 appeared in the dotted position, rather than its correct location!

KENILWORTH JUNCTION

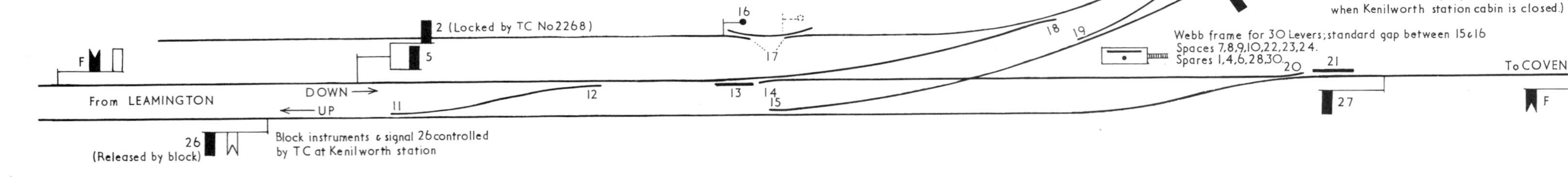

Right Looking from the 'V' of the junction towards Warwick, with the Coventry line on the left and the Berkswell curve on the right. The line dropping away to the right of the Kenilworth embankment is the tannery and coal sidings spur. See how the linoleum on the signal box floor glistens.

Below Kenilworth Junction box looking towards Leamington in February 1966. Note the unused spaces, as well as spares, in the lever frame.

KESWICK

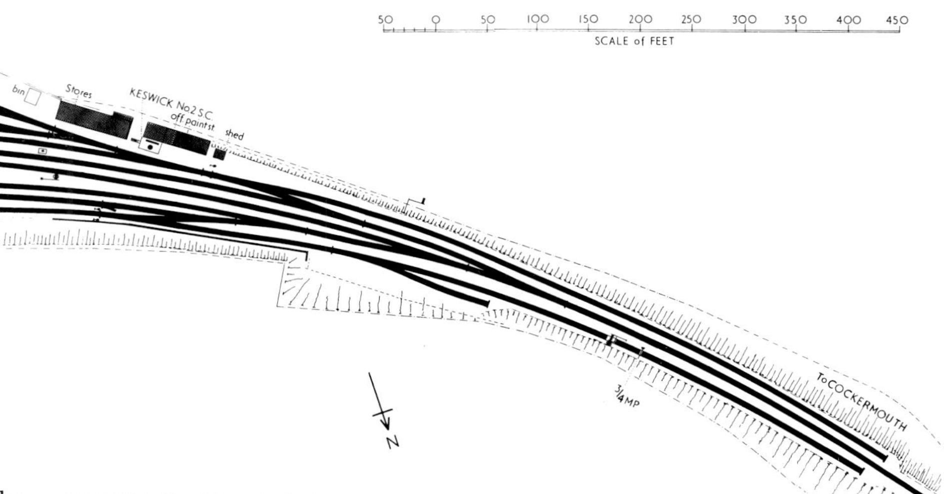

Keswick Station, in its last days, looking towards Penrith. Note the LMS hybrid box on the Down platform. The facilities, befitting the headquarters of an independent company, the CKPR, were generous.

KESWICK *(Map Ref. S12)*

Keswick was the principal intermediate station on the 31½ mile Cockermouth, Keswick and Penrith Railway. The CKPR was authorised, on 1st August 1861, to build a line from Penrith, on the LNWR West Coast main line, to Cockermouth Junction, where it again met the LNWR for the remaining way into Workington. At Penrith, the CKP also made a connection with the Stockton & Darlington (later NER), and although retaining its independence down to 1923, the CKP was worked by the LNWR and NE companies. The branch opened on 2nd January 1865 and became popular with tourists, as it passed within convenient distance of Bassenthwaite Lake, Derwent Water, Thirlmere and Ullswater. Keswick was the only intermediate place of any size, and was especially well frequented due to its proximity to Derwent Water. In 1873, plans were prepared for an 'underpassage' (i.e. a subway) to connect the platforms, rather than the more common footbridge. This was located at the west end of the station buildings, and remained in existence until closure. The main buildings were on the Down or westbound platform, and, in independent days, housed the CKP offices.

Part of the line was doubled in the 1890s, but most of the CKP stayed single, and was worked by electric train tablet. In Keswick Station, there were three passenger lines, the Up and Down platforms and No. 1 loop together with a through road, the Jubilee siding, for goods traffic. Absolute block working was in force on the passenger lines, and no block on the goods road. Under the LMS, the western box, Keswick A, became No. 2 and Keswick B, which was replaced by an LMS 'hybrid' cabin with a Derby frame, Keswick No. 1.

In the LNWR working timetable for 1922, the CKP is recorded as a foreign line. Six ordinary passenger trains ran in each direction, augmented by a return workmen's train from Keswick to Threlkeld. One Maryport & Carlisle passenger train ventured down from Brigham in the morning, returning after an hour in Keswick! Freight services included several local goods commencing or terminating at Keswick, together with through NER mineral trains. Passenger services west of Keswick ceased on 18th April 1966, and after a few years of basic railway the last train (a chartered 8 car DMU) ran on 4th March 1972.

KESWICK

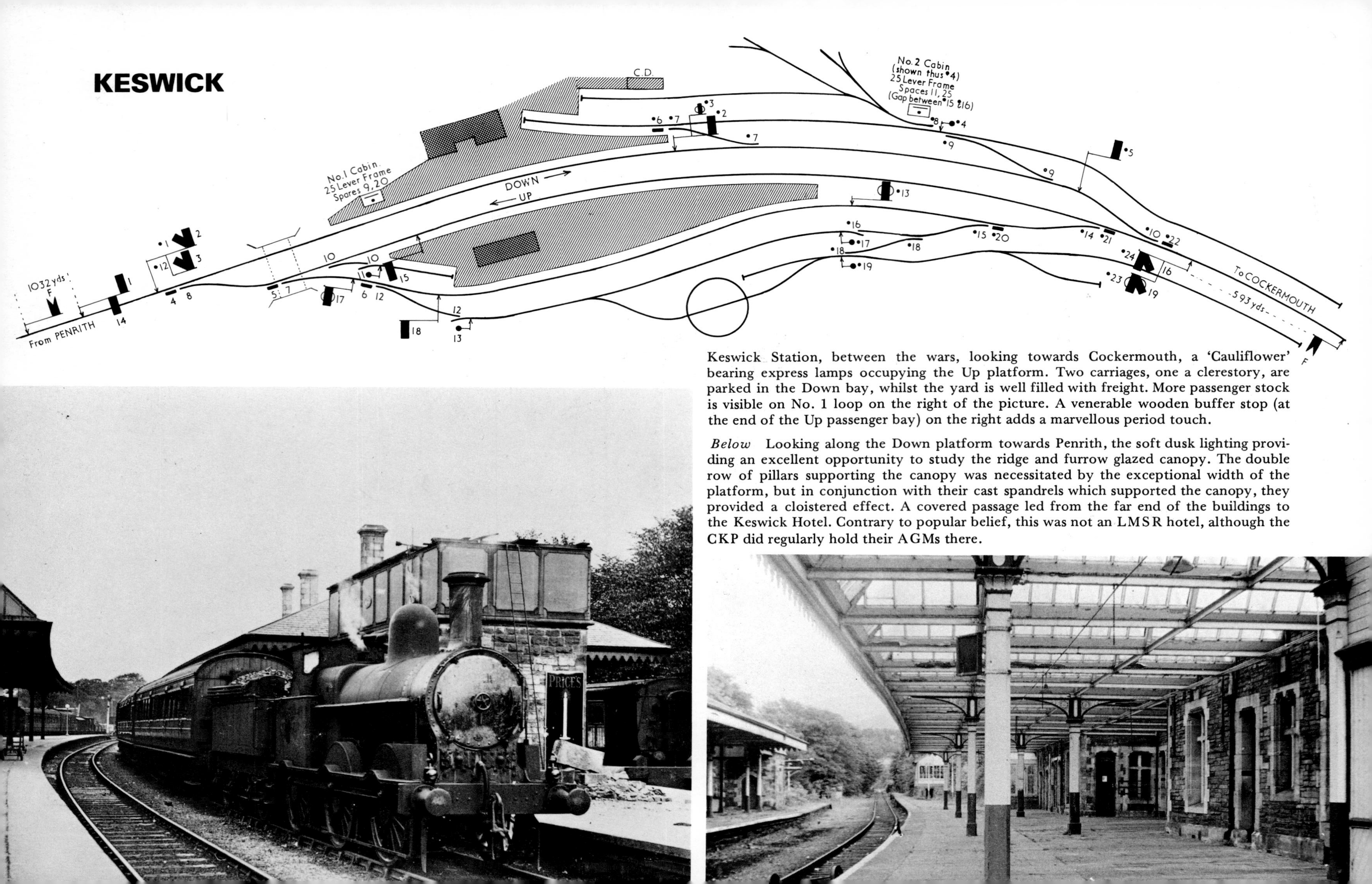

Keswick Station, between the wars, looking towards Cockermouth, a 'Cauliflower' bearing express lamps occupying the Up platform. Two carriages, one a clerestory, are parked in the Down bay, whilst the yard is well filled with freight. More passenger stock is visible on No. 1 loop on the right of the picture. A venerable wooden buffer stop (at the end of the Up passenger bay) on the right adds a marvellous period touch.

Below Looking along the Down platform towards Penrith, the soft dusk lighting providing an excellent opportunity to study the ridge and furrow glazed canopy. The double row of pillars supporting the canopy was necessitated by the exceptional width of the platform, but in conjunction with their cast spandrels which supported the canopy, they provided a cloistered effect. A covered passage led from the far end of the buildings to the Keswick Hotel. Contrary to popular belief, this was not an LMSR hotel, although the CKP did regularly hold their AGMs there.

KETTERING

Plan dated 25 SEP 1896

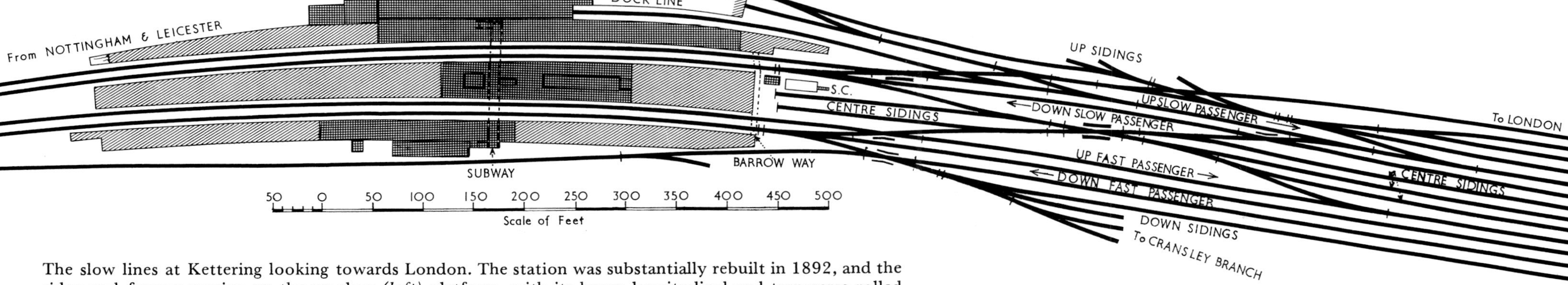

The slow lines at Kettering looking towards London. The station was substantially rebuilt in 1892, and the ridge and furrow awning on the up slow *(left)* platform, with its heavy longitudinal and transverse rolled steel joists in clear view, is quite different from the other platforms.

KETTERING *(Map Ref. K6)*

The network of routes serving Kettering is an impressive example of the relentless drive which went into the creation of the Midland empire. In 1855, Kettering was not even on the railway map; in 1880, lines radiated from the town in five directions. The build-up began in 1857 with the opening of the MR Leicester–Bedford–Hitchin line through the town. The sharply graded Huntingdon branch followed in 1866 and the mineral-only Cransley branch in 1877. In 1880, the Manton–Nottingham line opened, putting Kettering in direct communication with Nottingham and Melton Mowbray. The actual junction with the main line was at Glendon, only a short distance to the north of the town, and both Leicester and Nottingham expresses called at Kettering.

With all this activity at Kettering and elsewhere, quadrupling of the main line became a necessity, and this work was pressed forward from the late 1870s. The MR engineer's report for 1882 noted that work was well advanced on the Kettering–Sharnbrook section, and by 1895 continuous quadruple track existed from London to Glendon Junction, where the two double track main lines diverged, giving (in effect) a continuation of the four roads to the north.

Over most of the quadruple section, the new lines were to the east of the original tracks, but between Kettering and Wellingborough, the fast lines were transferred to a new formation on the western side of the old lines, and the old fast roads given over to freight traffic. At both Kettering and Wellingborough stations, the fast lines reverted to their old formation, and the new tracks were to the east.

Although primarily goods lines, the new roads were used for passengers in the vicinity of the larger stations, and Kettering was provided with four main platforms.

In the 1920s about a dozen trains departed from Kettering on the Nottingham line, including certain restaurant car expresses; the Huntingdon branch carried about five trains each way daily, whilst there were about twenty departures in the London direction. By 1942, the Huntingdon service had declined to two workings, and ceased altogether in 1959, to be followed in 1966 by the ending of the direct Nottingham service. Nottingham trains continue to run by way of Leicester, and the station remains an important railhead for the south-east corner of Northamptonshire.

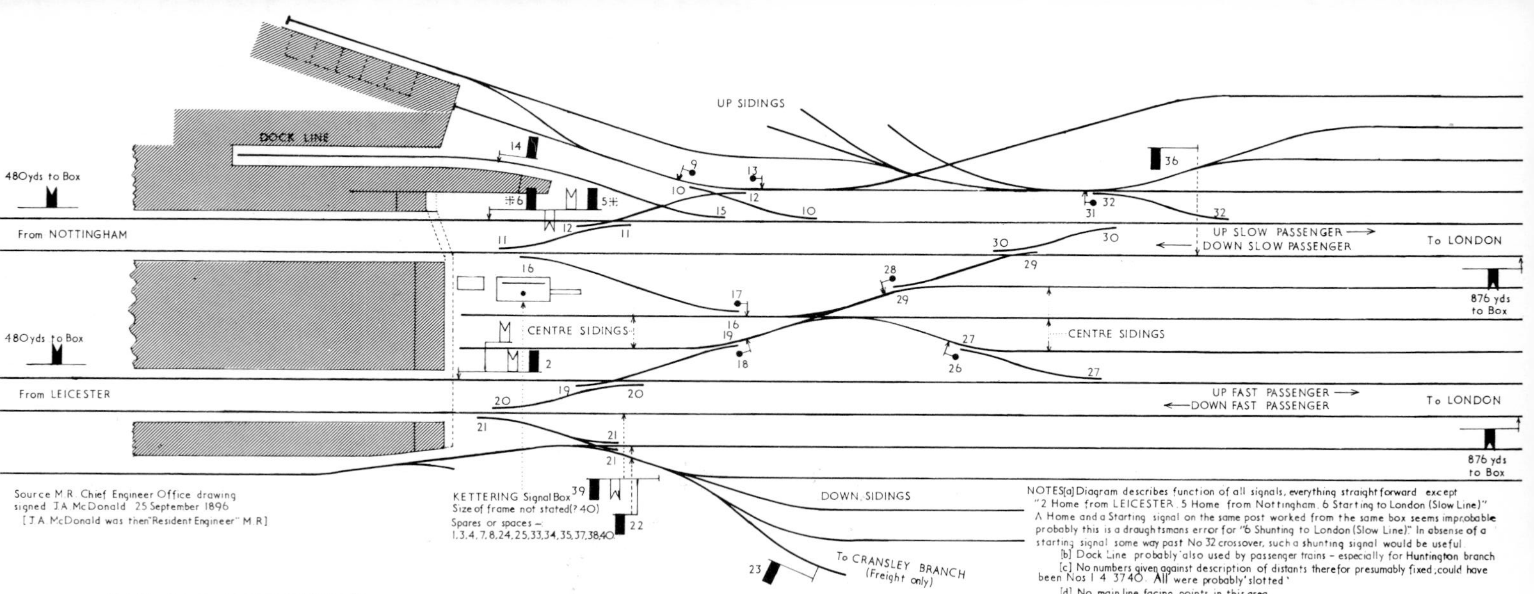

KETTERING

Looking from the Down fast platform towards London.

Although the main features of the track layout have altered remarkably little since the date of the scale and signalling plans, there have been a number of changes. Most notable being the replacement of the old signal box which was on a cramped location between the short centre sidings and the Down slow, by a new box in the wider space about the middle of the long series of cross overs and slips from the Down to the Up side of the station. As well as providing more generous space, this was a more logical location for the box, as the signalman's view would be markedly improved, whilst the distance of pull for the points would not be as extreme as would be the case with a box at one end of the track layout. This would, in turn, make for easier maintenance and reduce the effort needed to pull the points. The layout is, in fact, a classic example of the effect of the Board of Trade, and practical limits on the distance at which points could be worked from a box, as the whole of the connections are compressed into a remarkably compact area. For ease in shunting the various yard points are, of course, hand-worked, and not controlled by the signalman. Connections from the yards to the running lines are worked from the box, and the signalling of such connections has always presented problems. At Kettering, all moves from the yards on to the running lines were controlled from shunt signals in the 1896 diagram, but no shunt signals were provided for moves between the running lines, or from the running lines to the various sidings. (Signals 17, 18, 26 and 28, although controlling a move between running lines, are primarily to regulate movements out of the centre sidings.

KETTERING

Above left The Down fast platform and awning looking towards Leicester. The partially hidden plain timbering of the subway and platform buildings make a contrast to the ridge and furrow awning on the platform, with its delicate leaf pattern motif. Although the filigree work at the end is visible, the gable ends are filled in with plain vertical boarding. Fortunately the ornate gable castings on the opposite platform are seen in all their glory.

Above right Looking towards Leicester from the centre platform, with the fast lines on the left and the slow lines on the right. The original formation is on the left, and the piecemeal ancestry of the station is apparent in the different length of span between the end columns of the island canopy, the spandrels on the left being to the full length, those on the right being shortened and bolted together. The rebuilding must have been somewhat like playing with a giant 'meccano' set.

Left Despite the unequal spans, the awning on the centre platform represents Victorian use of steel and glass at its finest. Just look at the gable ends with their delicate castings when compared to the top heavy boarding applied to the Down fast platform. One difference caused by the rebuilding not immediately apparent, is that the Down fast platform retains arched spandrels throughout its length, whilst the island platform is supported by transverse lattice girders joining the columns, except at the ends, where the decorative arches appear.

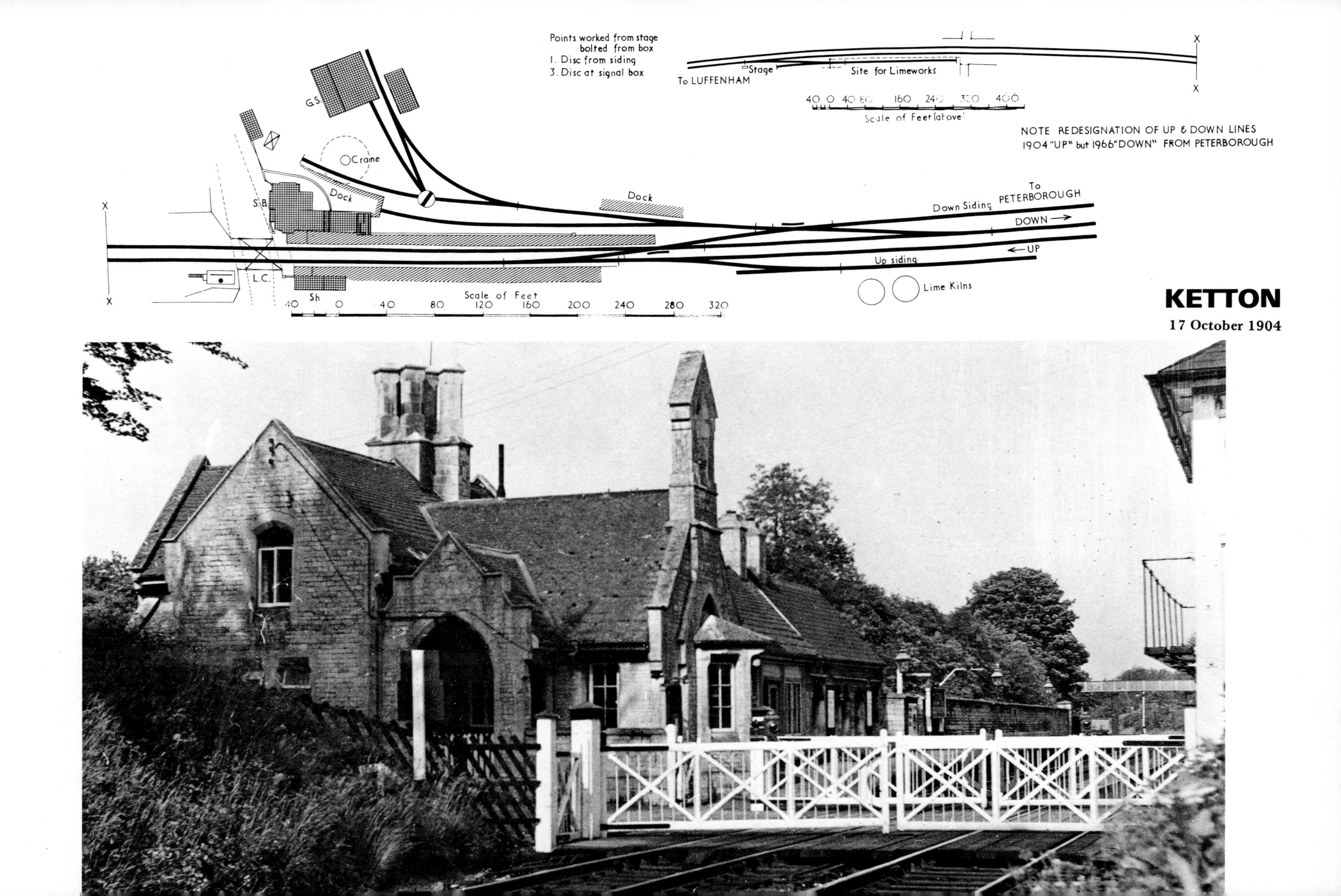
Points worked from stage
bolted from box
1. Disc from siding
3. Disc at signal box
To LUFFENHAM
Stage
Site for Limeworks
40 0 40 80 160 240 320 400
Scale of Feet (above)
NOTE REDESIGNATION OF UP & DOWN LINES
1904 "UP" but 1966 "DOWN" FROM PETERBOROUGH
G.S.
Craine
Dock
S.B.
Dock
To PETERBOROUGH
Down Siding
DOWN
UP
Up siding
Lime Kilns
L.C.
Sh
Scale of Feet
40 0 40 80 120 160 200 240 280 320

KETTON

17 October 1904

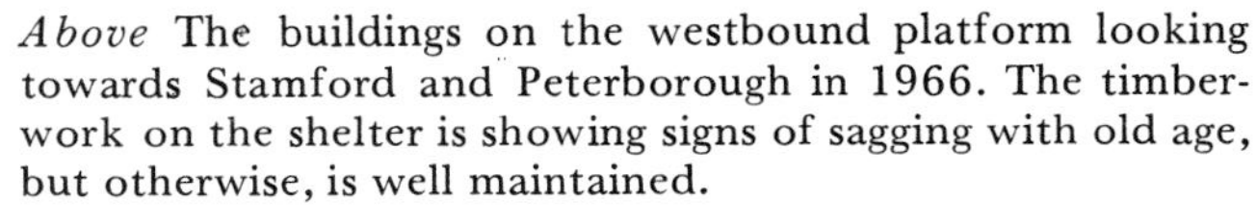

Above The buildings on the westbound platform looking towards Stamford and Peterborough in 1966. The timber-work on the shelter is showing signs of sagging with old age, but otherwise, is well maintained.

Opposite page The early railway builders adopted a variety of styles from Classical, through Florentine to Tudor and Gothic. The main buildings at Ketton looking towards Peterborough were Victorian ecclesiastical Tudor.

Above The signal cabin and crossing looking towards Peterborough. The signal box is of the type built by the Midland from the 1890s, with deep front windows and shallow end windows. In the early 1900s deep windows all-round were adopted.

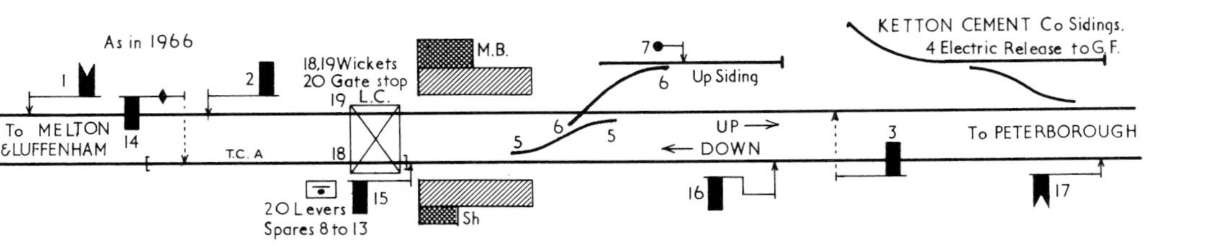

KETTON *(Map Ref. K8)*

Ketton Station was on the Syston & Peterborough branch of the Midland Railway, between Melton Mowbray and Stamford. Owing to a dispute with Lord Harborough over the course of the line near Saxby, this section was not opened until 1st May 1848, almost two years after the eastern and western extremities came into use.

Ketton Station, renamed Ketton & Collyweston from July 1935, was situated by a level crossing over a minor road connecting its two name villages. The main buildings on the west-bound platform were of local stone with a roof of Collyweston tiles. These were not unlike the better known Cotswold roofing stone. It was a refreshing case of a national company using local materials and traditions in construction work to good effect, and is an example which could be followed more often today. The designs used on the Syston & Peterborough were very varied and of extremely high quality, by and large. Architectural responsibility is commonly divided between William Parsons and Sancton Wood, with a belief that the latter may well have tacked Ketton. The building was essentially Tudor with a delightful little belfry thrown in for good measure. The shelter on the other side was a composite building in stone and timber, but despite the mixture of styles blended effectively.

From 1851 until 1966, the portion of the Syston line between Luffenham (q.v.) and Stamford (q.v.) carried LNWR services to and from Seaton, as well as Midland trains. In 1905, six or seven MR trains called at Ketton, whilst the LNWR provided five workings between Seaton and Stamford. In 1944, the LMS operated five services over the main route, with a further five on the Seaton line. Not all of the latter trains called at Ketton however.

When comparing the scale plan of 1904 and the signalling plan of 1966, it will be seen that Up and Down designations have been reversed. This is covered more fully under Luffenham. A small goods yard was located on the north side of the line. Access to one siding was via a wagon turntable or a very sharp connecting curve, a most unusual arrangement.

The station closed to goods traffic in 1965, and to passengers on 6th June 1966.

KINETON

Engineer's Plan of 24/9/84

Station
(deleted on 1884 plan)
[Cabin]
DOWN →
G.S.
To TOWCESTER
← UP
Shelter
Cabin
20 0 20 40 60 80 100 140 180 240
Scale of Feet
From STRATFORD

KINETON *(Map Ref. F4)*

From June 1871 until July 1873, Kineton acted as the western terminus and headquarters of the East & West Junction Railway. For the first two years, the Fenny Compton–Kineton section was worked under the one engine in steam system, using a round red train staff. As Kineton was the E&WJ headquarters, the rules stated that, in the event of an engine breakdown, the fireman was to take the staff to Kineton and accompany any assisting engine back to where he left his own locomotive. A footnote provided that the staff was to be 'fixed in a socket on the engine or tender, or carried over the shoulder by means of a cross-belt'.

When the extensions to Towcester and Stratford opened, Kineton lost much of its importance, and Stratford became the headquarters of the enlarged system. Absolute block working was introduced after a short while, and electric train staff working was adopted from 1894 onwards.

As Kineton was larger than the average SMJ village, the station was larger than the standard pattern. The main yard was on the south side of the line, and was reached off a long head shunt which formed a continuation of the Down loop. The loop was later extended and this process was repeated during the Western Region modernisation of the signalling in 1959. The scale plan shows the layout in 1884, the 'B' signalling plan as at July 1959.

The ordinary weekday passenger service in 1942 consisted of two through trains in each direction. These were augmented on Saturdays by two short-workings from Stratford, one of which returned to Stratford as a passenger train, the other as empty coaching stock in the evening. The line closed to passenger traffic in 1952, and to through freight services in 1965.

The main buildings on the Down platform looking towards Stratford, a few weeks after nationalisation, and when notice boards, still headed LMS, carried a poster about the Transport Act 1947. The building with its twin pavilions, although modest, was substantially larger and more ornate than the wayside E&WJ stations, and boasted quoined

Above Kineton Station looking towards Stratford in 1967, after the sidings had been lifted (although the points remain in situ). This view shows the station with the platforms scarified, but the loop extended under the Western Region re-signalling plan for long through freight workings. The remains of the leads from the cattle siding and goods shed road trail into the Down loop, whilst the auxiliary token hut, starter and loop points are almost on the skyline, right of centre. As befitted a place of greater importance than the average E & WJ station, the goods shed is an enlarged version of the common design.

Below No. 43822, a former Midland '3F', with a raised power class numeral still on the cab sidesheet, has the right of way to Stratford in 1951, when the loop was in its intermediate form, longer than in 1884, but much shorter than after the 1959 alterations. Comparing this view with the scale plan, it will be seen that the Down loop to main cross over has been moved out beyond the cattle dock siding, but is short of the goods shed siding, which is reached off a long head shunt. The ground signal by the Down loop starter, controls access into the yard head shunt, whilst a similar signal controls moves ex the head shunt. Further ground signals regulate movements ex the Up siding and over the trailing cross over. Judging by the number of wagons in the yard, Kineton still made good use of its railway at the start of the 'fifties.

KINETON

Diagram dated JULY 1959

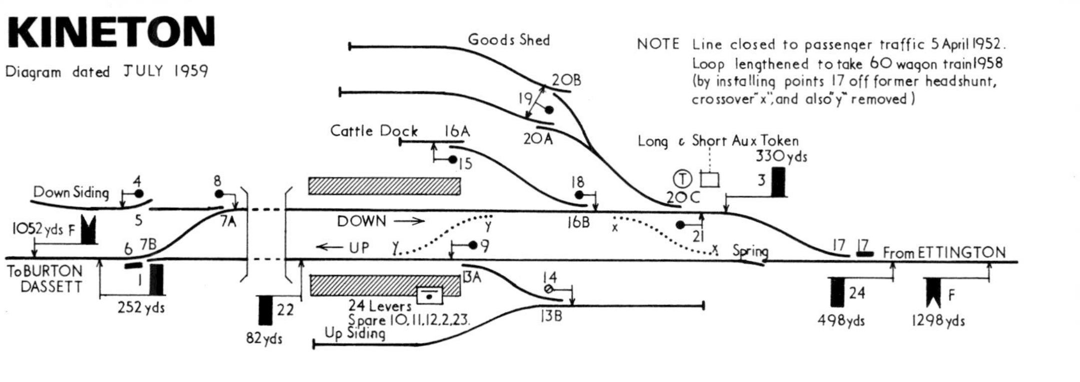

Below Kineton Station after closure to all traffic, forlorn and awaiting its fate, a sorry contrast to the bustling scene left, but one which has been repeated all too often. In the distance, the line curves round towards Burton Dassett, where the long abandoned Edge Hill Light Railway made connection with the SMJ, and eventually on to Towcester. Architecturally the building was strange with hipped roofs facing towards the track and stepped gables facing the approach drive. The low block at this end was the Ladies and Gents, plus store facilities. Note the diamond-shaped SMJ bridge warning notices each side of the bridge.

LAIRG

50 0 50 100 150 200 250 300 350
Scale of Feet

South S.C. tablet catcher store W.R. W.T. tablet catcher 67MP To WICK →
← From INVERGORDON p.w. huts w.col'n refreshments lamp r. Station offices Agents house left luggage toilets lamp r. coal G.S. North S.C. Workmen's houses
pump house tanks cattle pens loading bank tanks Anglo American oil store Scottish Oils & Shell Mex oil store auction mart

LAIRG *(Map Ref. Q20)*

When the Inverness—Wick line was being laboriously created, the object was not to find the shortest possible route, but to open up the countryside, and in this context Lairg was important, not so much on account of the population (1,000), but as a road junction. Five roads led away from the town into the wilds of North West Sutherland, and the station thus served an immense hinterland.

Lairg was on the Sutherland Railway, and opened to passengers in 1868. Its original purpose as a railhead for the north west was fulfilled, and despite the vast changes in transport patterns over the past 100 years, that significance still exists. In the right distance of ur illustration is a small red and cream bus, belonging to the Sutherland Transport & Trading Co. In the centenary year of the railway, four such buses would appear daily in Lairg from Balchrick, Tongue, Durness and Lochinver (none of them less than a two hour journey away). After the departure of the Up and Down midday trains, they would depart for the north west.

The station facilities included four goods sidings with provision for traffic to the Anglo-American Oil and Scottish Oils/Shell Mex depots. A locomotive turntable was reached off the head shunt. Limestone traffic was formerly brought by barge from quarries on Loch Shin to the village, and then carted to the station where it was burnt in a kiln on the station loading bank. In addition to the general yard facilities, a very short siding holding about five wagons came off the main line just outside the station, a few yards beyond the north signal box.

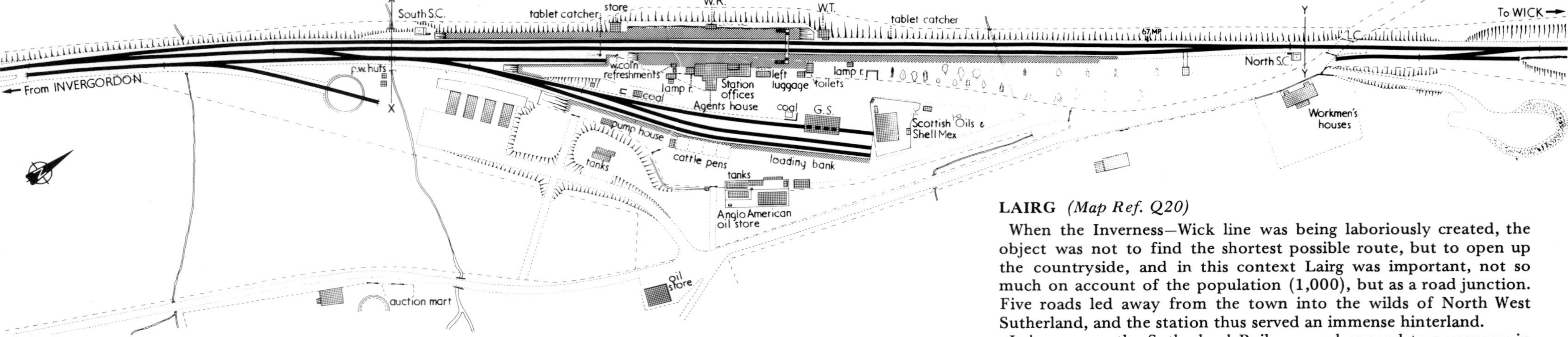

Left The main building at Lairg looking from the footbridge towards Invergordon and the south. The Agent's house is at right angles to the station building. Together the whole building is most peculiar, for it is in three clear sections. The nearest portion with a low roof level possesses a dormer window, which is neither ground nor first floor. The next section with a higher roof level possesses two normal dormer windows providing light to the living quarters, whilst the building concludes with a final low portion. Even in pre-war days, the station handled a good deal of petrol traffic, and this still remained the case in the 'sixties, as can be seen opposite. The bus commented upon above, is a Bedford J4LZI 16-seater, and when leaving would drive along between the station house and petrol depot to reach the highway.

LEA HALL

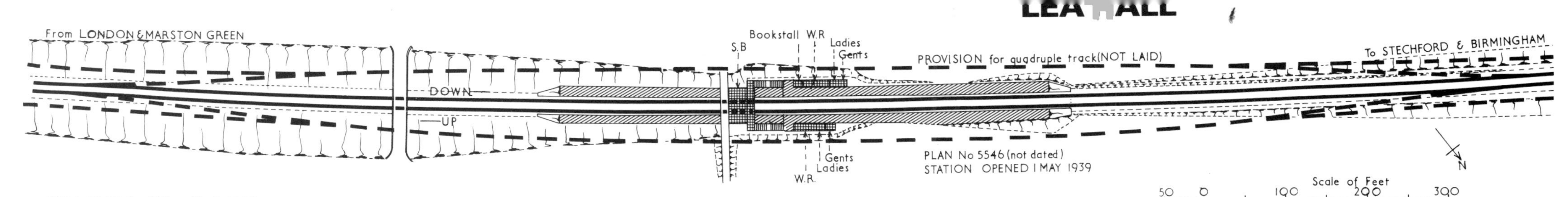

LEA HALL *(Map Ref. D6)*

By the time the LMS had been formed, railways had ceased to enjoy an effective monopoly on inland transport, due to the advent of the motor bus, the car and the lorry. Unsettled conditions immediately after World War I, the grouping and assimilation process, road competition, the general strike and the Wall Street crash all retarded the development of new lines and stations during the early years of the LMS. It was not until the 'thirties that a recognisable LMS-style appeared. As had customarily been the case with railways, it followed the contemporary mode in building. In Victorian times, this had embraced Gothic, Italianate, Classical, Cottage Orne and a host of other styles. In the 'thirties, architects were venturing into reinforced concrete. Functional design was a key idea, with the elimination of projecting crevices and pillars where possible. These new stations tended to be located in the suburbs of the larger cities, where new housing development, away from existing stations, offered fresh traffic, or where new projects, such as the Wirral electrification, offered a dramatic increase in business.

Lea Hall Station depicts the later style of LMS station design, and was opened on 1st May 1939 to serve new housing developments on the Eastern outskirts of Birmingham. The station is located in a shallow cutting, with the booking office carried above the tracks. Access to the platform is via reinforced concrete stairways. In 1938, the LMS had built a number of replacement stations in the Wirral in conjunction with electrification (see Meols), and these made use of a reinforced concrete framework with brick filling and metal framed windows. The concrete roof and awnings were supported by cantilever beams from above. By 1939, the LMS had improved this system sufficiently to eliminate the heavy roof beams. Lea Hall was to this improved design. When new, the platform buildings were fully fronted with doors, windows and brick in-filling, but such has been the level of vandalism in recent years, that the fronts have been removed, leaving brick pillars in lieu.

The LMS provided thirteen to fifteen workings each way, the rush hour peaks and limited off-peak service being typical of a commuter station. Quadrupling of this stretch of the L&B was considered by the LMS, as indicated on the plan, and the station was designed accordingly, but the work was never carried out.

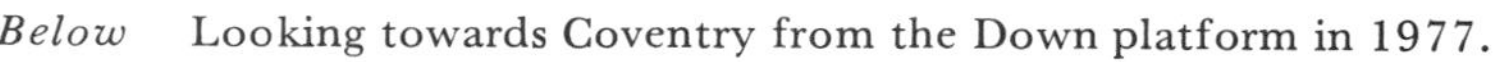
Below Looking towards Coventry from the Down platform in 1977.

Below The Up shelter after rebuilding by BR to anti-vandal form.

LEAMINGTON SPA (AVENUE)

NOTE: Leamington Upper Coal Yard was located *between* Avenue and Milverton Stations.

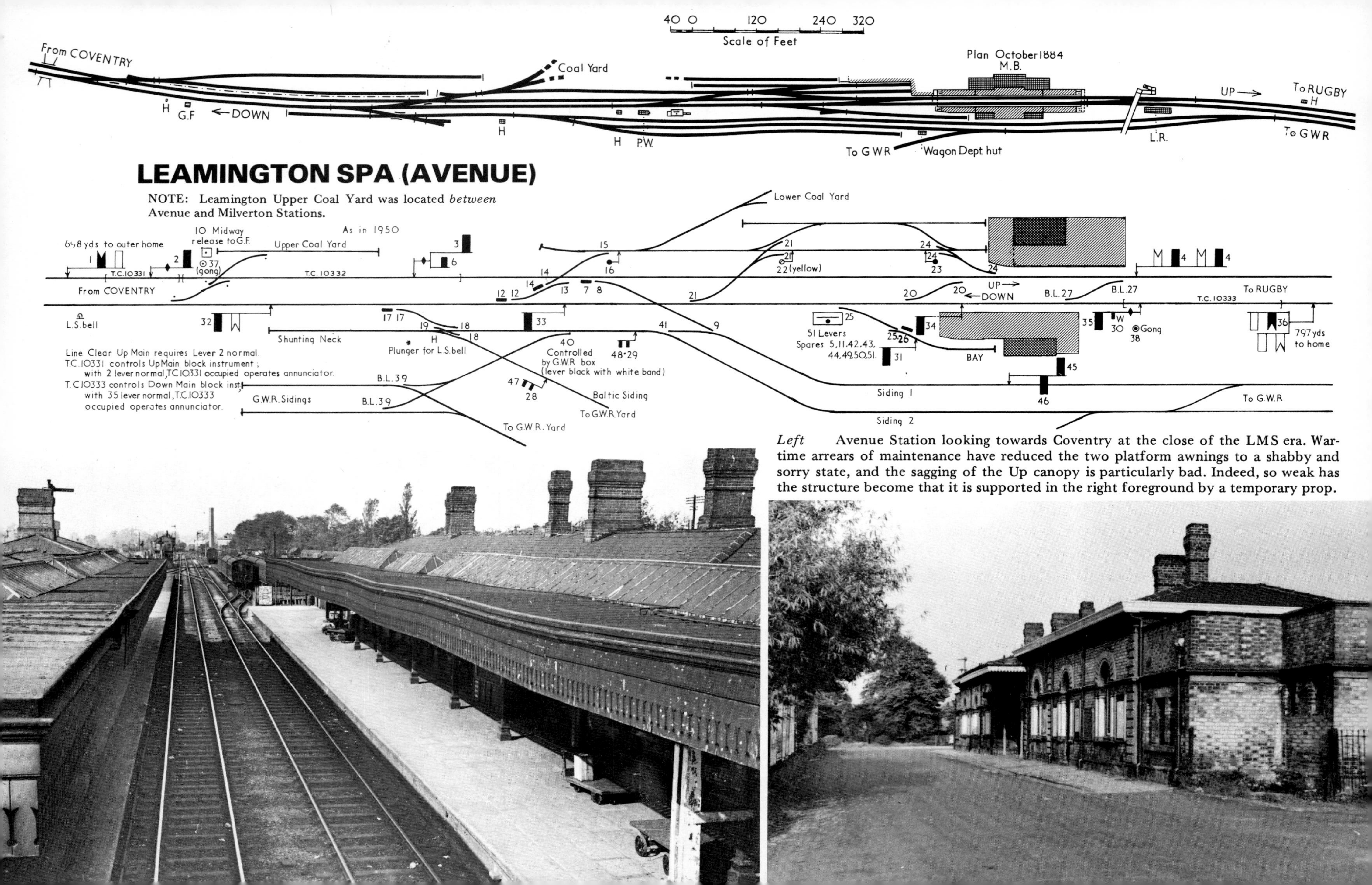

Left Avenue Station looking towards Coventry at the close of the LMS era. War-time arrears of maintenance have reduced the two platform awnings to a shabby and sorry state, and the sagging of the Up canopy is particularly bad. Indeed, so weak has the structure become that it is supported in the right foreground by a temporary prop.

Above No. 6609, a 'Webb' 5 ft. 6 in. 2-4-2 tank, pulls into Leamington Spa Avenue Station from Warwick Milverton at the head of a two coach motor train in the 'thirties. Compared to the scale plan, it will be seen that the Down platform has been extended and the Up and Down cross over moved further out.

Below No. 25393 *Loyalty* heads an excursion through Leamington towards Warwick and Birmingham in the mid 'thirties. It will be seen that the buildings were in much better condition than immediately after the war. A variety of LMS, LNER and GWR poster boards are to be seen on the Down platform.

Above (previous page) The main buildings on the Up platform looking towards Rugby from the station approach. The buildings have now gone, and the road serves as a bus station. Ironically, passengers to Rugby, by bus, board their vehicle only yards from where they formerly entered the station to make the same journey.

LEAMINGTON SPA *(Map Ref. F5)*

The first line to be authorised in the Leamington area was the Warwick & Leamington Union Railway of 1842. This company proposed to build a line from Coventry to Milverton, which was duly opened as a part of the L&B in 1844. The Rugby & Leamington Railway was authorised in 1846, and taken over by the LNWR the same year. This line opened from Milverton to Rugby on 1st March 1851. At first Leamingtonians had to put up with the Milverton station (between Leamington and Warwick), but in February 1854, the LNWR belatedly opened *Leamington Avenue* on a site adjoining the 1852 Great Western Railway station. The station repeatedly changed its name, *Leamington* being the common ingredient, but *Spa, Avenue* or both were added or deleted.

In 1864, a connection was laid in at the western end of the station to the GWR, over which a certain amount of traffic was exchanged. A running connection, at the eastern end, worked by an additional box, *Leamington GW Junction* was installed in July 1908. The curvature of this connection was so tight that trains were restricted to 5 mph.

Considerable changes took place in the layout between 1880 and 1895. They are recorded to remind us that this was a period of great expansion of railway facilities. In 1883, the Rugby line was still single, east of the station, and was worked by staff and ticket. When a new connection was laid in half a mile out of Leamington to serve a canal wharf and malting works, the points were locked by means of a key on the staff. The branch was doubled shortly thereafter, and operations greatly eased. A new bay siding was laid in at the back of the Down platform in 1884, but was not used as a passenger line until 1892, at which time a full sized signal, instead of a shunt signal, was installed. Additional connections were added in 1884 on the Down side, and the Up yard and landing were modified four years later.

As both Avenue and Milverton stations acted as termini for the Coventry–Leamington and Rugby–Leamington–Warwick services respectively (the two lines being customarily treated as separate branches rather than a through route), the station was a hive of activity for much of the day. The opening of the direct Birmingham spur from Kenilworth Junction to Berkswell in 1884, and the Marton Junction–Daventry branch on 1st August 1895, contributed yet further traffic.

In 1927, there were nineteen departures from Avenue for Coventry and three direct workings to Birmingham over the Berkswell line. Ten trains came in from Rugby, the majority being motor services. Two of these terminated at Avenue, the remainder running on to Milverton, although one of the latter was not so advertised! Six trains came from the Weedon line, four from Weedon itself, and two from Napton & Stockton. Of these, four terminated at Milverton, one ran on to Atherstone, and the other expired at the Avenue Station. When one adds freight movements, transfer traffic to and from the GWR and sundry light engines to and from Milverton shed, one gains some idea of how busy Avenue Station once was.

Sadly, the Weedon branch closed in September 1958 and the Rugby line in 1959. Coventry–Leamington services ended on 18th January 1965 and freight traffic (except private siding) in 1969. The Avenue Station has now been demolished, and all that remains are a few sidings and the Coventry–Leamington section which has been re-aligned on to a direct junction with the ex-GWR station. This is traversed by freight traffic, the occasional excursion and certain Paddington–Birmingham services as well, timetabled passenger workings resuming from 2nd May 1977.

Above Looking towards Rugby in 1953, with a modern tubular post starting signal.

Below The same scene in the 'forties with LNWR tall signals and gong post *(right)*.

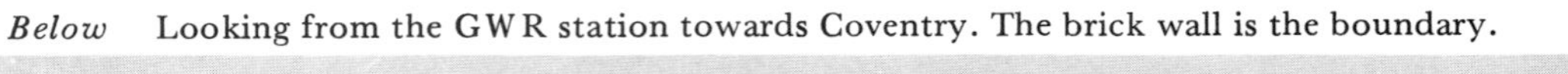

Above 'How are the mighty fallen' – the end of an LNWR signal in 1952.

Below Looking from the GWR station towards Coventry. The brick wall is the boundary.

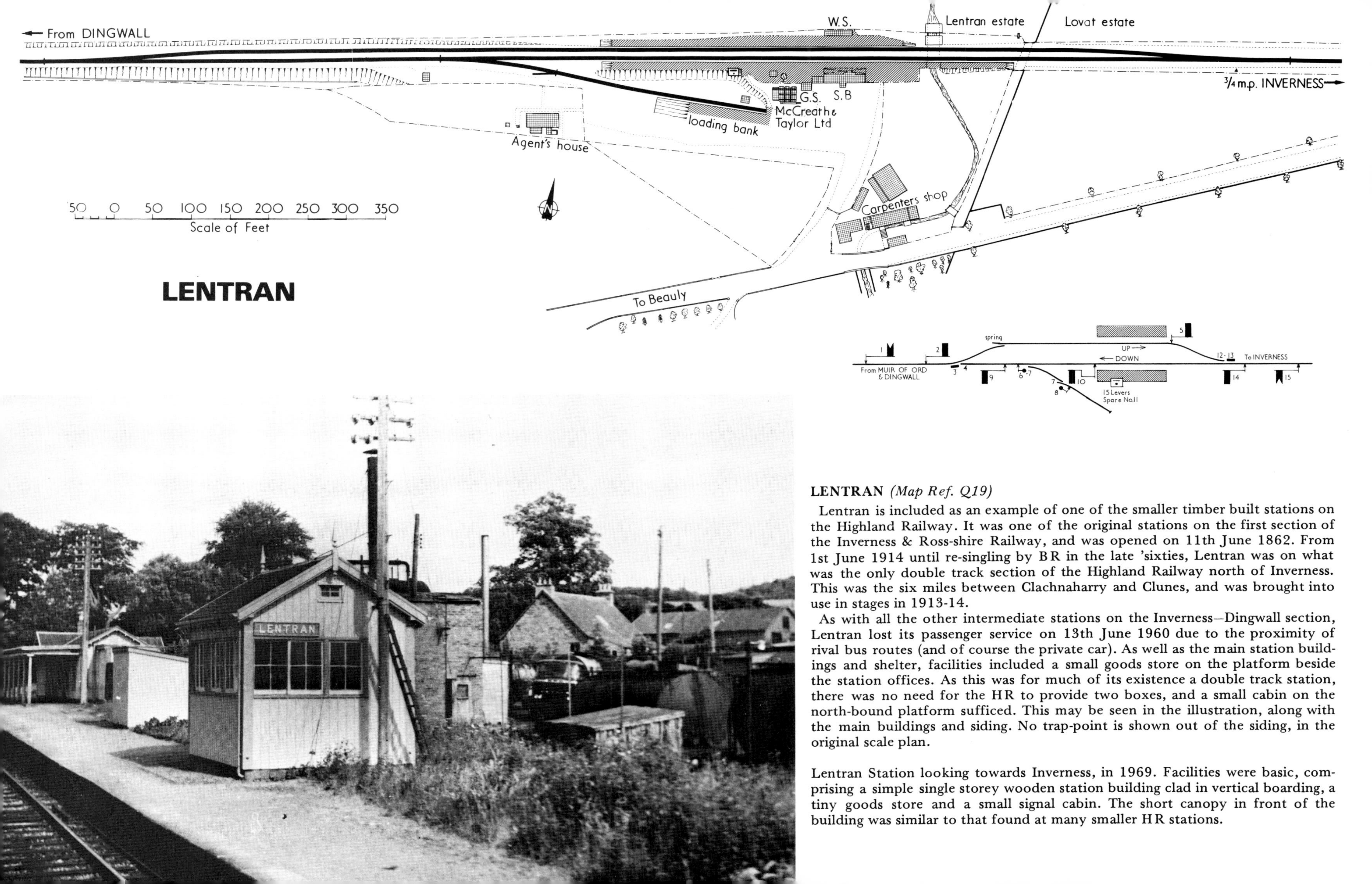

LENTRAN *(Map Ref. Q19)*

Lentran is included as an example of one of the smaller timber built stations on the Highland Railway. It was one of the original stations on the first section of the Inverness & Ross-shire Railway, and was opened on 11th June 1862. From 1st June 1914 until re-singling by BR in the late 'sixties, Lentran was on what was the only double track section of the Highland Railway north of Inverness. This was the six miles between Clachnaharry and Clunes, and was brought into use in stages in 1913-14.

As with all the other intermediate stations on the Inverness–Dingwall section, Lentran lost its passenger service on 13th June 1960 due to the proximity of rival bus routes (and of course the private car). As well as the main station buildings and shelter, facilities included a small goods store on the platform beside the station offices. As this was for much of its existence a double track station, there was no need for the HR to provide two boxes, and a small cabin on the north-bound platform sufficed. This may be seen in the illustration, along with the main buildings and siding. No trap-point is shown out of the siding, in the original scale plan.

Lentran Station looking towards Inverness, in 1969. Facilities were basic, comprising a simple single storey wooden station building clad in vertical boarding, a tiny goods store and a small signal cabin. The short canopy in front of the building was similar to that found at many smaller HR stations.

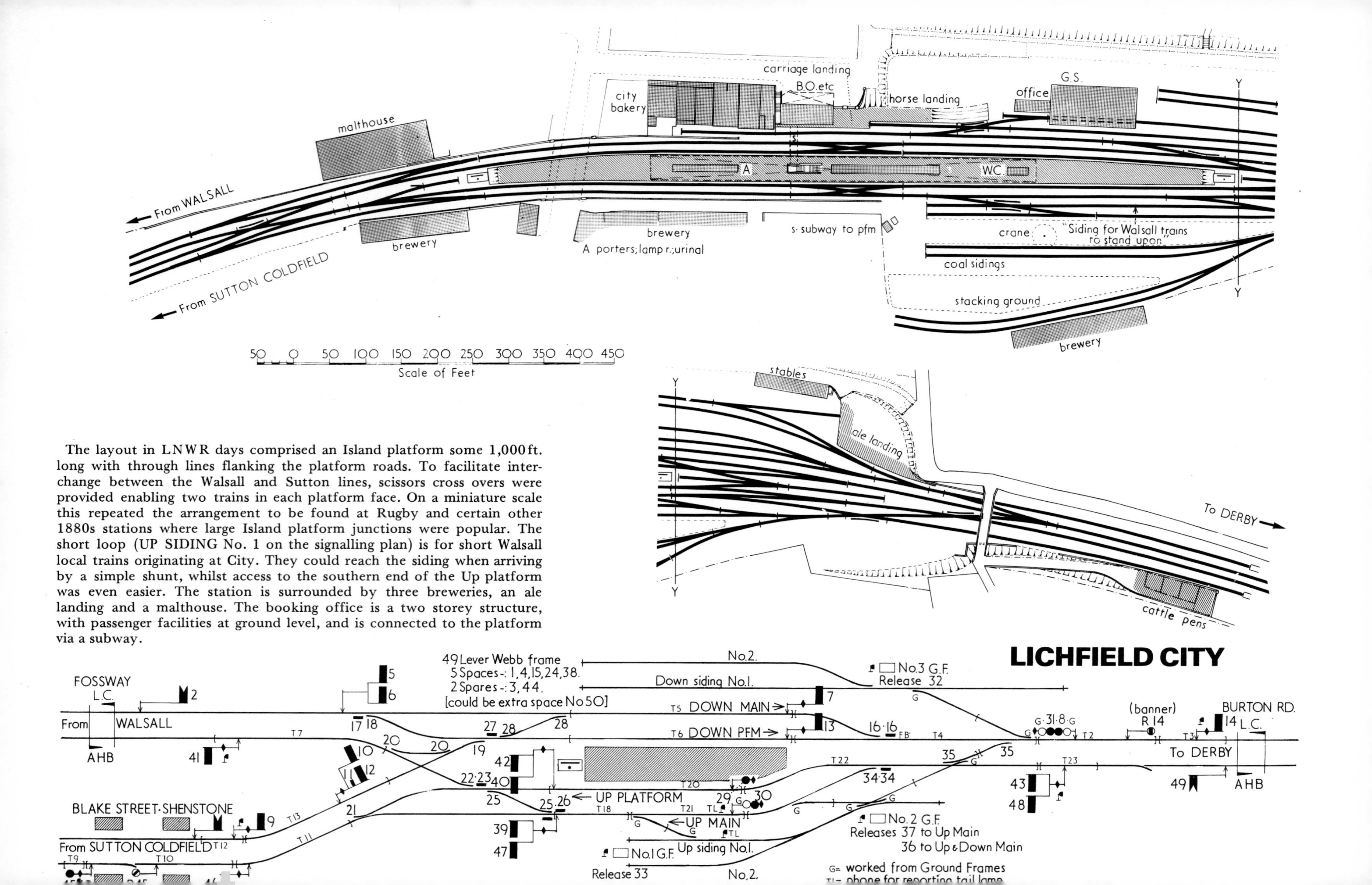

The layout in LNWR days comprised an Island platform some 1,000 ft. long with through lines flanking the platform roads. To facilitate interchange between the Walsall and Sutton lines, scissors cross overs were provided enabling two trains in each platform face. On a miniature scale this repeated the arrangement to be found at Rugby and certain other 1880s stations where large Island platform junctions were popular. The short loop (UP SIDING No. 1 on the signalling plan) is for short Walsall local trains originating at City. They could reach the siding when arriving by a simple shunt, whilst access to the southern end of the Up platform was even easier. The station is surrounded by three breweries, an ale landing and a malthouse. The booking office is a two storey structure, with passenger facilities at ground level, and is connected to the platform via a subway.

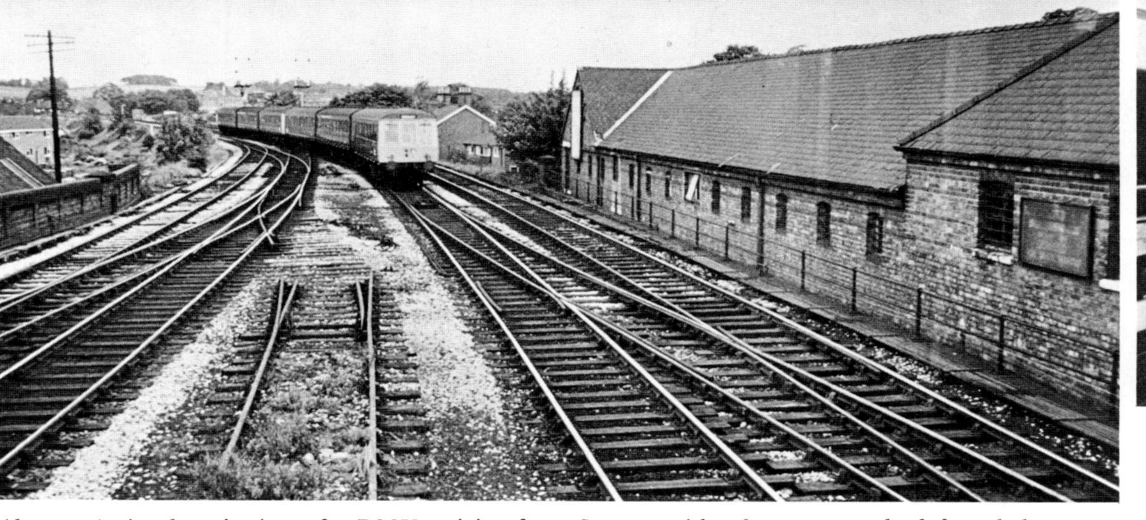

Above A signalman's view of a DMU arriving from Sutton, with a brewery on the left and the malthouse on the right. The only change since LNW days has been the partial dismantling of the short siding.

Above right Looking along the Up platform towards Burton.

Below The booking office looking from the forecourt towards Sutton.

LICHFIELD CITY *(Map Ref. D8)*

Lichfield, although a cathedral city with important historical links, is of modest size, but despite its limited traffic potential, boasts a complex railway history, and various stations over the years. The town was served by two LNWR routes crossing at right angles, and forming a large X. The best known is the Trent Valley route, running approximately north west, and represented by other stations in this selection. A lesser known route, from Walsall to Burton ran in a north-easterly direction. A third line came up from Sutton Coldfield to join the Walsall–Burton line completing the railway map of the town.

The Walsall–Burton line was authorised as the Trent Valley, Midland and Grand Junction railway in 1846 and merged with the South Staffordshire Junction Railway to form the South Staffordshire Railway in 1847. The 17½ miles from Walsall to Wichnor Junction (where the SSR made connection with the MR Whitacre–Burton route) was opened on 9th April 1849. The original Lichfield Station was about a mile south of where the SSR was carried over the Trent Valley, but a high level junction station was added a few months later. The SSR history was complex, but the line eventually passed into LNWR control.

From the days of the railway mania, there was continual agitation for a line striking north from Birmingham, and this was partially satisfied by the LNWR Aston–Sutton Coldfield line in 1862. North of Sutton, the empty countryside offered little inducement to the LNWR, but after further outside efforts to build a line, the LNWR obtained powers in 1880 for a Sutton–Lichfield link. This would considerably increase demands on the original SSR 'City' Station, and on 3rd November 1884, a new Lichfield City Station was partially brought into use a short distance away from the first station. The Lichfield–Sutton passenger service commenced on 15th December 1884.

Passenger workings at City Station fell into two categories, the Wolverhampton–Walsall–Lichfield–Burton services over the original SSR, and the Sutton line trains from 1884. As was frequently the case, the agitation for a line was more pronounced than the use made of the facility, and as late as 1921, the LNWR found nine trains on the SSR and twelve on the Sutton route adequate. Although housing development has been marked south of Walsall and Sutton, there has been little residential development along the lines into Lichfield, and the SSR services ceased on 18th January 1965, leaving only the Sutton passenger workings. The Walsall–Burton route remains open to freight.

LIVERPOOL EXCHANGE

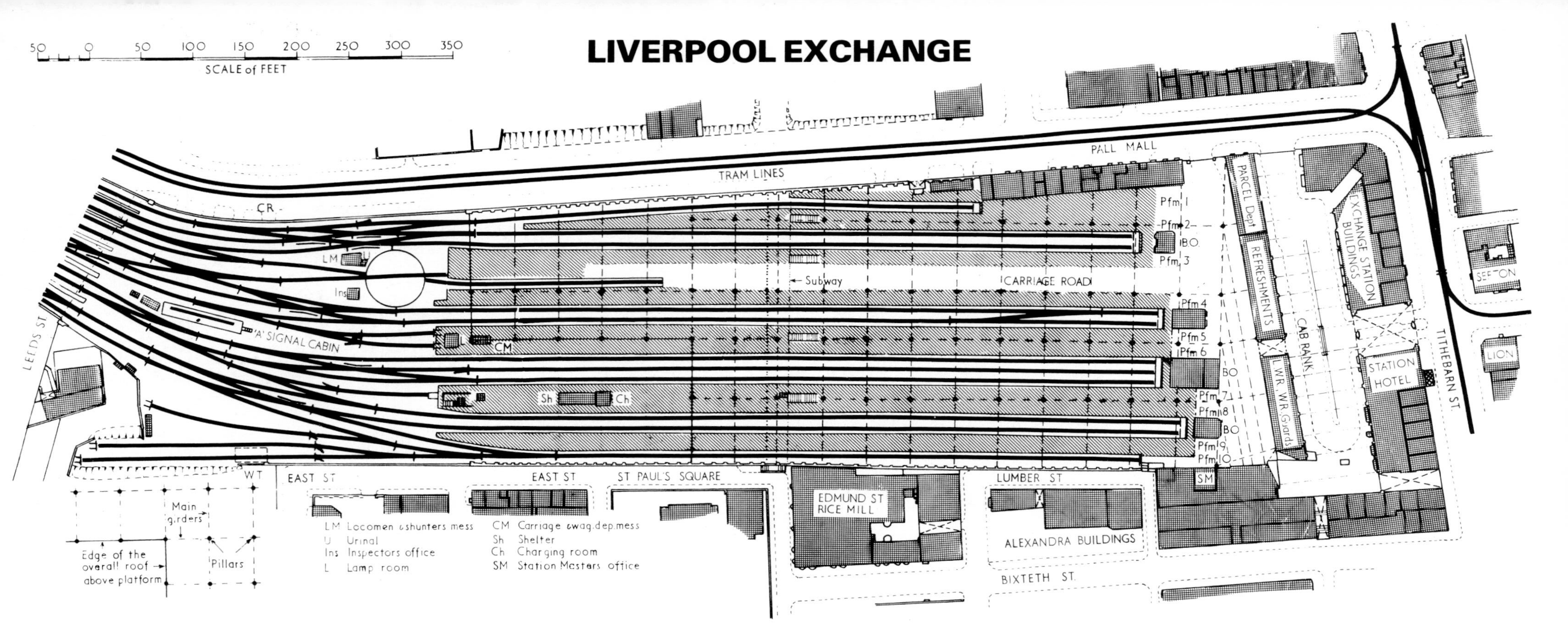

LIVERPOOL EXCHANGE *(Map Refs. A1, S9)*

The first steps in the creation of what eventually became the L&YR network of routes serving Liverpool were taken in 1845, when the Liverpool & Bury Railway was authorised from a terminus at Great Howard Street, Liverpool, to a junction with the Bolton & Preston Railway (see under Chorley) at Lostock. On 3rd August 1846 the L&B obtained powers to extend their line from Great Howard Street, to a central site on Tithebarn Street near the Exchange. A few days prior to this, the Liverpool & Bury had amalgamated with Manchester & Leeds to form the Lancashire & Yorkshire Railway. During this period discussions took place with the Liverpool, Ormskirk & Preston Railway, whose act, also of August 1846, sanctioned a line from a junction with the L&B at Walton to the outskirts of Preston. In October 1846, the LO&P was amalgamated with the East Lancashire Railway, and it was under the auspices of the ELR and LYR that the lines into Great Howard Street opened in 1848-49. The extension from Great Howard Street to Tithebarn Street opened on 13th May 1850.

The new station fronted on to Tithebarn Street and the main facade rose 90ft. above street level. Approach to the platforms, of which there were five, was by an inclined ramp, for in order to keep open a number of minor roads which ran at right angles to the course of the line, the approach to the station had to be elevated, and the rails were 25ft. above street level at the terminus. A few weeks after the new terminus opened, the Liverpool, Crosby & Southport Railway was completed from Waterloo to a junction with the L&Y at Sandhills, and Tithebarn Street thus had to cope with traffic on three routes.

By the mid 'seventies, the station was quite inadequate for the traffic flowing over the three main lines, and plans were prepared to erect a new station (authorised in 1876). In 1881, a station design competition was held, the plans at that time calling for the retention of the high level approach, but the idea of a street level station came to the fore the following year, and in 1883, the L&Y obtained powers to lower the station and approach lines, so closing off the old streets. The new station was to be enlarged to ten passenger platforms, and to cope with the steadily expanding traffic, the old approach via Great Howard Street was supplemented by a new four track loop line from Liverpool Exchange Junction to Exchange 'B' cabin, just outside the station area. The loop line and the first half of the new Exchange Station came into use on 12th December 1886, at which date the old high level station was closed for rebuilding. The work was completed in July 1888, and the following month the magnificent Exchange Hotel came into operation.

Exchange Station was well situated in the city centre, and with the goods and motive power facilities out of town, was on a remarkably compact site for its traffic and flexibility. Ease of operation and economy of space were the cardinal features in the design, and overall the station was an excellent compromise between these two mutually opposing ideals. Exchange 'B' box was situated on pillars above one of the subsidiary roads, whilst 'A' was sandwiched between the lines serving Nos. 5 and 6 platforms.

The old L&Y 'B' box was eventually replaced by a smaller BR cabin on the opposite side of

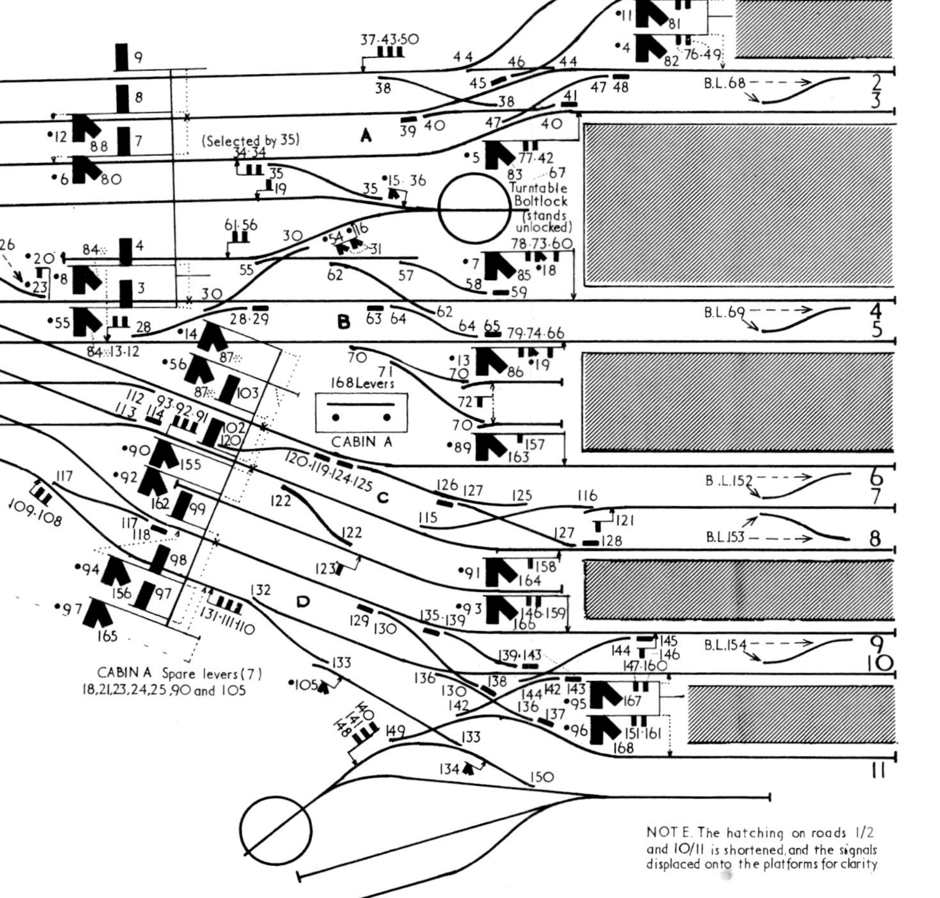

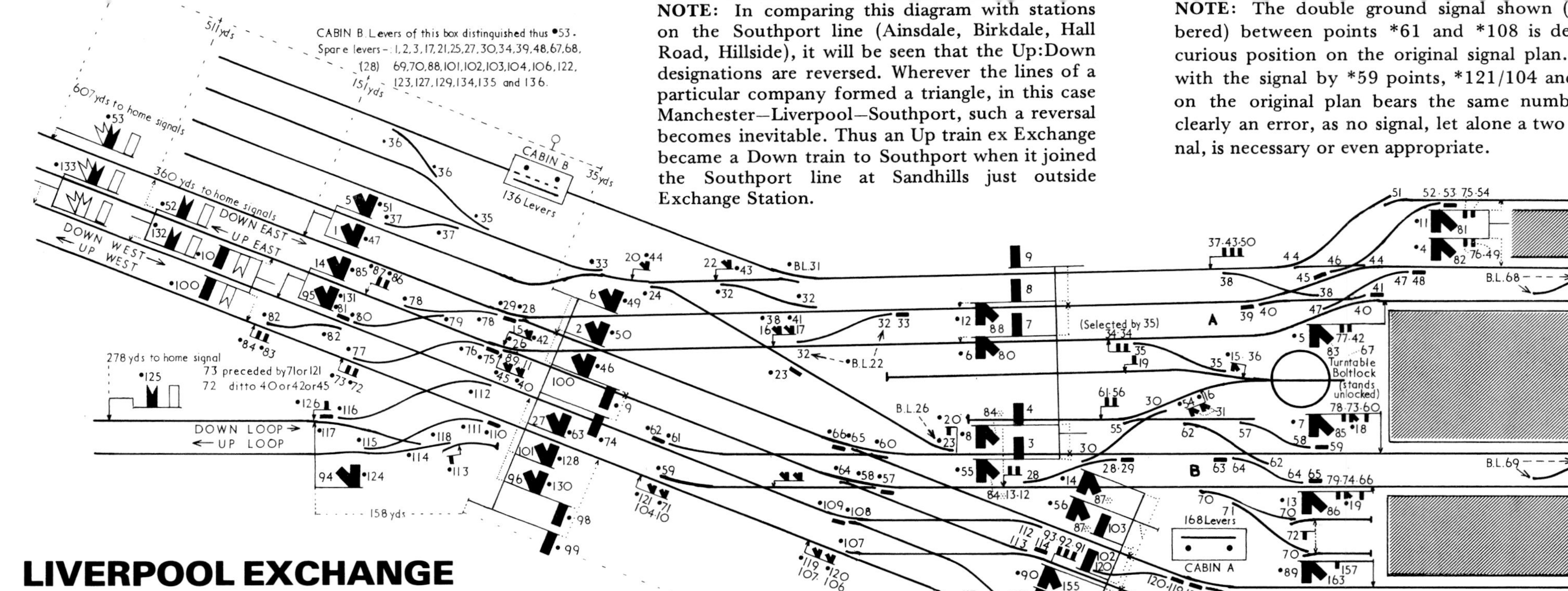

LIVERPOOL EXCHANGE

As at 23 MAY 1898

NOTE: In comparing this diagram with stations on the Southport line (Ainsdale, Birkdale, Hall Road, Hillside), it will be seen that the Up:Down designations are reversed. Wherever the lines of a particular company formed a triangle, in this case Manchester—Liverpool—Southport, such a reversal becomes inevitable. Thus an Up train ex Exchange became a Down train to Southport when it joined the Southport line at Sandhills just outside Exchange Station.

NOTE: The double ground signal shown (but not numbered) between points *61 and *108 is depicted in this curious position on the original signal plan. It is identical with the signal by *59 points, *121/104 and *71/10, and on the original plan bears the same numbers. This was clearly an error, as no signal, let alone a two arm shunt signal, is necessary or even appropriate.

the line. This became No. 1 box, whilst the old station 'A' box became No. 2. Two turntables were installed to minimise conflicting movements within the station area. One of these, reached off Nos. 8 to 10 platforms, became superfluous when the Southport line was electrified in 1904. In 1906, both lines to Aintree, via Marsh Lane and via Kirkdale, were electrified, and in 1913 electric trains reached Ormskirk. This marked the completion of the electrification programme, the remaining services being steam (later diesel) worked until Exchange Station was closed on 29th April 1977 as a part of an extensive revision of suburban services on Merseyside. Former L&Y trains were diverted from the loop line and crossed the site of Great Howard Street yard before burrowing beneath central Liverpool to new stations at Moorfields and Central.

The working of Exchange Station in mixed steam and electric days was fascinating, with electric trains arriving and departing every few minutes in platforms 7 to 10 (roads 8 to 11), and steam trains with all their concomitant noise and bustle on the remaining lines. The west turntable site and related sidings (which were all very short) were used for electric train storage during the off-peak periods, and care had to be taken when shunting into the sidings, on account of the steep gradients.

One of the authors has vivid memories of the illuminated indicators on the electric side of the station. These indicated in a tall display frame the nature of the next four departures, the destinations, platforms and the stations served. A stopping train to Southport was a particularly impressive display, with line after line illuminated. With an express, the majority of the intermediate stations would, of course, remain unlit. The four sets of up and down lines leading from the platforms towards the station throat were given letter designations for ease of reference.

'A' route led to and from platforms 1 to 3; 'B' route to Nos. 4 and 5; 'C' route to Nos. 6 and 7, and 'D' route Nos. 8, 9 and 10.

The large space between platforms 3 and 4 was occupied by a cab road, whilst further facilities existed in the forecourt beyond the circulating area. Impressive iron gates closed off the entrances when not required. An exit from Exchange Hotel led on to the forecourt, whilst another exit led on to Tithebarn Street.

Exchange was one of the most elegant stations on the L&Y, perhaps because rebuilding in the 1880s was so comprehensive, and the facilities then provided were so generous as to obviate the need for the piecemeal additions which have disfigured other large stations.

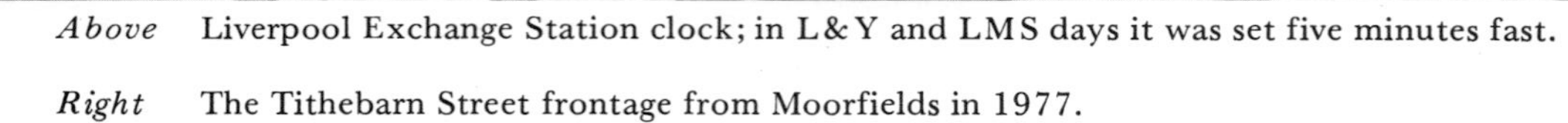

Above Liverpool Exchange Station clock; in L&Y and LMS days it was set five minutes fast.

Right The Tithebarn Street frontage from Moorfields in 1977.

Below The cab rank looking towards Pall Mall. Exchange Hotel is on the right.

Above The concourse looking towards Pall Mall. The dotted lines on the scale survey show the principal roof girders. Owing to the triangular shape of the site, the main vertical pillars, on the left, support one continuous girder at right angles to the train shed, and separate girders (one to each pillar) which run parallel to the parcels dept, refreshment and waiting rooms.

Below Looking towards the country end of platforms 6 and 7. The different nomenclature of the various tracks, approach lines and even signal cabins, at differing periods is apparent from the scale and signalling plans. The greater length of overall roof above platforms 1 to 5 compared to platforms 6 to 10, as indicated on the scale plan, is apparent.

Above The Southport line booking office at the foot of platforms 6 and 7. The reduced number of ticket hatches still in use is a sad reminder of the steady decline suffered by Exchange. A few days after this photograph was taken, the station closed for ever.

Below Looking towards the buffer stops from platforms 5 and 6, LMSR-built Southport electric stock being drawn up on platforms 5 and 7. The railings on the left protect the steps leading down to the subway which passed beneath the station. The positioning of the roof pillar partially blocking the head of the stairs was extraordinary, but illustrations and plans confirm the feature. The wide platforms were invaluable in bygone times.

Above By 1977, successive retrenchments had reduced the number of working levers to just a handful.

Below Despite the cutbacks, both lever frame and the surviving block instruments were typically 'Lanky'.

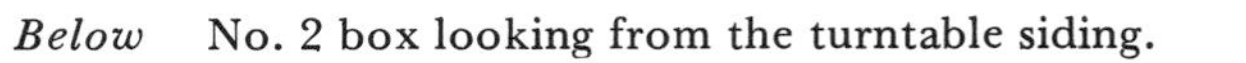

LIVERPOOL EXCHANGE
No. 2 Signal Box
(originally 'A' cabin)

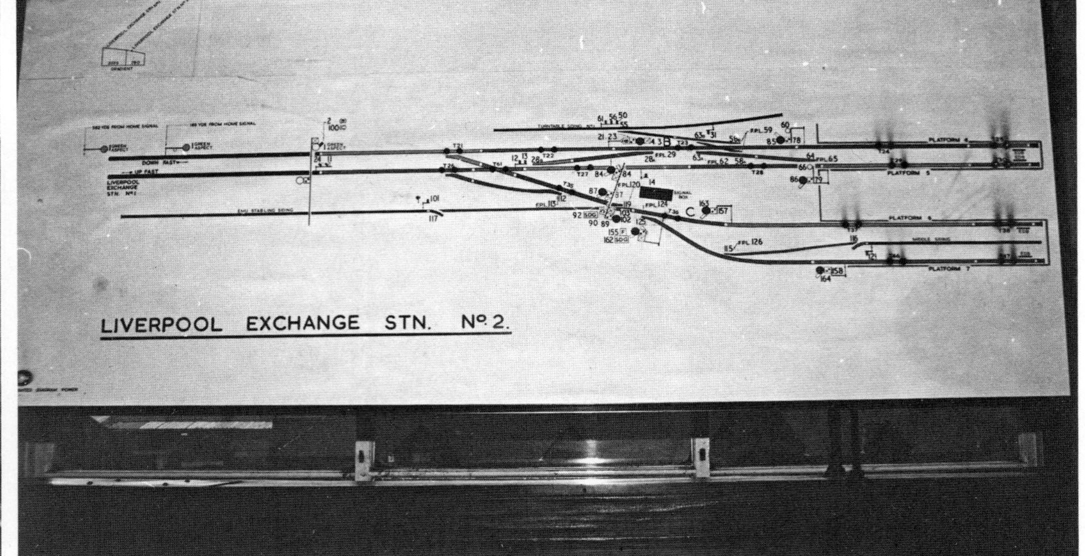

Above No. 2 box diagram in 1977. The discolouration of the diagram above the track circuits in the platforms (which are on for long periods) is interesting. The track circuits on the approach lines are only on briefly, so this effect is not apparent.

Below No. 2 box looking from the turntable siding.

Above Looking towards No. 2 box from platforms 5 and 6.

Below Signalman's view from No. 2 box looking towards the stops. The greater length of the overall roof above platforms 1 to 5 is clearly apparent, as is the different widths of the various spans. The turntable pit at the foot of platforms 3/4 has been filled in, but the curved coping can still be seen just beyond the inspector's hut by the turntable siding. The distant white column visible above the huts is the first roof pillar on platforms 1/2. (see scale plan).

Above From No. 2 box looking towards Southport. The modern Exchange No. 1 box is visible through the angled supports of the near signal gantry. The L&Y Exchange 'B' cabin (see signal plan) was carried on the masonry pillars visible above the DMU on the right, and straddled one of the carriage siding roads.

Below Exchange No. 1 box in 1977 showing the divergence of the Southport and Kirkdale lines at Sandhills. Although No. 2 box controls the platform connections, the lines appear on No. 1 diagram, as arrival and departure signals are slotted.

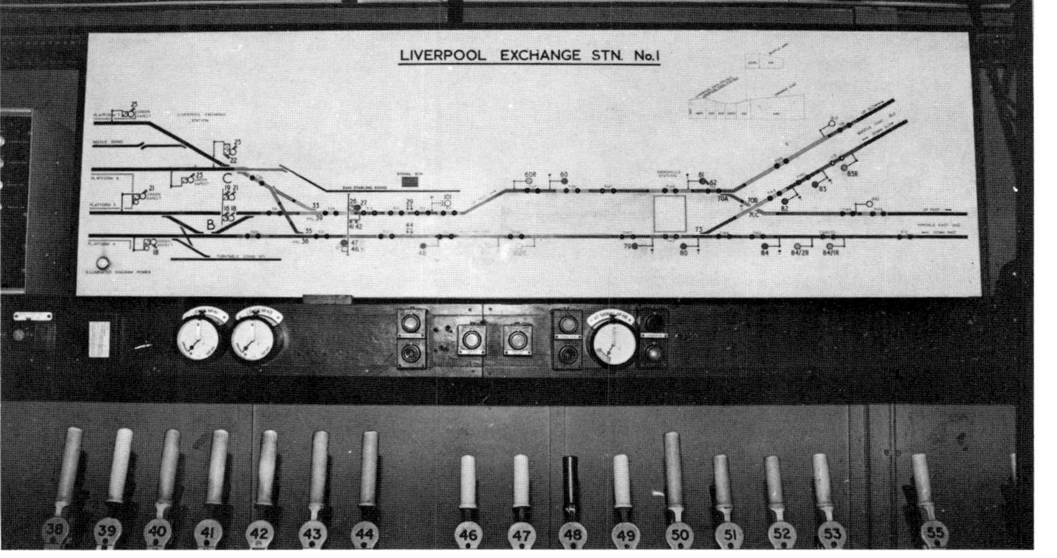

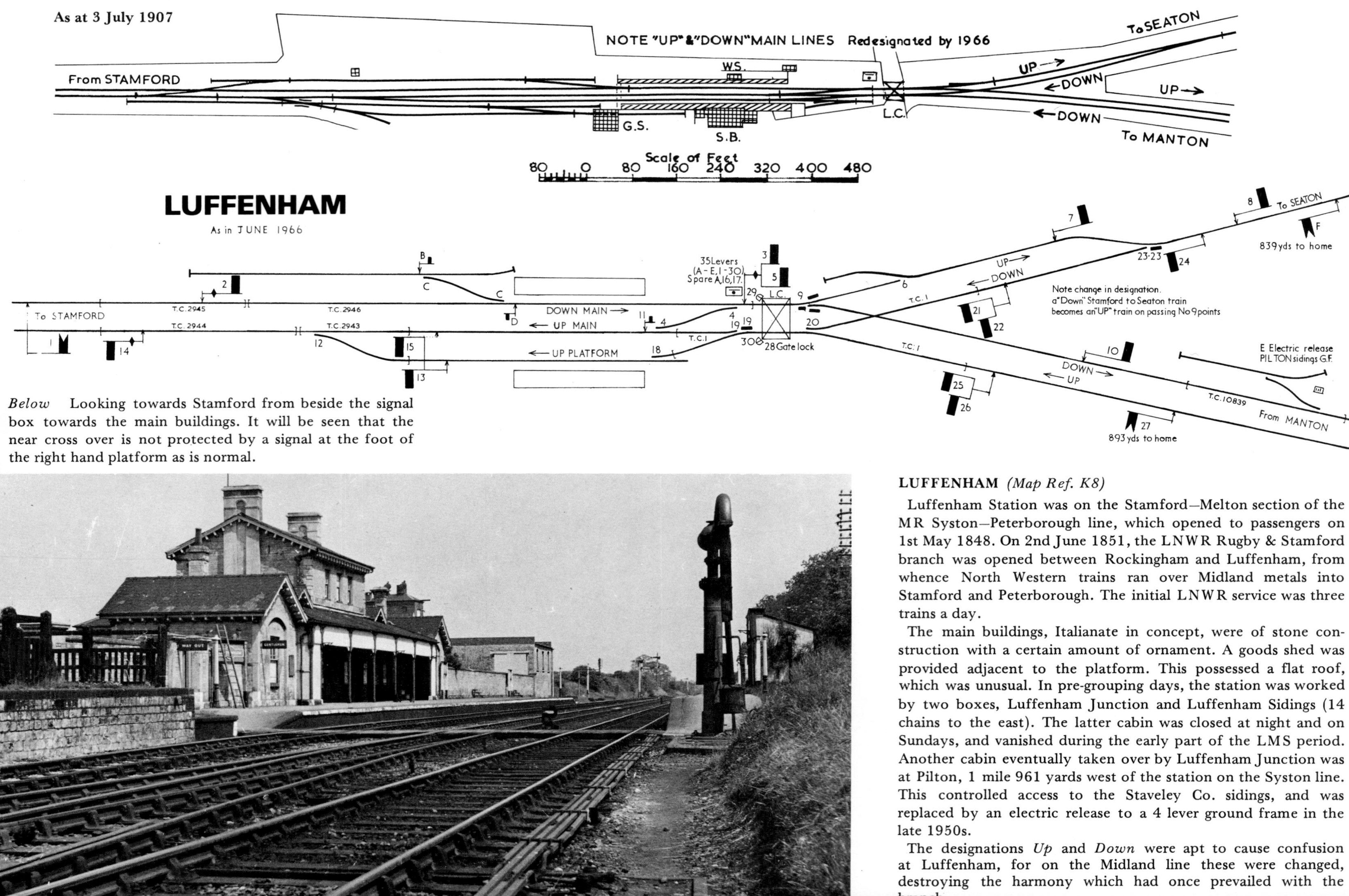

Below Looking towards Stamford from beside the signal box towards the main buildings. It will be seen that the near cross over is not protected by a signal at the foot of the right hand platform as is normal.

LUFFENHAM *(Map Ref. K8)*

Luffenham Station was on the Stamford–Melton section of the MR Syston–Peterborough line, which opened to passengers on 1st May 1848. On 2nd June 1851, the LNWR Rugby & Stamford branch was opened between Rockingham and Luffenham, from whence North Western trains ran over Midland metals into Stamford and Peterborough. The initial LNWR service was three trains a day.

The main buildings, Italianate in concept, were of stone construction with a certain amount of ornament. A goods shed was provided adjacent to the platform. This possessed a flat roof, which was unusual. In pre-grouping days, the station was worked by two boxes, Luffenham Junction and Luffenham Sidings (14 chains to the east). The latter cabin was closed at night and on Sundays, and vanished during the early part of the LMS period. Another cabin eventually taken over by Luffenham Junction was at Pilton, 1 mile 961 yards west of the station on the Syston line. This controlled access to the Staveley Co. sidings, and was replaced by an electric release to a 4 lever ground frame in the late 1950s.

The designations *Up* and *Down* were apt to cause confusion at Luffenham, for on the Midland line these were changed, destroying the harmony which had once prevailed with the

Thus a Stamford–Seaton train was *Down* between Stamford and Luffenham, but *Up* for the remainder of its journey. Trains service details were as for Ketton, except that being a more important station, all locals and the occasional semi-fast called at Luffenham. The station closed to goods in 1964, and to passengers on 6th June 1966. The Seaton Junction line was subsequently lifted, but the MR line remains open as a through route for both passengers and goods.

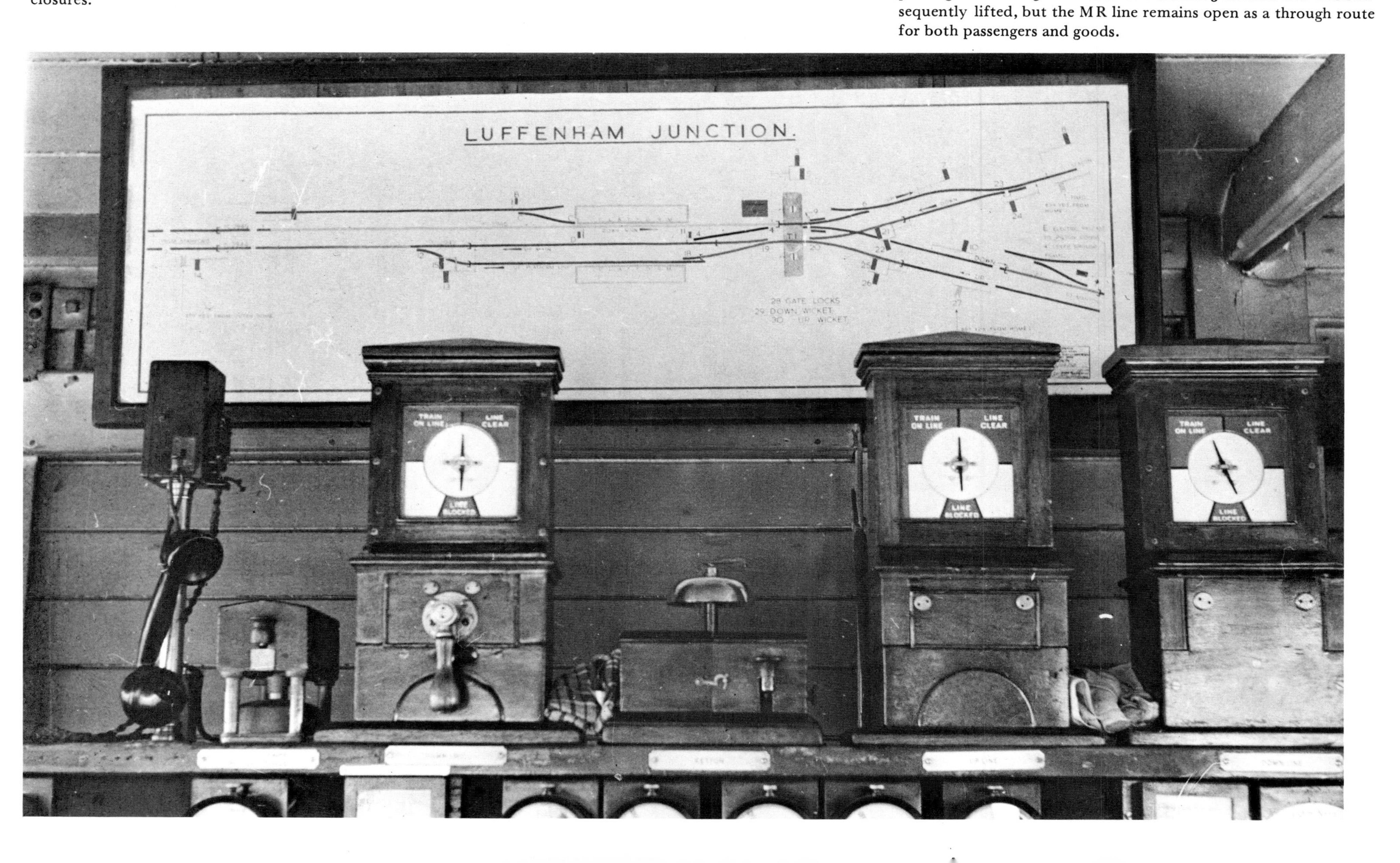

Luffenham Junction signal box diagram, block instruments, signal repeaters and track circuits, a vignette of traditional signalling equipment now sadly on the wane, due to power box working or line closures.

The North Western platforms looking towards Peterborough in 1966. The end of the canopy has been cut away revealing its construction. The inclined covered way from the station building to the platforms is visible on the right.

MARKET HARBOROUGH *(Map Ref. J7)*

Before the coming of the railways, Market Harborough was an important coaching station, and at first sight, it might appear that this significance had lingered on into the railway age, for lines radiated from the town in six directions, to Leicester, Nottingham, Peterborough, St. Pancras, Northampton and Rugby. The importance was, however, potential rather than actual, due to the existence of alternative routes and to company politics. The first line into Harborough was the LNWR Rugby–Stamford branch which was formally opened from Rugby on 27th April 1850. On 1st June this was extended five miles to Rockingham, and on 2nd June 1851, connection was made with the MR Peterborough line at Luffenham. In 1857, the MR Leicester–Bedford–Hitchin line was opened. Midland trains ran over North Western metals for three quarters of a mile in the vicinity of Harborough, and as traffic grew on the Midland, these flat junctions became an intolerable nuisance. Finally, on 3rd June 1881, the companies obtained powers to build a flyover to take the MR over the LNWR and to erect a new joint station south of the flyover. The station, in the 'V' of the divergence of the Rugby and Bedford lines, was opened on 14th September 1884 and the flyover in June 1885.

In the meantime, there had been various other developments. On 16th February 1859, the LNWR Market Harborough–Northampton branch came into use. On 15th December 1879, the GN & LNWR Joint line was completed from Melton Mowbray to a junction with the Peterborough line at Welham, just outside the town. The joint line gave the LNWR access to Nottingham and its coalfields, and a heavy traffic passed south from the coalfields onto the LNWR via Northampton. The GNR were granted rather pointless running powers over the LNWR into Northampton.

For passengers, the position was less satisfactory, for the Rugby, Peterborough, Northampton and Joint lines were all minor cross country routes with around five to seven trains each way daily. The Midland provided a more intensive service, but no attempt was made to provide through services, and there was in fact a difference between the level of the running rails until after the grouping, when the LMS redesigned the layout. Even this did not make a great difference, and passenger services ceased over the joint line in 1953. Except for certain night express workings, passenger services to Northampton ended in 1960, and the Rugby line closed in 1966, leaving only the Midland line as a regular passenger route.

Although Market Harborough did not become a major junction, it was nevertheless a busy station and was extensively re-signalled by the LMS who replaced the old MR and LNW boxes in the station area by two new cabins, Nos. 2 and 3 which worked the station and LMS connections to the north. The junction between the Rugby and Northampton lines was controlled from No. 1 box, which was replaced in 1957 by a modern BR mechanical box. After the various closures, the layout was greatly simplified, and the remaining trackage worked from the old No. 2 box.

MARKET HARBOROUGH

The approach to Market Harborough as seen from a Rugby–Peterborough train. The sharp curve into the Up bay platform over bridges 35A and 35 is most noticeable. It is also possible to study the relationship, to one another, of the station buildings, inclined way and platforms.

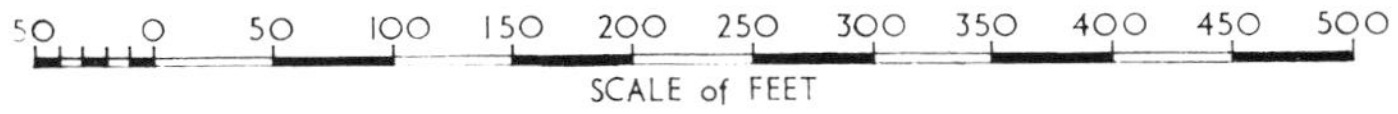

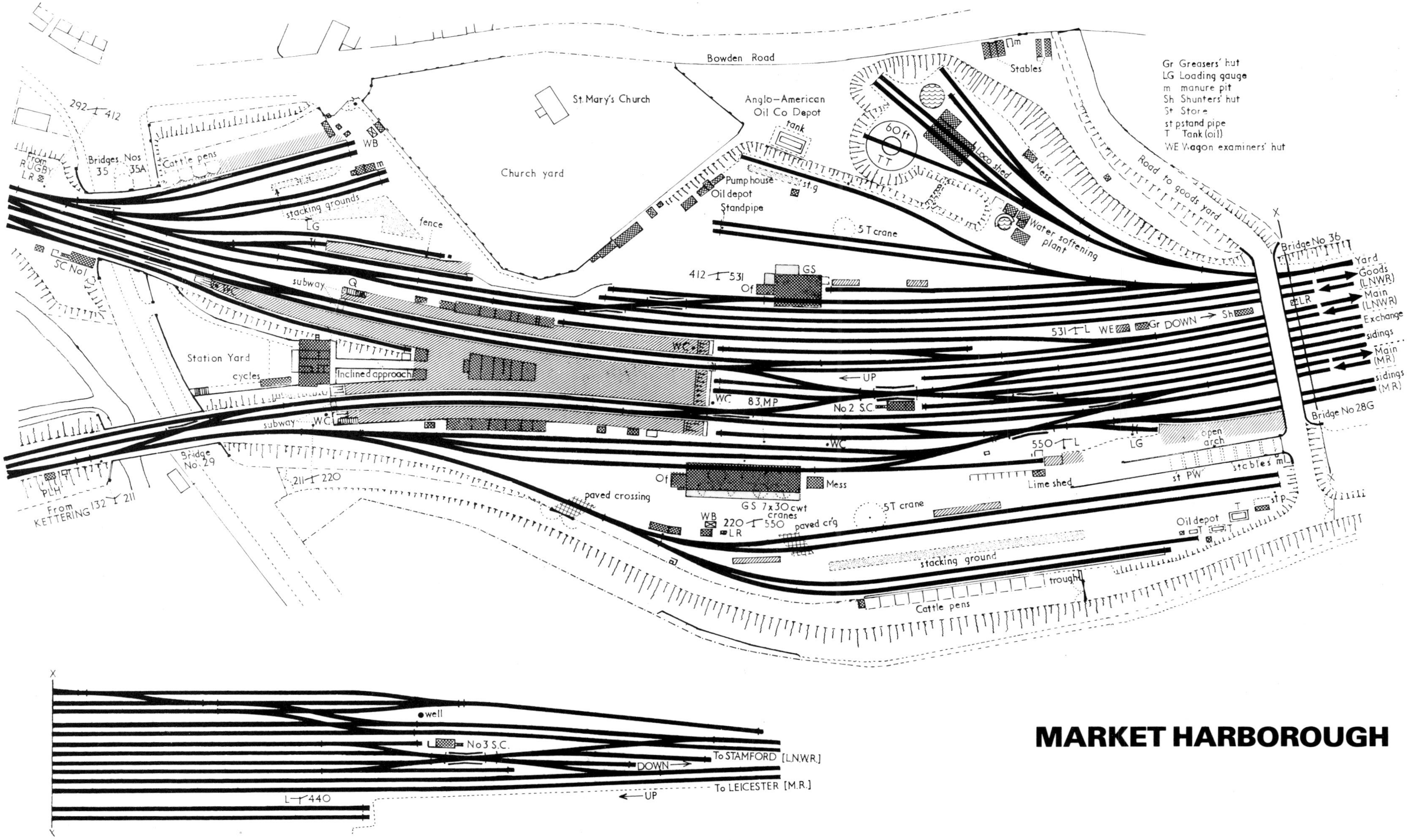

SCALE of FEET

Gr Greasers' hut
LG Loading gauge
m manure pit
Sh Shunters' hut
St Store
st p stand pipe
T Tank (oil)
WE Wagon examiners' hut

Left The forecourt and main office block looking from the station yard in 1966. The LNW line is on the left, the Midland on the right. The main building is a red brick Queen Anne mansion with stone pilasters and a delightful dormer window. It is not quite symmetrical, an external staircase being provided on the Midland *(right hand)* side.

Above Market Harborough No. 2 signal cabin looking towards ex Midland Yard.

Left Looking from the foot of the Down North Western platform towards Peterborough (LNWR) and Leicester (Midland). The tracks on the extreme left are the LNWR goods; the line in the foreground is the Down LNWR passenger. The exchange sidings double slips can be seen opposite No. 2 signal box, whilst the Midland running lines are on the extreme right, beyond the right hand signal post. The access bridge to the yard, a very long centre span flanked by two shorter spans, is visible on the skyline. Beyond the right hand span, the approach road forked, one access descending to track level, the upper arches being used as stables. (One wonders if the horses were stabled in order of size!) The second access road swept round outside the yard giving access to the cattle pens, and a further gate into the yard, and finally rejoined the public highway. The bridge eventually became unsafe, eliminating direct access from Bowden Road. The LNWR had their own small yards on their side of the station sidings, facing towards Rugby and Peterborough. The Up and Down LNW goods lines displayed one extraordinary feature in consequence, a diamond crossing at the Rugby end of the platforms, so that the two roads changed sides. A trailing connection between the Up and Down goods at this point made the trackwork even odder. As a result of this freakish arrangement an Up goods could shunt the Up LNW yard, although it was on the Down side, without fouling the Down goods line. On the other hand *all* through trains fouled the opposite running line, producing the equivalent of single line working. The cure seemed infinitely worse than the disease! This bizarre layout is indicated by the letter 'Q' on the scale plan.

The Midland platforms looking towards Leicester. The inclined ramp (with stables) to the Midland yard is visible beyond the platforms, but the bridge (28G) had gone by the 'seventies.

MARSTON GREEN

Proposed widening & underpass (plan 3874-36) NOT CARRIED OUT

The Down buildings looking towards Birmingham; note the contrasting styles of the lower and upper portions of the footbridge as described in the text.

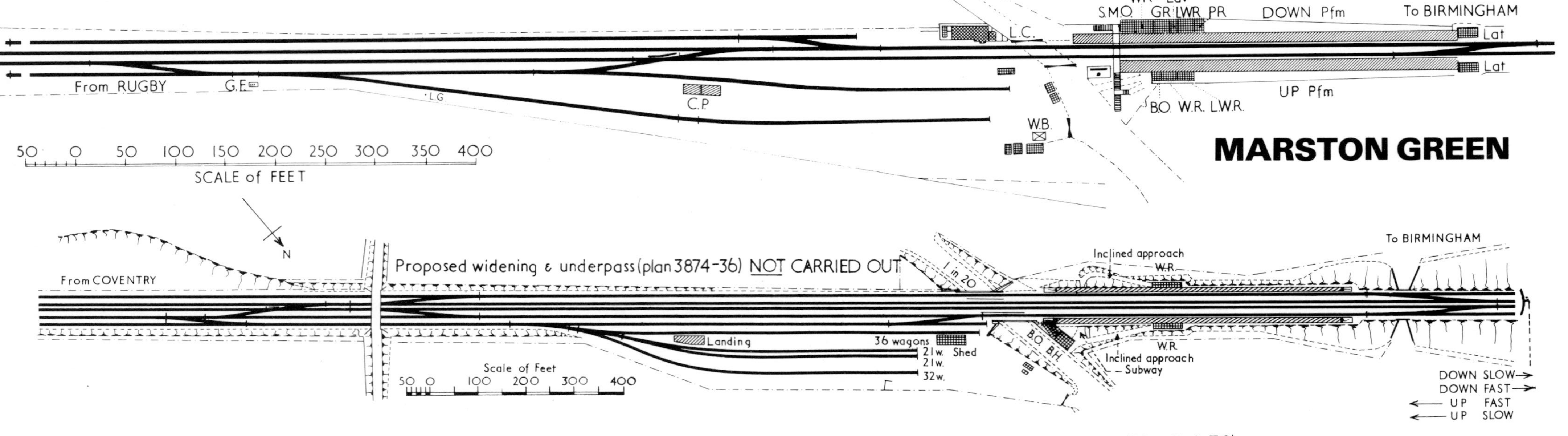

MARSTON GREEN *(Map Ref. E6)*

Marston Green Station is on the London & Birmingham main line between Hampton-in-Arden and Lea Hall. It marks the present easterly limits of the almost continuous urban/suburban sprawl which radiates outwards from Birmingham. The original decision to open Marston Green, then serving a tiny village community, was taken in October 1844 and a platform and booking hut authorised the following month. Until recently, Elmdon Lane crossed the line on the level just to the east of the station. The road has now been closed and the stump of the roadway converted into a bus terminal, giving the station considerable value as a road-rail interchange point in the West Midlands PTE area. The crossing was controlled from Marston Green box, which remained in use as a crossing frame after the commencement of power box working. The box was officially closed in August 1976, although it had been disused for some time prior to this.

As the line passed close to Elmdon aerodrome a short distance to the east of the station, emergency colour light signals were installed. These were normally out, but in the event of the down line becoming obstructed or damaged by aircraft, the emergency colour light signals could be illuminated by the signalman to stop any Down train. These signals, when lit, gave yellow and red aspects, and should a train be stopped at the emergency stop signal, the driver was not to proceed until the light had been extinguished and permission had been received by telephone from the signalman.

One result of electrification was the modification of the various station structures including the footbridge and canopies. The lower half of the former is pure LNWR, as evidenced by the design of the lower stairway railings. The upper half is BR. The trimming back of the awning on the up side gives one the opportunity to study the window frames and ornate iron spandrels fitted in the central opening.

Under Lea Hall (see page 103) reference was made to the proposed quadrupling of the approach to Birmingham by the LMSR in the 1930s. This was one of several schemes examined in the late 'thirties, many of which fell victim to the Second World War. At Marston Green the plan envisaged providing a road underpass approached by inclines of 1 in 20, a two track and two single track spans across the lowered road, and a much enlarged goods yard as well. The existing buildings were to be replaced by a modern booking office facing the road with inclined approaches to the platforms and waiting rooms. The construction of a booking office facing the road avoided the need for Up and Down booking offices and thus saved staff, and was a feature of contemporary LMS thinking, as at Lea Hall and Meols. In addition to the four main running lines, there would have been an Up goods loop.

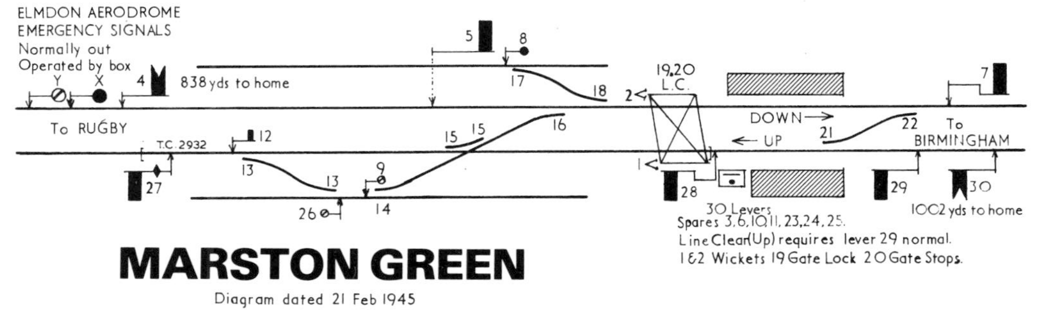

The Up building and platform looking towards Birmingham in the evening sun. The BR alterations to the canopy and valance have rather spoiled the lines of a once pretty building.

Marston Green signal box and Up buildings looking towards Birmingham. The extent to which the footbridge has had to be raised is noteworthy.

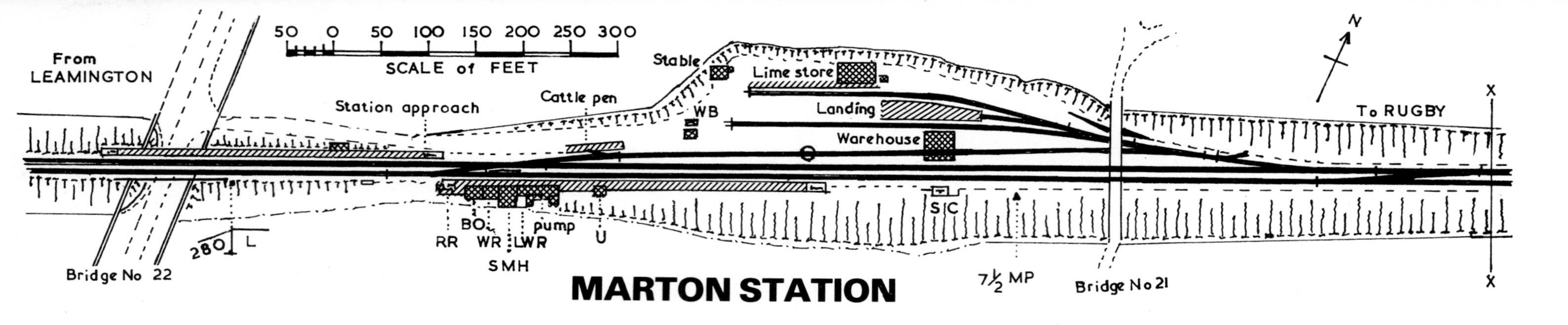

Above A scale survey of Marton Station in the 1880-1895 period. The isolated wagon turntable is a relic of an even earlier layout.

Below The station building on the Down platform looking towards Leamington, in 1959. As was often the case with old buildings, the station house was not properly damp-proofed, and even in summer, it was common to find a fire in the hearth to keep ground damp at bay. Judging by the number of chimneys, the station was well-equipped for this task.

MARTON *(Map Ref. F6)*

Marton was one of the original wayside stations on the Rugby & Leamington branch of the LNWR, which opened on 1st March 1851. Initially the line was single, but was doubled in the 1880s, the Marton–Leamington section being completed on 28th January 1884. As the station yard was on the Up side of the line opposite the old platform, the new platform had to be staggered, with the result that it was constructed outwards across the bridge carrying the railway over the Southam–Coventry road. The use of viaducts to carry platforms in urban areas was not uncommon, but this must have been one of the few rural locations to be so graced. The signal box diagram (see page 126) shows the layout in latter days. It is interesting to note that despite the abandonment of black and white striped painting of distant signal posts after the war, both the Up and Down tubular post isolated distants at Marton were still striped when the station closed to passengers on 15th June 1959.

The Southam–Daventry branch opened on 1st August 1895, and ran from Marton Junction (just over two miles west of the station) to Daventry where it joined the existing LNWR branch to Weedon. This line was single track, worked by Webb & Thompson electric train staff. The layout at Marton Junction is given to complete the coverage of the railway facilities in the Marton area. Prior to the opening of the branch, Marton was the nearest LNWR station to Southam, and between 1853-60 and 1877-95, Southam was added to the station title. A horse bus ran between two places four times a day until the opening of the new line in 1895.

Train services on the main line in 1895 comprised eight trains in each direction. All of the east-bound trains, including two semi-fasts, called at Marton, but in the reverse direction two ran non-stop. By 1927 ten trains to Rugby and nine to Leamington called at Marton.

Below Nelson's Sidings, Marton, in the early 1890s, from an engineers' survey. The scale plan is to the same size as the contemporary Marton survey. The plain track between Marton and Nelson's Sidings has been omitted to save space, the distance between the points 'XX' and 'YY' on the two plans being 700 ft. The scale plan of Marton Junction is from the same survey which pre-dated the Southam line, the latter being added to bring the diagram up to date. Collectively, the three layouts trace the development of railway facilities serving a small community residing over a wide area, and with suitable shortening of the countryside stretches could make the basis of an interesting model railway, especially when it remembered that the Rugby–Leamington–Berkswell (or Coventry) route was used as a diversion for engineering works – or accident – on the main line.

Y [XX & YY 700 feet apart]
From LEAMINGTON
LC
Y
1/4 MP
Nelson's Siding S.C.
Lever stage
2'0" culvert
Cottages
NELSON'S Cement Depot
Warehouse
S P
Fog hut
6'0" culvert
To RUGBY
L
519
Bridge No 20
7 MP

Left Marton goods yard looking towards Rugby, in 1959. From left to right the facilities comprise the lime bank and lime store, horse and carriage landing, goods shed and signal cabin. Although the station was still open for passengers, the usual trains were two-coach push-pulls and these stopped further along by the station buildings, this portion of the platform only being used by the signalman or station staff en route for the box. As a result it became heavily overgrown. At the time of the scale survey, a windmill existed in the fields to the north of the station, and was visible from the platform, but had gone when this view was taken. Marton Up advanced starting signal is visible through the arch of the bridge.

MARTON STATION

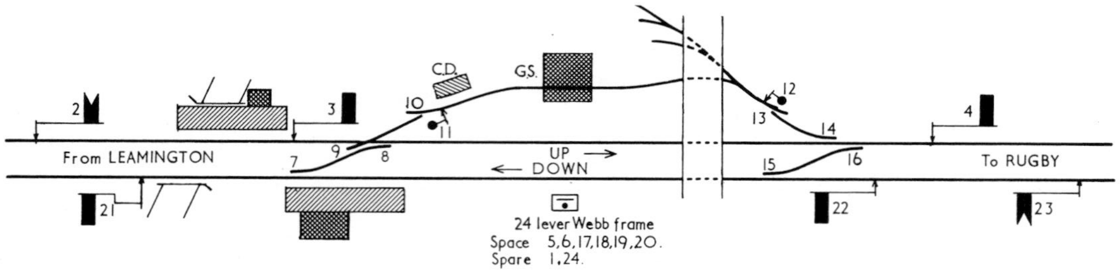

Marton signal box layout in the 'fifties, long after the removal of the Nelson's Sidings complication.

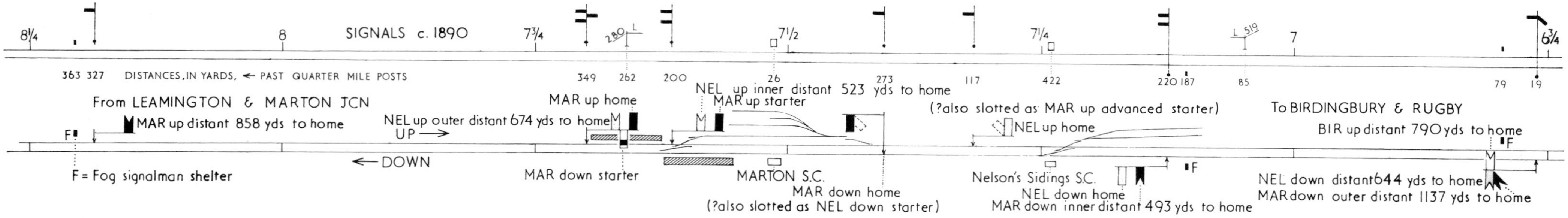

The engineers' signal plan is for an early signalling arrangement current with the scale plan, and shows an additional signal box and outdoor lever frame about 22 chains on the Rugby side of Marton Station cabin. This box, Nelson's Siding signal box, was adjacent to a minor occupation crossing, and controlled access to two private sidings on the Up side of the line. These sidings probably closed in the late 1890s when the Leamington–Southam–Daventry branch opened, as this passed close to Nelson's works and there would seem to be little point in continuing to haul loads along the highway to the Marton sidings. The signalling arrangements are from an engineers' plan which shows the number of arms, but does not differentiate distant or stop arms, or make clear to which line a signal refers. In the absence of any further information, and given the interest of this early installation, the reconstruction in the 'C' plan has been prepared from the best available data, and in the light of known physical features. The existence of the outer distants for Marton Station on the Down line would appear to be confirmed by the lever pull plates, lever 24 (even after many years disuse) requiring 23 etc. on its pull plate though painted white.

MARTON JUNCTION

Right Marton Junction signal cabin looking towards Rugby, on 5th March 1966.

MARTON JUNCTION

MARTON JUNCTION

Left Marton Junction looking towards Rugby, with some dubious shunting moves in progress, in 1959. A passenger train is signalled on the Down Rugby line, yet the '8F' on the Weedon branch has not only passed the branch home signal, but the trap had been set to permit this!

NOTE – AN HISTORICAL ACCOUNT OF MARTON JUNCTION IS GIVEN ON PAGE 124

Below Marton Junction and Honingham Hill road bridge looking towards Rugby in 1966.

MATLOCK

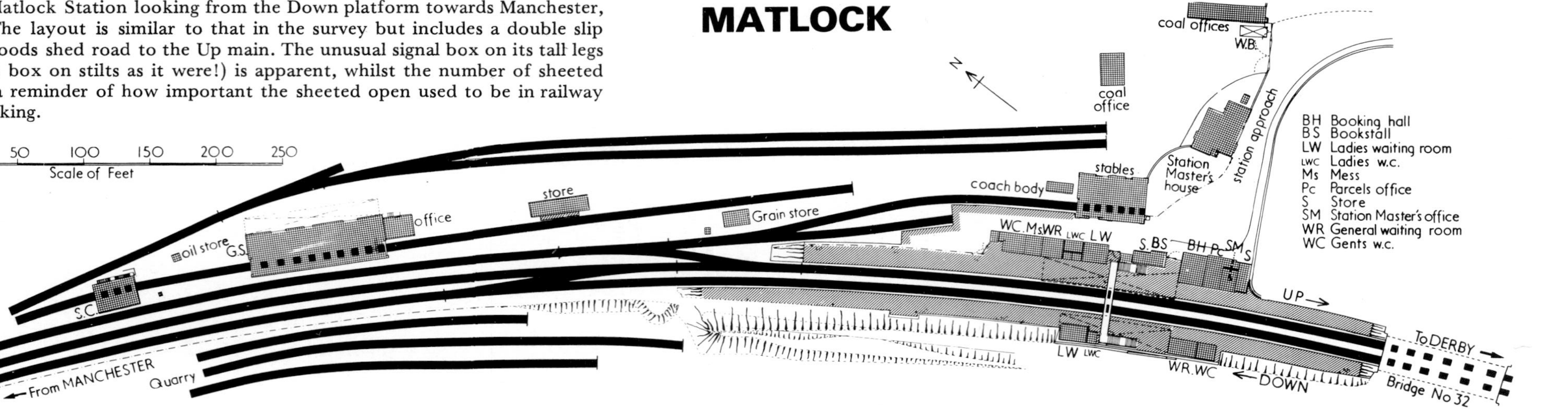

Bottom Matlock Station looking from the Down platform towards Manchester, in 1911. The layout is similar to that in the survey but includes a double slip from the goods shed road to the Up main. The unusual signal box on its tall legs (a Midland box on stilts as it were!) is apparent, whilst the number of sheeted wagons is a reminder of how important the sheeted open used to be in railway freight working.

MATLOCK *(Map Ref. U8)*

Nowadays Matlock is the northern terminus of the one-time MR Derby–Manchester route, the first section of which, between Ambergate on the Derby–Chesterfield line, and Rowsley, was opened on 4th June 1849 by the Manchester, Buxton, Matlock & Midlands Junction Railway. This company was absorbed into the Midland Railway in 1871, some years after the opening of the Buxton extension.

Local passenger services consisted of six to seven trains a day. In the case of Matlock, these were augmented by a number of expresses booked to call at the station. In 1944, there were, consequently, twelve northbound and eleven southbound trains. Local services north of the town ceased on 6th March 1967 and through expresses on 1st April 1968. Multiple-unit *pay trains* from Derby, augmented by the occasional excursion, continue to run as far as Matlock. The line, which has been singled, extends a short distance beyond the station to some quarry sidings, and the connections on this section can be used to stable excursion stock.

At Matlock, the end of the platforms was immediately adjacent to a bridge, and, in its main-line state, would make an interesting and convenient station to model. The scenic possibilities, with Matlock Tor as a backdrop, would be considerable.

Above Matlock Station looking towards Derby, in 1977, when the station had reached its nadir. A preservation project hopes to see tracks stretching north from the town once again, as in the view on the previous page.

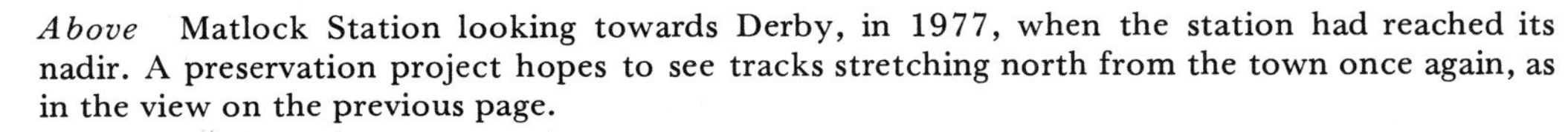

Below The main buildings looking from the station approach in 1977.

Above Looking from the approach to the landing, towards the station forecourt in 1977.

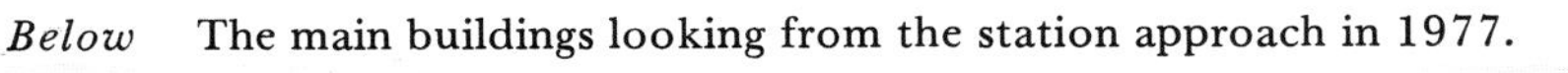

Below The Up platform looking towards the present end of track, which is a quarry a short distance beyond the station. Note the variety of awnings.

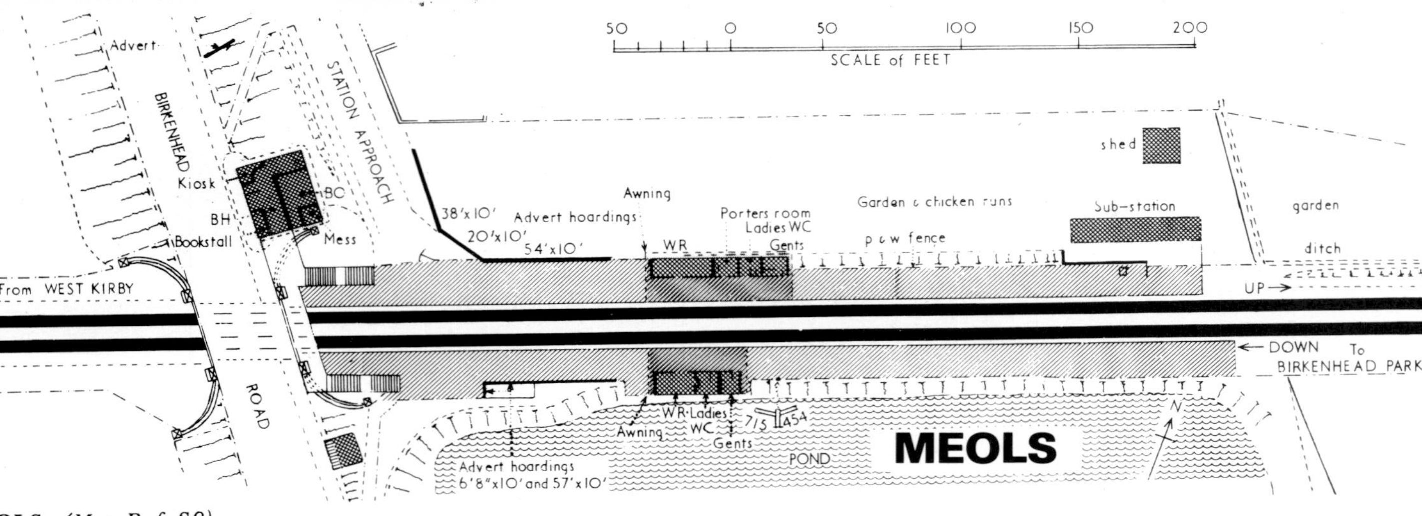

Left The scale plan provides exceptional detail about the LMS-built station, and is therefore reproduced to a large scale so as not to lose the finer points. The proximity of the station to a large pond is noteworthy, but the pond was nearly obscured in practice by the numerous robust advertisement hoardings. Facilities on the platforms were confined to waiting rooms, toilets and a porter's room, the booking office being in the twin storey blocks illustrated below.

Below The road frontage of Meols Station with the BR and Merseyside passenger transport executive insignia co-existing on display signs, indicating the close liaison which now prevails between the PTEs and BR over commuter lines in the metropolitan counties (i.e. the highly built-up industrial areas).

MEOLS *(Map Ref. S9)*

Meols Station, although not a new station created by the LMS, as was the case with Lea Hall (see page 103), was so drastically rebuilt by the company as to typify LMS design-work of the 1930s, with its emphasis upon reinforced concrete functionalism. The original Meols Station, with timber buildings and low cinder platforms, opened as a part of the Hoylake Railway on 2nd July 1866, and passed via the Seacombe, Hoylake and Deeside Railway to the Wirral Railway. Despite the residential development of the north Wirral as a suburb of Liverpool and Birkenhead, these companies were customarily impoverished, and Meols was as outmoded as the rest of the WR when it passed into LMS ownership in 1923. New rolling stock and other improvements ensued, but it was not until 1938, and the introduction of electric services that the Wirral section was transformed. The new electric trains operated over the independent Mersey Railway into Liverpool, and to coincide with this development, the LMS modernised the stations at Leasowe, Moreton, Meols and Hoylake. Meols was provided with concrete slab platforms, whilst the buildings were framed in reinforced concrete with brick and glass in-filling. Concrete awnings were provided for the two storey station office and the waiting rooms on the platforms, the awnings being supported *from above* by reinforced concrete cantilever beams. Access to the station was via the adjacent road bridge, the booking hall being on the upper floor, with access to the platforms via a footbridge. The road elevation was functional in the extreme, with a typically 1930s curved canopy (seen opposite). The new station was opened in 1938, and unlike Lea Hall had been little altered by the start of the 'eighties.

Initially the Hoylake Railway provided six trains in each direction, and with gradual residential development, the number rose to fourteen by 1877, and twenty by the 1880s. The momentum continued, and by the 1940s the LMS was providing a ten minute service during rush hours, with trains every fifteen to twenty minutes out of peak. In 1944, the first train to call was at 6.02 am for Liverpool, and the last train, the 11.22 pm to West Kirby, the outer terminus of the line.

Right Looking from the Up platform towards Birkenhead Park. The concrete cantilever beams supporting the platform canopies on the two buildings are prominent even from platform level, as is the relatively flat roof over the building, and sharp slope of the canopy section. Well tended gardens helped to remove something of the stark functional look.

Lower right Looking from the Down platform towards West Kirby and the outer end of the line, as a window cleaner gives some attention to the stairway leading to the Up platform. The metal framed windows, divided into numerous horizontal panes by prominent glazing bars, are typical not only of LMS architecture of the period, but of 1930s building in general.

Below A variety of heavily built timber seats characterised the modernised stations. Some had a completely plain two plank back, others were framed as shown below. Many were provided with two intermediate legs, but a few shorter seats, with one intermediate leg, were to be found. Regrettably this seat at Meols has suffered from the attentions of that worthless and inexcusable creature of modern times, the vandal.

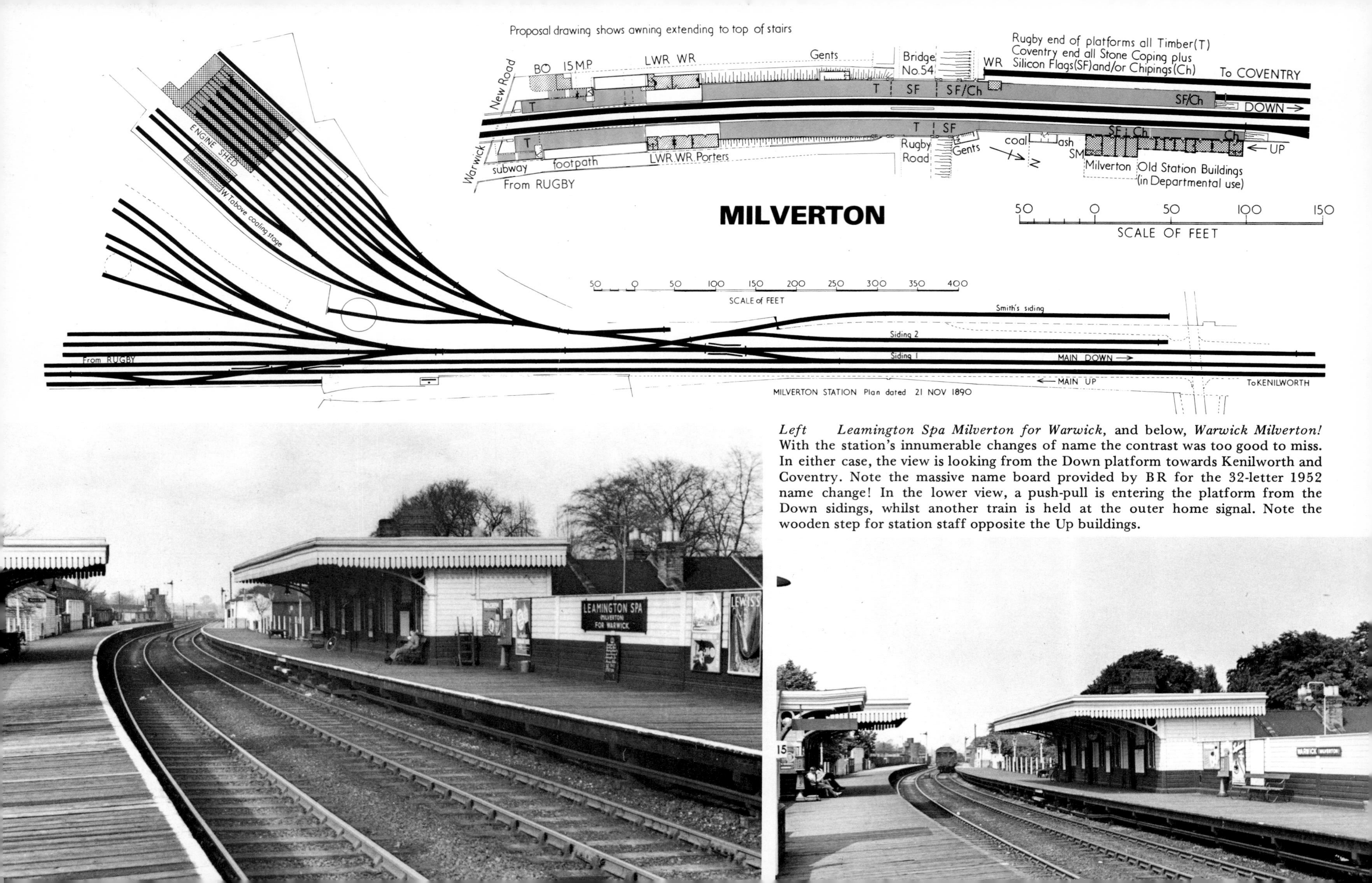

Left *Leamington Spa Milverton for Warwick*, and below, *Warwick Milverton!* With the station's innumerable changes of name the contrast was too good to miss. In either case, the view is looking from the Down platform towards Kenilworth and Coventry. Note the massive name board provided by BR for the 32-letter 1952 name change! In the lower view, a push-pull is entering the platform from the Down sidings, whilst another train is held at the outer home signal. Note the wooden step for station staff opposite the Up buildings.

MILVERTON

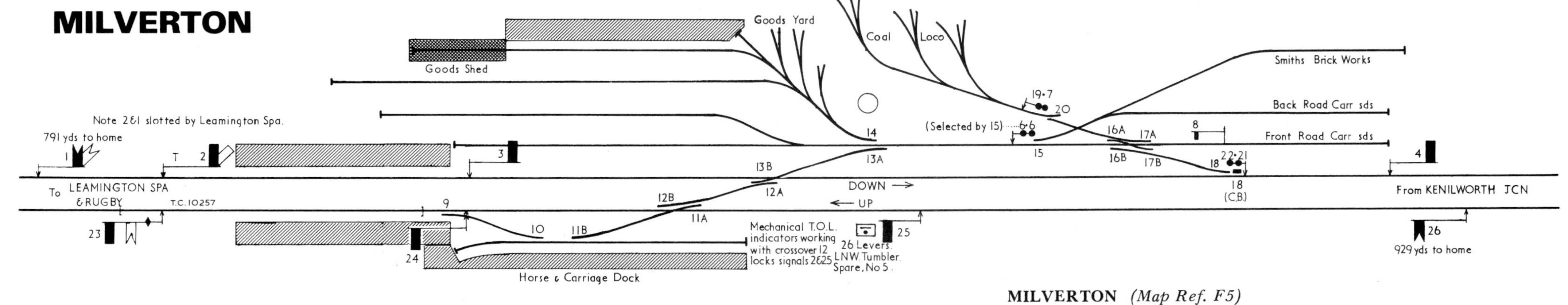

Looking from the driving cab of the Warwick–Rugby push-pull, stabled between turns in the Down sidings clear of No. 13 points. From left to right, the horse and carriage dock, passenger station, yard and water softener.

MILVERTON *(Map Ref. F5)*

Construction of a branch from Coventry on the L&B to Warwick (Old Milverton) was authorised in the Warwick and Leamington Union Railway Act of 18th June 1842. The W&LU was sold to the L&B in 1843 and the line opened to the first Milverton Station on 9th December 1844. This was at first known as *Leamington.* In 1851, the Rugby–Milverton line opened, and a station was provided at Leamington (Avenue) in 1854, and Leamington Station was renamed *Warwick (Milverton)*. In due course the attractions of this name paled and the station successively became *Warwick, Warwick (Milverton), Leamington (Milverton), Leamington Milverton (Warwick)* and *Milverton (for Warwick)*. In 1883, a new station was opened, and in 1884 this assumed the title *Warwick (Milverton)*, which it bore until 1952, when BR adopted the most impressive title yet, *Leamington Spa (Milverton) for Warwick*. The line was constructed as a single track branch, but was doubled in the 'eighties.

A general account of the services radiating from Leamington and Warwick has been given under Leamington (Avenue), but a few matters of particular relevance to Milverton are of interest. Milverton shed (in LNWR days a sub-shed of Rugby, code 8) provided much of the motive power for trains over this group of branches, although Rugby and Coventry also provided locomotives. As engine and staff movements between Avenue and Milverton were frequent, the section was specially exempted from the staff riding pass regulations, under which an employee had to apply for a pass if he required to ride from one station to another prior to going on duty, or after leaving work. These passes were normally issued by station masters or foreman, and had to be attached to the guards'/breaksmen's working sheets etc. after use, for forwarding to the relevant District Superintendent.

Most Coventry services started and terminated at Avenue Station, serving Milverton en route, whilst the majority of the Rugby or Weedon trains started from Milverton, serving Avenue en route. The section between the two stations thus carried a service of epic proportions, some 38 trains each way in 1927! During the week, Milverton box was extremely busy, with locomotives on and off shed and the terminating and through passenger workings, plus goods, but on Sundays only the Coventry line was in operation, and as these trains terminated at Leamington, the station was little more than an ordinary wayside station.

MORCOTT

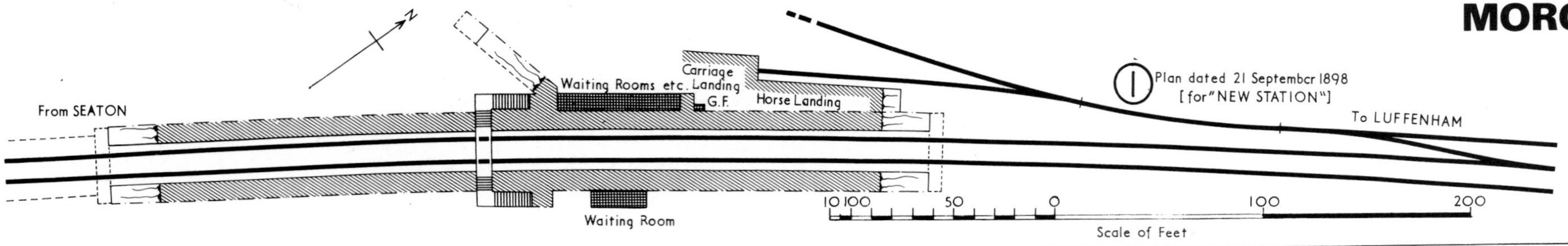

① Plan dated 21 September 1898 [for "NEW STATION"]

From SEATON

Waiting Rooms etc.

Carriage Landing

G.F.

Horse Landing

To LUFFENHAM

Waiting Room

10 100 50 0 100 200

Scale of Feet

Between 1898 and 1907 a cross-over plus a single slip connection to the goods yard were added, and the ground frame replaced by a signal box

In 1907 the track was singled, and the redundant platform, waiting room, footbridge & barrow-ways, and also the signal box were removed.

See diagram ②

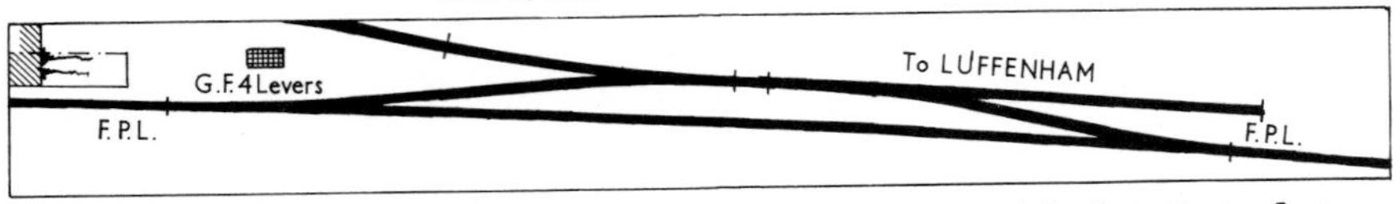

G.F. 4 Levers

To LUFFENHAM

F.P.L.

F.P.L.

③ AFTER ALTERATION TO SINGLE LINE WORKING COMPLETION 21 JULY 1907

A new pair of points — in lieu of the single slip, two Facing Point Locks and a 4 Lever Ground Frame — in lieu of the Signal Box — were installed; the G.F. was locked by the Tablet

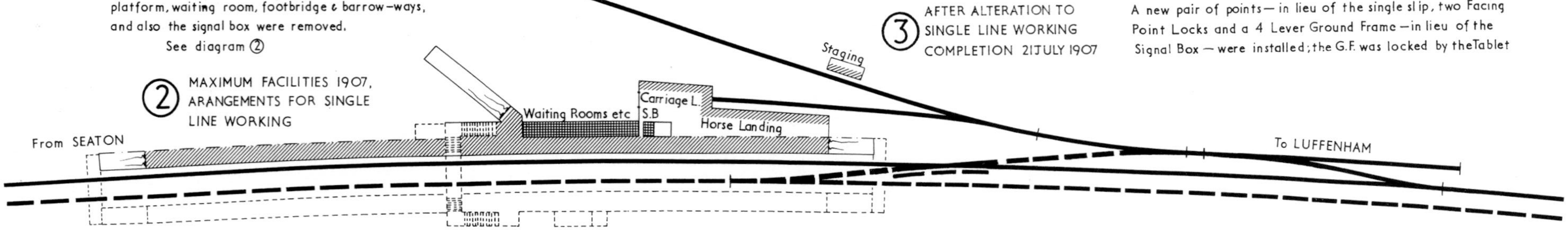

Staging

② MAXIMUM FACILITIES 1907, ARANGEMENTS FOR SINGLE LINE WORKING

From SEATON

Waiting Rooms etc

Carriage L.

S.B

Horse Landing

To LUFFENHAM

MORCOTT *(Map Ref. K8)*

At first sight, Morcott Station looked to be a typical sleepy backwater with little or no history. In fact, the reverse was true, but like the celebrated legend of Northampton and its supposed opposition to the London & Birmingham line, fiction overtook fact. Morcott Station was located on the Rugby–Luffenham branch of the LNWR between Seaton and Luffenham, at which place the LNWR trains forsook their own metals for the Midland route into Peterborough. The line was opened in 1851, but in the 'seventies the LNWR tired of their long way round and obtained powers for a cut-off from Seaton Station to Yarwell Junction on the LNWR Northampton–Peterborough branch. The cut-off opened to freight on 2nd July 1879 and to passengers on 1st November. The Seaton–Luffenham section was thus reduced to an insignificant link with an infrequent connecting service into Stamford. It has been alleged that the Seaton–Luffenham section was singled at this time, and by inference that Morcott Station, which did not open until 1898, was a single platform effort. Like many legends it has been oft repeated, but there is abundant evidence to the contrary. Board of Trade *signal arrangements and systems of working* returns of the 1880s persist in describing the line as a double track section, 3 miles 60 chains in length. It is so shown on an LNWR plan of 1894, and when the LNWR finally provided a station it was still double. Plans were issued in September 1898 for a double track station with a small yard on the Down side. On 20th October, the LNWR notified the Board of Trade of their intention to open the station in *eleven days* time, seeking provisional approval pending inspection. Colonel H. A. Yorke of the Board of Trade was deputed to inspect the new station, and in his report of February 1899 he observed that two ground frames had been provided, one on the platform to work the signals, and one in the yard to control the points, the yard frame being unlocked by a key withdrawn from the platform frame, which in turn locked the Down platform starting signal at danger. Although key locking of this description had been perfected by E. M. G. Eddy of the LNWR (he later went out to Australia as a State Commissioner of Railways), its use in the UK was frowned on by the Board of Trade, as it was cumbersome, and, as installed at Morcott, it meant that a train shunting between the platform and yard would be likely to pass the platform starter at danger, unless the station staff were scrupulous in taking the key from frame to frame. Colonel Yorke disapproved, but his only requirements were a clock visible from the platforms and the addition of Up line catch points a train's length behind the Up home signal, both of which had been complied with by May 1899. Subsequently a yard connection was laid in to the Up line and the ground frames replaced by a proper signal box, but with five passenger trains each way and an infrequent freight service, these facilities were excessive, and the line was singled in 1907, 28 years after this might reasonably have been done! The Up platform, signal box and footbridge at Morcott all went, and the station resembled many other basic LNWR stations. Freight services ceased on 4th May 1964 and passenger services on 6th June 1966.

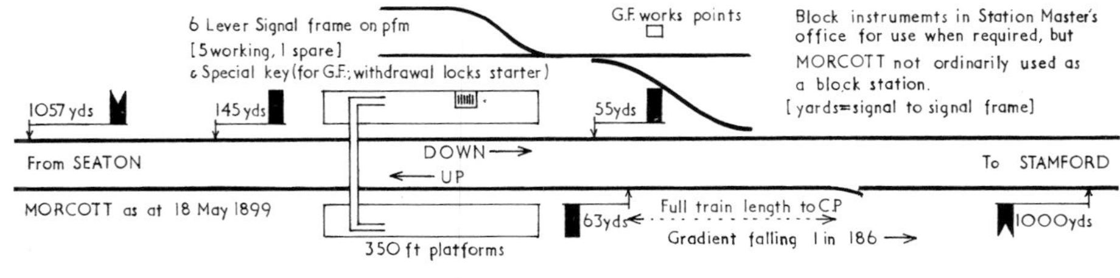

Opposite page The station forecourt on the last day of services, 4th June 1966.

Below Morcott Station looking towards Stamford, a few minutes before the last train, on 4th June 1966. Trees occupy the site of the long removed Up platform.

NARBOROUGH

16 June 1877

From LEICESTER
W.S.
L.C.
UP →
To NUNEATON
S.M.
M.B.
← DOWN
G.S.
40 0 40 80 120 160 200
Scale of Feet

1128 yds
To GLEN PARVA JCN.
DOWN →
← UP
L.C.
T.C.3
T.C.2
T.C.4
T.C.1
From CROFT SIDINGS
Up sidings
Siding 1
1459 yds
Siding 2
Siding 3
Siding 4
Ⓣ Treadle, 1¼ miles, operates Annunciator
21 Gate Stops
22 Gate Lock
22 Levers (Webb)
Spares 2,7,8,14,15.
One engine in steam
Train Staff
ENDERBY BRANCH
"stop & await instructions"
DOWN →
← UP

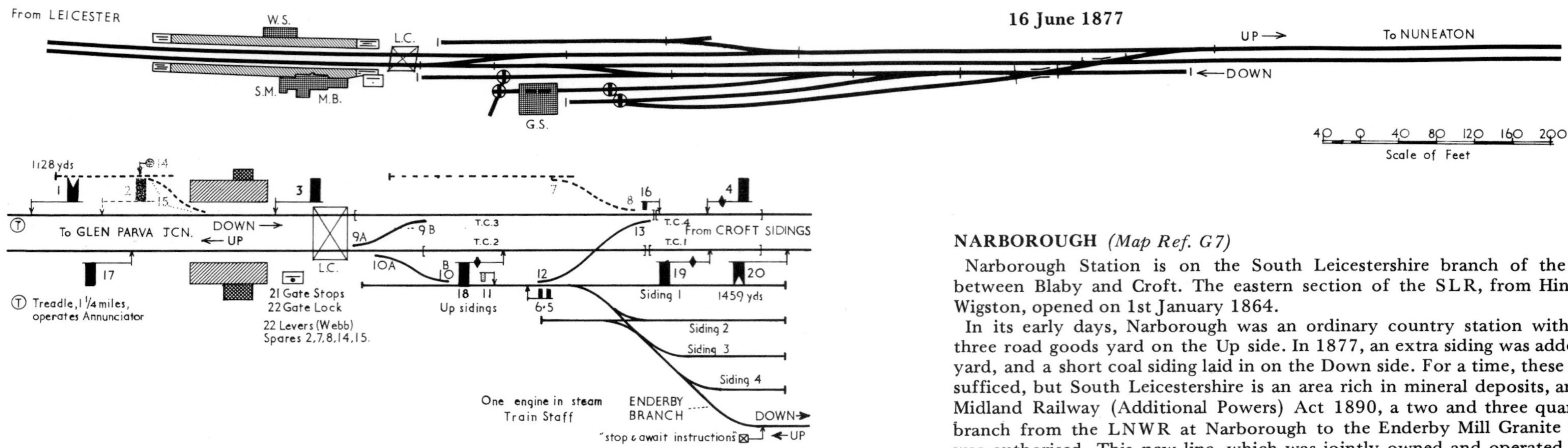

NARBOROUGH *(Map Ref. G7)*

Narborough Station is on the South Leicestershire branch of the LNWR between Blaby and Croft. The eastern section of the SLR, from Hinckley to Wigston, opened on 1st January 1864.

In its early days, Narborough was an ordinary country station with a small three road goods yard on the Up side. In 1877, an extra siding was added in the yard, and a short coal siding laid in on the Down side. For a time, these facilities sufficed, but South Leicestershire is an area rich in mineral deposits, and in the Midland Railway (Additional Powers) Act 1890, a two and three quarter mile branch from the LNWR at Narborough to the Enderby Mill Granite Quarries was authorised. This new line, which was jointly owned and operated, was for freight traffic only. It commenced at a set of exchange sidings beyond the LNWR yard. The old level crossing box became Narborough No. 2, and a new cabin, No. 1, was added to control the connections off the new branch on to the main line. The maximum number of wagons which was authorised on to the branch was fifty, and off the branch seventy five. Prior to 1923, both LNWR and Midland engines worked out to Enderby, and some of the freight rosters on the South Leicester branch were extremely complex. One required an LNWR six-coupled goods engine to be in traffic for almost 16 hours without any opportunity of going on shed.

The station closed to passengers on 4th March 1968, but re-opened as a result of local demand on 5th January 1970. Narborough No. 1 box was demolished, but No. 2 remained in being to control the remaining trackage at the station, including access to the Enderby branch, worked under the one engine in steam principle. A 'Stop and Await Instructions' board was provided at which trains off the branch came to a stand. If a shunter was on duty, enginemen worked according to his directions. If not, the fireman was required to telephone the signalman at the station cabin.

Note: The official length of the Enderby branch varies from 2 m 16 ch of a BR 1955 WTT to the 2 m 56 ch of the 1890 Act. The BOT record it as 2 m 18 ch in 1895, and BR appendices postulate 2 m 31 ch and 2 m 48 ch.

Narborough level crossing and goods yard looking towards Nuneaton. From left to right, the site of the short coal road, the main lines, Up siding, Enderby branch exchange sidings and goods shed. Although many LNWR goods sheds had flat-topped sliding or hinged doors, round-topped arches were to be found on the South Leicester branch, with hinged doors, as at Narborough, or sliding doors, as at Hinckley. The manner in which the goods yard track has been slewed, to provide clearance for the inner home signal, is unusual. It suggests that the predecessor to this signal could at one time have been placed on the far side of the Down line, perhaps combined with a Down signal, as was once common, or even in the yard itself, right away from the running lines.

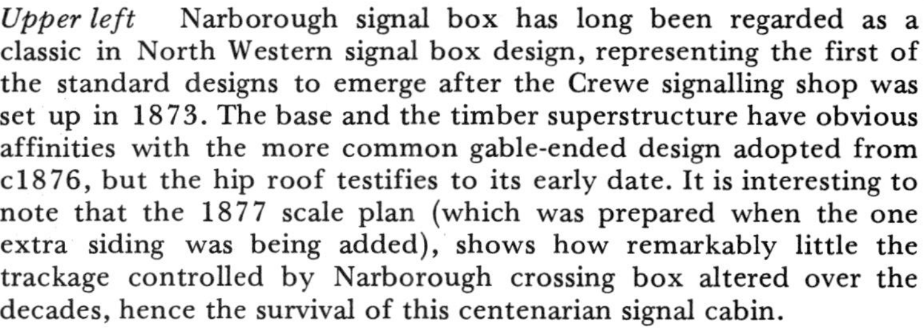

Upper left Narborough signal box has long been regarded as a classic in North Western signal box design, representing the first of the standard designs to emerge after the Crewe signalling shop was set up in 1873. The base and the timber superstructure have obvious affinities with the more common gable-ended design adopted from c1876, but the hip roof testifies to its early date. It is interesting to note that the 1877 scale plan (which was prepared when the one extra siding was being added), shows how remarkably little the trackage controlled by Narborough crossing box altered over the decades, hence the survival of this centenarian signal cabin.

Above Narborough Station shortly after re-opening to passengers in 1970. In LNWR days the Up direction followed usual London & Birmingham Railway policy of facing towards the main line. However, the South Leicestershire branch, although LNWR in origin, was increasingly absorbed into the Midland division of the LMS and LMR, and the designations reversed. The main buildings, on what had once been the Down platform, thus became the Up buildings in which guise they are illustrated. Such changes were highly confusing and served little real purpose.

Left The Station Master's house and station office looking from the diminutive forecourt. The buildings, which are devoid of ornament, reflect the economical policy pursued by the LNWR under Sir Richard Moon's long chairmanship. They cannot be compared in splendour to Atherstone, Wansford or Fenny Stratford, all of which were much earlier, but from the shareholders point of view, they were much better, for it is questionable whether the ornamentation really paid for itself in extra traffic, whatever its appeal to a later generation.

NEWPORT

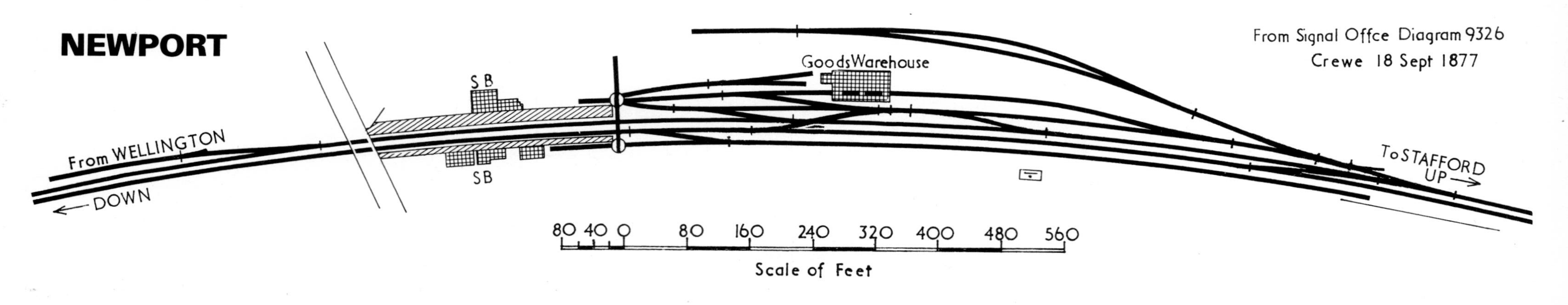

Newport Station looking from the Down platform towards Stafford on 10th September 1963. Contrasting this layout with the scale plan of 1877, there are a number of changes. The wagons turntables and square crossings have gone as might be expected, along with the lead to the Down turntable. The third cross over from the Up main to the yard (the one nearest the platform) has vanished, and the track nearest the running line has been made into a dead end instead of merging into a three way wagon turntable. The short siding reached off the Up turntable, with the strangely placed blades almost at the end, has also gone. It could hardly have been a loss as it must have been most awkward to work, and the additional trackage further down the yard was much more suited to operation.

NEWPORT *(Map Ref. 17)*

East Shropshire is renowned as one of the cradles of the industrial revolution, and one of the companies constructing railways in that area dated not from the railway age, but from the canal era. The Shropshire Union Railways & Canal Co., although not known by that title until 1846, dated back to 1793, when its parent, the Ellesmere & Chester Canal came into being. The SUR proposed in the 1840s to construct some 200 miles of railway, using, in many places, its own canal formations, but all that actually materialised was a 29 mile route between Stafford and Shrewsbury, and of this, the Shrewsbury–Wellington section was jointly owned!

The SUR Act was passed on 3rd August 1846, and the line opened on 1st June 1849, by which time, the SUR had been leased by the LNWR. Between Shrewsbury and Wellington, the new line carried GW as well as LNWR traffic and was correspondingly busy, but east of Wellington, traffic was much lighter and the places served en route, other than Newport, of minor importance. Even Newport, with a population of under 4,000, could not be described as a major centre, and passenger services ceased over the Stafford–Wellington section on 7th September 1964. Goods workings east of Newport came to an end in 1966 and freight traffic over the Donnington–Newport section on 22nd November 1969, so severing the town's rail link after 120 years.

In 1895, nine trains called at Newport in each direction. These were mostly locals, but did include a few semi-fasts, whose only stop between Stafford and Wellington it was. As the station was on the edge of town, 'Omnibuses and Flys' met all trains, except the night mails and on Sundays. As the westbound mail ran through at 2.27am, the omission was understandable!

In 1927, there were ten westbound and twelve eastbound services; once again the majority were locals.

Below left The main buildings on the Up platform, looking towards Stafford from the forecourt. Their construction spans a considerable period, the rectangular two storey building on the left being much older, with its classical upper storey windows, frieze and pantiled roof. The single storey extension displays the familiar LNWR window which could be found on timber, pre-fabricated and brick structures, with an elongated central pane and narrow side panes. The footbridge, on the right, with its timber and corrugated iron stairway is also of interest, adding up to a diverse mixture of periods and styles.

Warehouse
Siding 2
Grain silo
"Stop and await instructions"
Engine BV & 47 wagons
(motor worked)
1277 yds to home
Gong
Siding 1
200yd
T.C.1
From WELLINGTON
T.C.2154
T.C.2155
UP MAIN →
← DOWN MAIN
To STAFFORD
Down siding
R 26
28 Levers
LNWR Tumbler
Spares 5,8,9,12,13,14,18,24.
NOTE
7 gong to platform
R 26 banner repeater
22 clearance bar
1034 yds to home

NEWPORT

Below right Looking towards Stafford from the footbridge with yet more variation in style apparent, even the construction of the canopies differing in this view. The Down canopy is in two separate sections, one much lower than the other. This illustration provides an excellent opportunity to study this particular pattern of LNWR valancing (how many modellers remember the painting date!), and also the pantiled roof of the original block. Today all has gone.

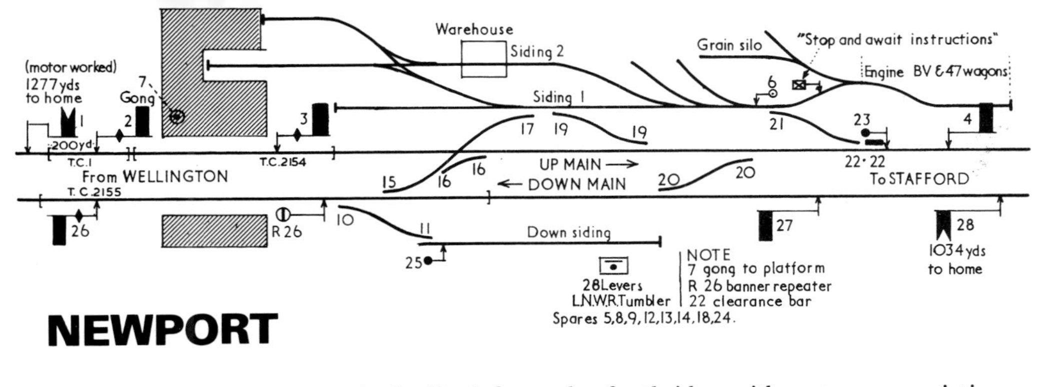

Right Looking from the Down platform towards Stafford in September 1963. As with almost every aspect of Newport Station, its piecemeal ancestry is immediately apparent, the most obvious feature being the remarkable difference in window levels between the new single storey block on the Up platform and the old rectangular building, the windows of which are so much lower that they suggest that the station was originally provided with a very modest platform indeed. It is surprising however, how well the platform canopy holds such a dissimilar building together. The long high brick wall to the right of the building was typical of early stations, where the main building was often positioned centrally with a symmetrical wall at each side. It is quite likely that a similar wall once ran across the site of the later structure, which, it should be noted, post-dates the 1877 survey.

NEWPORT

Lower right It is frequently forgotten that many stations, even quite small ones, were provided with additional entrances for the convenience of passengers, and Newport was no exception. The main approach was via the forecourt, but a subsidiary approach fronted the main road bridge which crossed the line by the Wellington end of the platforms. This led on to the passenger footbridge, and even in the early 'sixties, one could still visualise a spic and span carriage and pair turning into the tiny forecourt to pick up or deliver one of the line's more affluent travellers.

Below The cattle dock and goods shed looking towards Stafford from beyond the platform wall referred to above.

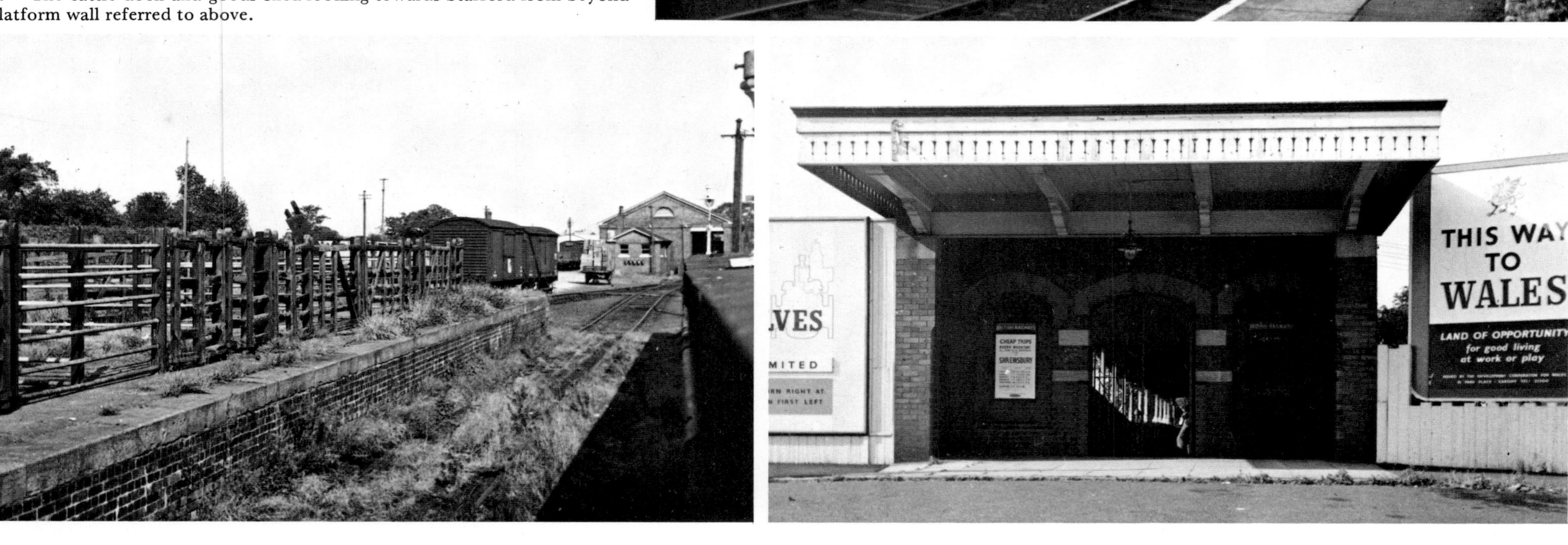

PADBURY

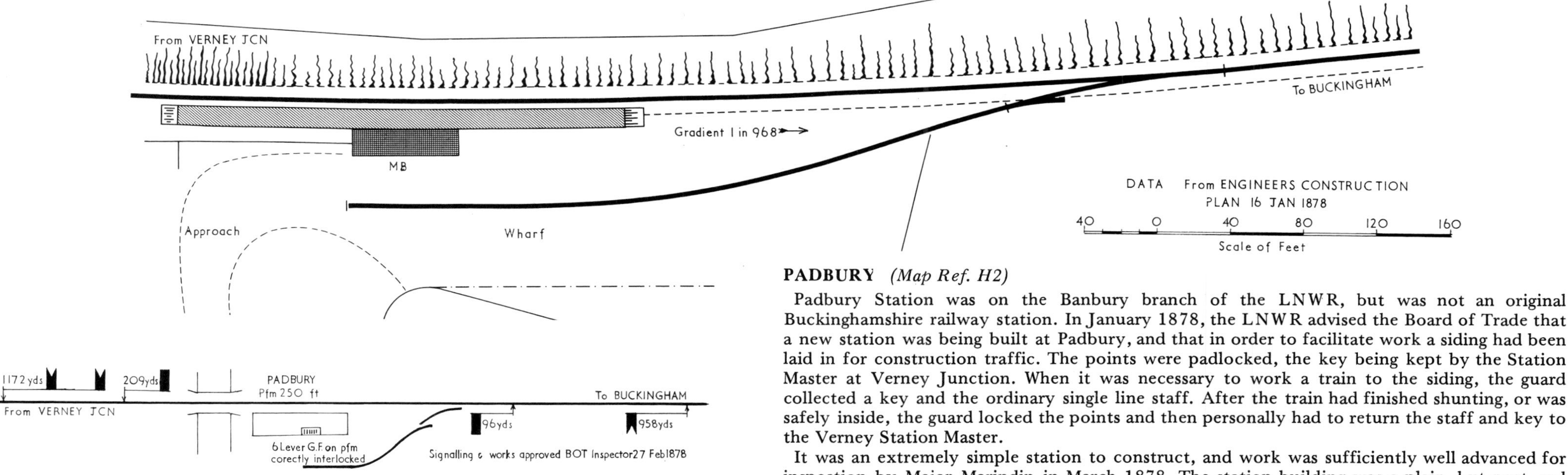

PADBURY *(Map Ref. H2)*

Padbury Station was on the Banbury branch of the LNWR, but was not an original Buckinghamshire railway station. In January 1878, the LNWR advised the Board of Trade that a new station was being built at Padbury, and that in order to facilitate work a siding had been laid in for construction traffic. The points were padlocked, the key being kept by the Station Master at Verney Junction. When it was necessary to work a train to the siding, the guard collected a key and the ordinary single line staff. After the train had finished shunting, or was safely inside, the guard locked the points and then personally had to return the staff and key to the Verney Station Master.

It was an extremely simple station to construct, and work was sufficiently well advanced for inspection by Major Marindin in March 1878. The station building was a plain, but neat, red brick structure without awning, and was situated on a 250ft. long platform. The running signals and siding connections were worked from a six lever ground frame locked by the train staff.

The station closed to goods on 6th January 1964, and to passengers on 7th September 1964.

Below Looking from the end of the platform towards Verney Junction in 1966. The goods yard had gone by this time, but the site of the ground frame can be made out from the opening in the platform for the point rodding and signal wires. Ornamental shrubs along the side of the building and the ruins of a once delightful flower garden reveal that nature is fast gaining the ground now that there is no one to tend the bushes and plants.

Below Looking from the station approach towards Banbury in 1966. The station altered little throughout its 86 year life, and apart from the grounds, unkempt in this post-closure scene, it must have looked very much this way to Major Marindin back in March 1878.

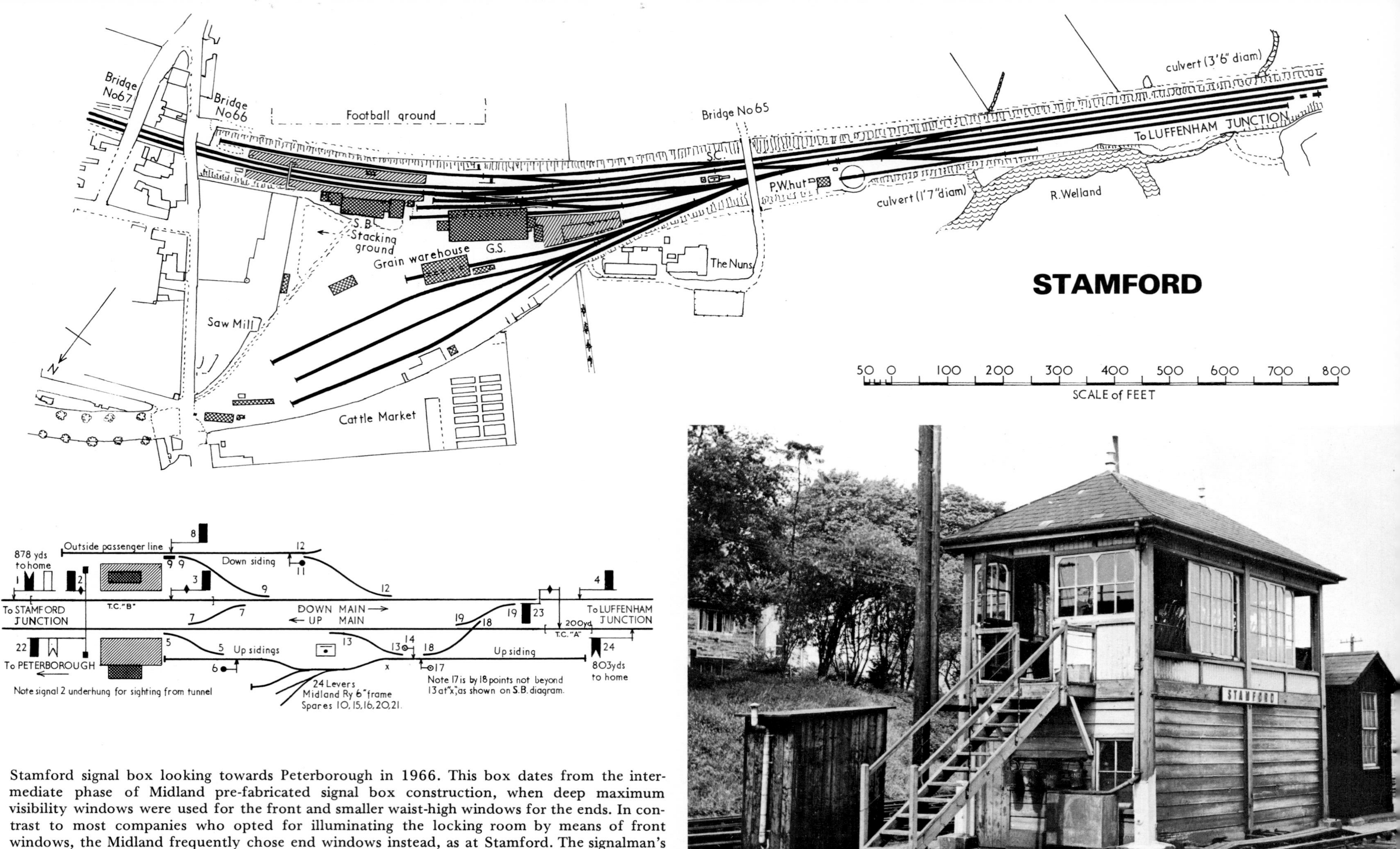

Stamford signal box looking towards Peterborough in 1966. This box dates from the intermediate phase of Midland pre-fabricated signal box construction, when deep maximum visibility windows were used for the front and smaller waist-high windows for the ends. In contrast to most companies who opted for illuminating the locking room by means of front windows, the Midland frequently chose end windows instead, as at Stamford. The signalman's closet is visible to the left of the steps and the enginemen's hut to the right of the box. The near corner posts have both been repaired, a new section being spliced in at the bottom to combat rot – the Achilles heel of Midland boxes.

STAMFORD *(Map Ref. L8)*

The MR branch from Syston to Peterborough was opened in three sections (as recounted under Melton Mowbray). The Stamford–Peterborough portion came into use on 2nd October 1846, but as the Midland did not have access to this part of its system until the line was completed as a through route on 1st May 1848, the eastern section was worked first by the LNWR, and later by the Eastern Counties Railway.

From 1851, the LNWR operated through Stamford once more, this time reaching the town via their own Rugby–Luffenham branch. The LNWR trains continued on to Peterborough over Midland metals, but in 1879 the North Western opened a cut-off between Seaton and Wansford and the Stamford service became an unimportant shuttle working from Seaton Junction. From 1856, the Midland station was subject to competition from the Stamford & Essendine Railway, whose two branches served Essendine on the GNR main line and Wansford on the LNWR. Neither was particularly important, and the effect on the MR, with its through services to Peterborough and Leicester, was minimal.

The main buildings at Stamford (Town) Station were in the MR 'Baronial' theme, and both they and the shelter on the opposite platform boasted highly ornate (and quite dissimilar) awnings.

The MR service was of the order of five to seven trains each way, augmented by the occasional short-working from the Leicester direction. The LNWR service was similar, five or six trains between Stamford and Seaton Junction. Under the LMS this level was maintained, though the occasional through train, including certain of the Harwich–Birmingham boat trains, was routed via the town instead of over the Wansford line.

The Seaton service ceased in 1966, but Stamford remains open as an intermediate station on the MR Syston–Peterborough route.

In the introduction, reference was made to occasional errors in signal box diagrams. At Stamford, the reader is referred to No. 17 shunt signal, which was shown at 'X' on the signal box diagram, but was, in reality, as shown on the signalling 'B' plan. The very unlikeliness of the 'X' siting persuaded the authors to photograph the signal concerned!

Above Stamford Station looking towards Luffenham. The commodious goods shed is visible between the platforms, whilst the signal cabin is just visible in the upper left corner. The DMU in the foreground has arrived from Seaton Junction on the last day of service, 4th June 1966, and will transfer to the outside line until departure time. Note the platform barrow by the Down shelter.

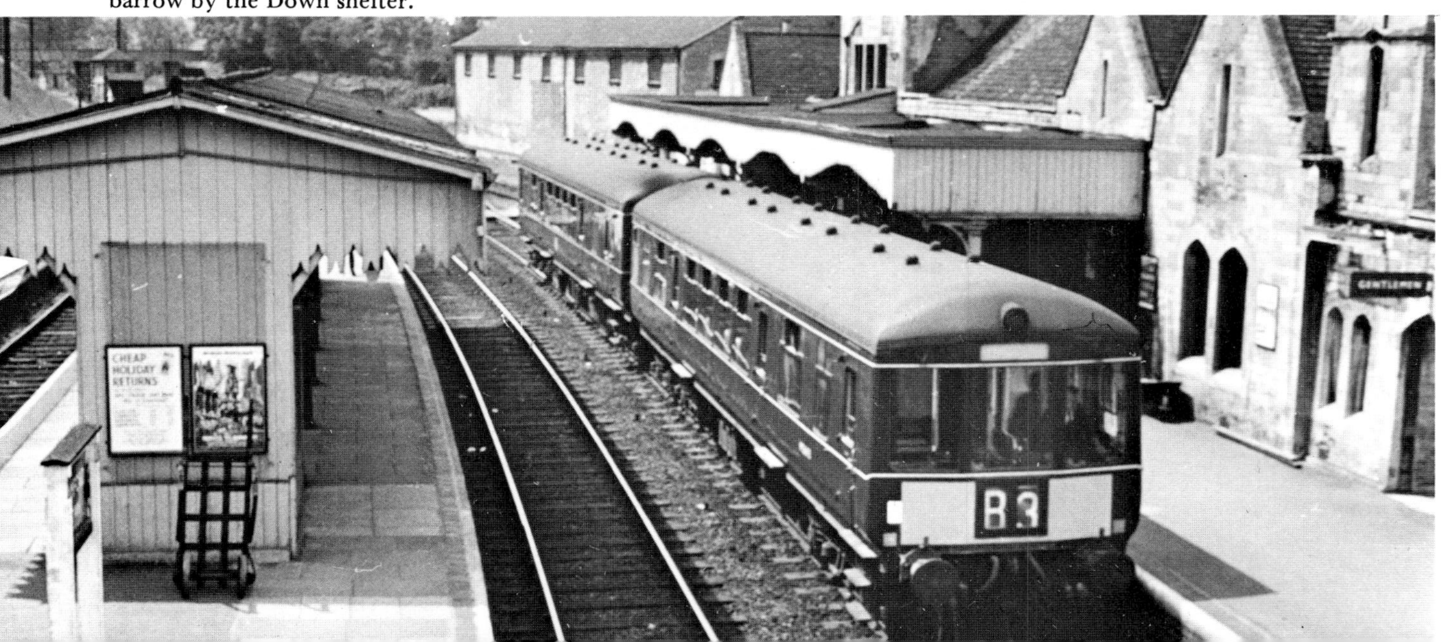

Below Looking towards Peterborough. The main buildings on the Up platform are customarily attributed to Sancton Wood, and are to a Tudor motif with a conical turret with a weather vane bearing the Syston & Peterborough initials. The LNWR services from Stamford to Seaton Junction used the near or outside line.

STONE

Above This LMS survey includes several unusual features, such as the isolated section of track by the stables and the wagon turntable unusually close to the cross over by the goods shed. Freight facilities are usually grouped together, but at Stone, there are sidings off the Up and Down Norton Bridge lines and off the Up and Down Colwich, i.e. all four possibilities, plus a private siding off the down headshunt! There are even three goods sheds!

Below The front elevation of Hunt's Jacobean station buildings looking from the 'V' of the junction towards Stoke. It is instructive to study the different treatment accorded to the centre gable compared to the side gables. The telephone kiosk, though useful, does not contribute to the symmetry, nor does the 1940 LMS concrete footbridge on the left.

Below The lamp hut on the Up Stafford platform looking to the approach road.

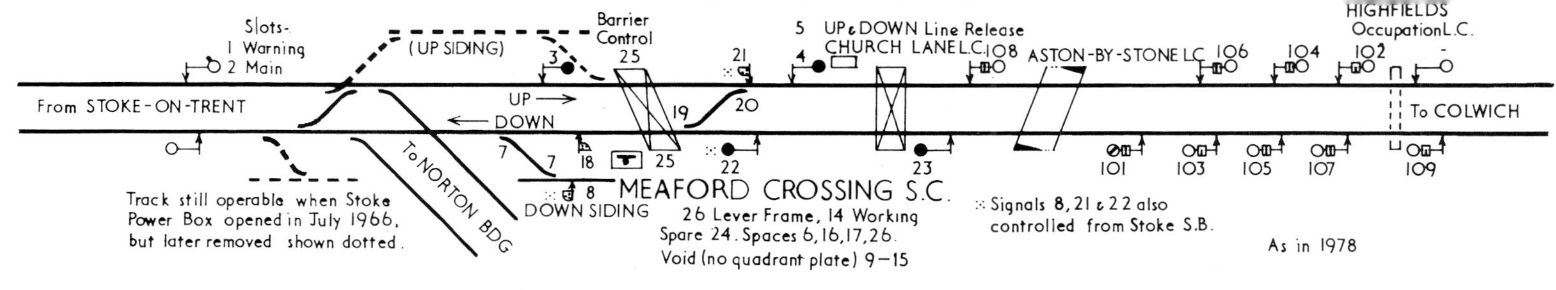

STONE *(Map Ref. T8)*

Stone Station is located at the divergence of the former North Staffordshire Railway, Norton Bridge–Stoke and Colwich–Stone lines, the two principal 'Knotty' arteries to and from the south. Both lines were authorised under the three acts of 26th June 1846 which created the backbone of the NSR. The Norton Bridge–Stoke route opened to passengers on 17th April 1848, and the Colwich route on 1st May 1849. Despite its important strategic location, there were no further significant developments affecting Stone. Local services on the Norton Bridge line continue to call at Stone, but the platforms on the Colwich line have been cut back, and the route only carries through traffic.

Stone is a modest town on the edge of the potteries, and the station is quite well situated, the principal approach being up a long drive paralleling the Colwich line. The main buildings front on to a small forecourt, and were designed by H. A. Hunt, who was also responsible for Stoke Station. They are in the Jacobean style and possess great vigour. LMS and BR additions, most notably a concrete footbridge have not been to the same aesthetic standard.

In its formative years, the NSR provided 4–6 trains on the Norton Bridge route and a couple to Colwich. Although local traffic was sparse on the latter route, the diversion of a number of LNWR Euston–Manchester expresses over this section provided much-needed traffic, though through traffic was of course its object when built. The introduction of steam rail motor services in 1905 augmented the already intensive train service around Stoke, but had a limited effect on Stone, as the station was on the fringe of the potteries 'suburban' network, and of railcar workings. Provision was made for terminating trains, and these survived into LMS days. By the late thirties, there were 18–20 trains south to Norton Bridge and Stafford, but 24–25 north to Stoke. The Colwich line saw a couple of workings in each direction. By 1944 the Colwich route had declined to one through local train and one running part way, and the intermediate stations were closed to passengers on 6th January 1947.

Below left Looking from the Down Stoke platform towards Colwich and Stafford. The footbridge was rebuilt by BR to provide added clearance for the 25 kV overhead, but retains the massive and rather crude lines of the LMS design, whose pillars it uses.

Below right Meaford Crossing box, with the approach drive in the background. The ornamental bargeboards were a feature of many NSR signal boxes.

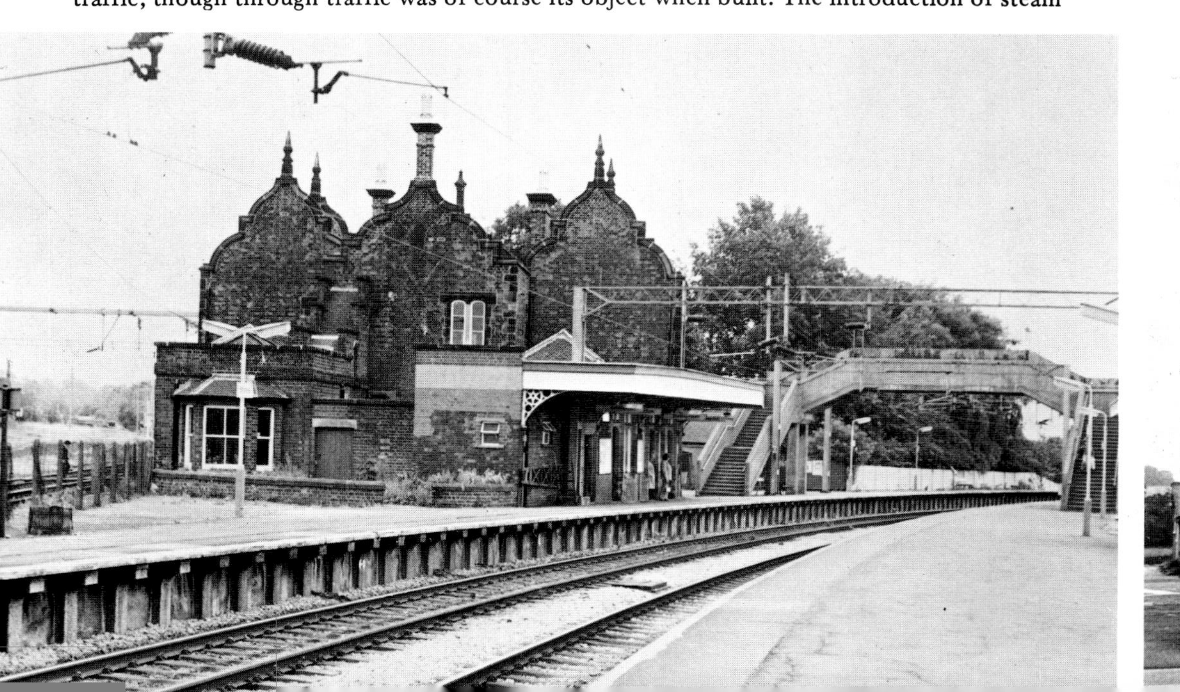

SUTTON COLDFIELD *(Map Ref. D7)*

Proposals to construct a railway from Birmingham to Sutton Coldfield were heard as early as the 1840s, but it was not until 1859 that real progress was made, with the LNWR obtaining powers for a branch from Aston to Sutton. This opened on 2nd June 1862 and brought Sutton firmly into the West Midlands suburban area. Population increased dramatically and in 1880, an extension to the cathedral city of Lichfield was authorised. This opened to goods in September 1884, and to passengers on 15th December. A new passenger station, on a 15 chain radius curve, replaced the original one, and the new line plunged into a 171 yard long tunnel immediately beyond the end of the platforms.

After the Lichfield extension was opened, a proportion of trains ran right through, others terminating at Sutton or the next station to the north, Four Oaks (q.v.).

On Sunday 23rd January 1955, Sutton Station was the scene of a serious derailment in which seventeen lives were lost. Diversionary working was in force on the Midland Derby–Gloucester main line, and the 12.15 York–Bristol express was diverted via Sutton. The train, driven by a conductor-driver who knew the route, entered the station curve at 55-60mph instead of the regulation 30mph, and was derailed. The reason for the excessive speed was never ascertained.

Goods facilities were withdrawn from Sutton on 1st May 1967, and a Motor Rail terminal for services to Scotland and the West Country established in the yard. The authors travelled from the terminal a short time after it had been opened on the Stirling service. Sadly, Sutton (and also Newton-le-Willows) was closed in 1972 in favour of Crewe, which was a poor substitute for the West Midlands area. The sidings and loading facilities were still in situ in 1976, but have since been lifted.

The station continues to handle ordinary passenger traffic.

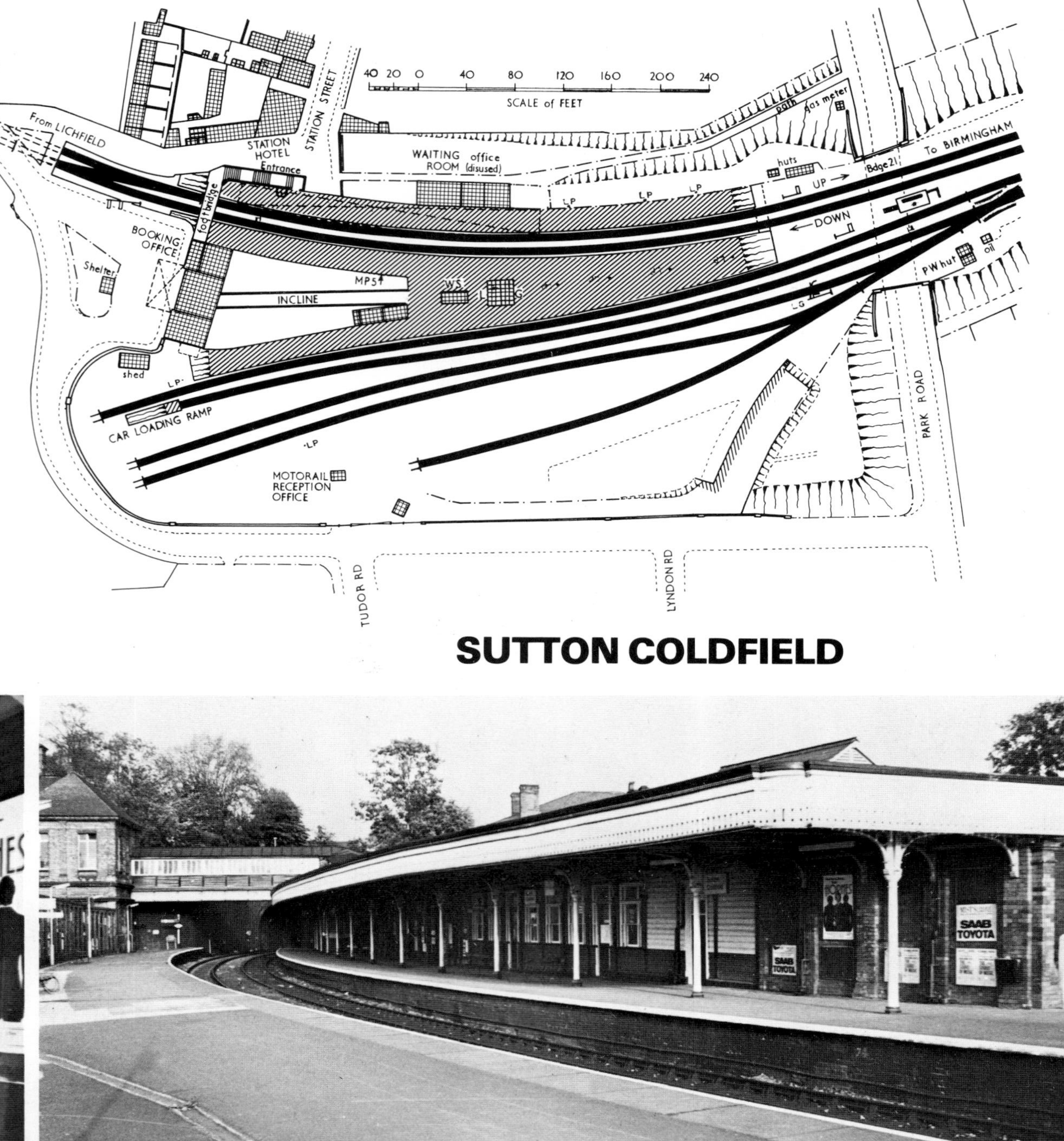

Opposite page left 'Underneath the arches' – looking towards Lichfield from the Up platform. In contrast to many stations previously described, there is a measure of uniformity in this arcade.

Opposite page right Looking, on a Sunday afternoon, towards Lichfield from the Down side. Much of this platform was swept by wreckage from the 1955 crash. Had the accident happened when the station was in use (it was closed on a Sunday) the consequences could have been even more terrible.

Right Seldom does one see a scene like this on a prototype station, with the tracks curving so sharply out of sight. For a corner station on a model railway, the station has much to commend it, even including a convenient tunnel!

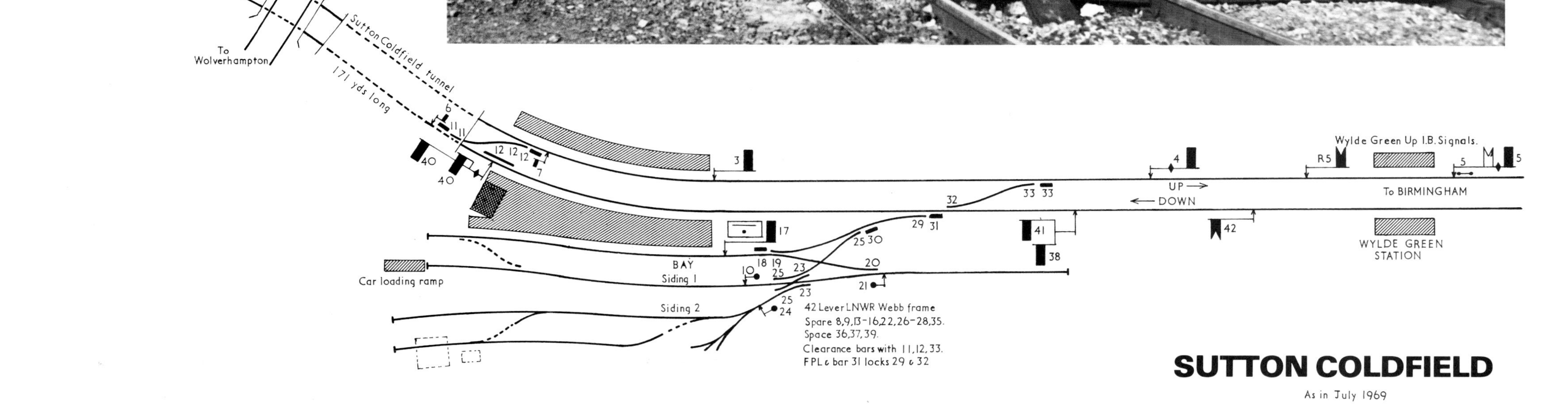

SUTTON COLDFIELD

As in July 1969

SUTTON PARK

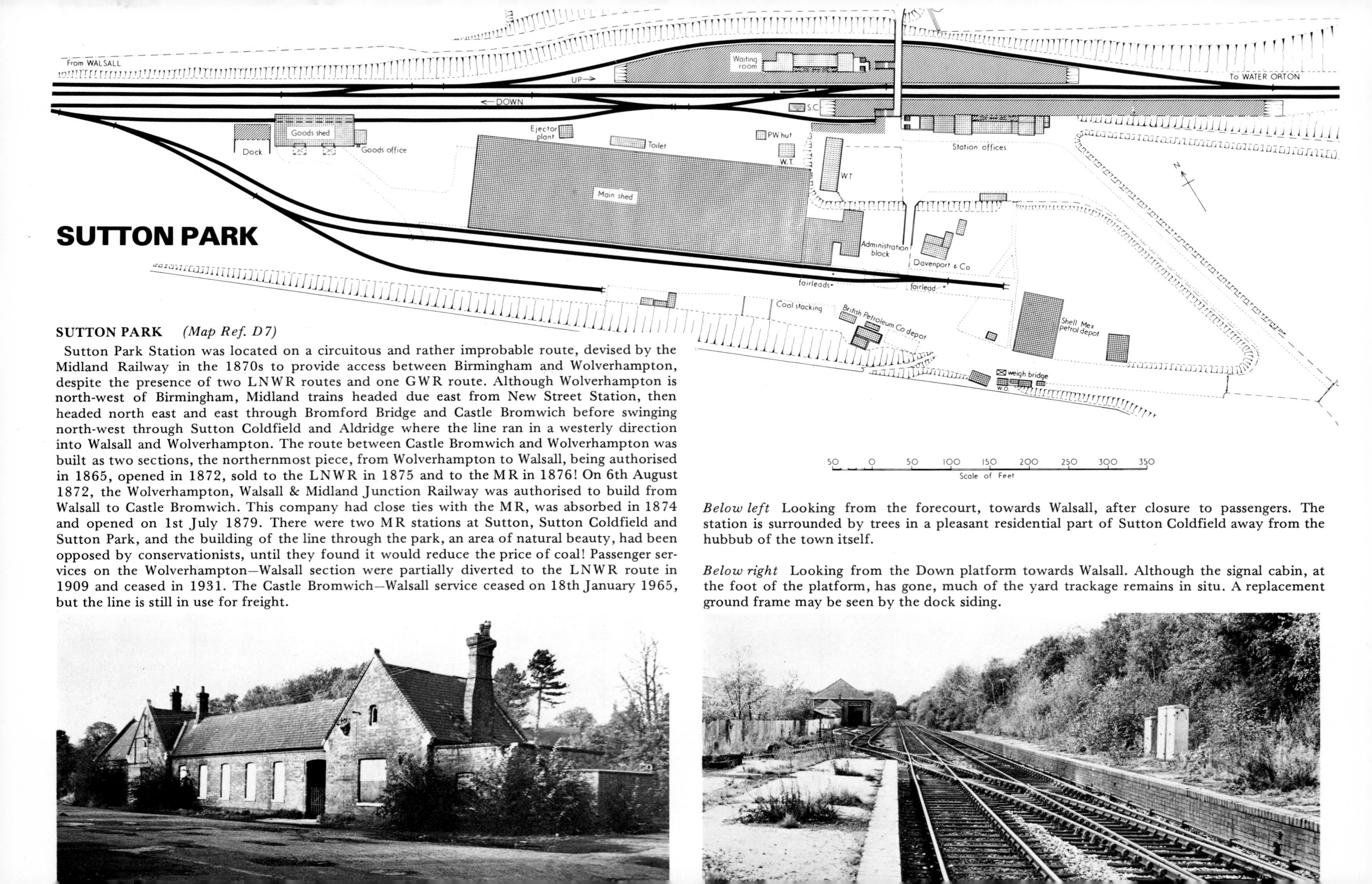

SUTTON PARK *(Map Ref. D7)*

Sutton Park Station was located on a circuitous and rather improbable route, devised by the Midland Railway in the 1870s to provide access between Birmingham and Wolverhampton, despite the presence of two LNWR routes and one GWR route. Although Wolverhampton is north-west of Birmingham, Midland trains headed due east from New Street Station, then headed north east and east through Bromford Bridge and Castle Bromwich before swinging north-west through Sutton Coldfield and Aldridge where the line ran in a westerly direction into Walsall and Wolverhampton. The route between Castle Bromwich and Wolverhampton was built as two sections, the northernmost piece, from Wolverhampton to Walsall, being authorised in 1865, opened in 1872, sold to the LNWR in 1875 and to the MR in 1876! On 6th August 1872, the Wolverhampton, Walsall & Midland Junction Railway was authorised to build from Walsall to Castle Bromwich. This company had close ties with the MR, was absorbed in 1874 and opened on 1st July 1879. There were two MR stations at Sutton, Sutton Coldfield and Sutton Park, and the building of the line through the park, an area of natural beauty, had been opposed by conservationists, until they found it would reduce the price of coal! Passenger services on the Wolverhampton–Walsall section were partially diverted to the LNWR route in 1909 and ceased in 1931. The Castle Bromwich–Walsall service ceased on 18th January 1965, but the line is still in use for freight.

Below left Looking from the forecourt, towards Walsall, after closure to passengers. The station is surrounded by trees in a pleasant residential part of Sutton Coldfield away from the hubbub of the town itself.

Below right Looking from the Down platform towards Walsall. Although the signal cabin, at the foot of the platform, has gone, much of the yard trackage remains in situ. A replacement ground frame may be seen by the dock siding.

TAMWORTH

Above Looking towards Derby from the end of the Up Midland platform, with a Midland water column, notice and signal in the foreground.

Below The Up low level buildings looking towards Stafford. These, and a magnificent twin storey building on the Down side, were in a lively Jacobean style by John William Livock, architect to the Trent Valley line (see Atherstone). The shadow of one of Livock's splendid gables is visible in the left foreground, whilst one of the graceful columns supporting the LNW canopy is seen in silhouette on the right hand side.

Above Tamworth High Level, looking south, in 1911 showing the Down Midland platform and lifts, the further lift being largely obscured by the nearer structure. The LNWR line passed beneath the MR between these two lifts.

Below Tamworth Low Level in 1953, looking north. The structure on the extreme right is the Down Midland to Up LNWR mail lift which dominated the previous view. The pinnacles of Livock's twin storey building for the LNWR station are just visible on the left, beyond the bridge carrying the Midland main line. The view is taken from the Down LNW platform.

TAMWORTH *(Map Ref. E8)*

The railway facilities at Tamworth comprise two separate stations at right angles to one another, connected by lifts for mail interchange and by a sharply-curved and steeply-graded spur for exchange of vehicles. In point of age, premier place must go to Tamworth (High Level) Station, which is located on the Birmingham–Derby main line of the Midland Railway. The B&DJR was authorised in 1836 and opened to regular traffic on 12th August 1839. Tamworth was one of the original stations, and was a short distance north of the Anker Viaduct. The B&DJR was absorbed into the Midland Railway in the great amalgamation of 1844.

In July 1845, the Trent Valley Railway was incorporated to build a line from Rugby to Stafford. The TVR was taken over by the LNWR, and opened on 15th September 1847. The LNWR line ran at right angles to, and passed beneath the MR station by means of a bridge. A chord line from the LNWR to the Midland was completed as early as June 1847.

Tamworth was a small market town, but its location astride the West Coast and MR Bristol main lines gave it immense strategic importance as a postal exchange point. Mails were first conveyed over the B&DJR in 1840, but it was several years later that the TPO services became properly organised. In the early days the Midland TPO ran from Rugby to Newcastle and connections had to be made via the Rugby–Birmingham line for the south west. In 1850, a Gloucester–Tamworth service was established, and two years later came a through Gloucester–Tamworth–Newcastle working. The inauguration of a separate West Coast postal train, in 1885, was a measure of the growth in traffic. Prior to this time, the postal had carried a limited number of passengers. In 1927, the Down postal left Euston at 8.30pm. It connected with the northbound Midland TPO at Tamworth about 10.40pm, whilst the Up West Coast postal connected with the southbound Midland TPO some hours later. Apart from these workings, there were various railway and GPO parcels exchanges, and the night shift at Tamworth was often hard pressed to cope. When the new Tamworth

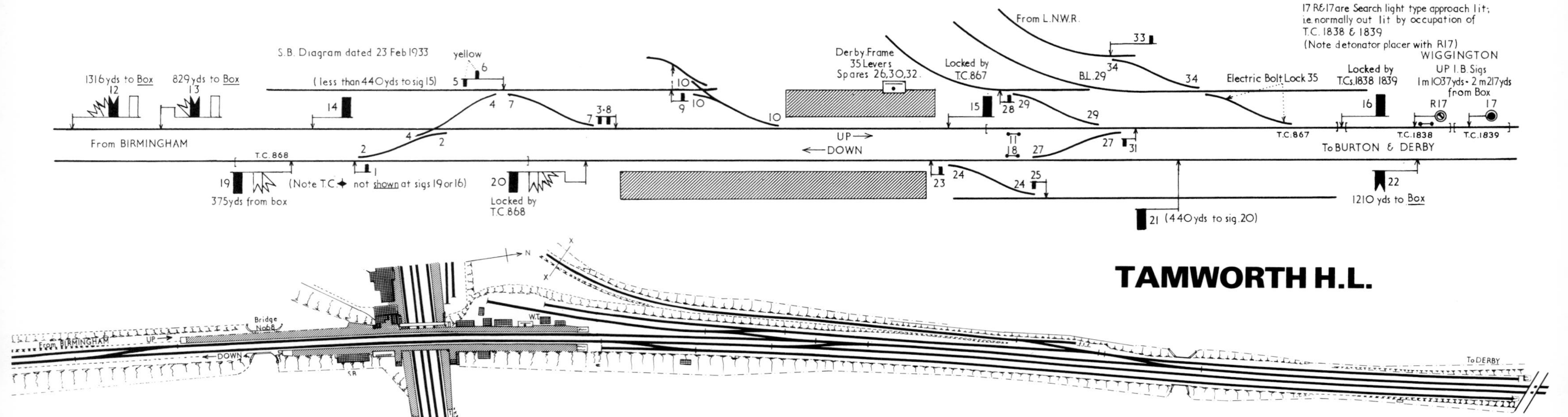

The 1935 'B' plan presents a number of interesting features. The Wiggington Up IB was a searchlight approach-lit colour light. In the early days of colour light signalling, two basic types emerged, the Multi-unit type with a separate bulb and lens for each aspect, and the Search-light type which had one bulb and lens.

The aspect shown was determined by the position of a moving spectacle glass, as in traditional semaphore signalling. Approach lighting was applied to certain IB signals and reduced power consumption and bulb wear. The lights in the signal were not illuminated until a train entered upon the track circuit, in advance of the signal controlling the entrance to the intermediate block section. In the case of Tamworth, the Wiggington signal was illuminated by the occupation of TCs 1838-1839. The IB distant was automatically returned to danger upon the passage of the train, and the IB home released by the block instruments.

A detonator placer was provided in conjunction with the IB distant, and in the event of the failure of the signal light, this would operate. Normally however, it was held off the rails, and the position of the detonator placer, along with the aspect the signal was showing, the proving of the lamp and the track circuit indications, were all detected in the box. In the event of the TCs 1838-1839 becoming occupied and then clear with 17 (the IB) in the ON position, a train running away on right line alarm bell sounded in the cabin.

With its convenient interchange between the Midland and LNWR services, Tamworth secured a passenger service which was far better than might otherwise have been the case. On the Midland division, the LMS provided some 18 trains each way including a number of expresses.

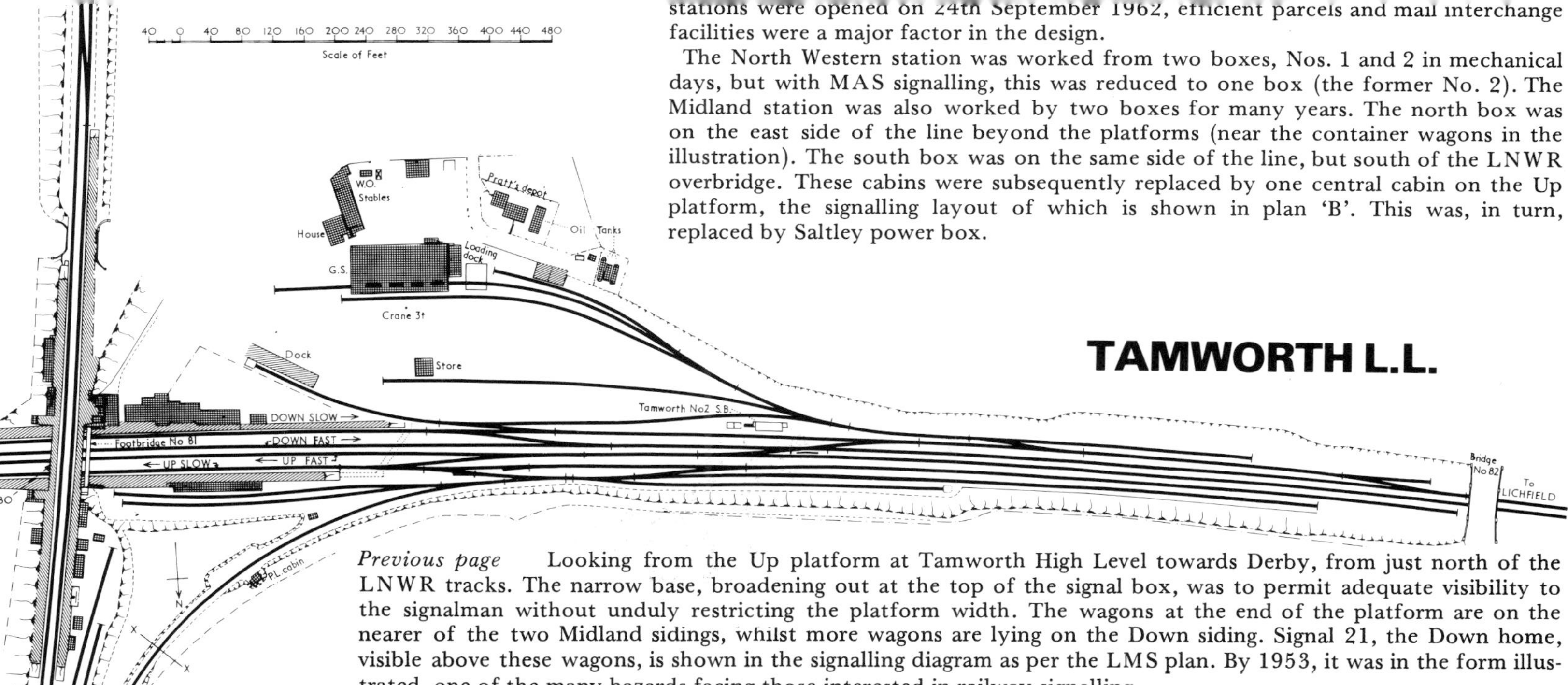

stations were opened on 24th September 1962, efficient parcels and mail interchange facilities were a major factor in the design.

The North Western station was worked from two boxes, Nos. 1 and 2 in mechanical days, but with MAS signalling, this was reduced to one box (the former No. 2). The Midland station was also worked by two boxes for many years. The north box was on the east side of the line beyond the platforms (near the container wagons in the illustration). The south box was on the same side of the line, but south of the LNWR overbridge. These cabins were subsequently replaced by one central cabin on the Up platform, the signalling layout of which is shown in plan 'B'. This was, in turn, replaced by Saltley power box.

Previous page Looking from the Up platform at Tamworth High Level towards Derby, from just north of the LNWR tracks. The narrow base, broadening out at the top of the signal box, was to permit adequate visibility to the signalman without unduly restricting the platform width. The wagons at the end of the platform are on the nearer of the two Midland sidings, whilst more wagons are lying on the Down siding. Signal 21, the Down home, visible above these wagons, is shown in the signalling diagram as per the LMS plan. By 1953, it was in the form illustrated, one of the many hazards facing those interested in railway signalling.

Below Looking from the Up Midland platform along the LNWR station towards Lichfield and the north. The freight train occupies the Up exchange siding nearest the running lines, the other roads being already occupied by wagons. The chord to the Midland station commenced just beyond the right hand platform end.

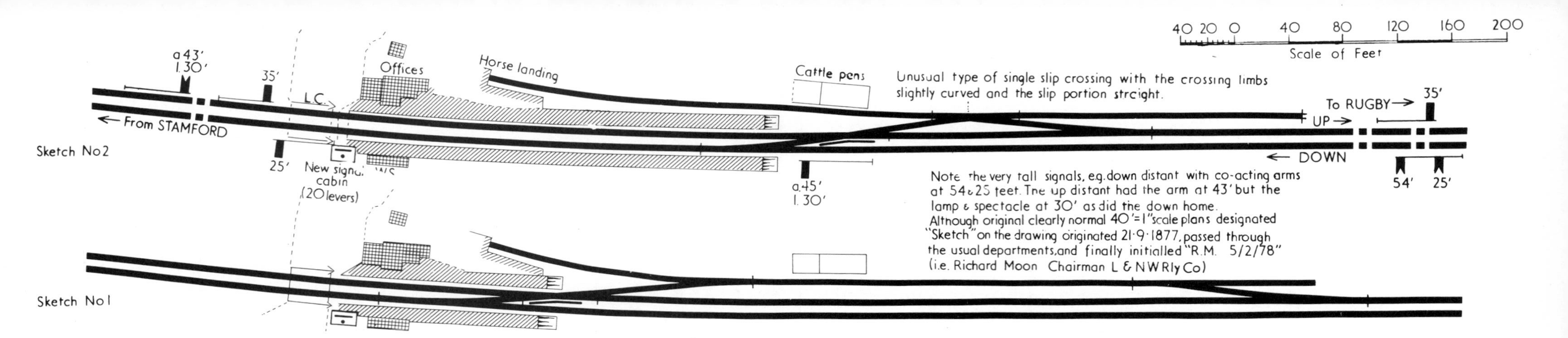
40 20 0 40 80 120 160 200
Scale of Feet
a43'
1.30'
35'
L.C.
Offices
Horse landing
Cattle pens
Unusual type of single slip crossing with the crossing limbs slightly curved and the slip portion straight.
To RUGBY→
35'
UP→
← From STAMFORD
Sketch No2
25'
New signal cabin (20 levers)
a45'
1.30'
← DOWN
54'
25'
Note the very tall signals, e.g. down distant with co-acting arms at 54 & 25 feet. The up distant had the arm at 43' but the lamp & spectacle at 30' as did the down home.
Although original clearly normal 40'=1" scale plans designated "Sketch" on the drawing originated 21·9·1877, passed through the usual departments, and finally initialled "R.M. 5/2/78"
(i.e. Richard Moon Chairman L & NWRly Co)
Sketch No1

THEDDINGWORTH (*Map Ref. H6*)

Construction of the Rugby & Stamford branch was approved by the proprietors of the London & Birmingham Railway in February 1846, and work began the following month, although parliamentary approval was not secured until June. Theddingworth was one of the original stations on the Rugby—Market Harborough section which was formally opened on 27th April 1850. Although some trains may have run on 29th April, in conjunction with the Market Harborough fair, timetabled services commenced on 1st May, with three trains each way. The Rugby & Stamford line joined the MR at Luffenham (q.v.), LNW trains reaching Peterborough via Midland metals. The Rugby—Market Harborough section was originally single, but by 1877 the LNWR was considering doubling the branch, and a series of station plans were prepared. The original proposal for Theddingworth, sketch No. 1, envisaged two short platforms each about 150ft. long with access to the yard from both directions, with over 260ft. in the clear accessible from either direction, and with a short side and end loading road as well. The yard would have been convenient to work, but the Up end cross over would have been more than 250 yards from the box, and second thoughts prevailed. The platforms, as envisaged, would also have been unacceptable, and the length was more than doubled to about 300ft., the Up and Down cross over, as a result, being moved towards Rugby. The effect of these two changes was to create the awkward layout shown (a feature which appeared at other Rugby & Stamford line stations). Had there been no level crossing, this would have been unnecessary, as the box could have been positioned at the Rugby end of the platforms or part way down the yard. Other than by resorting to a level crossing ground frame and signal box, this was impracticable at Theddingworth, so that yard shunting was ever after hampered.

Under Morcott it will have been noted that the date of singling of that section commonly quoted is in error (by over 20 years). By a strange coincidence, the date of *doubling* of another part of the Rugby & Stamford line, from Rugby to Market Harborough is also incorrect, albeit only by a few months! Some sources give a July 1878 date, but on 9th December 1878 the LNWR notified the Board of Trade that the works would be ready for inspection in a few days time, 'As the new works cannot be made ready for inspection without connecting the points and signals to the signal cabins, and as they must necessarily pass into use from such time, the new line will, in effect, be opened on the 16th inst'. The doubled section commenced at Rugby Locomotive Junction, 580 yards south of the booking office, and ran for 17 miles 284 yards to Market Harborough. Theddingworth was 12 miles 32 chains from Rugby and received a 20 lever box (7 spares or spaces).

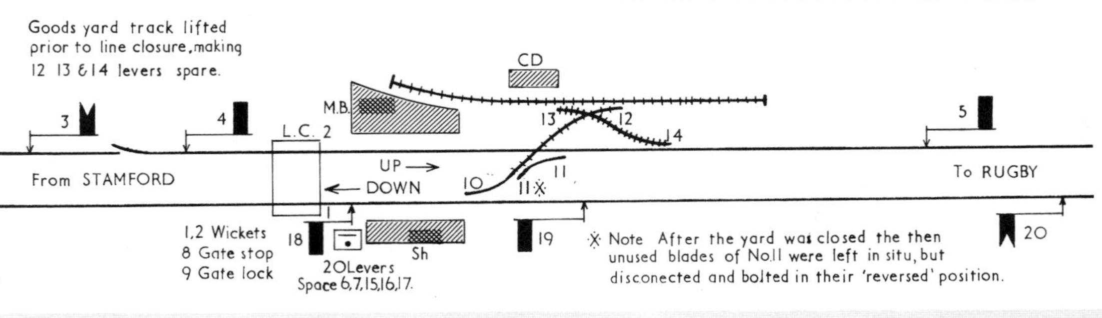
THEDDINGWORTH
Goods yard track lifted prior to line closure, making 12 13 & 14 levers spare.
CD
M.B.
3
4
L.C. 2
13
12
14
5
From STAMFORD
UP→
← DOWN
10
11
11※
To RUGBY
1
1,2 Wickets
8 Gate stop
9 Gate lock
18
20Levers
Space 6,7,15,16,17.
Sh
19
※ Note After the yard was closed the then unused blades of No.11 were left in situ, but disconected and bolted in their 'reversed' position.
20

In the 1890s eight trains traversed the Rugby–Market Harborough line, four or five of which called at the minor stations. By the 1940s the stopping passenger service had increased to six or seven trains. Freight services were withdrawn on 6th April 1964 and passenger services on 6th June 1966.

Opposite page Looking from the signal cabin towards Rugby, 29th January 1966. The Down platform building is an example of the pre-fabricated modular timber buildings introduced by the LNWR in the mid-'seventies. Originally the valancing continued round the front of the building, but was latterly cut back at several stations on the branch to comply with a more generous structure gauge. The area adjacent to the buildings on both platforms is surfaced with blue paving bricks. The restricted site available for the yard is apparent, hemmed in by the long platforms provided in 1878, rising ground to the left, and the road bridge in the distance.

Right Looking from beyond the level crossing towards Rugby. The signal cabin suffered fire damage, and was rebuilt to a curious hybrid design spanning the decades, with an LNWR brick base and lever frame and a modern superstructure and flat roof. In contrast to most LNWR boxes, where small handrails bolted to the windows were the rule, it also received adequate railings along the outside of the walkways. The Up home signal remains a fine example of the tall LNWR running signal, and could even be the original 1878 signal. By 1966, it had been extensively braced with a subsidiary strain post on the Down side.

Above Looking from the Up end of the yard towards Market Harborough in 1966. Although timber posts were favoured by the LNWR and LMS, and concrete posts latterly, the rail built loading gauge possesses a certain functional simplicity. The cattle pens are to the right of the station buildings.

Right The Up buildings looking towards Market Harborough on 29th January 1966. The station was some distance from the village, and was never connected to the water mains. Instead, water was delivered in milk churns off a convenient train, one being seen so employed on the platform. The absence of running water, apart from making life inconvenient, must have contributed materially to the success of the signal box fire. The modern hut in the foreground is singularly lacking in charm.

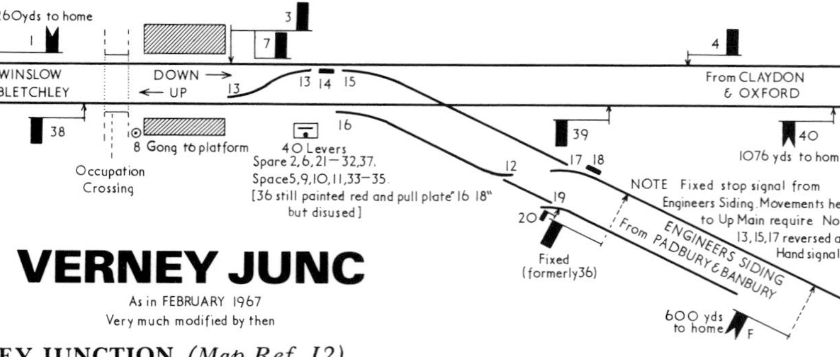

VERNEY JUNC

As in FEBRUARY 1967
Very much modified by then

VERNEY JUNCTION *(Map Ref. J2)*

Verney Junction was a railway crossroads in the middle of open countryside, named not after a place, but after a family. In the Victorian era, the Verney family were influential landowners in Buckinghamshire, and Sir Harry Verney a staunch advocate of railways. He was a leading figure in the inception of the Buckinghamshire Railway, and with the line crossing his territory, it was appropriate that the divergence of the Oxford and Banbury branches should have been named Verney Junction.

The Bletchley–Banbury line opened on 1st May 1850, and the Verney–Islip section on 1st October. The line was extended to Rewley Road Station, Oxford the following year. From the outset, the workings at Verney Junction were peculiar. It was the physical divergence of the two routes, but the actual junction and staff station was at Winslow, from whence two parallel single lines ran as far as Verney, where the Banbury branch turned northwards. By 1870, junction connections existed at Verney, but it was not until 1875 that conventional working was implemented, and Verney finally became the staff station for the single line section.

In 1868, an additional route was added in the shape of the independent Aylesbury & Buckingham Railway. Trains from Aylesbury terminated at a single platform on the south side of the line, and the station was enlarged at this time to cope with the extra workings, which ran about three times a day. The impecunious A&BR was taken over by the Metropolitan Railway in 1891 in their drive to the north, and was in turn transferred to the Metropolitan & GC joint committee, and the southern extremity used as a part of the GCR London Extension. Verney Junction and the northern portion of the A&B line remained a rural backwater, and passenger services were withdrawn in 1936 by London Transport. It was the most northerly point on the Metropolitan/London Transport rail system.

On 7th September 1964 the Verney–Buckingham section closed to passengers, and after freight traffic ceased over this section in 1966, the branch was demoted to an engineers' siding, and the incredible signalling layout shown in plan 'B' adopted. This included a *fixed* stop signal, which is naturally extremely rare, but to add to the confusion, the lever which formerly worked the signal (No. 36), was not painted as a spare, (i.e. white), but left in red!

The final stage in the run-down came with the cessation of passenger services on the Oxford line on 1st January 1968. Verney soon fell into decay, and the signal box and buildings were demolished.

For many years, an outstanding feature of Verney Junction was a colourful display of cement animals and pixies, created by a former Station Master. The figures included a duck, visible in one of the illustrations. The duck was close to a bird bath, but whether his martial bearing attracted birds to the bath, or repelled them is an unknown factor. Some may say that a duck does not look martial – if so, they did not meet the Verney duck! Be that as it may, the Verney duck is an enduring memory of a once delightful station which is now no more.

Above The Down LNWR buildings looking towards Bletchley in 1967. This was an island platform, Metropolitan trains using the back face until the service was abandoned in 1936. Access to the station was via the footbridge which can be seen on the left of this view and below. The main building is typically LNWR design, but one wonders whether the number of passengers using the station really justified such a lavish expenditure.

Above Verney Junction looking from the barrow crossing at the east end of the station. From left to right; the footbridge spanning the Metropolitan tracks, and permitting passengers to gain access to Verney Junction without crossing the lines, the Metropolitan and Down LNWR platform and buildings, the Oxford line, Verney Junction signal box and the Up LNWR platform and shelter. The martial duck stands out in white against a dark backdrop to the right of the Verney Junction nameboard on the Down platform.

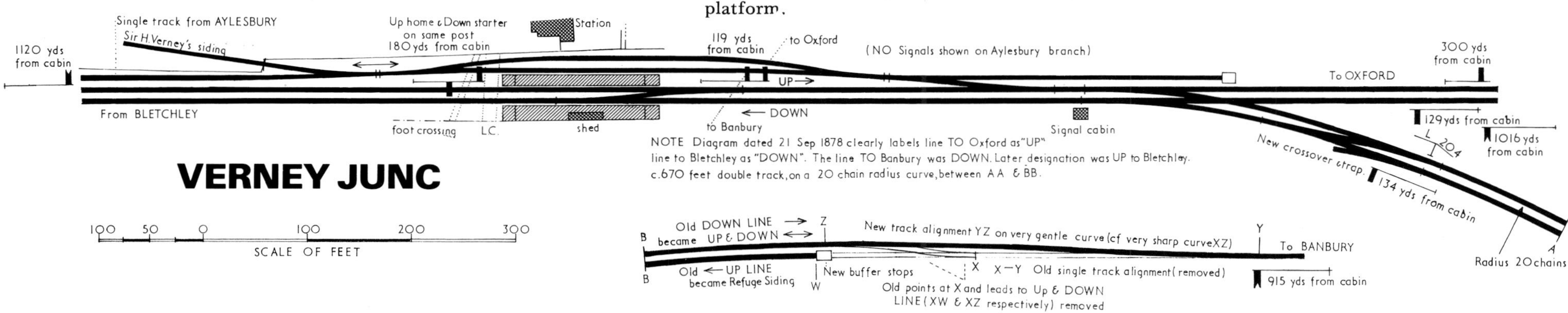

No. 42155 pulls into Verney Junction with a local from Bletchley in 1953, with the Metropolitan Railway signal box and sidings visible on the right. The platform lamps are inscribed VERNEY JUNCTION, whilst the rockery and flower beds in the foreground are a part of the Station Master's handiwork. Mermaids, pixies, animals and ducks testified to his skills.

Looking from the Metropolitan platform towards Oxford, permanent way wagons occupying the disused Metropolitan run-round loop. The Banbury connections can be seen just to the left of the timber hut in the foreground. The home signal ex Oxford is to the left of the lamp, whilst the Banbury home is just to the right. The North Western short arms and dwarf signals on the left, ex the Metropolitan, are especially attractive.

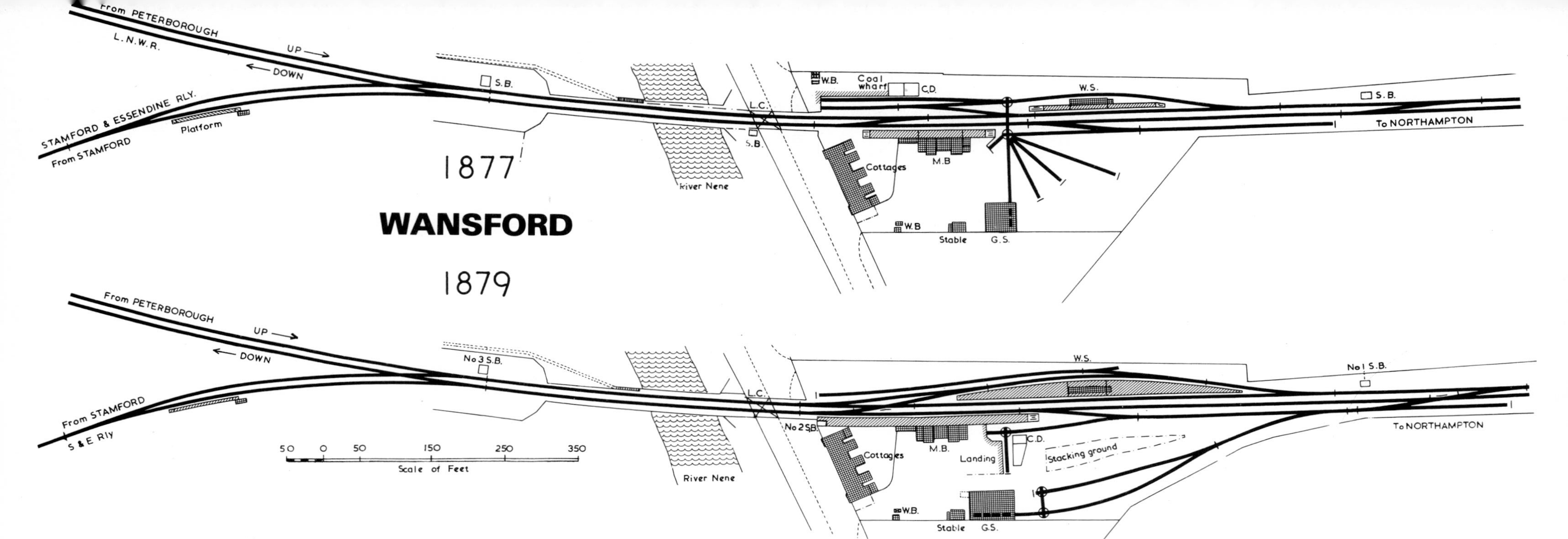

WANSFORD *(Map Ref. L7)*

Wansford is a small village (pop. 400), situated about 6¾ miles west of Peterborough. The L&B Northampton & Peterborough branch ran near to the village and opened on 2nd June 1845. A station was provided where the line crossed the Great North Road by a level crossing. The crossing remains to this day, but the main road has, mercifully, been diverted. The initial service was three trains a day, and the line was single, but doubling was instituted almost immediately, and was completed by September 1846. The main stations on the line were splendid Elizabethan or Jacobean structures designed by J. W. Livock, Wansford, in stone, and being outstanding.

In 1867, the Stamford & Essendine Railway (worked for most of its life by the GNR) opened a single track branch from Stamford to a junction with the LNWR on the east side of the Nene Bridge. S&ER trains shared the North Western station facilities, but this happy arrangement did not last for long. The two companies had a row, and S&ER trains henceforth terminated at a new one-platform station set amongst the fields, but on S&E land. In 1877, Stephen Reay, secretary of the LNWR, notified the Board of Trade that 'the junction with the Stamford line at Wansford, which has been for some time disused, has been reinstated'. Colonel Yolland inspected the work, and was not impressed with either company's efforts. The junction with the S&E was controlled by a cabin on the south side of the line, and the Colonel noted that the points from the short stretch of double S&E track on to the single line were too far from the box for safe working (198 yards). He was more scathing about the LNWR station. A second box by the level crossing controlled the eastern end of the station. The levers were in the open, and both at this cabin and at the junction box, the interlocking was incomplete. The platform was but 50 yards in length, and the Colonel felt that he could not recommend the connections as safe for passenger traffic.

After this sad blow, the LNWR prepared a proper rebuilding plan which involved lengthening both platforms, eliminating the old wagon turntables and square crossings, and improving the yard access. They also proposed to install parallel rails at the S&E/LNWR junction in order to bring those points within working distance of the level crossing box. This would have enabled the junction box to be closed, but how it was proposed to deal with the points from the double track to the single track on the S&E itself was not clear. Perhaps as that was the S&E's problem, the LNWR did not really care. The Board of Trade agreed that the connections could come into use, subject to a final inspection once the work was completed. The station was re-inspected in September 1879, and in the event the LNWR retained three cabins. No. 1 (24 levers) controlled the yard connections at the west end of the station. No. 2 (34 levers), the station crossing area, and No. 3 (15 levers) the junction.

In the early years of this century, a new cabin was erected by the level crossing, to control all movements. Services over the Stamford line — usually about four workings a day — ended on 1st July 1929, and the Peterborough line trains ceased calling at Wansford on 1st July 1957, several years before the branch was abandoned.

Up to this point, the story was the all-too-familiar one of decline, but in 1974, the Peterborough Railway Society leased the line from Yarwell Junction to Orton Longueville from the Peterborough Development Corporation, who had bought it from BR. Wansford became the headquarters of the Nene Valley Railway, and by 1977 amazing progress had been made, including the construction of a replacement Up platform upon which the station buildings from the now closed Barnwell Station were sited. Although this new platform is opposite the main buildings rather than staggered as was formerly the case, the atmosphere is decidedly North Western, that is, until one sees a French, Danish, Swedish or German locomotive drift into the station. The NVR have exploited the generous clearances on the preserved section to good — if unusual — effect.

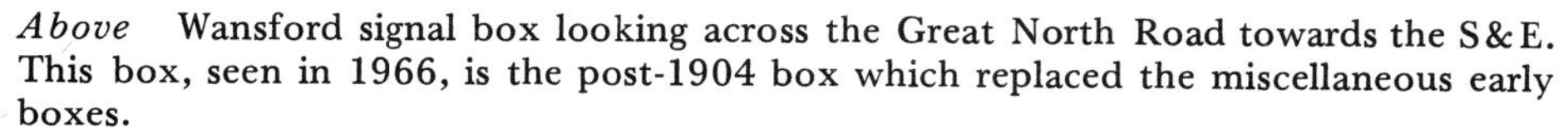

Above Wansford signal box looking across the Great North Road towards the S&E. This box, seen in 1966, is the post-1904 box which replaced the miscellaneous early boxes.

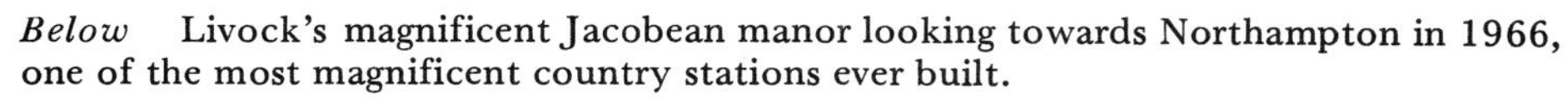

Below Livock's magnificent Jacobean manor looking towards Northampton in 1966, one of the most magnificent country stations ever built.

Above In the preservation era in the 'seventies. Livock's building on the left, the level crossing centre, and the LNWR building ex Barnwell on the right.

Below Although not precisely where the original Up platform or buildings were, the efforts of the preservationists set off Livock's building admirably.

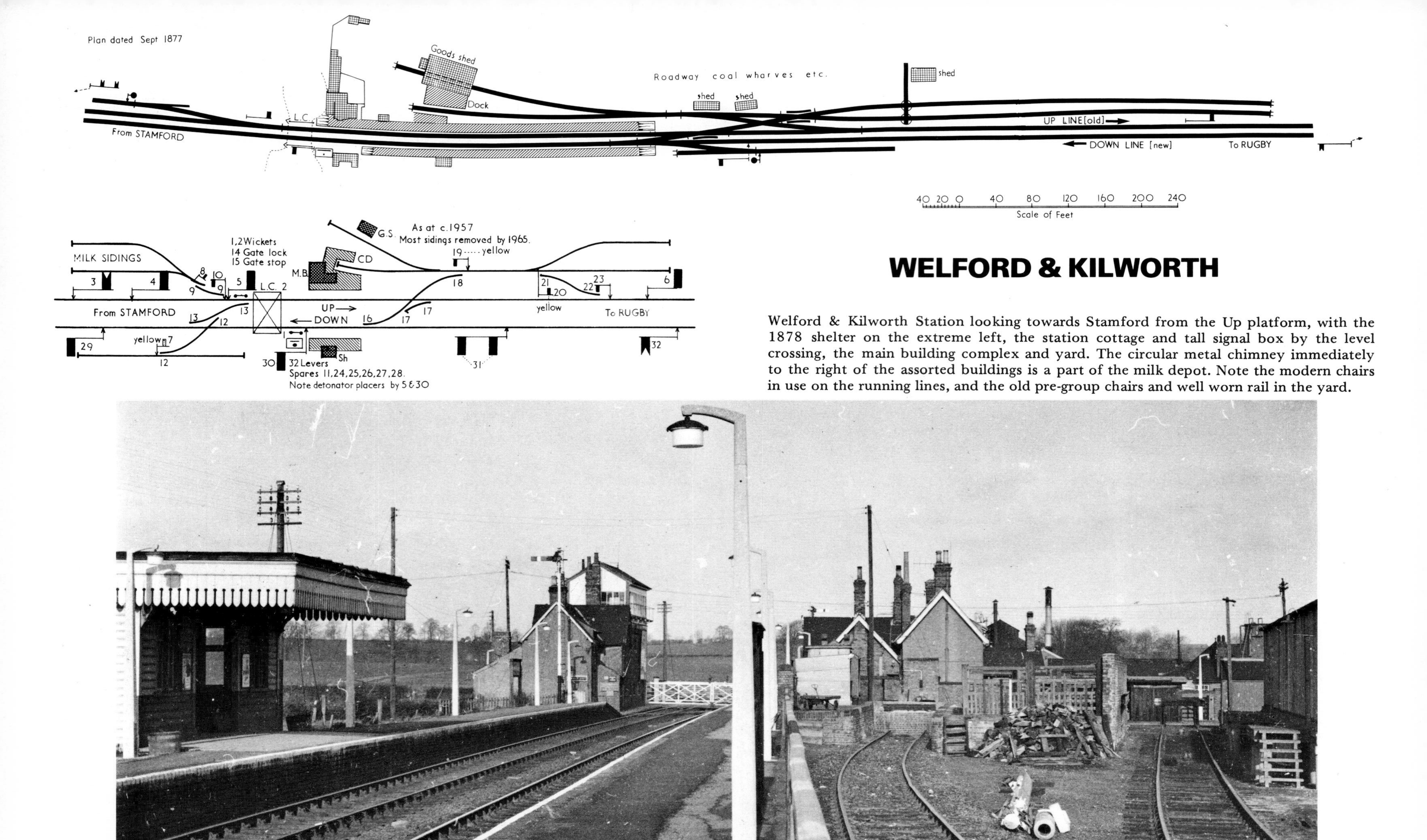

WELFORD & KILWORTH

Welford & Kilworth Station looking towards Stamford from the Up platform, with the 1878 shelter on the extreme left, the station cottage and tall signal box by the level crossing, the main building complex and yard. The circular metal chimney immediately to the right of the assorted buildings is a part of the milk depot. Note the modern chairs in use on the running lines, and the old pre-group chairs and well worn rail in the yard.

WELFORD & KILWORTH *(Map Ref. H6)*

The design of Welford & Kilworth Station clearly indicated its antiquity, and it was in fact one of the original stations on the LNWR Stamford branch, which opened in 1850. The main buildings were on the Up platform and were at ground level. When normal height platforms were provided, the bay window looking out on to the platform was at ankle-height vis-à-vis passengers standing on the platform. Further extensions included a selection of outbuildings and a wooden waiting room, which in no way matched the rest of the structure. On the opposite platform, a house was provided very close to the track. A diagonal board walk ran from this platform over to the Up platform, whilst a second narrow walk way continued past the cottage and the signal box, which was positioned between the house and the road. In order to give the signalman visibility in the Rugby direction it was necessary to make the cabin exceptionally tall for a country station, with the floor at roof height relative to the cottage.

The Dairy sidings on the Stamford side of the level crossing contributed their quota of traffic. The milk ran out from Rugby about 3.30am, and the empties used to return about 5.00am. Welford was used for many years as a convenient disposal point for milk tanks which developed a defect en route. Although a long distance run at high speeds might not be possible, such cripples could often be run at low speed the short distance to Welford, so saving their load.

The station was closed on 6th June 1966, and the line lifted, and buildings eventually demolished. The local pronunciation is Kill'erth, the 'W' being silent.

For the first three years the station was known as Welford, and from 1897 until 1913 as Welford and Lutterworth, after which Kilworth was restored. (It was referred to in any case as Killerth!) The change was a response to the GCR 'London Extension' with its Lutterworth Station which was convenient to the village. As the LNWR rival was over 5 miles away, the value of the change is debatable!

The cottage, signal box and Up buildings looking towards Stamford in 1966. The provision of two home signals so close together is unusual on a minor line. The outer home protects the milk sidings, whilst the inner home protects the crossing. Such an arrangement was hardly an asset, as exit from the milk sidings was controlled by a shunt signal, and the outer signal was really enough. The buildings, which developed over a century from 1850, fall into no recognisable architectural style. 'Welfordian All-sorts' might be the best label to apply!

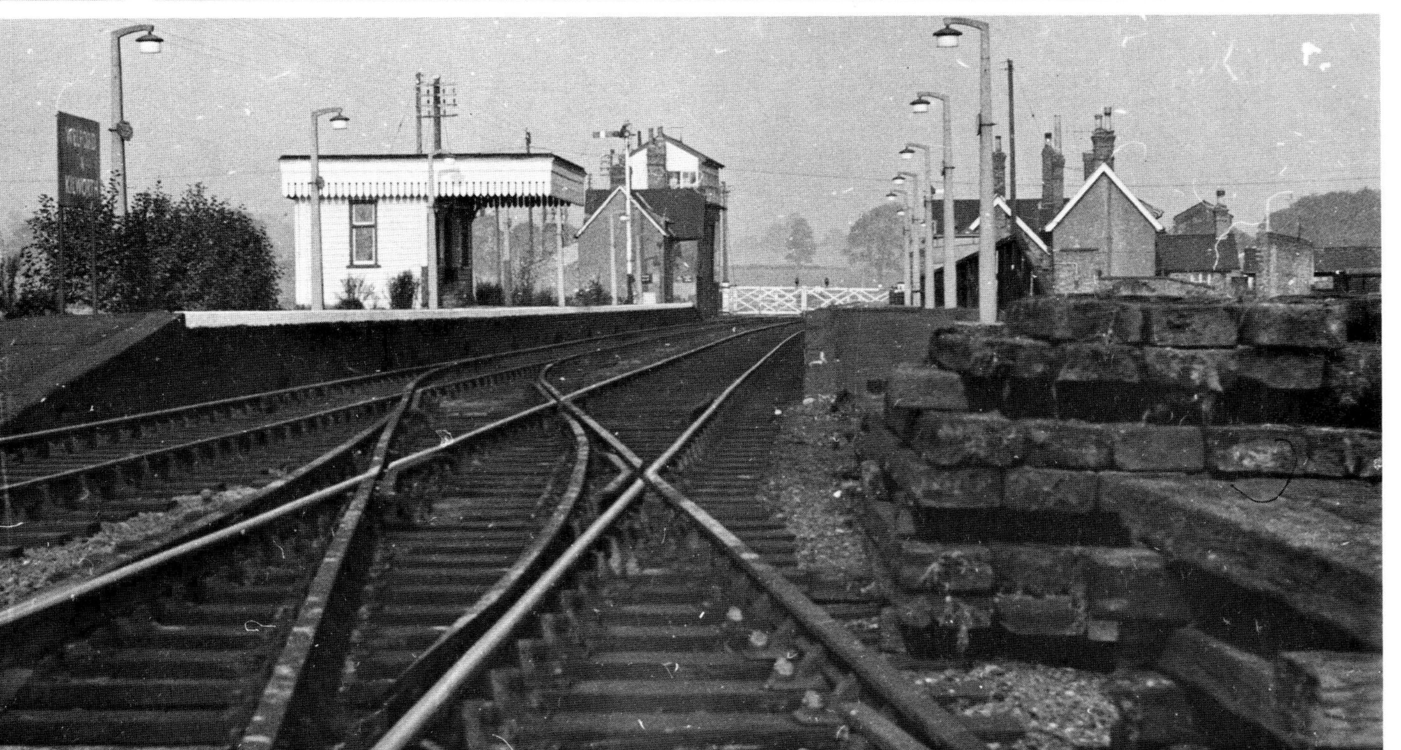

Looking towards Stamford from the yard connection. The shelter on the Down platform is one of the pre-fabricated buildings which the LNWR developed from about 1876, this being an 1878 example. The forest of tall concrete lamp posts add an incongruous touch of modernity to what is, otherwise, a traditional scene, albeit one which had but weeks to live when this view was taken.

WELLINGBOROUGH

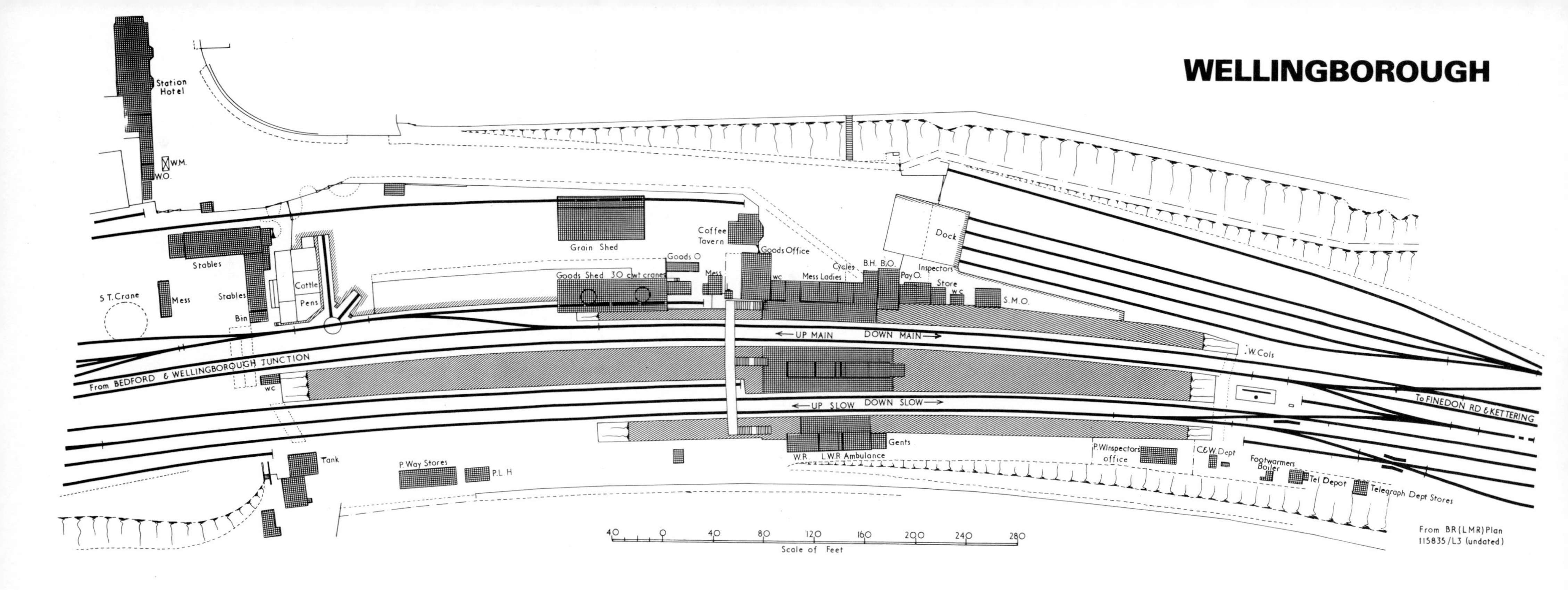

The main buildings at Wellingborough looking from the approach road towards Kettering and the north. The round headed windows, mostly grouped in pairs within a blind arcade of multi-coloured bricks, became a Midland house-style, as did the diamond and lozenge pattern iron frame glazing.

WELLINGBOROUGH *(Map Ref. K5)*

Two factors dominated the development of Wellingborough, rail communications and the ironstone industry. Both went hand in hand, and through them, the town reached its present size of about 37,000. The first line into Wellingborough was the LNWR Northampton–Peterborough branch which opened in 1845. It was not until 1857, however, that the town achieved main line status with the opening of the MR Hitchin line.

Initially the main line was double track, but the rapid increase in traffic over the Midland system made quadrupling necessary by the late 'seventies, and one of the priority stretches was from just south of Wellingborough to Sharnbrook, where the heavy climb to Sharnbrook summit provided a serious obstacle to freight trains. This work was completed in the early 'eighties.

As well as main line services, including expresses, Wellingborough was served by the Higham Ferrers branch trains and also Midland workings over the LNWR branch to Northampton, where the MR opened their own passenger and goods station. The MR and LNWR lines at Wellingborough were connected by a curve which diverged from the main line to the south of the platforms. The usual level of services was about twelve to fourteen trains in each direction, and these continued until the LNW branch was closed to passengers on 4th May 1964. In the early 1900s the Higham Ferrers branch carried ten trains in each direction, and still did so in 1942. Regular services ended on 15th June 1959.

WELLINGBOROUGH

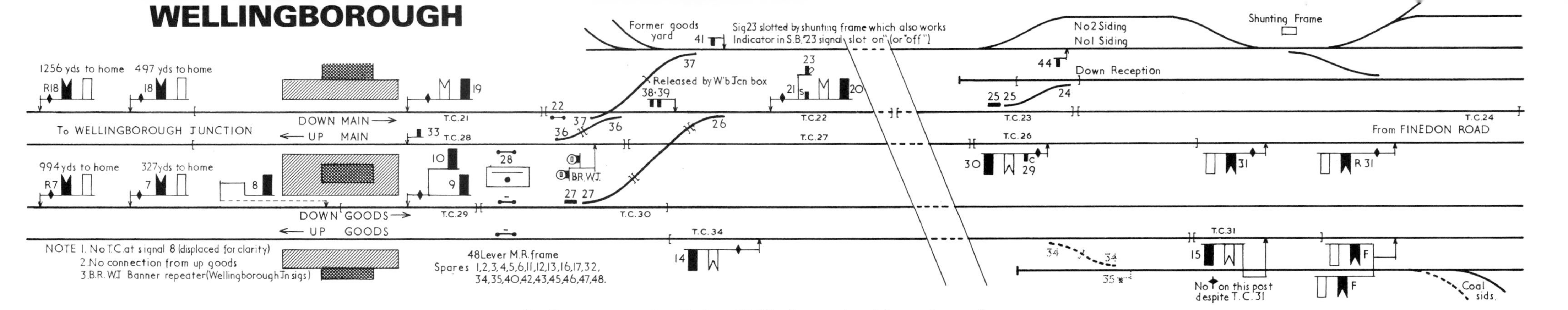

Right On 2nd September 1898, the 6.45pm Down express ex St. Pancras was derailed at Wellingborough with tragic results. The train comprised a 4-4-0 tender engine and five carriages, and as it was running through the station at about 60mph, the engine struck a mail trolley which had fallen from the platform onto the line. The engine derailed, and at the yard connections at the north end, the entire train left the rails. The driver, fireman and five passengers lost their lives. A contributing factor was that the platform sloped towards the line, the Down platform being just 2ft. above rail level. If a trolley was incorrectly parked or tampered with, it would roll on to the line with the slope this way. Ironically, the Up platform had been raised and a reverse slope created to throw off rain water when the Higham Ferrers branch was opened in 1893-94, but nothing had been done on the Down. This was attended to shortly after the accident, but other than for these alterations and incidentals, the scene at Wellingborough moments before that fateful evening so long ago, could not have differed greatly from the scene on the right with a mail barrow loaded and waiting for its train.

Below The Down main platform looking towards the north, showing the original buildings designed by C. A. Driver, and matching ridge and furrow canopy, a marked contrast to the later building and timber awning on the right hand side. This canopy is similar to the original canopies at Kettering, but sadly, the last row of glazing and decorative gable ends have been removed, destroying much of its beauty.

WELLINGBOROUGH

Right Looking north from the Down main platform towards Kettering. On the previous page, mention was made of the 1898 derailment. The locomotive, after derailing in the platform, continued along the permanent way more or less straight, until it encountered the connection into the yard off the Up fast. The locomotive was forced violently to the left into the yard, and was swung through 180 degrees by the force of its impact with obstructions in the yard, and by carriages, the first three of which passed between engine and tender. The locomotive came to rest against a slope of the cutting, approximately opposite the blades of the yard points (37 in the modern signalling plan). The tender finished up on its side a few yards further on, between the Down fast and the yard, whilst the carriages had bisected them as they were brought to a standstill. One vehicle, a six-wheel saloon, was deflected inwards, obstructing the Up fast line. Fortunately there was no train approaching on the Up line at the time. In this 1970s study, the yard sidings on the left have been lifted along with the centre siding, but the site is otherwise little altered. Note the banner repeater signals referring to the Up main line just to the left of the box. These are not worked by the station box, but by Wellingborough Junction signal box at the south end of the station. As the station is on the curve, and the buildings obscure the running signals, these banners are necessary to give the driver advance warning of the signals.

Lower right Looking northwards across the station from the Down main platform, a few yards short of the start of the derailment. The Up main platform was substantially upgraded when the Higham Ferrers branch was added, and a short bay provided at the south end (see scale plan). The facilities on this platform thus bear little relationship to the original 1857 station, the building being much plainer without the lozenge-windows, circular headings or other flourishes. The canopy is totally different, and the graceful cast columns so much in favour in the 1850s have been almost totally eliminated, with cast brackets springing from the building instead. These in turn support steel joists. The comparison with Kettering, where lattice girders were used for the major rebuild, is of interest in tracing changing ideas and policies. This arrangement was less elegant, but provided a less cluttered platform for passengers, luggage and barrows.

Below Wellingborough goods shed looking from the footbridge towards Bedford. In comparing this view with the scale plan, it will be noted that the Down main platform, which was originally quite short, has been extended, as has the goods shed, the trailing connection from the yard to the Down fast (shown on the scale plan), having been moved. The goods shed is similar in style to the 1857 station with its round headed narrow windows with lozenge and diamond panes, but as is so often the case with Midland structures, appearances are deceptive. Comparison with earlier views will reveal that whilst the road elevation of the station buildings is decorated with a semi-circular blind arcading, the platform elevation boasts slightly pointed arches. The rail elevation of the goods shed harmonises with the latter, with blind arcades each containing a single window. Despite superficial similarities between the arcading, there are important differences, the station building being in patterned multi-colour brick, whilst the goods shed is plain. The window arches also differ, the goods shed again being much the plainer.

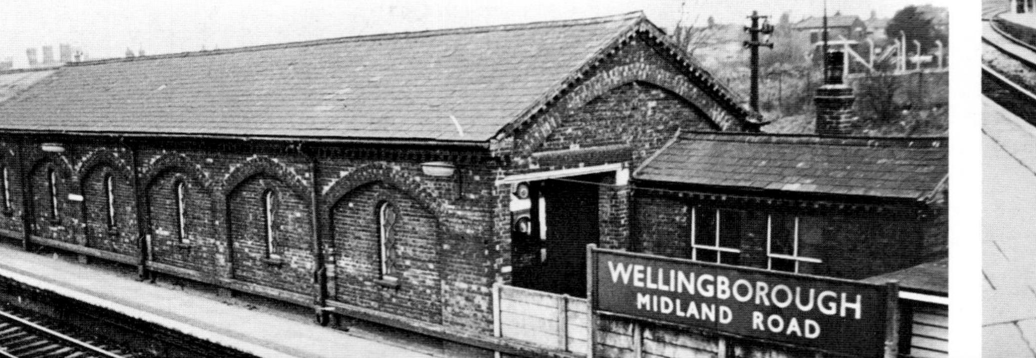

WIND RMERE

7 July 1911

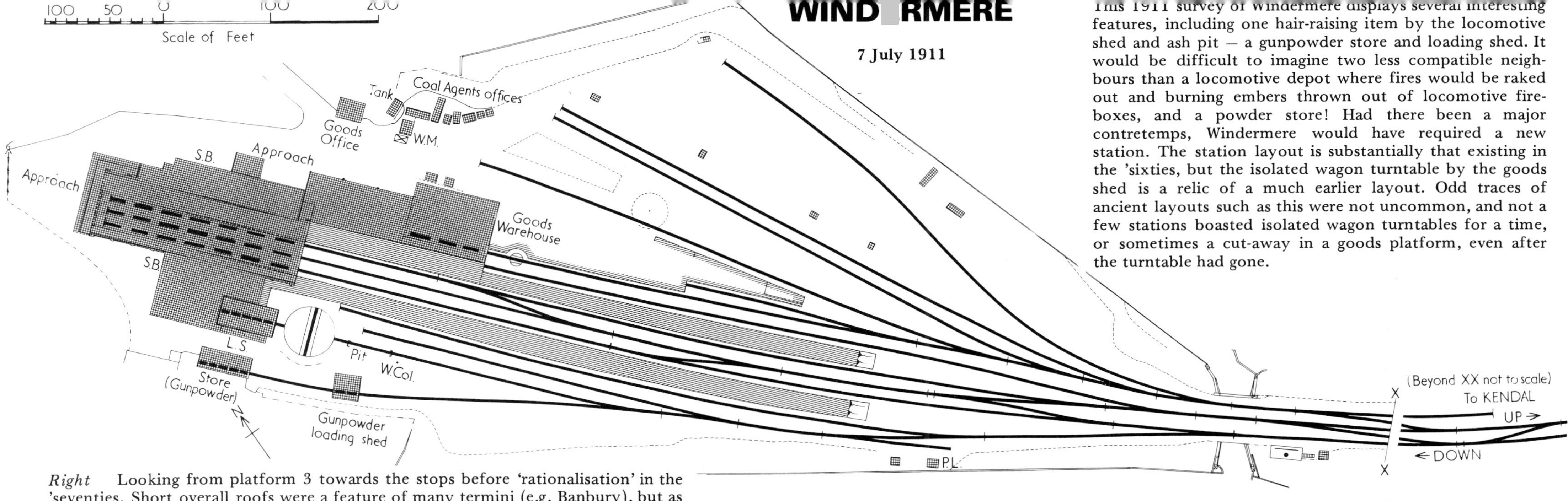

This 1911 survey of Windermere displays several interesting features, including one hair-raising item by the locomotive shed and ash pit – a gunpowder store and loading shed. It would be difficult to imagine two less compatible neighbours than a locomotive depot where fires would be raked out and burning embers thrown out of locomotive fireboxes, and a powder store! Had there been a major contretemps, Windermere would have required a new station. The station layout is substantially that existing in the 'sixties, but the isolated wagon turntable by the goods shed is a relic of a much earlier layout. Odd traces of ancient layouts such as this were not uncommon, and not a few stations boasted isolated wagon turntables for a time, or sometimes a cut-away in a goods platform, even after the turntable had gone.

Right Looking from platform 3 towards the stops before 'rationalisation' in the 'seventies. Short overall roofs were a feature of many termini (e.g. Banbury), but as trains became longer, platform canopies gained in popularity for all but the largest stations. This is a classic example of the 'Euston roof' standard on the LNWR for many years.

Below After rationalisation, looking from platform 2. The removal of the end screen and much of the cladding exposes the constructional technique.

K. A. Miller

WINDERMERE *(Map Ref. S11)*

The Kendal & Windermere Railway was incorporated in 1845 to build a line from Oxenholme on the Lancaster & Carlisle Railway, via Kendal to Birthwaite, as Windermere town was then commonly called. For over twenty years – until the FR Ulverston–Lakeside branch was opened – the K&W was the sole convenient access for tourists to Lake Windermere. The opening of the Furness branch with its genuine Lakeside terminus must have been a great blow to the LNWR (who had taken over the K&W), as Windermere Station and town were about 1½ miles from the Lake, and the journey from Bowness Pier involved a considerable climb. The LNWR TOURIST GUIDE of 1875 (a 662 page mini-encyclopaedia) commented 'The rail from Oxenholme Junction to Windermere affords an easy and delightful means of access to the Lake District'. In the early days, five or six trains ran from Oxenholme to Windermere, augmented by short-workings between Oxenholme and Kendal. This had risen to about a dozen trains by the turn of the century, augmented in summer by excursion traffic from afar. A regular coach service, originally horse, later motor, ran from Windermere to Ambleside and Keswick, and in 1895 there were three through coaches a day, the journey taking from 3 to 4 hours. Further routes ran to Ullswater, Coniston and the Langdales. The LNWR Programme of Tours for 1895 noted that 'Omnibuses meet all the Trains at Windermere. Fares from the station to Bowness 6d'.

The 1927 summer timetable provided thirteen departures, four of which were expresses. Of the remainder, some went as far as Oxenholme, others to Grange, Carnforth or Preston. A staff of carriage cleaners was employed in summer to clean out excursion stock during its lie-over. In pre-group days, stock from a variety of companies could be seen in the station, and to take just one example from the LNWR September Trains notice of 1909, an advertised excursion ran on Mondays and Wednesdays from Blackpool Central to Windermere. The LNW provided the stock and guard, and also motive power from Blackpool to Preston, where the stock was attached to the 9.42 am Preston to Windermere.

Goods traffic ceased in April 1969, but the station continues to handle passenger traffic, albeit now reduced to single track, and with one instead of four passenger platforms and no siding or run round connections.

Above Looking towards the stops from beside No. 18 points after the closure of the goods yard in 1969. The trap ex the centre road, the far half of No. 22 points, is visible adjacent to the two ground discs 16 and 21, ex the one-time run-round. The limited value possessed by early overall roofs, as at Windermere, is apparent in this view, with a short piece of platform well protected, a further short canopy on platforms 1 and 2, and then bare to the elements. A cheaper but longer roof along both platforms would have been infinitely more satisfactory.

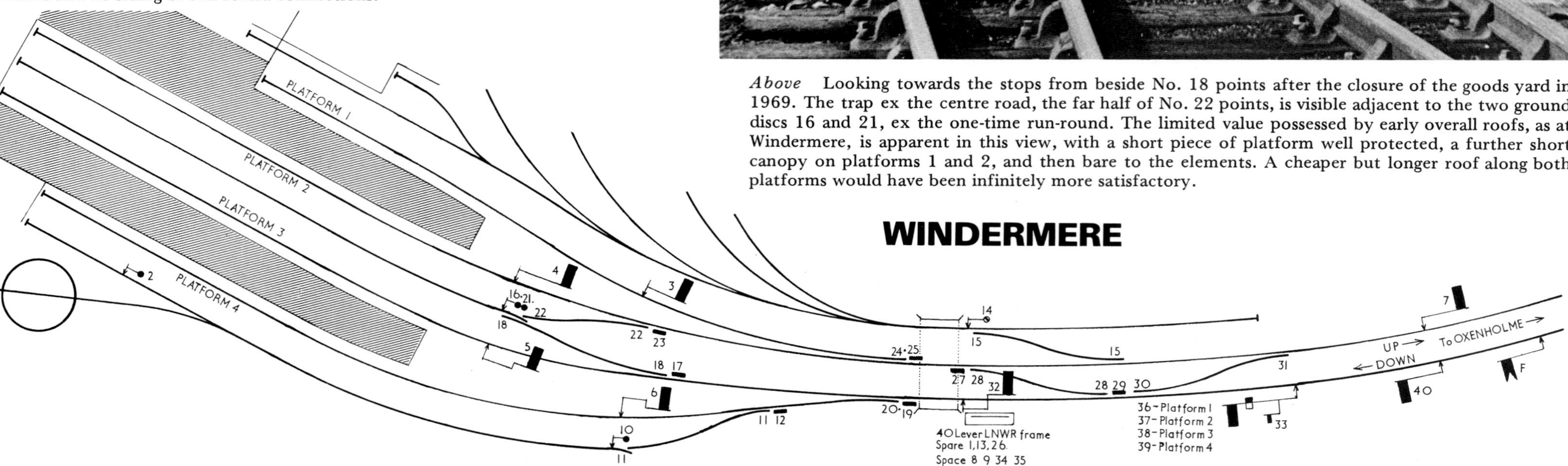

Right Looking towards the end of Windermere No. 2 platform in 1963, with the goods yard on the left, Nos. 1 and 2 platforms, the signal box, centre road, 3 and 4 platforms and locomotive road. No fewer than fourteen signals can be made out, commencing with the advance starter No. 7 (above the right hand end of the mineral wagon), then No. 3, the back of the inner home (with its four route indicators 36, 37, 38 and 39) and subsidiary signal 33, the platform starter No. 4, starter No. 32 (by the box), disc signals 21 and 16, No. 6, disc signal No. 10 and finally platform starter No. 5. One wonders if the permanent way trolley by No. 5 signal is the same one as appears on the later view on the previous page! In the smaller gauges, a station such as this would make an attractive model, especially with the excuse to operate a variety of stock on summer excursions to supplement local passenger and freight services.

Below A Stanier 'Black Five' awaits a crowd of holidaymakers on a dull afternoon in 1963, when excursion traffic — to the seaside or inland resorts — was still very much a part of the summer scene. The yard was still in use, and the generous covered accommodation for goods is noteworthy.

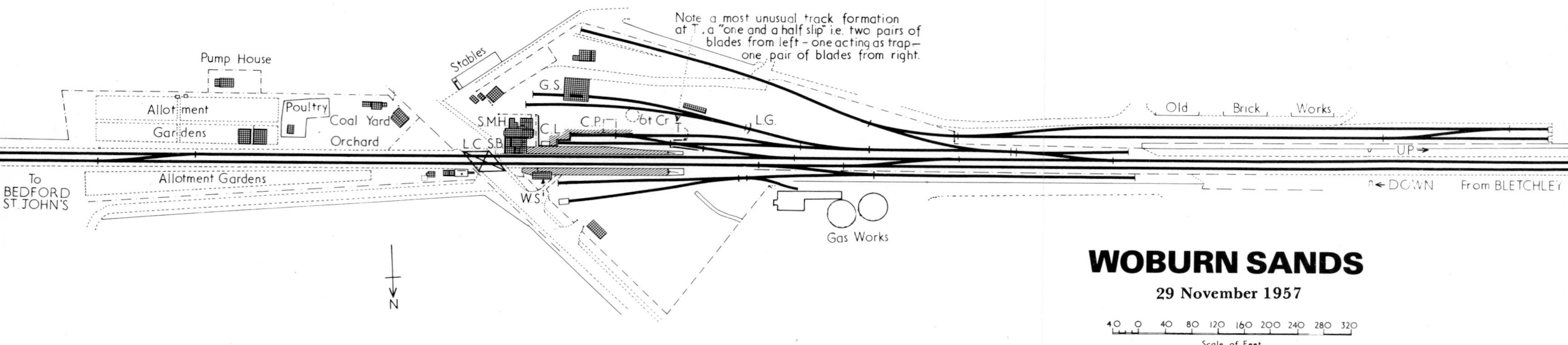

WOBURN SANDS *(Map Ref. K3)*

Woburn Sands is an intermediate station on the LNWR Bletchley–Bedford branch. Construction of the Bedford Railway began in 1845, the first sod being lifted by the Duchess of Bedford in the Woburn area. The line was formally opened on 17th November 1846, public traffic commencing the following day. It was worked by the LNWR from the outset.

An undated drawing shows the station layout at one time to have been similar to Fenny Stratford (see page 74) with sidings on both sides of the line connected by wagon turntables and square crossings. These were ultimately removed and ordinary trailing yard connections had to suffice. A rail connected ballast pit once existed a short distance to the east of the station. A siding ran from the pit to the main line, and although the points were removed, the isolated siding track remained in situ for a considerable period.

At several stations on the branch, a gong lever was provided from the box to the platform so that the signalman could communicate with the station staff. As the box at Woburn was separated from the main buildings by no more than the width of the roadway, the gong lever was dispensed with, and a large bell was hung outside the cabin for the signalman to ring. On a cold wet day, a gong lever was infinitely more desirable!

As befitted a station serving one of the stately homes of England, the buildings at Woburn Sands were of excellent quality, the design being in part dictated by a stipulation from the Duke of Bedford, that it should harmonise with various buildings on the estate. It is possible that the main stations, which were in the rustic or Cottage Orné style with timber framework and ornate fretted bargeboards, were the work of J. W. Livock, several of whose structures have been illustrated earlier.

Below Looking from the Up platform at Woburn Sands towards Bedford, in May 1967. The existence of separate goods facilities on both sides of the line, and of sidings serving two industrial concerns was remarkable at a relatively small station, especially one so near an important residence such as Woburn. The shelter on the left is a most peculiar structure with its decorative false canopy, sloping roof and vertical boarding. The signal box bell is at the right hand corner of the box, reached from the open window.

WOBURN SANDS

As in April 1967

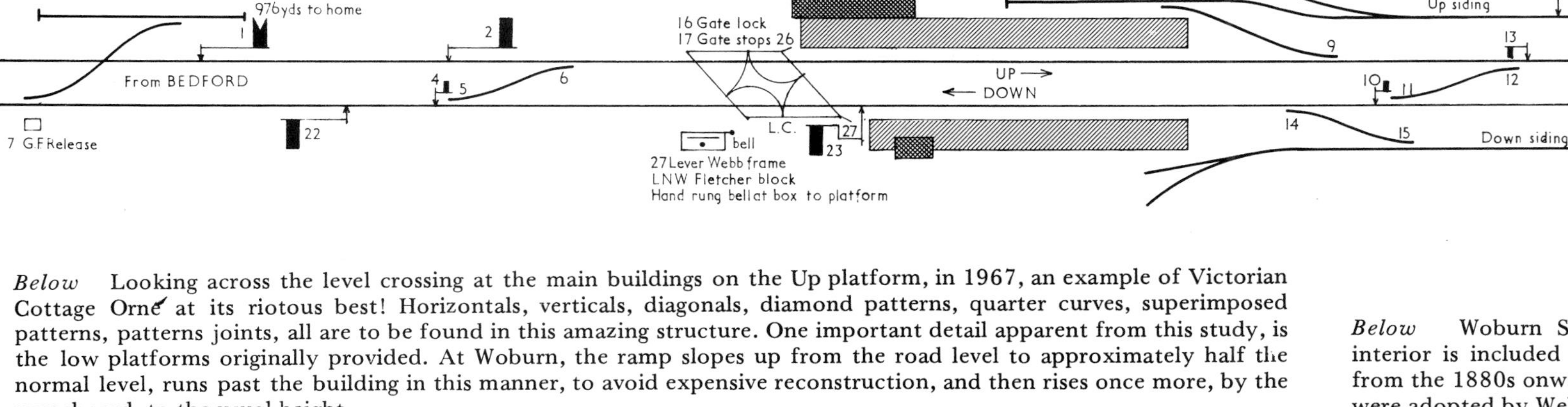

Below Looking across the level crossing at the main buildings on the Up platform, in 1967, an example of Victorian Cottage Orné at its riotous best! Horizontals, verticals, diagonals, diamond patterns, quarter curves, superimposed patterns, patterns joints, all are to be found in this amazing structure. One important detail apparent from this study, is the low platforms originally provided. At Woburn, the ramp slopes up from the road level to approximately half the normal level, runs past the building in this manner, to avoid expensive reconstruction, and then rises once more, by the nameboard, to the usual height.

Below Woburn Sands signal box in May 1967. This signal box interior is included as it so typifies the facilities in an LNWR box from the 1880s onwards. The levers with their front-mounted stirrup were adopted by Webb in preference to the catch handle at the back, which was commonly adopted elsewhere. Most North Western men swore *by* the frames; outsiders drafted in to work LNWR boxes generally swore *at* them, but it was largely a matter of experience and taste. Wooden footrests, one solid, one open, are provided by the distant levers as the long pulls required considerable physical effort. Most levers still bear the long narrow cast number plates of LNWR days, but 25 and 26, the nearest two levers, have received BR replacements. The smaller numbers below the lever number refer to other levers required to set a route. The back-board contains a mixture of LNW description plates at the far end, and BR plates at the near end.

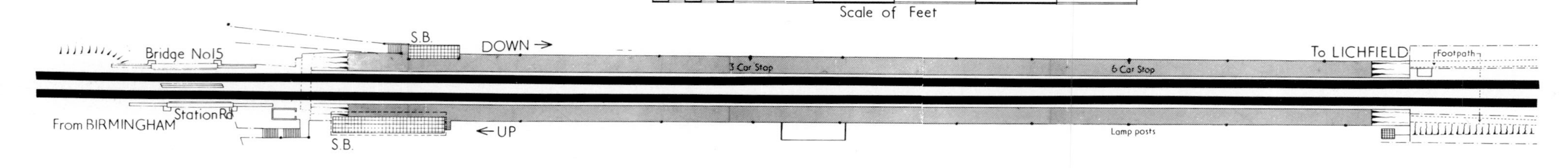

WYLDE GREEN

Wylde Green Station looking towards Sutton Coldfield in 1977, from bridge 15 across Station Road. Access to the station is via a flight of steps on the right hand or Up side, an inclined slope on the Down side and via footpaths which run along the side of the line to flights of steps leading up to the road overbridge in the distance. Despite the busy suburban service, there was no passenger overbridge, as the station was opened early enough to avoid Board of Trade demands for such a facility.

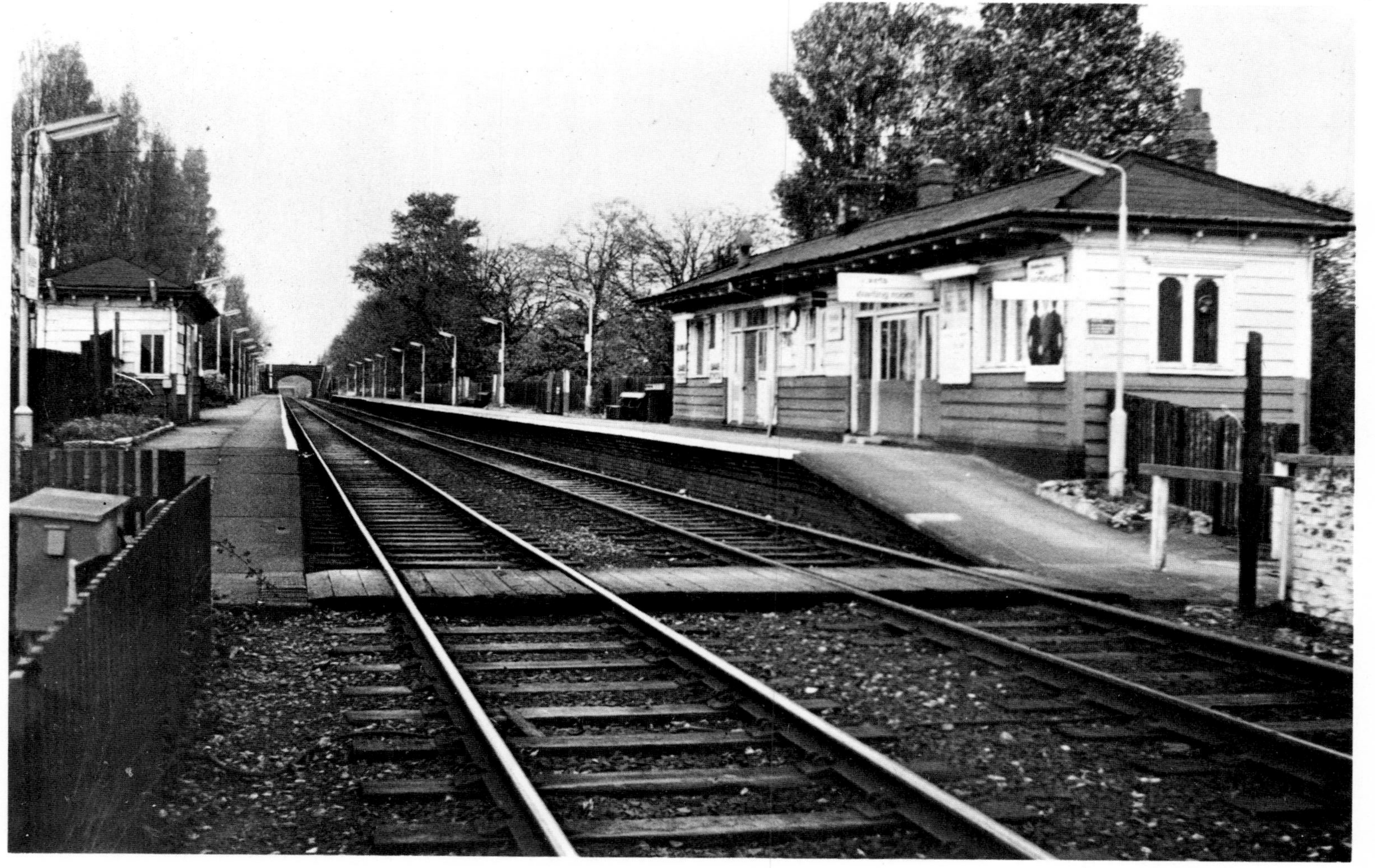

WYLDE GREEN *(Map Ref. D7)*

Wyld Green, as it was known when the Aston–Sutton Coldfield branch of the LNWR was opened on 2nd June 1862, was the last station before Sutton. In 1864, the present spelling, with an 'e' was adopted.

The unusual signalling system with its semaphore IBs, installed between Aston No. 2 and Sutton has already been described. Wylde Green Station was provided with two IB signals. The northbound signal was controlled from Erdington, the southbound from Sutton. In both cases, the IB distants were returned to danger automatically on the passage of the train.

For further details of the signalling, see plan 'B' Erdington and Sutton Coldfield.

The buildings on both platforms were similar to those provided at other stations on the branch, i.e. an early type of wooden building with horizontal rusticated boarding. In common with a number of these buildings provided elsewhere, the eaves were extended outwards over the platform to provide a miniscule canopy. It was more a gesture than a practical attempt at keeping passengers dry, but this design quirk can be seen on both buildings in the illustration opposite. The doors and their surrounds on the right hand or Up building are a later style, as is the end window on the Down shelter. The hipped roof, which characterised these early rusticated buildings, was replaced by a flat roof and later by a roof with plain gable ends, but the LNW later returned to a modified hipped roof.

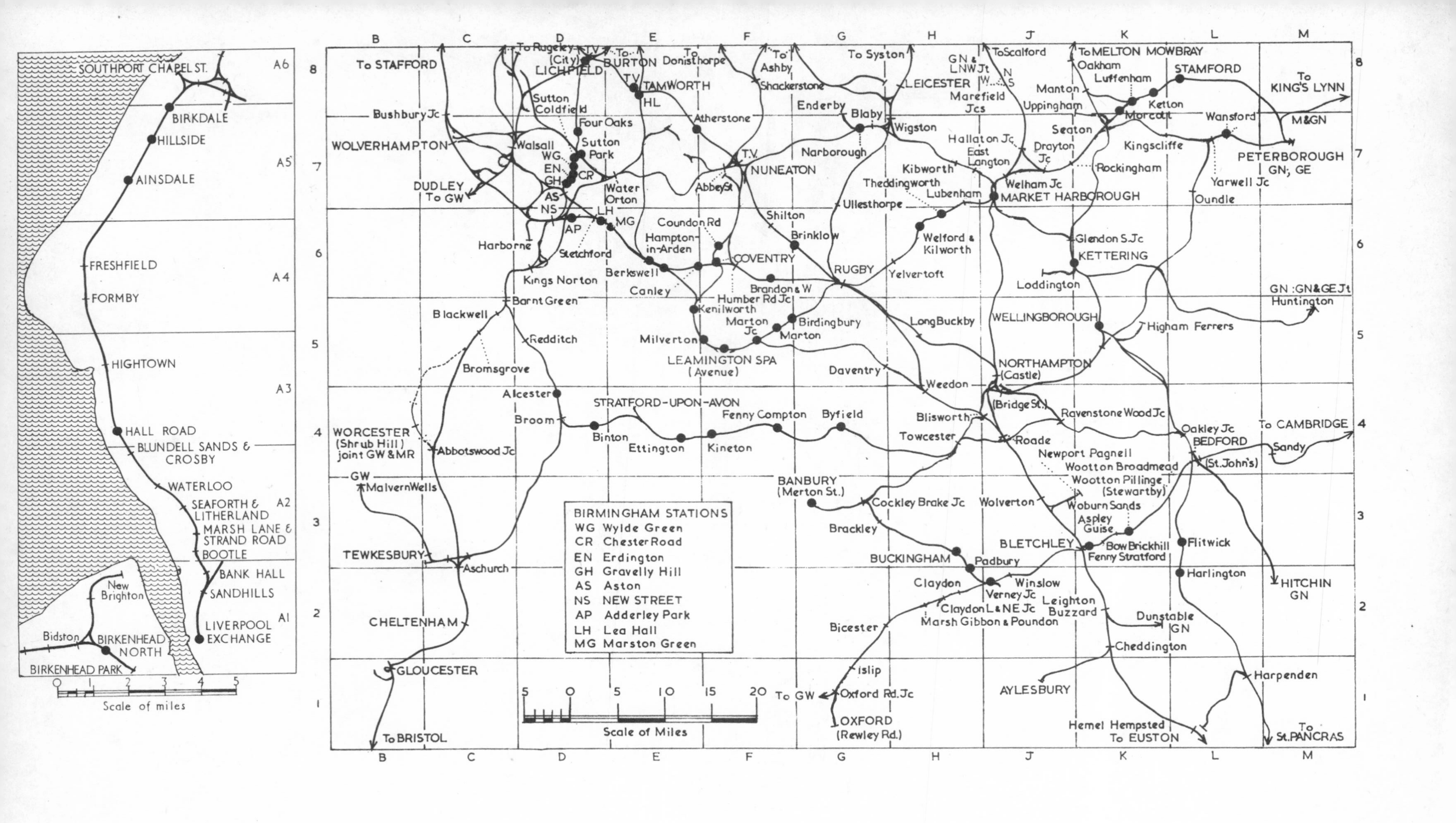
SOUTHPORT CHAPEL ST.
BIRKDALE
HILLSIDE
AINSDALE
FRESHFIELD
FORMBY
HIGHTOWN
HALL ROAD
BLUNDELL SANDS & CROSBY
WATERLOO
SEAFORTH & LITHERLAND
MARSH LANE & STRAND ROAD
BOOTLE
BANK HALL
SANDHILLS
LIVERPOOL EXCHANGE
New Brighton
Bidston
BIRKENHEAD NORTH
BIRKENHEAD PARK
A6
A5
A4
A3
A2
A1
0 1 2 3 4 5
Scale of miles
To STAFFORD
Bushbury Jc
WOLVERHAMPTON
DUDLEY To GW
To Rugeley
LICHFIELD (City)
T.V.
To BURTON
TAMWORTH
HL
To Donisthorpe
To Ashby
Shackerstone
To Syston
LEICESTER
GN & LNW Jt
Marefield Jcs
To Scalford
To MELTON MOWBRAY
Oakham
Luffenham
STAMFORD
To KING'S LYNN
M&GN
Manton
Uppingham
Ketton
Morcott
Wansford
Seaton
Kingscliffe
PETERBOROUGH GN; GE
Yarwell Jc
Oundle
Drayton Jc
Rockingham
Hallaton Jc
East Langton
Welham Jc
MARKET HARBOROUGH
Sutton Coldfield
Four Oaks
Sutton Park
Walsall
WG
EN
GH
CR
AS
NS
AP
LH
MG
Water Orton
Atherstone
Enderby
Blaby
Wigston
Narborough
NUNEATON
Abbey St
Kibworth
Theddingworth
Lubenham
Ullesthorpe
Shilton
Brinklow
Welford & Kilworth
Yelvertoft
RUGBY
Coundon Rd
Hampton-in-Arden
COVENTRY
Stetchford
Harborne
Berkswell
Kings Norton
Canley
Brandon & W
Humber Rd Jc
Kenilworth
Barnt Green
Blackwell
Redditch
Marton Jc
Birdingbury
Marton
Milverton
LEAMINGTON SPA (Avenue)
Bromsgrove
Glendon S.Jc
KETTERING
Loddington
GN: GN & GE Jt
Huntington
WELLINGBOROUGH
Higham Ferrers
Long Buckby
Daventry
NORTHAMPTON (Castle)
Weedon
Alcester
STRATFORD-UPON-AVON
Broom
Binton
Ettington
Kineton
Fenny Compton
Byfield
(Bridge St.)
Blisworth
Ravenstone Wood Jc
Towcester
Roade
Oakley Jc
BEDFORD
(St. John's)
To CAMBRIDGE
Sandy
WORCESTER (Shrub Hill) joint GW & MR
Abbotswood Jc
GW
Malvern Wells
BANBURY (Merton St.)
Cockley Brake Jc
Wolverton
Newport Pagnell
Wootton Broadmead
Wootton Pillinge (Stewartby)
Woburn Sands
Aspley Guise
Brackley
BLETCHLEY
Bow Brickhill
Fenny Stratford
Flitwick
TEWKESBURY
Aschurch
BUCKINGHAM
Padbury
Claydon
Winslow
Verney Jc
Claydon L & NE Jc
Marsh Gibbon & Poundon
Leighton Buzzard
Harlington
HITCHIN GN
Dunstable GN
CHELTENHAM
Bicester
Cheddington
GLOUCESTER
Islip
To GW
Oxford Rd. Jc
OXFORD (Rewley Rd.)
AYLESBURY
Harpenden
Hemel Hempsted
To EUSTON
To St. PANCRAS
To BRISTOL
BIRMINGHAM STATIONS
WG Wylde Green
CR Chester Road
EN Erdington
GH Gravelly Hill
AS Aston
NS NEW STREET
AP Adderley Park
LH Lea Hall
MG Marston Green
5 0 5 10 15 20
Scale of Miles
B C D E F G H J K L M
1 2 3 4 5 6 7 8